# Essentials of
# KTEA™-3 and WIAT®-III Assessment

# Essentials of Psychological Assessment Series

## Series Editors, Alan S. Kaufman and Nadeen L. Kaufman

# Essentials

## of KTEA™-3 and

## WIAT®-III Assessment

Kristina C. Breaux
Elizabeth O. Lichtenberger

WILEY

Published by John Wiley & Sons, Inc., Hoboken, New Jersey.
Published simultaneously in Canada.

For general information on our other products and services, please contact our Customer Care Department within the U.S. at 800-956-7739, outside the U.S. at 317-572-3986, or fax 317-572-4002.

Wiley publishes in a variety of print and electronic formats and by print-on-demand. Some material included with standard print versions of this book may not be included in e-books or in print-on-demand. If this book refers to media such as a CD or DVD that is not included in the version you purchased, you may download this material at http://booksupport.wiley.com. For more information about Wiley products, visit www.wiley.com.

**Library of Congress Cataloging-in-Publication Data**

Names: Breaux, Kristina C., author. | Lichtenberger, Elizabeth O., author.
Title: Essentials of KTEA™-3 and WIAT®-III assessment / Kristina C. Breaux, Elizabeth O. Lichtenberger.
Description: Hoboken, New Jersey : John Wiley & Sons, Inc., [2016] | Series: Essentials of psychological assessment | Includes bibliographical references and index.
Identifiers: LCCN 2016025373 (print) | LCCN 2016037821 (ebook) | ISBN 9781119076872 (pbk.) | ISBN 9781119077091 (epdf) | ISBN 9781119076834 (epub)
Subjects: LCSH: Kaufman Test of Educational Achievement. | Wechsler Individual Achievement Test. | Ability—Testing.
Classification: LCC LB3060.33.K38 B74 2016 (print) | LCC LB3060.33.K38 (ebook) | DDC 371.26—dc23
LC record available at https://lccn.loc.gov/2016025373

Cover Design: Wiley
Cover Image: © Greg Kuchik/Getty Images

Printed in the United States of America

FIRST EDITION

*PB Printing*   10 9 8 7 6 5 4 3

*To Gary, Jane, and Donovan,*
*Thank you for giving me the time I needed,*
*encouraging me in wonderful ways*
*(like French press coffee, artwork, and silly songs),*
*and sustaining me with your love.*
*—Kristina*

*To Mike, Hannah, and Lauren,*
*Thank you for your unwavering support,*
*your steadfast encouragement,*
*and your unconditional love.*
*—Liz*

# CONTENTS

# SERIES PREFACE

I n the *Essentials of Psychological Assessment* series, we have attempted to provide the reader with books that will deliver key practical information in the most efficient and accessible style. Many books in the series feature specific instruments in a variety of domains, such as cognition, personality, education, and neuropsychology. Other books, like *Essentials of KTEA-3 and WIAT-III Assessment*, focus on crucial topics for professionals who are involved in any with assessment—topics such as specific reading disabilities, evidence-based interventions, or ADHD assessment. For the experienced professional, books in the series offer a concise yet thorough review of a test instrument or a specific area of expertise, including numerous tips for best practices. Students can turn to series books for a clear and concise overview of the important assessment tools, and key topics, in which they must become proficient to practice skillfully, efficiently, and ethically in their chosen fields.

Wherever feasible, visual cues highlighting key points are utilized alongside systematic, step-by-step guidelines. Chapters are focused and succinct. Topics are organized for an easy understanding of the essential material related to a particular test or topic. Theory and research are continually woven into the fabric of each book, but always to enhance the practical application of the material, rather than to sidetrack or overwhelm readers. With this series, we aim to challenge and assist readers interested in psychological assessment to aspire to the highest level of competency by arming them with the tools they need for knowledgeable, informed practice. We have long been advocates of "intelligent" testing—the notion that numbers are meaningless unless they are brought to life by the clinical acumen and expertise of examiners. Assessment must be used to make a difference in the child's or adult's life, or why bother to test? All books in the series—whether devoted to specific tests or general topics—are consistent with this credo. We want this series to help our readers, novice and veteran alike, to benefit from the intelligent assessment approaches of the authors of each book.

We are delighted to include *Essentials of KTEA-3 and WIAT-III Assessment* in our series. In this book, the authors provide readers with succinct, straightforward, theory-based methods for competent clinical interpretation and application of the most recent editions of two widely used tests of individual achievement. Both the KTEA-3 and WIAT-III are normed for children, adolescents, and adults, and these tests are used in a wide variety of settings. This book helps ease the transition of examiners who have been longtime users of the earlier editions of these tests, and provides a solid foundation for new examiners who are first discovering the abundance of information that can be gathered from these two individual assessment instruments. These tests of achievement both tap the important domains of academic ability required for an assessment of learning disabilities. This book thoroughly integrates theory, research, clinical history, and clinical inference with sets of guidelines that enable the examiner to administer, and then systematically interpret and apply, the KTEA-3 and the WIAT-III. The digital resources offered with this book supplement the comprehensive information provided in the text, offering examiners a cutting-edge resource that will optimize and extend KTEA-3 and WIAT-III assessment results and interpretation.

*Alan S. Kaufman, PhD, and Nadeen L. Kaufman, EdD, Series Editors*
Yale Child Study Center, Yale University School of Medicine

# ACKNOWLEDGMENTS

We would like to acknowledge several people for their special and extraordinary contributions. We are particularly grateful to Ron Dumont and John Willis, whose expert opinions and eagle eyes helped evaluate both the KTEA™-3 and WIAT®-III to create an unbiased chapter on the strengths and weaknesses of these instruments. We also appreciate the expertise and assistance that Thomas Witholt and James Henke gave in helping develop rich content for our chapter on Q-interactive. Invaluable data analysis was provided by psychometrician Xuechun Zhou, which allowed us to add new composite scores for both the KTEA™-3 and WIAT®-III. We are grateful for the contributions of interesting clinical case reports by Michelle Lurie and Debra Broadbooks, which helped bring the use of the two tests to life. Finally, the contributions of Marquita Flemming, Tisha Rossi, and the rest of the staff at John Wiley & Sons are gratefully acknowledged. Their expertise and pleasant and cooperative working style made this book an enjoyable and productive endeavor.

# Essentials of
# KTEA™-3 and WIAT®-III Assessment

# One

## OVERVIEW

Over the past few years, there have been many changes affecting those who administer standardized achievement tests. New individually administered tests of achievement have been developed, older instruments have been revised or renormed, and new electronic methods of test administration have been developed. The academic assessment of individuals from preschool to post–high school has increased over the past years due to requirements set forth by states for determining eligibility for services for learning disabilities. Individual achievement tests were once primarily norm-based comparisons with peers but now serve the purpose of analyzing academic strengths and weaknesses via comparisons with conormed or linked individual tests of ability. In addition, the focus of academic assessment has been broadened to include not only reading decoding, spelling, and arithmetic but also areas such as reading comprehension, arithmetic reasoning, arithmetic computation, listening comprehension, oral expression, and written expression (Smith, 2001).

These changes in the field of individual academic assessment have led professionals to search for resources that would help them remain current on the most recent instruments. Resources covering topics such as how to administer, score, and interpret frequently used tests of achievement and on how to apply these tests' data in clinical situations need to be frequently updated. Thus, in 2001, Douglas K. Smith published a book in the *Essentials* series titled *Essentials of Individual Achievement Assessment,* which devoted chapters to four widely used individually administered tests of achievement.[1] Smith's book was the inspiration for writing this book, which focuses on the most recent editions of two of the instruments written about in *Essentials of Individual Achievement Assessment*: the Wechsler Individual Achievement Test (WIAT) and the Kaufman Test of Educational Achievement (KTEA). Because both of these instruments are widely used achievement tests in school psychology and related fields,

---

1. Another widely used achievement test, the Woodcock Johnson–Fourth Edition (WJ-IV; Schrank, Mather, & McGrew, 2014) is the topic of its own book in the *Essentials* series entitled *Essentials of WJ-IV Tests of Achievement Assessment* (Mather & Wendling, 2015).

the third editions of the WIAT and KTEA are deserving of a complete up-to-date book devoted to their administration, scoring, interpretation, and clinical applications. *Essentials of KTEA-3 and WIAT-III Assessment* provides that up-to-date information and includes rich information beyond what is available in the tests' manuals. Digital administration and scoring through the Q-interactive system is the focus of a chapter designed to benefit new, novice, and even experienced Q-interactive users. An entire chapter is devoted to illustrative case reports to exemplify how the results of the KTEA-3 and WIAT-III can be integrated with an entire battery of tests to yield a thorough understanding of a student's academic functioning. In a chapter devoted to clinical applications of the tests, the following topics are discussed: the integration of the KTEA-3 and WIAT-III with tests of cognitive ability, focusing on the conceptual and theoretical links between tests, and the assessment of special populations, including specific learning disabilities (under IDEA 2004) and attention-deficit/hyperactivity disorder, or hearing impairments. Expanding on the topic of learning disabilities, the identification of common reading disability subtypes using the KTEA-3 and WIAT-III is discussed. Gender differences in writing are also addressed. Key information on using the WIAT-III and KTEA-3 to monitor a student's response to intervention further enriches the chapter on clinical applications.

## PURPOSES AND USES OF ACHIEVEMENT TESTS

The WIAT-III and KTEA-3 are used for many reasons, including diagnosing achievement, identifying processes, analyzing errors, making placement decisions and planning programs, measuring academic progress, evaluating interventions or programs, and conducting research. Some pertinent applications of these tests are described next.

### Diagnosing Achievement

The WIAT-III and KTEA-3 provide the following types of information for diagnosing academic achievement:

- A general estimate of academic achievement, which may include the WIAT-III Total Achievement composite, the KTEA-3 (Comprehensive or Brief Form) Academic Skills Battery composite, or the Brief Achievement composite from the KTEA-3 Brief.
- An analysis of a student's academic strengths and weaknesses in reading, mathematics, spelling, written expression, and oral language (listening and speaking). This assessment data may be used as part of a comprehensive assessment for identifying a learning disability.

- Investigation of related factors that may affect academic achievement, such as Phonological Awareness, Naming Facility (RAN), and Associational Fluency on the KTEA-3 and Early Reading Skills (includes items for assessing phonological awareness), Oral Word Fluency, Expressive Vocabulary, and Receptive Vocabulary on the WIAT-III.

## Identifying Processes

Pairwise subtest comparisons on both the WIAT-III and KTEA-3 allow examiners to better understand how students comprehend language (Reading Comprehension versus Listening Comprehension) and express their ideas (Written Expression versus Oral Expression).

## Analyzing Errors

The KTEA-3 provides a detailed quantitative summary of the types or patterns of errors a student makes on 10 of the 19 KTEA-3 subtests, including Letter & Word Recognition, Nonsense Word Decoding, Phonological Processing, Spelling, Reading Comprehension, Listening Comprehension, Written Expression, Oral Expression, Math Concepts & Applications, and Math Computation. Tracking error patterns can help examiners plan appropriate remedial instruction specifically targeting the difficulties that a student displays.

The WIAT-III provides skills analysis capabilities that also yield a detailed quantitative summary of the types of errors a student makes on seven of the 16 subtests. This information helps examiners evaluate a student's error patterns and skill strengths and weaknesses. Each subtest includes sets of items that measure a specific skill or set of skills. Analyzing the student's errors through the skills analysis yields information that can then be used in the design of an instructional plan or specific intervention for a student.

The KTEA-3 and WIAT-III score reports accessible through Q-global or Q-interactive provide detailed error analysis assessment data to summarize the skills a student needs to be taught and provide recommendations for teaching those skills. In addition, the new Q-global Intervention Guide for LD Subtypes takes into account the student's pattern of performance across cognitive, language, and achievement areas to identify potential learning disability subtypes and make recommendations about how to tailor an intervention approach. The recommendations from this Intervention Guide consider a student's areas of relative strength when remediating relative weaknesses.

## Making Placement Decisions and Planning Programs

The WIAT-III and KTEA-3 norm-referenced scores, along with the error analysis information, indicate an examinee's approximate instructional level. These results can inform decisions regarding appropriate educational placement as well as appropriate accommodations or curricular adjustments for new student admissions or transfers from other educational settings. The information can also assist in the development of an individualized education program (IEP) based on a student's needs. For adolescents and adults, the results can help inform decisions regarding general equivalency diploma (GED) preparation, appropriate vocational training, or job placement decisions.

## Measuring Academic Progress

As a general guideline, wait about 8 months to 1 year before readministering the same form of an achievement test. For the WIAT-III, academic progress can be measured by retesting after enough time has passed between administrations, taking into consideration any potential practice effects.

The two parallel forms of the KTEA-3 Comprehensive Form allow an examiner to measure a student's academic progress while ensuring that changes in performance are not due to the student's familiarity with the battery content. The KTEA-3 Brief (which is identical to the core battery of Comprehensive Form B) may also be alternated with the KTEA-3 Comprehensive Form A to reduce practice effects when measuring progress over time.

Reporting growth scale values (GSVs) is highly recommended when evaluating an examinee's performance across administrations. GSVs and GSV charts are available on both the KTEA-3 and the WIAT-III to facilitate a comparison of performance over time.

## Evaluating Interventions or Programs

The WIAT-III and KTEA-3 can provide information about the effectiveness of specific academic interventions or programs. For example, one or more of the composite scores could demonstrate the effectiveness of a new reading program within a classroom or examine the relative performance levels between classrooms using different math programs.

## Conducting Research

The WIAT-III and the KTEA-3 Comprehensive Form are reliable, valid measures of academic achievement that are suitable for use in many research designs. Indeed, a brief search of the literature yielded hundreds of articles that utilized the WIAT or the

KTEA. The two parallel forms of the KTEA-3 make it an ideal instrument for longitudinal studies or research on intervention effectiveness using pre- and post-test designs.

The KTEA-3 Brief Form is also a reliable, valid measure of academic achievement that is ideal for research designs that call for a screening measure of achievement. The brevity of the KTEA-II Brief Form makes it useful in estimating the educational achievement of large numbers of prisoners, patients in a hospital, military recruits, applicants to industry training programs, or juvenile delinquents awaiting court hearings, where administering long tests may be impractical.

## Screening

The KTEA-3 Brief Form is intended for screening examinees on their basic skills in mathematics, reading, and writing. The results of the screening may be used to determine the need for follow-up testing. The KTEA-3 Brief Form and Comprehensive Form (A or B) may be integrated efficiently without readministering subtests. In this way, the Brief Form is ideally suited for contributing information about basic academic skills to a more comprehensive evaluation.

## SELECTING AN ACHIEVEMENT TEST

Selecting the appropriate achievement test to use in a specific situation depends on a number of factors.[2] The test should be reliable, valid, and used only for the purposes for which it was developed. The *Code of Fair Testing Practices in Education* (Joint Committee on Testing Practices, 2004) outlines the responsibilities of both test developers and test users. Key components of the Code are outlined in Rapid Reference 1.1.

### ≡ *Rapid Reference 1.1*

**Excerpts from the Code of Fair Testing Practices in Education**

#### A. Selecting Appropriate Tests

Test users should select tests that meet the intended purpose and that are appropriate for the intended test takers.

1. Define the purpose for testing, the content and skills to be tested, and the intended test takers. Select and use the most appropriate test based on a thorough review of available information.

*(continued)*

---

2. Portions of this section were adapted from Chapter 1 of *Essentials of Individual Achievement Assessment* (Smith, 2001).

*(Continued)*

2. Review and select tests based on the appropriateness of test content, skills tested, and content coverage for the intended purpose of testing.
3. Review materials provided by test developers and select tests for which clear, accurate, and complete information is provided.
4. Select tests through a process that includes persons with appropriate knowledge, skills, and training.
5. Evaluate evidence of the technical quality of the test provided by the test developer and any independent reviewers.
6. Evaluate representative samples of test questions or practice tests, directions, answer sheets, manuals, and score reports before selecting a test.
7. Evaluate procedures and materials used by test developers, as well as the resulting test, to ensure that potentially offensive content or language is avoided.
8. Select tests with appropriately modified forms or administration procedures for test takers with disabilities who need special accommodations.
9. Evaluate the available evidence on the performance of test takers of diverse sub-groups. Determine to the extent feasible which performance differences may have been caused by factors unrelated to the skills being assessed.

## B. Administering and Scoring Tests

Test users should administer and score tests correctly and fairly.

1. Follow established procedures for administering tests in a standardized manner.
2. Provide and document appropriate procedures for test takers with disabilities who need special accommodations or those with diverse linguistic backgrounds. Some accommodations may be required by law or regulation.
3. Provide test takers with an opportunity to become familiar with test question formats and any materials or equipment that may be used during testing.
4. Protect the security of test materials, including respecting copyrights and eliminating opportunities for test takers to obtain scores by fraudulent means.
5. If test scoring is the responsibility of the test user, provide adequate training to scorers and ensure and monitor the accuracy of the scoring process.
6. Correct errors that affect the interpretation of the scores and communicate the corrected results promptly.
7. Develop and implement procedures for ensuring the confidentiality of scores.

## C. Reporting and Interpreting Test Results

Test users should report and interpret test results accurately and clearly.

1. Interpret the meaning of the test results, taking into account the nature of the content, norms or comparison groups, other technical evidence, and benefits and limitations of test results.

*(continued)*

(*Continued*)

2. Interpret test results from modified test or test administration procedures in view of the impact those modifications may have had on test results.

3. Avoid using tests for purposes other than those recommended by the test developer unless there is evidence to support the intended use or interpretation.

4. Review the procedures for setting performance standards or passing scores. Avoid using stigmatizing labels.

5. Avoid using a single test score as the sole determinant of decisions about test takers. Interpret test scores in conjunction with other information about individuals.

6. State the intended interpretation and use of test results for groups of test takers. Avoid grouping test results for purposes not specifically recommended by the test developer unless evidence is obtained to support the intended use. Report procedures that were followed in determining who were and who were not included in the groups being compared and describe factors that might influence the interpretation of results.

7. Communicate test results in a timely fashion and in a manner that is understood by the test taker.

8. Develop and implement procedures for monitoring test use, including consistency with the intended purposes of the test.

## D. Informing Test Takers

Test users should inform test takers about the nature of the test, test taker rights and responsibilities, the appropriate use of scores, and procedures for resolving challenges to scores.

1. Inform test takers in advance of the test administration about the coverage of the test, the types of question formats, the directions, and appropriate test-taking strategies. Make such information available to all test takers.

2. When a test is optional, provide test takers or their parents/guardians with information to help them judge whether a test should be taken—including indications of any consequences that may result from not taking the test (e.g., not being eligible to compete for a particular scholarship)—and whether there is an available alternative to the test.

3. Provide test takers or their parents/guardians with information about rights test takers may have to obtain copies of tests and completed answer sheets, to retake tests, to have tests rescored, or to have scores declared invalid.

4. Provide test takers or their parents/guardians with information about responsibilities test takers have, such as being aware of the intended purpose and uses of the test, performing at capacity, following directions, and not disclosing test items or interfering with other test takers.

(*continued*)

(Continued)

5. Inform test takers or their parents/guardians how long scores will be kept on file and indicate to whom, under what circumstances, and in what manner test scores and related information will or will not be released. Protect test scores from unauthorized release and access.

6. Describe procedures for investigating and resolving circumstances that might result in canceling or withholding scores, such as failure to adhere to specified testing procedures.

7. Describe procedures that test takers, parents/guardians, and other interested parties may use to obtain more information about the test, register complaints, and have problems resolved.

Note: The Code was developed in 1988 and was revised in 2004 by the Joint Committee of Testing Practices, a cooperative effort of several professional organizations that has as its aim the advancement, in the public interest, of the quality of testing practices. The Joint Committee was initiated by the American Educational Research Association (AERA), the American Psychological Association (APA), and the National Council on Measurement in Education (NCME). In addition to these three groups, the American Association for Counseling and Development/Association for Measurement and Evaluation in Counseling and Development and the American Speech-Language-Hearing Association also now sponsor the Joint Committee.

Source: Code of Fair Testing Practices in Education (Joint Committee on Testing Practices, 2004).

The first factor to consider in selecting an achievement test is the purpose of the testing. Discern whether a comprehensive measure (covering the areas of achievement specified in the Individuals with Disabilities Improvement Act of 2004 [Public Law (PL) 108-446]) is needed or whether a less specific screening measure is appropriate. Another issue is whether an analysis for the identification of a specific learning disability will need to be examined. Although PL 108-446 does not require the presence of an achievement-ability discrepancy for determining eligibility for learning disabilities services, states still have the option to include this discrepancy if they choose. For this purpose, using achievement tests with conormed or linked ability tests is best. To gather diagnostic information and information about the level of skill development, you should use a test with skills analysis procedures.

The second factor to consider in selecting an achievement test is whether a particular test can answer the specific questions asked in the referral concerns. The specificity of the referral questions will help guide the test selection. For example, if the referral concern is about a child's reading fluency, the test you select should have one or more subtests that directly assess that domain.

The third factor to consider in selecting an achievement test is how familiar an examiner is with a certain test. Familiarity with a test and experience with scoring and interpretation is necessary to ethically utilize it in an assessment. If you plan to use a new test in an assessment, you should ensure that you have enough time to get proper training and experience with the instrument before using it.

The fourth factor to consider in selecting an achievement test is whether the test's standardization is appropriate. Consider the recency of the test's norms. Most recent major tests of academic achievement are well standardized, but you should still review the manual to evaluate the normative group. For example, verify that the sample size was adequate and appropriate stratification variables were used in the standardization sample. When evaluating an individual with a clinical or special group classification, consider whether a special study was conducted with the target classification group and the strength of the results.

The fifth factor to consider in selecting an achievement test is the strength of its psychometric properties. Consider whether the test's data have adequately demonstrated its reliability and validity. A test's internal consistency, test-retest reliability, and correlations with other achievement tests and tests of cognitive ability should all be examined. Additionally, consider the floor and ceiling of a test across age levels. Some tests have poor floors at the youngest age levels for the children with the lowest skills, and other tests have poor ceilings at the oldest age levels for the children with the highest skill levels. You can judge the adequacy of the floors and ceilings by examining the standard score range of the subtests and composites for the age range of the student you are assessing.

In Chapter 5 of this book, Ron Dumont and John Willis review what they feel are the strengths and weaknesses of the WIAT-III and KTEA-3, respectively. We encourage examiners to carefully review the test they select to administer, whether it is the WIAT-III, KTEA-3, or another achievement test, to ensure that it can adequately assess the unique concerns of the student for whom the evaluation is being conducted. Rapid Reference 1.2 summarizes the key points to consider in test selection.

## ≋ Rapid Reference 1.2

### Key Points to Consider in Test Selection

- Consider the Purpose of the Assessment and What Type of Test(s) It Demands
  - Comprehensive assessment
  - Screening assessment
  - Identification of a learning disability
  - Skills analysis

(continued)

*(Continued)*

- **Consider Your Experience With the Assessment Instrument You Are Planning to Administer**
  - Administration (extensive, some, or no experience?)
  - Scoring (extensive, some, or no experience?)
  - Interpretation (extensive, some, or no experience?)
- **Consider the Adequacy of the Test's Standardization**
  - Are norms recent?
  - Was the standardization sample appropriate?
  - Were studies conducted with students with learning disabilities?
  - Was the norm sample appropriately stratified according to age, gender, geographic region, ethnicity, and socioeconomic status?
- **Consider the Psychometric Qualities of the Test**
  - Is the test's reliability adequate (internal consistency and test-retest reliability)?
  - Is the test's validity adequate (correlations with other achievement tests, correlations with ability tests)?
  - Does the test have an adequate floor for the age of the student you are assessing?
  - Does the test have an adequate ceiling for the age of the student you are assessing?

## ADMINISTERING STANDARDIZED ACHIEVEMENT TESTS

The WIAT-III and KTEA-3 are standardized tests, meaning that they measure a student's performance on tasks that are administered and scored under known conditions that remain constant from time to time and person to person. Standardized testing allows examiners to directly compare the performance of one student to the performance of many other students of the same age who were tested in the same way. Strict adherence to the rules allows examiners to know that the scores obtained from the child they tested are comparable to those obtained from the normative group. Violating the rules of standardized administration renders norms of limited value. Being completely familiar with the test, its materials, and the administration procedures allows examiners to conduct a valid assessment in a manner that feels natural, comfortable, and personal—not mechanical. The specific administration procedures for the KTEA-3 are discussed in Chapter 2, those for the WIAT-III are discussed in Chapter 3, and administration and scoring through Q-interactive for these instruments are discussed in Chapter 7.

### Testing Environment

Achievement testing, like most standardized testing, should take place in a quiet room that is free of distractions. The table and chairs that are used during the assessment should be of appropriate size for the student being assessed. That is, if you are assessing a preschooler, then the table and chairs used should be similar to those that you would find in a preschool classroom. However, if you are assessing an adolescent, adult-size table and chairs are appropriate.

When administering the KTEA-3 or the WIAT-III with Q-interactive on iPad devices, the examiner should make sure that the testing environment has a power outlet in case the iPads need to be charged before or during the assessment. Prior to administration, your iPad should be connected to a secure Wi-Fi or 3G connection, so you can transfer your assessments from Q-interactive Central to Q-interactive Assess. Generally, set up the testing environment in the same manner as you do for a traditional assessment session. Consider the client's iPad as the stimulus book, and the examiner's iPad should be propped up with its case so that the screen is out of view of the client.

For the WIAT-III administration with easels, the seating arrangement should allow both the examiner and the student to view the front side of the easel. For the KTEA-3 administration with easels, the seating arrangement should allow the examiner to see both sides of the easel. The examiner must also be able to write responses and scores discreetly on the record form (out of plain view of the examinee). Many examiners find the best seating arrangement is to be at a right angle from the examinee, but others prefer to sit directly across from the examinee. The test's stimulus easel can be used to shield the record form from the student's view, but if you prefer, you may also use a clipboard to keep the record form out of view. Sit wherever is most comfortable for you and allows you easy access to all of the components of the assessment instrument.

## Establishing Rapport

In order to ensure that the most valid results are yielded from a test session, try to create the best possible environment for the examinee. Perhaps more important than the previously discussed physical aspects of the testing environment is the relationship between the examiner and the student. In many cases, the examiner will be a virtual stranger to the student being assessed. Thus, the process of establishing rapport is a key component in setting the stage for an optimal assessment.

Rapport can be defined as a relationship of mutual trust or emotional affinity. Such a relationship typically takes time to develop. To foster the development of positive rapport, you need to plan on a few minutes of relaxed time with the student before diving into the assessment procedures. Some individuals are slow to warm up to new acquaintances, whereas others are friendly and comfortable with new people from the get-go. Assume that most students you meet will need time before being able to comfortably relate to you.

You can help a student feel more comfortable through your style of speech and your topics of conversation. Adapt your language (vocabulary and style) to the student's age and ability level (i.e., don't talk to a 4-year-old as you would a teenager, and vice versa). Use a friendly tone of voice, and show genuine personal interest and responsiveness. For shy children, rather than opening up immediately with conversation, try an ice-breaking activity such as drawing a picture or playing with an age-appropriate toy. This quiet interaction with concrete materials may provide an opening to elicit conversation about them.

In most instances, it is best not to have a parent, teacher, or other person present during the assessment, as it can affect the test results in unknown ways. However, when a child is having extreme difficulty separating, it can be useful to permit another adult's presence in the initial rapport-building phase of the assessment to help the child ease into the testing situation. Once the child's anxiety has decreased or once the child has become interested in playing or drawing with you, encourage the student to begin the assessment without the adult present.

Maintaining rapport requires diligent effort throughout an assessment. Watch students for signs of fatigue, disinterest, and frustration. These signs are clues that you need to increase your feedback, give a break, or suggest a reward for completing tasks. Using good eye contact will help you show interest and enthusiasm for the student's efforts. Use your clinical judgment about how much praise a child needs for his or her efforts. Some children will need more pats on the back than others. Always praise students for their efforts, not the correctness of their responses.

## SUMMARY INFORMATION ABOUT THE TESTS AND THEIR PUBLISHERS

The KTEA-3 Comprehensive and Brief Forms and the WIAT-III are published by Pearson under the brand PsychCorp. In Rapid Reference 1.3 and Rapid Reference 1.4, we provide a summary of important information about the WIAT-III, KTEA-3 Comprehensive Form, and KTEA-3 Brief Form. These Rapid References provide information on the following topics: test author, publisher, publication date, what the test measures, age range covered by the test, administration time, and test price. To be qualified to purchase either the KTEA-3 or the WIAT-III individuals must meet one of the following standards:

- A master's degree in psychology, education, occupational therapy, social work, or in a field closely related to the intended use of the assessment, and formal training in the ethical administration, scoring, and interpretation of clinical assessments.

## ≡ *Rapid Reference 1.3*

### Basic Information About the Wechsler Individual Achievement Test–Third Edition

| | |
|---|---|
| Author | WIAT-III: Pearson |
| Publication Date | 2009<br>Adult norms: 2010 |
| What the Test Measures | Basic Reading, Reading Comprehension, Reading Fluency, Mathematics Calculation, Mathematics Problem Solving, Written Expression, Listening Comprehension, and Oral Expression. |
| Age Range | 4–50 years |
| Administration Time | Estimates based upon the time it took for 50% of the standardization sample to administer all grade-appropriate subtests.<br>Pre-K–Kindergarten: 35–45 minutes<br>Grades 1–3: 80–94 minutes<br>Grades 4–12+: 104 minutes |
| Publisher | Pearson<br>800.627.7271<br>www.pearsonclinical.com/ |
| Price<br>(Pricing is subject to change) | **WIAT-III Kit**<br>**Without Q-Global scoring: $545**<br>**With Q-Global scoring: $699**<br>Includes Examiner's Manual, Technical Manual CD, Stimulus Book, Scoring Workbook, Oral Reading Fluency Book, Word Card, Pseudo Word Card, Audio CD, Response Booklets (25), Record Forms (25), and optional Q-global Score Reports (75).<br><br>**WIAT-III Printed Tech Manual: $30**<br>ISBN 0158984722<br>*Note: Consumers must call to order this item*<br><br>**WIAT-III Q-interactive:**<br>Pricing options are available per subtest or by subscription (see www.helloq.com/pricing/Price-Options.html) |

## ⪑ *Rapid Reference 1.4*

### Basic Information About the Kaufman Test of Educational Achievement–Third Edition

| | |
|---|---|
| Author | Alan S. Kaufman and Nadeen L. Kaufman |
| Publication Date | KTEA-3 Comprehensive Form: 2014<br>KTEA-3 Brief Form: 2015 |
| What the Test Measures | The following achievement domains are measured in both the Comprehensive and Brief Forms: Reading, Mathematics, and Written Language. The Comprehensive Form measures an additional fourth domain: Oral Language. |
| Age Range | 4–25 years (Comprehensive & Brief Forms) |
| Administration Time | Academic Skills Battery Composite: 15 min. for Pre-K to 85 min. for grades 3+<br>Brief Form BA-3 composite: 20 minutes |
| Publisher | Pearson<br>800.627.7271<br>www.pearsonclinical.com |
| Price<br>*(Pricing is subject to change)* | **KTEA-3 Comprehensive Form A or B Kit**<br>**Without Q-Global Scoring: $420.50**<br>**With Q-Global Scoring : $625.25**<br>Includes Administration Manual, Scoring Manual, 2 Stimulus Books, USB Flash Drive (contains Technical Manual, Audio Files, Scoring Keys, Hand Scoring Forms, Letter Checklist, Qualitative Observations Form, Error Analysis Forms), Form A Record Forms (25), Form A Response Booklet (25), 3 Form A Written Expression booklets (2 each), soft-sided carrying bag, and optional Q-global Score Reports (100).<br><br>**KTEA-3 Brief Form Kit: $297**<br>Includes Administration Manual, Stimulus Book, USB Flash Drive (contains Technical Manual, Audio Files), Record Form (25), Response Booklet (25), and Form B Written Expression Booklet (2 each of Levels 2-4).<br><br>**KTEA-3 Printed Tech Manual: $30**<br>Product Number 32442<br>*Note: Consumers must call to order this item*<br><br>**KTEA-3 Q-interactive:**<br>Pricing options are available per subtest or by subscription (see www.helloq.com/pricing/Price-Options.html) |

- Certification by or full active membership in a professional organization (such as ASHA, AOTA, AERA, ACA, AMA, CEC, AEA, AAA, EAA, NAEYC, NBCC) that requires training and experience in the relevant area of assessment.
- A degree or license to practice in the healthcare or allied healthcare field.
- Formal, supervised mental health, speech/language, and/or educational training specific to assessing children, or in infant and child development, and formal training in the ethical administration, scoring, and interpretation of clinical assessments.

# Two

# KTEA™-3

T he Kaufman Test of Educational Achievement–Third Edition (KTEA-3) was developed to assess the academic achievement of individuals ages 4 through 25 (prekindergarten through adult). The KTEA-3 has two versions: the Brief Form (Kaufman & Kaufman, 2015a) and the Comprehensive Form (Kaufman & Kaufman, 2014a). The Brief Form assesses three academic domains (reading, math, and written expression). The Comprehensive form assesses a fourth domain (oral language) as well as additional reading-related, oral, and cross-domain areas. The Comprehensive Form includes two independent parallel forms, A and B, which were designed with very few to no overlapping items.

The six KTEA-3 Brief subtests are exactly the same as the core subtests from Comprehensive Form B. Examiners who need to build on the KTEA-3 Brief results for a more in-depth academic evaluation are able to integrate the results from the KTEA-3 Brief and the KTEA-3 Comprehensive (Form A or B) without readministering subtests.

Much of the information in this chapter pertains specifically to the Comprehensive Form; however, administration and scoring information for the subtests included in both the Brief Form and Comprehensive Form applies to both tests. Additional information specific to the Brief Form is discussed in two sections in this chapter: *Overview of the KTEA-3 Brief Form* summarizes its benefits and uses, psychometric properties, and differences from the Comprehensive Form. *Using the KTEA-3 Brief Form* provides further information about using the Brief Form for various purposes and in conjunction with the Comprehensive Form.

## HISTORY AND DEVELOPMENT

Over a 4-year period beginning in 1981, Drs. Alan and Nadeen Kaufman developed the first edition of the Kaufman Test of Educational Achievement (K-TEA). The K-TEA was standardized in both the Spring and Fall of 1983. The normative groups were composed of 1,409 students in the spring and 1,067 in the fall. Upon completion of the standardization, the K-TEA was published in 1985. Then, in the mid-1990s, American Guidance Service, publisher of the K-TEA, restandardized the original K-TEA to match the 1994 U.S. Bureau of the Census estimates of the population. No changes were made to the items and scales of the K-TEA during the restandardization, but the norms were thoroughly updated. The renorming project involved four achievement batteries: the K-TEA, the Peabody Individual Achievement Test–Revised (PIAT-R), KeyMath–Revised (KeyMath-R), and the Woodcock Reading Mastery Tests–Revised (WRMT-R). The instruments all measured one or more domains of academic achievement. During the renorming, each student was administered one of the primary batteries along with subtests from the other instruments. Thus, each of the primary batteries was administered to approximately one-fifth of the standardization sample. The renorming of the K-TEA was finalized with the publication of the K-TEA/Normative Update (K-TEA/NU) by Nadeen and Alan Kaufman in 1997.

Because professionals in school psychology and related fields used the K-TEA and K-TEA/NU so frequently, the test authors decided to revise the test beginning in 1995. Indeed, studies of test usage have shown that both the K-TEA and the K-TEA/NU were used frequently in educational and clinical settings (Archer et al., 1991; Hammill, Fowler, Bryant, & Dunn, 1992; Hutton, Dubes, & Muir, 1992; Laurent & Swerdlik, 1992; Stinnett et al., 1994; Wilson & Reschley, 1996). To ensure that the KTEA-II provided the most useful and practical information to clinicians, the Kaufmans developed their plan for the second edition based on current research and clinical practice. Four main goals were targeted in the revision of the K-TEA: (1) improve the measurement of the achievement domains measured by the original K-TEA; (2) add content that is appropriate for preschool and college-age students; (3) add subtests to assess written and oral expression, listening comprehension, and reading-related skills; (4) make error analysis more informative through the systematic representation of skills, and, on some subtests, a more fine-grained approach to classifying errors.

Generally, the first step in the development of each KTEA-II subtest was to define at a conceptual level which skills should be measured for a particular academic domain (Kaufman & Kaufman, 2004a). Both literature reviews and expert opinion were used to determine what should be measured within each academic domain. The original K-TEA items were reviewed to determine which item formats should be retained and which should be modified. Since four new achievement areas were added in the KTEA-II, expert advisors contributed suggestions for content and item formats for written expression, oral expression, listening comprehension, and reading-related skills. Part of the content development of the subtests involved making sure that certain skills were systematically represented. Developing subtests in this manner helped to make error analysis more informative and also allowed a more fine-grained approach to classifying errors on some subtests.

In 2009, planning and conceptual development of the KTEA-3 began. Several key goals and primary considerations were identified for the revision of the KTEA-II and development of the KTEA-3, which are outlined in Rapid Reference 2.1

(Kaufman & Kaufman, 2014b). Pilot testing of new subtests and items was conducted in 2010 and then a national tryout of the full KTEA-3 was conducted in 2011. The KTEA-3 was standardized in the fall of 2012 and the spring of 2013.

---

### ≡ Rapid Reference 2.1

.........................................................................................................................

#### Goals of KTEA-3 Development

- Add subtests to assess reading vocabulary, reading fluency, writing fluency, and math fluency.
- Extend the age range downward, from 4:6 in the KTEA-II to 4:0 in the KTEA-3 by adding content appropriate for young 4-year-olds.
- Extend the administration grade range on several subtests downward to assess children in prekindergarten, kindergarten, and grade 1.
- Simplify the administration rules for Reading Comprehension, Listening Comprehension, and Oral Expression.
- Revise the Oral Expression subtest to provide an engaging item type that is easy to administer and score for the examiner, and that minimizes demands on listening comprehension and working memory for the examinee.
- Incorporate measures of skills that are clinically sensitive.

---

## CHANGES FROM KTEA-II TO KTEA-3

The Comprehensive Form of the KTEA-II was modified in a number of ways to create the KTEA-3. The age range assessed was increased from 4:6 to 25:11 on the KTEA-II to 4:0 to 25:11 on the KTEA-3. All 14 subtests from the KTEA-II were retained and updated. However, one subtest from the KTEA-II, Naming Facility (RAN), was divided into two separate subtests on the KTEA-3: Object Naming Facility and Letter Naming Facility. New subtests were also added to the KTEA-3 to measure reading vocabulary and fluency, writing fluency, and math fluency. By retaining 14 subtests from the KTEA-II, dividing the Naming Facility subtest into two subtests, and adding four new subtests, the KTEA-3 includes 19 subtests for assessing academic skills and areas related to learning disabilities. Further, the KTEA-3 continues to provide error analysis classification as well as error analysis norms for the same 10 subtests as in the previous edition. The composite structure, however, was substantially revised from the KTEA-II to the KTEA-3. The Don't Forget box reminds readers of these changes from the KTEA-II to the KTEA-3.

### Subtests

The KTEA-3 provides much flexibility for examiners. If only one particular domain of academic functioning is of concern, examiners may choose to administer a single subtest or any combination of subtests in that domain in order to assess an examinee's academic achievement. If multiple domains need to be measured, then all of the age-appropriate subtests can be administered to obtain the desired composite score(s). Succinct descriptions of the KTEA-3 Comprehensive Form subtests are given in Rapid Reference 2.2, which is organized by content area. The age range for each subtest varies, so the table indicates the age range at which each subtest may be administered. Regardless of whether grade or age norms are being used, examiners should use student's grade level to guide selection of subtests.

# DON'T FORGET

## Changes From the KTEA-II to the KTEA-3

### Increased Age Range

| KTEA-II Age Range: | KTEA-3 Age Range: |
|---|---|
| 4:6 to 25:11 | 4:0 to 25:11 |

### Modified Composite Structure

| KTEA-II Composites: | KTEA-3 Composites: |
|---|---|
| *Comprehensive Achievement Composite* | *Academic Skills Battery Composite* |
| Reading | Reading |
| Mathematics | Mathematics |
| Written Language | Written Language |
| Oral Language | |
| | *Reading-Related Composites* |
| *Reading-Related Composites* | Sound-Symbol |
| Sound-Symbol | Decoding |
| Decoding | Reading Fluency |
| Oral Fluency | Reading Understanding |
| Reading Fluency | |
| | *Oral Composites* |
| | Oral Language |
| | Oral Fluency |
| | |
| | *Cross Domain Composites* |
| | Comprehension |
| | Expression |
| | Orthographic Processing |
| | Academic Fluency |

### Modified Existing Subtests and Added New Subtests

| Number of KTEA-II Subtests: | Number of KTEA-3 Subtests: |
|---|---|
| 14 | 19 |

*Note:* Subtests of the KTEA-II and KTEA-3 are listed in Rapid Reference 2.2.

# ≡ Rapid Reference 2.2

## Brief Description of KTEA-3 Comprehensive Form Subtests

| Reading Subtest | Age Range | Description |
|---|---|---|
| Letter & Word Recognition | 4–25 | The examinee identifies letters and pronounces words of increasing difficulty. |
| Nonsense Word Decoding | 6–25 | The examinee reads aloud a list of nonsense words. |
| Reading Comprehension | 6–25 | Early items require matching a symbol or word(s) with a corresponding picture, or reading a simple instruction and then performing the action. Later items involve reading passages and answering comprehension questions. |
| Reading Vocabulary* | 6–25 | Early items require the examinee to point to one of three words with a similar meaning as the target word. Remaining items require the examinee to read a sentence and select the word that has a similar meaning as the target word. |

| Reading Fluency Subtest | Age Range | Description |
|---|---|---|
| Word Recognition Fluency | 6–25 | The examinee reads aloud a list of words as quickly as possible during two 15-second trials. |
| Decoding Fluency | 8–25 | The examinee reads aloud a list of nonsense words as quickly as possible during two 15-second trials. |
| Silent Reading Fluency* | 6–25 | The examinee silently reads simple sentences and marks yes or no to indicate whether the statement is true or false, completing as many items as possible within a 2-minute time limit. |

| Math Subtest | Age Range | Description |
|---|---|---|
| Math Concepts & Applications | 4–25 | The examinee responds orally to test items that focus on the application of mathematical principles to real-life situations. |

*(continued)*

(Continued)

| Math Subtest | Age Range | Description |
|---|---|---|
| Math Computation | 5–25 | The examinee writes the answers to printed math calculation problems. |
| Math Fluency* | 6–25 | The examinee writes answers to as many addition, subtraction, multiplication, and division problems as possible in 60 seconds. |

| Written Language Subtest | Age Range | Description |
|---|---|---|
| Written Expression | 4–25 | Young children trace and copy letters, and write letters, words, and a sentence from dictation. At grade 1 and higher, examinees complete writing tasks in the context of an age-appropriate storybook format. Tasks at those levels include writing sentences from dictation, adding punctuation and capitalization, completing or combining sentences, and writing an essay. |
| Spelling | 5–25 | Early items require students to write single letters that represent sounds. Later items involve spelling words from dictation. |
| Writing Fluency* | 7–25 | The examinee writes one sentence about each picture presented in the response booklet and completes as many items as possible within a 5-minute time limit. |

| Oral Language Subtest | Age Range | Description |
|---|---|---|
| Listening Comprehension | 4–25 | The examinee listens to a sentence or recorded passages and then responds orally to comprehension questions asked by the examiner. |
| Oral Expression | 4–25 | The examinee responds orally with a complete sentence to describe each photograph. Later items require the use of one or two target words or a beginning phrase. |
| Associational Fluency | 4–25 | The examinee says as many words as possible in 60 seconds that belong to a semantic category. |

(continued)

(Continued)

| Language Processing Subtest | Age Range | Description |
|---|---|---|
| Phonological Processing | 4–25 | The examinee responds orally to items that require manipulation of sounds within words. |
| Object Naming Facility** | 4–25 | The examinee names pictured objects as quickly as possible. |
| Letter Naming Facility** | 5–25 | The examinee names a combination of upper and lowercase letters as quickly as possible. |

Note: Fourteen KTEA-II Comprehensive Form subtests were retained and expanded to create the KTEA-3 and the four new subtests indicated above with an asterisk (Reading Vocabulary, Silent Reading Fluency, Math Fluency, and Writing Fluency) were added for the KTEA-3. In addition, the subtests listed with a double asterisk, Naming Object Facility and Letter Naming Facility, were previously combined in one subtest on the KTEA-II (Naming Facility). Subtest descriptions were adapted from Table 1.3 of the KTEA-3 Administration Manual (Kaufman & Kaufman, 2014c, p. 5).

Generally, scores from the KTEA-II Comprehensive Form correlate very highly with comparable scores from the KTEA-3 Comprehensive Form. For example, in a sample of 92 examinees in grades 2 through 12, the KTEA-II Comprehensive Achievement Composite and the KTEA-3 Academic Skills Battery composite correlated .93. These correlations are quite strong despite the fact that the KTEA-3 Academic Skills Battery composite for that age range has a slightly different combination of subtests from the previous edition (i.e., contains Spelling rather than Listening Comprehension).

The three KTEA-3 core composites also correlated very highly with their like-named composites on the KTEA-II Comprehensive. For example, the correlations between the KTEA-3 and KTEA-II Reading, Math, and Written Language Composites were .87, .93, and .87, respectively. Similarly, the like-named reading related composites also correlated highly across both the second and third editions of the test: Sound Symbol (.88), Decoding (.91), and Reading Fluency (.83). The KTEA-II and KTEA-3 correlations on the Oral Language and Oral Fluency Composites were slightly lower (.60 and .64, respectively), which was likely due to the new changes made to the subtests within these composites. Correlations at the subtest level were moderate to high, and generally ranged from the mid-.60s to the low-.90s. However, there were three subtests that displayed lower correlations due to the changes to the subtests across editions (e.g., Oral Expression and Associational Fluency were below .50). KTEA-II Naming Fluency correlated in the mid-.50 to mid-.60 range with the KTEA-3's new Object Naming Facility and Letter Naming Facility subtests. Rapid Reference 2.3 provides the correlations between KTEA-3 and KTEA-II subtests of the same (or similar) name.

## ≡ Rapid Reference 2.3

### Correlations Between KTEA-II and KTEA-3 Comprehensive Form Subtests of the Same Name

| Subtest | Corrected r |
| --- | --- |
| Math Concepts & Applications | 0.91 |
| Spelling | 0.88 |
| Math Computation | 0.87 |
| Nonsense Word Decoding | 0.86 |
| Letter & Word Recognition | 0.85 |
| Word Recognition Fluency | 0.82 |
| Written Expression | 0.79 |
| Reading Comprehension | 0.74 |
| Decoding Fluency | 0.71 |
| Phonological Processing (KTEA-II Phonological Awareness) | 0.66 |
| Object Naming Fluency (KTEA-II Naming Fluency) | 0.64 |
| Listening Comprehension | 0.63 |
| Letter Naming Fluency (KTEA-II Naming Fluency) | 0.55 |
| Associational Fluency | 0.48 |
| Oral Expression | 0.37 |

Note: Coefficients are from Table 2.10 of the KTEA-3 Technical & Interpretive Manual (Kaufman & Kaufman, 2014b, p. 61).

### DESCRIPTION OF THE KTEA-3

The KTEA-3 Comprehensive Form has 19 subtests that are grouped into three core composites, 10 supplemental composites, and an overall Academic Skills Battery composite. The three core composites are Reading, Mathematics, and Written Language. The 10 Supplemental composites are divided into four Reading-Related composites, two Oral composites, and four Cross-Domain composites. The composition of the KTEA-3 Comprehensive varies slightly according to grade level (or age). For example, the Academic Skills Battery composite includes six subtests for grades 1 through 12 and above, five of the six subtests for kindergarten, and only three of the six subtests for prekindergarten. Figure 2.1 details which subtests contribute the Academic Skills Battery composite and the core composites.

The ages at which core subtests may first be administered vary from Pre-K to grade 1. Three subtests are administered beginning at the Pre-K level: Letter & Word Recognition, Math Concepts & Applications, and Written Expression. Two additional subtests are first administered at the kindergarten level: Math Computation

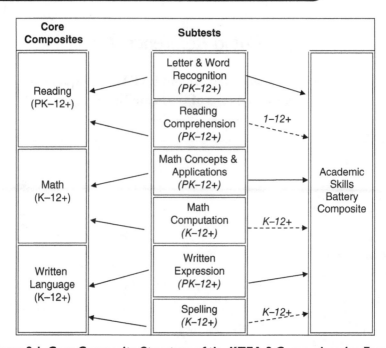

**Figure 2.1  Core Composite Structure of the KTEA-3 Comprehensive Form**

*Source:* Adapted from Figure 1.1 of the *KTEA-3 Administration Manual* (Kaufman & Kaufman, 2014c, p. 14).

and Spelling. Reading Comprehension is first administered at the grade 1 level. From kindergarten on, all three core composites can be obtained.

For children in prekindergarten (Pre-K is defined as children who have not yet begun kindergarten), the KTEA-3 Comprehensive yields only one Core composite: Reading. Although no Math or Written Language Core composites are calculated at the Pre-K level, the Math Concepts & Applications subtest and the Written Expression subtest are available for children in Pre-K. In addition, four Supplemental Composites can be calculated for the Pre-K level: Oral Language, Oral Fluency, Comprehension, and Expression. Nine subtests can be administered to examinees at the Pre-K level.

For kindergarteners, the KTEA-3 Comprehensive yields three Core composites: Reading, Math, and Written Language. Four Supplemental composites can also be calculated: Oral Language, Oral Fluency, Comprehension, and Expression. Twelve subtests can be administered to examinees at the kindergarten level.

For examinees in grades 1 through 12 and above, the three aforementioned Core composites are calculated based upon scores yielded from six subtests. From grades 1 to 12+, eight of the Supplemental composites are available; however, two of the composites, Reading Fluency and Academic Fluency, are available only for grades 3 through 12 and above. Rapid Reference 2.4 lists which subtests contribute to the Supplemental composites.

## ≋ Rapid Reference 2.4

### Structure of the KTEA-3 Supplemental Composites

| Reading Related Composites | Grade | Subtests Administered | | |
|---|---|---|---|---|
| Sound-Symbol | 1–12+ | Phonological Processing | Nonsense Word Decoding | |
| Decoding | 1–12+ | Letter & Word Recognition | Nonsense Word Decoding | |
| Reading Fluency | 3–12+ | Silent Reading Fluency | Word Recognition Fluency | Decoding Fluency |
| Reading Understanding | 1–12+ | Reading Comprehension | Reading Vocabulary | |

| Oral Composites | | | | |
|---|---|---|---|---|
| Oral Language | PK–12+ | Associational Fluency | Listening Comprehension | Oral Expression |
| Oral Fluency | PK–12+ | Associational Fluency | Object Naming Fluency | |

| Cross-Domain Composites | | | | |
|---|---|---|---|---|
| Comprehension | PK–12+ | Reading Comprehension | Listening Comprehension | |
| Expression | PK–12+ | Written Expression | Oral Expression | |
| Orthographic Processing | 1–12+ | Spelling | Letter Naming Facility | Word Recognition Fluency |
| Academic Fluency | 3–12+ | Writing Fluency | Math Fluency | Decoding Fluency |

### Mapping KTEA-3 to Common Core State Standards

The KTEA-3 was not designed as a measure of Common Core State Standards (CCSS; National Governors Association Center for Best Practices & Council of Chief State School Officers, 2010). Rather, the KTEA-3 is intended for use in all 50 states, regardless of whether a state has adopted CCSS.

For practitioners interested in mapping the KTEA-3 to CCSS, the tables in Rapid Reference 2.5 show that the KTEA-3 measures many of the skills identified by the

Common Core State Standards (CCSS) as important for meeting grade level expectations. As explained in the *Technical & Interpretive Manual* (Kaufman & Kaufman, 2014b, p. 136), the KTEA-3 was designed to measure skills that are both clinically sensitive and correspond to CCSS whenever possible. However, certain CCSS are not measured by the KTEA-3 because the standards are not relevant to the purpose and intended use of the KTEA-3, or the skill would be difficult to measure with a norm-referenced clinical assessment (Kaufman & Kaufman, 2014b, pp. 136–137).

## ≡ Rapid Reference 2.5

### KTEA-3 and the Common Core State Standards

**KTEA-3 Content Map to English Language Arts CCSS**

| Subtest / CCSS Domain | K | 1 | 2 | 3 | 4 | 5 | 6 | 7 | 8 | 9–10 | 11–12 |
|---|---|---|---|---|---|---|---|---|---|---|---|
| **Letter & Word Recognition** | | | | | | | | | | | |
| Print Concepts | • | — | | | | | | | | | |
| Phonics and Word Recognition | • | • | • | • | • | • | | | | | |
| **Reading Comprehension** | | | | | | | | | | | |
| Craft and Structure | — | — | • | • | • | • | • | • | • | — | — |
| Key Ideas and Details | — | • | • | • | • | • | • | • | — | — | — |
| Phonics and Word Recognition | — | • | • | • | • | • | | | | | |
| Vocabulary Acquisition and Use | • | • | • | • | • | • | • | • | • | — | — |
| **Nonsense Word Decoding** | | | | | | | | | | | |
| Phonics and Word Recognition | — | • | • | • | • | • | | | | | |
| **Phonological Processing** | | | | | | | | | | | |
| Phonological Awareness | • | • | | | | | | | | | |
| **Word Recognition Fluency** | | | | | | | | | | | |
| Phonics and Word Recognition | • | • | • | • | • | • | | | | | |
| **Decoding Fluency** | | | | | | | | | | | |
| Phonics and Word Recognition | — | • | • | • | • | • | | | | | |
| **Silent Reading Fluency** | | | | | | | | | | | |
| Fluency | — | • | • | • | • | • | | | | | |
| Phonics and Word Recognition | — | • | • | • | • | • | | | | | |

*(continued)*

(Continued)

| Subtest | Grade | | | | | | | | | | |
|---|---|---|---|---|---|---|---|---|---|---|---|
| CCSS Domain | K | I | 2 | 3 | 4 | 5 | 6 | 7 | 8 | 9–10 | 11–12 |
| **Reading Vocabulary** | | | | | | | | | | | |
| Vocabulary Acquisition and Use | ● | ● | ● | ● | ● | ● | ● | ● | ● | ● | ● |
| **Written Expression** | | | | | | | | | | | |
| Conventions of Standard English | ● | ● | ● | ● | ● | ● | ● | ● | ● | ● | ● |
| Print Concepts | ● | ● | | | | | | | | | |
| Text Types and Purposes | — | ● | ● | ● | ● | ● | ● | ● | ● | — | — |
| **Spelling** | | | | | | | | | | | |
| Conventions of Standard English | ● | ● | ● | ● | ● | ● | ● | ● | ● | ● | ● |
| **Writing Fluency** | | | | | | | | | | | |
| Text Types and Purposes | ● | — | — | — | — | — | — | — | — | — | — |
| **Listening Comprehension** | | | | | | | | | | | |
| Comprehension and Collaboration | ● | ● | ● | ● | ● | ● | — | — | — | — | — |
| Vocabulary Acquisition and Use | ● | ● | ● | ● | ● | ● | — | — | — | — | — |
| **Oral Expression** | | | | | | | | | | | |
| Conventions of Standard English | ● | ● | ● | ● | ● | ● | ● | ● | — | — | — |
| Presentation of Knowledge and Ideas | ● | ● | ● | ● | ● | ● | ● | ● | — | — | — |
| **Associational Fluency** | | | | | | | | | | | |
| Presentation of Knowledge and Ideas | ● | ● | — | — | — | — | — | — | — | — | — |
| Vocabulary Acquisition and Use | ● | ● | ● | ● | — | — | — | — | — | — | — |
| **Object Naming Facility** | | | | | | | | | | | |
| Presentation of Knowledge and Ideas | ● | ● | — | — | — | — | — | — | — | — | — |
| **Letter Naming Facility** | | | | | | | | | | | |
| Print Concepts | ● | — | | | | | | | | | |

Note: If a cell is shaded, no Common Core State Standard is available for that domain at that grade level.

## KTEA-3 Content Map to Mathematics CCSS

| Subtest | Grade | | | | | | | | | |
|---|---|---|---|---|---|---|---|---|---|---|
| CCSS Domain | K | 1 | 2 | 3 | 4 | 5 | 6 | 7 | 8 | High School |
| **Math Concepts & Applications** | | | | | | | | | | |
| Counting and Cardinality | • | | | | | | | | | |
| Conditional Probability and the Rules of Probability | | | | | | | | | | • |
| Expressions and Equations | | | | | | | • | • | • | |
| Geometry | • | • | • | — | — | • | • | • | • | |
| Linear, Quadratic, and Exponential Models | | | | | | | | | | • |
| Measurement and Data | • | • | • | • | • | • | | | | |
| Number and Operations in Base Ten | — | • | • | • | • | • | | | | |
| Number and Operations—Fractions | | | | • | • | • | • | | | |
| The Number System | | | | | | | — | • | — | |
| Operations and Algebraic Thinking | • | • | • | • | • | • | • | | | |
| Ratios and Proportional Relationships | | | | | | | — | • | | |
| Similarity, Right Triangles, and Trigonometry | | | | | | | | | | • |
| Statistics and Probability | | | | | | | • | • | — | |
| Trigonometric Functions | | | | | | | | | | • |
| **Math Computation** | | | | | | | | | | |
| Counting and Cardinality | • | | | | | | | | | |
| Expressions and Equations | | | | | | | • | • | • | |
| Number & Operations in Base Ten | — | • | • | • | • | • | | | | |
| Number & Operations—Fractions | | | | — | • | • | | | | |
| The Number System | | | | | | | • | — | — | |
| Operations and Algebraic Thinking | • | • | • | • | • | • | • | | | |
| Seeing Structure in Expressions | | | | | | | | | | • |
| **Math Fluency** | | | | | | | | | | |
| Number & Operations in Base Ten | — | • | • | • | • | • | | | | |
| Operations and Algebraic Thinking | • | • | • | • | • | — | | | | |

Note: If a cell is shaded, no Common Core State Standard is available for that domain at that grade level.

# STANDARDIZATION AND PSYCHOMETRIC PROPERTIES OF THE KTEA-3

This section of the chapter describes the standardization sample and provides reliability and validity information for the KTEA-3.

## Standardization

The KTEA-3 Comprehensive Form was standardized with an age-norm sample of 2,050 examinees ages 4 through 25, and a grade-norm sample of 2,600 students in prekindergarten through grade 12. For each grade level, the sample size ranged from 150 to 200 students (with half of the examinees tested in the Fall and the other half in the Spring). For each age level, most sample sizes ranged from 120 to 160 examinees, except age 4 with a sample size of 100, and ages 19–20 and 21–25, each with a sample of 75.

The KTEA-3 Comprehensive Form contains two parallel forms, so approximately half of the norm sample was administered Form A and the other half was administered Form B. The standardization sample was stratified to closely match the U.S. population. Thus, on the variables of gender, ethnicity, parental education, geographic region, and special education or gifted placement, the standardization sample closely corresponded to data from the 2012 American Community Survey of the U.S. Census Bureau. Self-education was used instead of parent education for examinees ages 19–25.

## Reliability

The internal-consistency reliability of the KTEA-3 Comprehensive is strong for both Forms A and B. The average internal-consistency reliability value across grades and forms for the Academic Skills Battery Composite is .98. The averages for the Reading, Math, and Written Language Composites are .95, .97, and .94, respectively. The average reliability values by grade for the Supplemental Composites range from .72 to .98. Reliability values based on age groups are very similar to what was reported for the reliability values found with the grade-level samples. Table 2.1 presents the internal consistency reliability values of the Comprehensive Form subtests and composites averaged across forms.

Alternate-form reliability values were calculated by administering the two forms of the KTEA-3 Comprehensive to a sample of 306 examinees. The forms were administered 7.5 days apart, on average. Similar to the internal-consistency reliability values, the values for the alternate-form reliability are also high. The Academic Skills Battery Composites showed very high consistency across time and forms (mid-.90s). The Reading, Math, and Written Language Composites have alternate-form reliabilities in the high .80s to mid .90s. These strong values indicate that the alternate forms of the KTEA-3 will be useful for reducing practice effects when the test is administered more than once. Table 2.2 shows the alternate form reliability values.

**Table 2.1 Average Split-Half Reliability Coefficients for Subtests and Composites**

| KTEA-3 Subtest or Composite | Mean Grade-Based Reliability | Mean Age-Based Reliability |
|---|---|---|
| **Subtests** | | |
| Letter & Word Recognition | .97 | .97 |
| Reading Comprehension | .88 | .89 |
| Nonsense Word Decoding | .96 | .96 |
| Phonological Processing | .93 | .93 |
| Word Recognition Fluency | .86 | .87 |
| Decoding Fluency | .82 | .84 |
| Silent Reading Fluency | .82 | .84 |
| Reading Vocabulary | .93 | .93 |
| Math Concepts & Applications | .96 | .96 |
| Math Computation | .95 | .95 |
| Math Fluency | .90 | .91 |
| Written Expression | .86 | .85 |
| Spelling | .95 | .95 |
| Writing Fluency | .76 | .76 |
| Listening Comprehension | .85 | .85 |
| Oral Expression | .81 | .83 |
| Associational Fluency | .62 | .62 |
| Object Naming Facility | .69 | .71 |
| Letter Naming Facility | .67 | .68 |
| **Composites** | | |
| Reading | .95 | .96 |
| Math | .97 | .97 |
| Written Language | .94 | .94 |
| Academic Skills Battery | .98 | .98 |
| Sound Symbol | .96 | .96 |
| Decoding | .98 | .98 |
| Reading Fluency | .93 | .93 |
| Reading Understanding | .94 | .95 |
| Oral Language | .86 | .86 |
| Oral Fluency | .72 | .74 |
| Comprehension | .92 | .92 |
| Expression | .89 | .89 |
| Orthographic Processing | .91 | .92 |
| Academic Fluency | .91 | .91 |

*Note:* Adapted from Tables 2.1 and 2.2 of the *KTEA-3 Technical & Interpretive Manual* (Kaufman & Kaufman, 2014b). All reliabilities are based on the average of both forms combined. Mean grade-level values and mean age-level values were calculated using Fisher's *z* transformation.

**Table 2.2 Alternate Form Reliability Coefficients for Subtests and Composites**

| KTEA-3 Subtest or Composite | Grades PK–2 (n = 114) | Grades 3–6 (n = 80) | Grades 7–12 (n = 112) |
|---|---|---|---|
| **Subtests** | | | |
| Letter & Word Recognition | .95 | .91 | .83 |
| Reading Comprehension | .78 | .76 | .77 |
| Nonsense Word Decoding | .91 | .81 | .89 |
| Phonological Processing | .83 | .88 | .77 |
| Word Recognition Fluency | .86 | .82 | .89 |
| Decoding Fluency | | .81 | .83 |
| Silent Reading Fluency | .69 | .87 | .82 |
| Reading Vocabulary | .81 | .82 | .82 |
| Math Concepts & Applications | .86 | .91 | .95 |
| Math Computation | .87 | .89 | .90 |
| Math Fluency | .81 | .88 | .93 |
| Written Expression | .80 | .83 | .84 |
| Spelling | .91 | .92 | .87 |
| Writing Fluency | | .79 | .74 |
| Listening Comprehension | .74 | .74 | .69 |
| Oral Expression | .67 | .60 | .59 |
| Associational Fluency | .59 | .64 | .62 |
| Object Naming Facility | .73 | .72 | .65 |
| Letter Naming Facility | .60 | .54 | .76 |
| **Composites** | | | |
| Reading | .89 | .91 | .85 |
| Math | .87 | .94 | .95 |
| Written Language | .89 | .92 | .89 |
| Academic Skills Battery | .95 | .96 | .96 |
| Sound Symbol | .93 | .90 | .87 |
| Decoding | .96 | .92 | .90 |
| Reading Fluency | | .87 | .88 |
| Reading Understanding | .91 | .76 | .87 |
| Oral Language | .80 | .80 | .75 |
| Oral Fluency | .74 | .69 | .70 |
| Comprehension | .84 | .81 | .79 |
| Expression | .81 | .78 | .78 |
| Orthographic Processing | .83 | .84 | .88 |
| Academic Fluency | | .89 | .88 |

*Note:* Adapted from Table 2.4 of the *KTEA-3 Technical & Interpretive Manual* (Kaufman & Kaufman, 2014b). The KTEA-3 scores are based on grade norms. All reliability coefficients were corrected for the variability of the standardization sample.

## Validity

The validity of the KTEA-3 was demonstrated via multiple methods. Intercorrelations between the subtests and composites were calculated to show the relationships between the academic domains. Factor analyses were conducted to show that the structure of the test is empirically grounded. Correlations with other instruments were also conducted to evaluate the construct validity of the test. Finally, special population studies were conducted to show the efficacy of applying the KTEA-3 to the assessment of examinees with learning disabilities, language disorder, mild intellectual disability, attention-deficit/hyperactivity disorder, and academic giftedness. The results of these special studies are detailed in the Clinical Applications chapter in this book.

Confirmatory factor analysis was conducted to investigate the relationships between the KTEA-3 Comprehensive Form subtests and composites in a systematic manner. The factor analysis proceeded in a stepwise fashion with six subtests that compose the Reading, Math, and Written Language Composites, in addition to the three subtests that make up the Oral Language composite, yielding a final model comprised of four factors. The final model had good fit statistics and all subtests had high loadings on their factors. The results of the factor analysis are shown in Figure 2.2.

The KTEA-3 Comprehensive and Brief Forms were administered along with other tests of achievement and cognitive ability to a subset of the standardization sample. In addition to the results of the correlational data already reported with the original KTEA-II (see Rapid Reference 2.3), correlations were calculated between the KTEA-3 Comprehensive and Brief Forms. Further correlations were calculated between the KTEA-3 Comprehensive Form and the following achievement tests: WIAT-III, Woodcock-Johnson III Tests of Achievement (WJ III ACH; Woodcock, McGrew, & Mather, 2001), and the Clinical Evaluation of Language Fundamentals, Fourth Edition (CELF-IV; Semel, Wiig, & Secord, 2003). A summary of the KTEA-3 Comprehensive Form correlational studies with the WIAT-III and WJ III ACH are provided in Table 2.3. The results of the studies with the WIAT-III and WJ III ACH are very similar to those found with the KTEA-II. That is, most correlations between like-named composites were in the mid- to high-.80s, and correlations between most of the total achievement scores hovered between the high .80s and .95.

The tryout version of the KTEA-3 and the CELF-IV Formulated Sentences subtest were administered to 63 examinees to evaluate the validity of the newly revised KTEA-3 Oral Expression subtest. The CELF-IV Formulated Sentences and the KTEA-3 Oral Expression subtest correlated .64, which supported the validity of the newly revised KTEA-3 subtest.

In addition to the correlational data showing the relationships between the KTEA-3 and other tests of academic achievement, the *KTEA-3 Technical & Interpretive Manual* provides correlations between the KTEA-3 and two tests of cognitive ability: the KABC-II and the Differential Abilities Scales, Second Edition (DAS-II; Elliott; 2007). Sample sizes were 99 and 122 for the studies with the KABC-II and DAS-II, respectively. In addition, the *WISC-V Technical and Interpretive Manual* (Wechsler, 2014) provides correlations between the WISC-V and the KTEA-3 with a sample size of 207.

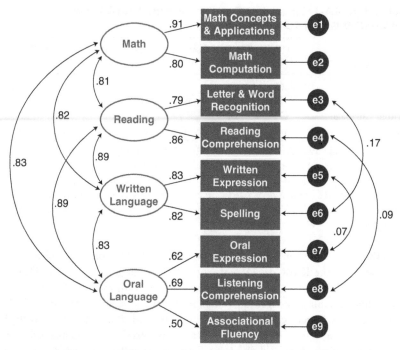

**Figure 2.2  Results of Confirmatory Factor Analysis of Nine KTEA-3 Comprehensive Form Subtests**

Source: Figure 2.1 of the KTEA-3 Technical & Interpretive Manual (Kaufman & Kaufman, 2014b, p. 53). Results are based on the age norm group between 6 and 25 (N = 1,727). Factors are shown in the ovals on the left, and subtests are in rectangles on the right. The numbers represent factor intercorrelations or factor loadings.

**Table 2.3  Correlations of KTEA-3 Comprehensive Composites With Other Achievement Test Composites**

| KTEA-3 Composite | WIAT-III | WJ III ACH |
|---|---|---|
| Reading | .86 | .82 |
| Mathematics | .90 | .83 |
| Written Language | .91 | .80 |
| Academic Skills Battery | .95 | .87 |

Note: Data are from Tables 2.11 and 2.12 of the KTEA-3 Technical & Interpretive Manual (Kaufman & Kaufman, 2014b). Sample sizes for N = 73 for the WIAT-III study and N = 68 for the WJ III ACH study.

**Table 2.4 KTEA-3 Composites Correlations With KABC-II, DAS-II, and WISC-V Global Scales**

| KTEA-3 Composite | KABC-II FCI | KABC-II MPI | KABC-II NVI | DAS-II GCA | DAS-II SRC | WISC-V FSIQ | WISC-V NVI |
|---|---|---|---|---|---|---|---|
| Reading | .60 | .54 | .57 | .55 | .52 | .75 | .61 |
| Math | .71 | .70 | .67 | .62 | .75 | .79 | .71 |
| Written Language | .71 | .67 | .59 | .49 | .57 | .69 | .56 |
| Academic Skills Battery | .75 | .71 | .67 | 65 | .72 | .82 | .69 |

*Note:* FCI = Fluid Crystallized Index; MPI = Mental Processing Index; NVI = Nonverbal Index; GCA = General Conceptual Ability; SRC = School Readiness Composite; FSIQ = Full Scale Intelligence Quotient. Data for the KABC-II and DAS-II are adapted from Tables 2.15 and 2.16 of the *KTEA-3 Technical & Interpretive* Manual (Kaufman & Kaufman, 2014b). Data for the WISC-V are adapted from Table 5.11 of the *WISC-V Technical and Interpretive Manual* (Wechsler, 2014b).

As shown in Table 2.4, correlations between the KTEA-3 core composite and the global scales of the KABC-II, DAS-II, and WISC-V range from .49 to .82. Generally, the KTEA-3 core composites correlate highest with measures of crystallized ability, fluid reasoning, and learning/school readiness. Correlations with the KTEA-3 Academic Skills Battery composite range from .69 and .82. Correlations with the KTEA-3 Reading composite are in the .50s and low .60s across the global scales with the exception of the WISC-V FSIQ (.75). Correlations with the KTEA-3 Math composite are mostly in the .70s with the exception of correlations with the KABC-II NVI (.67) and DAS-II GCA (.62). Correlations with the KTEA-3 Written Language composite range from .49 to .71.

The Reading, Math, and Academic Skills Battery composites correlated most strongly with the WISC-V FSIQ. The correlation was high (.69) between the WISC-V FSIQ score and the Written Language composite, although the Written Language composite correlated just slightly higher (.71) with the KABC-II FCI. As expected, the NVIs from the KABC-II and WISC-V correlate more strongly with the Math and Academic Skills Battery composites than the Reading and Written Language composites.

## OVERVIEW OF THE KTEA-3 BRIEF FORM

The KTEA-3 Brief offers many benefits to practitioners (adapted from Kaufman & Kaufman, 2015b, pp. 3–4), including the following:

- User friendly to administer and score
- Time efficient: the Brief Achievement (BA-3) composite may be obtained in about 20 minutes
- Flexible administration options: administer only the subtests you need
- Materials are engaging to examinees and child friendly
- Highly reliable and valid measure of basic academic skills

Like the Comprehensive Form, the KTEA-3 Brief Form has also been modified from the previous edition. The KTEA-3 Brief does not maintain the content or test structure of the KTEA-II Brief. Rather, the KTEA-3 Brief conceptualized and designed as a larger, more flexible battery of subtests. The following key changes were made to the KTEA-3 Brief Form from the previous edition, many of which are described in the *KTEA-3 Brief Form Administration Manual* (Kaufman & Kaufman, 2015b):

- The age range was changed from 4:6 to 90 years (KTEA-II Brief) to 4:0 to 25 years (KTEA-3 Brief). The grade norms were extended to include prekindergarten.
- There is only one form of the KTEA-3 Brief, which may be alternated with Form A of the Comprehensive Form for progress monitoring and re-evaluations.
- KTEA-3 Brief includes six subtests, which are exactly the same as the core subtests from the KTEA-3 Comprehensive Form B.
- The three subtests that contribute to the Brief Achievement composite include Letter & Word Recognition, Math Computation, and Spelling. Unlike the KTEA-II Brief, items that measure reading comprehension, math problem solving, and written expression are not included in the subtests that compose the three-subtest Brief Achievement (BA-3) composite. See Figure 2.3 to review the subtest structure of the Brief Achievement composite.
- Reading Comprehension, Math Problem Solving, and Written Expression subtests contribute only to the more extensive Academic Skills Battery (ASB) and domain composites.
- The ASB composite provided in the KTEA-3 Brief has the same structure as the ASB composite in the KTEA-3 Comprehensive Form.
- Five composite scores are available for the KTEA-3 Brief: the BA-3, ASB, and three domain composite scores: Reading, Math, and Written Language.
- To save time on a more comprehensive evaluation, KTEA-3 Brief scores may be incorporated into a Comprehensive Form score report and treated as part of the Comprehensive battery.
- In addition to the option of hand scoring, digital scoring of the KTEA-3 Brief is available on the Q-global web-based platform.

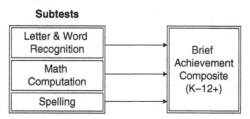

**Figure 2.3  Subtest Structure of the Brief Achievement (BA-3) Composite**

Despite a number of significant changes, the purposes and intended uses of the KTEA-3 Brief remain unchanged from the previous edition and include academic screening, evaluation of academic strengths and weaknesses, monitoring academic progress as part of a response-to-intervention program, and conducting research.

The KTEA-3 Brief subtests measure the same constructs as the KTEA-II Brief subtests (Reading, Writing, Math) but provide greater content coverage and clinical utility by providing separate subtest scores for domains within reading (Letter & Word Recognition, Reading Comprehension), writing (Written Expression, Spelling), and math (Math Concepts & Applications, Math Computation). The Don't Forget box summarizes key similarities and differences between the Brief Form and the Comprehensive Form.

# DON'T FORGET

## Comparing the KTEA-3 Brief Form with the Comprehensive Form

|  | Brief Form | Comprehensive Form |
|---|---|---|
| Grade and Age Range | Pre-K–12+<br>4:0 to 25:11 | Pre-K–12+<br>4:0 to 25:11 |
| Composites | 5 composites: | 14 composites: |
|  | Academic Skills Battery (ASB) composite | Academic Skills Battery (ASB) composite |
|  | Reading | Reading |
|  | Mathematics | Mathematics |
|  | Written Language | Written Language |
|  | Brief Achievement (BA-3) composite | Reading-Related Composites<br>Sound-Symbol<br>Decoding<br>Reading Fluency<br>Reading Understanding |
|  |  | Oral Composites<br>Oral Language<br>Oral Fluency |
|  |  | Cross Domain Composites<br>Comprehension<br>Expression<br>Orthographic Processing<br>Academic Fluency |

(continued)

(Continued)

|  | Brief Form | Comprehensive Form |
|---|---|---|
| **Subtests** | *6 subtests:* | *19 subtests:* |
|  | Letter & Word Recognition | See Rapid Reference 2.2 |
|  | Reading Comprehension |  |
|  | Written Expression |  |
|  | Spelling |  |
|  | Math Concepts & Applications |  |
|  | Math Computation |  |

### Brief Form Standardization and Technical Characteristics

The KTEA-3 Brief Form was standardized using the same sample of 2,050 examinees as the KTEA-3 Comprehensive Form. Since the KTEA-3 Brief Form is comprised of six subtests from Comprehensive Form B, it was standardized simultaneously with the parallel Comprehensive Form A of the KTEA-3. Hence, the standardization and psychometric properties described for the core subtests and composites of the Comprehensive Form also apply to the Brief Form. These data are summarized briefly in this section, although only the new data pertains to the Brief Achievement (BA-3) composite, which is unique to the Brief Form.

The KTEA-3 Brief Form has strong internal consistency reliability. The average split half reliability values were .97, .96, and .95 for the Letter & Word Recognition, Math Concepts & Applications, and Spelling subtests, respectively, by grade (grades Pre-K–12) and by age (ages 4:0–25). The split-half reliability values for the Brief Achievement Composite were .98 for both the grade and age norms. Alternate Form reliability was also strong (.94–.96 for the Brief Achievement composite).

The KTEA-3 Brief Form was administered along with other tests of achievement and cognitive ability during standardization. Correlations were calculated between the KTEA-3 Brief Form and KTEA-II Comprehensive Form. In a sample of 92 students administered both the KTEA-II Comprehensive and KTEA-3 Brief Forms, the correlation between the KTEA-II Comprehensive Achievement Composite (CAC) and the KTEA-3 Brief's Academic Skills Battery composite was .93 and the correlation between the CAC and Brief Achievement composite was .88.

The correlations between the KTEA-3 Brief Form and other achievement tests were also examined (Kaufman & Kaufman, 2015b). Specifically, the *Woodcock-Johnson III Tests of Achievement* (WJ III Ach; Woodcock, McGrew, & Mather, 2001) and the WIAT-III were each administered together with the KTEA-II Brief Form to samples of 68 and 73 students, respectively. The KTEA-3 Brief Achievement composite correlated .88 with the WJ III Brief Achievement Composite and .92 with the WIAT-III Total Achievement Composite.

Correlational data with two measures of Cognitive ability were also analyzed. The KTEA-3 Brief Achievement composite correlated .68 with the KABC-II Fluid Crystallized Index (FCI), .65 with the KABC-II Mental Processing Index (MPI), and .62 with the KABC-II Nonverbal Index (NVI) for the total sample. The Brief Achievement composite correlated .59 with the DAS-II General Conceptual Ability (GCA) score and .70 with the DAS-II School Readiness Composite.

## HOW TO ADMINISTER THE KTEA-3

As with any standardized test, when administering the KTEA-3 you should follow closely the test administration instructions contained in the test manual and stimulus books. The administration manuals for the Comprehensive Form and the Brief Form review the general administration procedures, and the stimulus books list specific administration directions.

The KTEA-3, both the Brief and Comprehensive Forms, offer much flexibility to examiners in terms of the subtests that can be administered and the order in which those subtests are administered. The entire battery may be administered or you may choose to administer only select composites or subtests. Once you have decided whether the KTEA-3 Brief Form battery or a complete or partial KTEA-3 Comprehensive Form battery will be administered, then you need to determine the sequence of the subtests. The stimulus books and record form provide the suggested administration order, but you may select a different administration order if you prefer. However, two subtests require a particular sequence, as noted in the Caution box shown later.

If the Academic Skills Battery composite is the only composite that is desired, then only three subtests from KTEA-3 Comprehensive Stimulus Book 1 are administered and three tests from Stimulus Book 2 are administered. Those subtests are as follows:

Subtest 2. Math Concepts & Applications
Subtest 3. Letter & Word Recognition
Subtest 4. Math Computation
Subtest 9. Reading Comprehension
Subtest 10. Written Expression
Subtest 12. Spelling

The three subtests of the Oral Language composite are also suggested for a comprehensive evaluation. Associational Fluency, Listening Comprehension, and Oral Expression are subtests 11, 16, and 18, respectively. Each is located in Stimulus Book 2.

# DON'T FORGET

..............................................................................................................................

## Get Up and Running Quickly With the KTEA-3: Tips for Veteran KTEA-II Users

Familiarize yourself with the four new KTEA-3 subtests: Reading Vocabulary, Silent Reading Fluency, Math Fluency, and Writing Fluency (the remaining 15 subtests were retained and expanded from the KTEA-II).

Familiarize yourself with the order of KTEA-3 subtest administration, which is different from KTEA-II.

- On the KTEA-II, Associational Fluency and Naming Facility (RAN) had to be administered intermittently throughout the battery even though they were the final subtests listed on the record form. However, on the KTEA-3 these subtests are the 11th and 13th subtests of the 19 subtests listed on the record form, so examiners do not need to actively decide at which earlier point to administer them.

- In addition, on the KTEA-II examiners were instructed to administer Letter & Word Recognition before Reading Comprehension because Letter & Word Recognition was used as a routing point for the Reading Comprehension subtest. However, this procedure is no longer used in the KTEA-3 administration.

Note that the KTEA-3 Flash drive contains forms that were previously part of the hard copies of forms in the kit:

- Subtest Composite Score Computation Form (previously front and back cover of the KTEA-II record form)

- Analysis Comparison Form (previously on page 3 and back cover of the KTEA-II record form)

- Graphical Profiles Form (previously on page 2 of the KTEA-II record form)

- Qualitative Observations Hand Scoring Form (previously page 4 of the KTEA-II record form)

- Error Analysis Summary Form

- Error Analysis Worksheets for Letter & Word Recognition, Math Computation, Nonsense Word Decoding, and Spelling

Print out the appropriate forms that you need prior to an assessment.

Locate the MP3 audio files on the KTEA-3 Flash Drive and find an audio device for playing the files. These files will be needed for:

- Administering Listening Comprehension

(continued)

(*Continued*)

- Exemplifying how to administer Phonological Processing, Letter & Word Recognition, and Nonsense Word Decoding

- Scoring Word Recognition Fluency and Decoding Fluency

Locate the *Technical & Interpretive Manual* on the KTEA-3 Flash Drive and familiarize yourself with how to navigate through the large PDF file using the "search" function and the page thumbnails.

# CAUTION

If you depart from the suggested subtest administration sequence, you must always:

- Administer Letter & Word Recognition before Word Recognition Fluency.
- Administer Nonsense Word Decoding before Decoding Fluency.

## Starting and Discontinuing Subtests

Like most standardized tests of individual achievement, the KTEA-3 items are ordered by difficulty with the easiest items first. Grade-based starting points are listed in the record form and on the first page of a subtest's directions in the stimulus book. If you have knowledge or suspicion based on clinical judgment that the examinee you are testing will benefit from an earlier or later start point, you may select a different start point.

If you have started administering a subtest from a starting point other than item 1, make sure that the examinee is able to achieve a basal. That is, the examinee must demonstrate proficiency on the task by getting the first few items correct in order to achieve the basal. If the examinee does not meet the basal criterion, then you must drop back to the preceding start point. The basal rules are listed in the record form as well as on the first page of the directions for a subtest in the stimulus book. Some subtests on the KTEA-3 do not have traditional basal rules because the items are grouped into item sets or because they are timed tasks. The Comprehensive Form subtests with item sets include Reading Comprehension, Listening Comprehension, Written Expression, and Word Recognition Fluency. Tests that do not have basal rules because they are timed include: Nonsense Word Decoding, Writing Fluency, Silent Reading Fluency, Math Fluency, Object Naming Facility, Letter Naming Facility, and Decoding Fluency. The Don't Forget box describes the administration procedures for these subtests that do not have traditional basal rules.

## Sample, Teaching, and Practice Items

Unlike many cognitive tests, such as the KABC-II, fewer KTEA-3 subtests include sample, teaching, and practice items. These items are intended to communicate the nature of the task by allowing the examiner to give feedback and explain the task further in order to teach the task. Most KTEA-3 subtests do not require instructional feedback because they resemble familiar academic tasks. However, nine Comprehensive Form subtests include sample, teaching, and practice items: Phonological Awareness, Nonsense Word Decoding, Spelling, Writing Fluency, Silent Reading Fluency, Reading Vocabulary, Object Naming Facility, Letter Naming Facility, and Oral Expression. Sample, teaching, and practice items are indicated on the record form by an apple icon.

# DON'T FORGET

## Comparing Sample, Teaching, and Practice Items

A *Sample* item may involve either of the following:

- The examiner demonstrates how to respond to the item type (e.g., Writing Fluency; Silent Reading Fluency).
- The examinee practices the task by responding to *unscored* items and receiving instructional feedback before the scored items are administered (e.g., Phonological Processing).

A *Teaching* item allows the examiner to give corrective or instructional feedback on *scored* items if the examinee responds incorrectly. This may involve rephrasing instructions, providing an example of a correct response, or explaining the correct answer.

A *Practice* item is included on two KTEA-3 subtests, Object Naming Facility and Letter Naming Facility, for the following purposes:

- Ensure that the examinee knows the correct names of the stimuli: If the examinee gives an incorrect name during the Practice item, the examiner teaches the correct name to use on the scored items. *Note:* Letter Naming Facility requires all letters to be named correctly on the Practice item; if one or more incorrect letter names are given, the subtest cannot be administered or scored.
- Give the examinee practice naming objects/letters sequentially in rows. The examiner may provide assistance performing the task during the Practice item only.

# DON'T FORGET

......................................................................................

### Starting Points, Basal Rules, and Discontinue Rules for Reading Comprehension, Listening Comprehension, Written Expression, and Oral Expression

| Subtest | Start Point | Basal | Discontinue |
|---------|-------------|-------|-------------|
| Reading Comprehension | Determined by grade (see Start Point Table on record form or stimulus book) | Must pass the first two items or drop back one start point. Administer all remaining items in the passage before dropping back for Sets D-H. | If there are five consecutive scores of 0 within a set, stop testing. |
| Listening Comprehension | Determined by grade (see Start Point Table on record form or stimulus book) | Must pass at least two items in the first passage administered. | If there are five consecutive scores of 0 within a set, stop testing. |
| Written Expression | Determined by grade (see Start Point Table on record form or stimulus book) | If the first several items seem difficult, drop back one level. | At stop point for level. For Level 1, discontinue if the examinee scores 0 on all of the items 3–10. |
| Oral Expression | Determined by grade (see Start Point Table on record form or stimulus book) | If Task is scored 0 on both of the first two items administered, drop back one start point. | At the item set stop point. If five consecutive items within a set are scored 0 for both Task and Grammar, stop testing. |

*Note:* Reading Comprehension and Listening Comprehension also include a "Decision Point" that states if there are three or fewer scores of 0 in a set, continue to next set.

### Recording Responses

Recording demands for the examiner range from minimal to very extensive, depending on the subtest (see Don't Forget box for an overview). Accurately recording responses during administration of KTEA-3 subtests is very important—especially if you intend to conduct error analysis after scoring the subtests is complete. On six of the 19 Comprehensive Form subtests, the examinees write their responses, requiring no recording on the examiner's part until scoring is conducted. Phonological Awareness and Math Concepts & Applications require simple recording of either a zero for incorrect or a one for correct, or recording a one-word response. Reading Comprehension and Listening Comprehension require that the gist of the examinee's responses are recorded with as much detail as possible, but Oral Expression and Associational Fluency require that an examinee's responses are recorded verbatim. Letter & Word Recognition and Nonsense Word Decoding require careful listening in order to correctly record the examinee's responses. Use of an audio recorder is highly recommended on all subtests that require verbatim responses to be recorded (see Don't Forget box). Mispronunciations on these two subtests should be recorded using the phoneme key provided on the record form or by writing the student's response phonetically. Recording responses either by the phonetic key or by phonetically spelling the examinee's response takes some practice. Chapter 3 of the *KTEA-3 Administration Manual* (Kaufman & Kaufman, 2014c) describes in more detail how to record responses for use with the error analysis system.

# DON'T FORGET

## Subtest Recording Demands

| Recording Demands | Subtest | Audio Recording |
|---|---|---|
| Minimal. Examinees write their responses. | Math Computation<br>Writing Fluency<br>Silent Reading Fluency<br>Math Fluency<br>Written Expression<br>Spelling | No |
| Score 0 or 1, record a brief response | Phonological Awareness<br>Math Concepts & Applications | No |
| Record the gist of the examinee's response, including key details | Reading Comprehension<br>Listening Comprehension | Helpful, but not typically needed |
| Verbatim recording of entire response | Oral Expression<br>Associational Fluency | Yes, strongly recommended |
| Verbatim recording of incorrect responses | Letter & Word Recognition<br>Nonsense Word Decoding | Yes, strongly recommended |

## Timing

Most subtests on the KTEA-3 are not timed. However, eight of the 19 subtests do require timing. Specifically, six fluency tasks have time limits: Writing Fluency, Silent

Reading Fluency, Math Fluency, Word Recognition Fluency, Decoding Fluency, and Associational Fluency. In these fluency tasks, the examinee's performance within the specified time is the basis of the score. For Object Naming Facility and Letter Naming Facility, examiners are required to record completion time. The time taken by the examinee to complete each trial of these tasks is converted to a point score.

### Queries and Prompts

Occasionally, examinees' responses may be missing an essential detail or qualifier to be 100% correct. These instances will most commonly occur during Reading Comprehension and Listening Comprehension and will require you to query the examinee to clarify his or her response. Specific queries are listed right in the stimulus book, and, when querying is done, a notation should be made on the record form (e.g., "Q"). Occasionally, examinees give multiple responses and it is unclear which response is the final answer. In such instances you should ask the examinee which is the intended response.

Prompts are used to encourage examinees or request clarification. For example, an examinee may give multiple responses and it is unclear which response is the final answer. In such instances you should ask the examinee which is the intended response. Unclear written responses are prompted sparingly. During standardization, most examiners did not clarify illegible responses, so written responses were scored based on what could be deciphered. Refer to the Don't Forget box for a summary of the recommended prompts to use in various circumstances.

## DON'T FORGET

### Recommended Prompts

| Circumstance | Prompt |
|---|---|
| Reluctant to respond | Just try your best.<br>Do the best you can. |
| Confusing response | What do you mean?<br>Tell me more. |
| Unclear response on Letter & Word Recognition or Nonsense Word Decoding | Do not ask the examinee to repeat the response. Instead, ask the examinee to respond more slowly on subsequent items. (Audio recording is especially beneficial in this circumstance.) |
| Unclear written response | I cannot read what this says.<br>(Use sparingly. If much of the examinee's writing is illegible, then decipher as best you can for scoring.) |

## Subtest-by-Subtest Notes on Administration

This section highlights pertinent information for administering each of the KTEA-3 subtests and points out common errors in administration. Subtests are listed in the order in which they appear in the KTEA-3 Comprehensive Form stimulus books. Because administrative procedures for the Brief Form are the same as the same-named Comprehensive Form subtests, examiners using the Brief Form can use the same guidelines that follow.

### *Phonological Awareness*

Phonological Awareness has five sections: (1) Blending; (2) Rhyming; (3) Sound Matching; (4) Deleting Sounds; and (5) Segmenting. All five sections can be administered to children in pre-K through grade 12. Examiners will find that listening to the audio file prior to administering the Blending Section and the Deleting Sounds section to be very useful as an example of how to proceed. Since this task is purely auditory (except for Rhyming and Sound Blending sections that have pictorial stimuli too), ensure that the examinee is paying attention prior to beginning an item. If necessary, you may repeat an item.

Subtle differences in regional dialect may affect the administration of some items. For example, consider Item 11 in Section 2 (Rhyming) of Form A. The examiner asks, "Which one doesn't rhyme with the others?" The two words that are intended to rhyme are *dog* and *log*. In general American English, *dog* and *log* rhyme, but in some regions of the United States the vowels in these words sound different. To give some approximations, *dog* may resemble *doge*

> **DON'T FORGET**
> ............................................
>
> ### Using Pepper the Puppet During Blending and Segmenting
>
> The KTEA-II provided the option of using Pepper, a hand puppet, during administration of the Blending and Segmenting Sections. Although the puppet is not provided in the KTEA-3 kit, examiners can still use a puppet during administration by following the modified instructions provided in the stimulus book.
>
> Most children find Pepper the puppet quite engaging, but some are distracted and seem to more easily go off task when it is their turn to make Pepper talk. With such children, remind them to stay on task, but suggest that they can have a few minutes to "play with Pepper" after the task is over (a nice built-in reward of the task). Occasionally, children may struggle with trying to make Pepper's mouth move. Encourage these children to focus on segmenting the word properly and worry less about getting Pepper to move his mouth.

(with a long o) in some areas of Louisiana, *daag* in some areas of Chicago, and *dwawg* in some areas of New York. Examiners should try to pronounce items using general American English, and encourage examinees with regional dialects to select the word that sounds *most* dissimilar.

For examinees who are easily distracted or overwhelmed by seeing more than one item on a page in the stimulus book, the examiner is permitted to use a blank sheet of paper to reveal one item at a time.

### Math Concepts & Applications

During administration of Math Concepts & Applications, you may find that some examinees require more concrete ways of processing the problems. Such examinees tend to count with their fingers or use the pictures to aid them in coming up with a response. Fingers are an acceptable tool for problem solving on this subtest, but calculators are not. Paper and pencil are allowed beginning with item 36, so examinees should be offered paper and pencil at that point should they wish to use them. In the latter half of the subtest, there are several word problems. Although the word problems are printed on the stimulus book for the examinee to see, you should read each of these problems aloud to the examinee.

### Letter & Word Recognition

The key to properly administering Letter & Word Recognition is having knowledge of the proper pronunciation of all the stimuli words. If you are unsure of how a word should be pronounced, you will undoubtedly struggle with whether an examinee correctly pronounced it and will therefore not know whether or not to continue. This problem is less of an issue when testing younger children, but when assessing older examinees and adolescents, they may be administered the highest levels of words, which are quite challenging. Thus, before administering the subtest, listen to the audio file provided with the test kit to hear the correct pronunciations of the most difficult words. In addition, consider using an audio recorder to capture examinee's responses, which can help facilitate scoring an error analysis.

Most of the stimuli words are presented six to a page, and examinees should be allowed to attempt to pronounce all words on a page, even if they have met the discontinue rule before reaching the sixth word on a page. Such administration methods will continue to foster good rapport. Sometimes examinees will pronounce words in disconnected pieces, but to receive credit, an examinee must pronounce words as a connected, relatively smooth whole. Thus, they should be instructed to "Say it all together" if they pronounce a word in disconnected pieces and then stop.

### Math Computation

The response booklet and a pencil with an eraser are needed to administer the Math Computation subtest. The response booklet should be folded so that the examinee can see only the page that they are currently working on. Some examinees will impulsively turn the page to see what comes next; if this happens, encourage the examinee not to worry about the later problems and instead just focus on finishing the page in front of them. Examinees may work out problems by counting on their fingers or by writing notes on the paper, but they may not use calculators. If necessary, remind examinees that it is okay to erase. Examinees with disabilities that cause difficulty with writing are allowed to respond orally.

It is important to closely observe examinees as they solve the problems. Some examinees will fill the entire square with scratch notes, and it may be unclear which number is their final response. If you are uncertain about which number the examinee intended as their final answer, ask the examinee to circle his or her final response before the next item has been started. As you are observing the examinee work out the problems make notes about repeated erasures, verbal mediation of the problems, or other notable behaviors.

For examinees who are easily distracted or overwhelmed by seeing more than one page or row of items at a time in the response booklet, the examiner is permitted to use a blank sheet of paper to reveal one page or row at a time.

## DON'T FORGET

### Reversing by Row/Page on Math Computation

The KTEA-3 manual recommends reversing by row/page on Math Computation in order to establish a basal because it's easier on the examiner and student during administration. Although reversing item by item does not invalidate the subtest, it can be awkward for the examinee who may wonder why they are continually being prompted to work backwards.

When applying the basal rule by page/row, the goal is to establish a basal at or as close to the grade appropriate start point as possible. For example, if we decide to start at Item 1 because we suspect math difficulties, but then the student performs well and surpasses the grade appropriate start point, go back and apply the basal rule by looking at the grade-appropriate start point to see if a basal was established there. If not, go back one item at a time to find three consecutive scores of 1 that are closest to the grade-appropriate start point: These items establish the basal (and all items preceding this basal are awarded credit).

### Nonsense Word Decoding

Similar to Letter & Word Recognition, the key to properly administering Nonsense Word Decoding is having knowledge of the proper pronunciation of all the stimuli words. Thus, it is crucial to listen to the audio file provided with the test kit that demonstrates how the words should be pronounced. Most of the stimuli words are presented in a group of six on an stimulus book page. To maintain rapport and minimize frustration for examinees, it is best to administer an entire stimulus book page (all six words) even if an examinee has discontinued before reading the sixth word. However, only the words read before the discontinue rule was met should be counted toward the final raw score. As the nonsense words become more challenging for examinees, some examinees will get stuck on a particular word with which they are struggling. In such cases, you should encourage examinees to try the next one so that the test continues without multiple lengthy delays.

Nonsense Word Decoding is one of the KTEA-3 subtests that allows teaching of the task. If the examinee responds incorrectly on items 1 or 2, tell the student the correct answer (the apple icons on the record form and stimulus book are reminders of which items allow teaching). Before you administer this subtest, it is advisable to practice how to record examinee's responses (whether you choose to do so using the phonemic key on the record form or another method). At times examinees will rapidly read the words, requiring you to increase your pace for recording their responses. For that reason, many examiners find that using an audio recorder to capture examinee's responses is beneficial and can aid in scoring. In addition to recording the responses to specific items, you may record what the student's general approach to pronouncing the nonsense words was by marking one of three boxes at the bottom of the record form (letter-by-letter, chunking, or whole word). However, if an examinee doesn't use the same general approach to most of the items, checking these "Response Style" boxes will not be that useful.

## Writing Fluency

The response booklet, a pencil, and a stopwatch are needed to administer Writing Fluency, in addition to the stimulus book. Although the examinee's pencil may have an eraser, you should remind the examinee to simply cross out a mistake rather than taking the time to erase it. The subtest includes two sample items and two teaching items because it is critical that examinees understand the task demands prior to starting this timed test. The key components of the examinee's written responses are that they are sentences (not fragments) and that they are short (not lengthy). Some examinees may seem particularly concerned about the neatness of their handwriting, which is not scored in this task. Examiners should make note of such methodical behaviors that may impact a student's score (and may affect how an examiner interprets the score).

## Silent Reading Fluency

Similar to the Writing Fluency subtest, Silent Reading Fluency requires the response booklet, a pencil, a stopwatch, and the stimulus book to administer the task. The speed of an examinee's response is critical on this fluency task, so examiners should instruct examinees to cross out their mistakes rather than taking the more time-consuming approach of erasing. Six items (two samples and four teaching items) are included to ensure that examinees understand the task demands. If the examinee answers three or four of the teaching items incorrectly, then the subtest should be discontinued. Some examinees appear to mark "yes" or "no" without reading the questions, and in such cases, examiners should remind the examinee to first read the questions. Items must be answered in order, so if an examinee skips items, remind them to answer every question in order without skipping any.

## Math Fluency

Similar to the Writing Fluency and Silent Reading Fluency subtests, the Math Fluency subtest requires the response booklet, a pencil, a stopwatch, and the stimulus book to administer the task. Some examinees may exhibit a look of nervousness or dislike when the response booklet reveals a page full of math problems on which they are asked to work on "as fast as you can." Make note of such behaviors, as they could be indicative of anxiety related to math. Although the directions that are given to the examinee include a reminder to "watch the signs," once the timing of the task has begun, examiners may not remind examinees to watch the addition, subtraction, multiplication, and division signs. However, if examinees attempt to answer the problems out of order, examiners must remind them immediately to answer the problems in order.

# DON'T FORGET

## Representing Division Problems

**Question:** Why does Math Fluency present division problems in only a vertical presentation, but Math Computation presents division problems in a variety of formats (horizontal, vertical, long division, etc.)?

**Answer:** The primary reason for using the vertical presentation for division in Math Fluency is to allow for a consistent presentation of items. Presenting all items vertically was meant to focus attention on the operation signs. Using a horizontal presentation for division would have made those items stand out. The test is designed to assess examinees' ability to attend to the sign and use flexible, efficient strategies, which is why a mixed operations math fluency subtest was developed as opposed to a single operation subtest like in the WIAT-III. If a student can't do division or is not familiar with the vertical presentation, a good strategy is to skip those problems. Students who don't attend to signs will spend time trying to solve those division problems using the wrong operation. If those problems had been presented horizontally, a student who doesn't know division well could have more easily skipped those items.

On the other hand, Math Computation is a power test, so we wanted to measure division skills using whatever presentation/method the students were taught. For this reason, we presented division problems using various formats.

## *Reading Comprehension*

Determine the starting point on the Reading Comprehension subtest based on the grade level of the examinee and the guide on the "Start Point" table KTEA-3 record form or on the first page of the Reading Comprehension subtest in the stimulus book. Items 1 through 4 require examinees to learn rebuses that symbolize objects, and the next three items ask examinees to recognize words that correspond to commonly seen signs. Items 8–20 require examinees to point to a picture of a word that they read, and items 21through 25 require the examinee to read a command and do what it says (e.g., "Stand up"). On items 21–25, some examinees may require you to encourage them to pretend or make believe in response to the command that they. Items 26 through 101 of Reading Comprehension require the examinee to read a sentence or a paragraph and answer questions about what they read. Examinees may read the paragraphs and questions silently or aloud, but they are not penalized if they make mistakes while they read aloud. However, such mistakes while reading aloud are noteworthy, especially if they are made frequently. In the remaining few items of Reading Comprehension, examinees must read a series of sentences and decide the correct order of the sentences, in addition to answering questions about the passage (items 102–105). Examinees are allowed to use paper and pencil to organize the sentence numbers for these two items if they wish. While reading the paragraphs or questions, examinees sometimes ask for clarification of a term or help to read a particular word. In such cases, you should not give them help, but rather encourage them to just try their best.

Some of the passage questions are multiple choice and require only recording a letter response (e.g., a, b, c, d). However, other questions are open-ended and in such cases the examinee's responses should be recorded verbatim. Generally, querying is not necessary for most responses, but if the examinee provides multiple responses and you are unsure which is their intended final response, then ask for clarification.

### Written Expression

Examinees' responses to items on the Written Expression subtest are recorded in the appropriate Written Expression Booklet (grades 1 through 12+) or in the response booklet (pre-K and kindergarten). The first stimulus book page of Written Expression lists which of the booklets examinees should use, based upon their grade level (the Caution box reminds examiners of an important point for administering to students in grade 1). The booklets, *Pam and Don's Adventure, The Little Duck's Friend, Kyra's Dragon, The Amazing Scrapbook, A Day on the Set*, and *The News at Six*, each tell a story with the goal of engaging the student in the writing tasks. Thus, when presenting the subtest, the examiner's directions written in the stimulus book emphasize the fact that the booklets are stories. Before administering any level of Written Expression, you should familiarize yourself with the Written Expression Booklet so that you know where to point to the words as you read them and so that you know where the student should write his or her response to each item (indicated by numbers printed in

## DON'T FORGET

### Spelling in the Written Expression Subtest

Spelling is not scored in the Written Expression subtest. If a student asks how to spell a word, you are allowed to tell him or her the correct spelling.

However, encouraging the student to try to spell the word on his or her own may yield clinically relevant information about spelling skills during contextual writing.

small boxes). The last item for each of the stories requires the examinee to write a summary of the story (items 37, 56, and 67). For each of these items the examinees are given 5 to 10 minutes to write their summary; thus, you will need a watch or clock to time these final items.

In Written Expression on the Comprehensive Form, you are allowed to repeat story segments or item instructions if it is necessary. As noted in the Don't Forget, you may also tell students how to spell a word, if they ask (spelling is not scored in this subtest). However, you should not spontaneously correct an examinee's spelling or offer similar assistance unless asked by the examinee.

## Associational Fluency

On the Associational Fluency tasks (naming foods and naming colors), you give examinees 60 seconds to say as many of the words in a category that they can think of. If examinees stop or say that they cannot think of more, you should encourage them to try to say more if they have more time left. You should attempt to record the examinee's words verbatim, but sometimes an examinee responds so rapidly that such recording is difficult. One recommended strategy for examiners is to use an audio recorder to capture all of the examinee's responses. If audio recording is not possible, if an examinee responds too quickly to record all of his or her words, you should simply make a checkmark on a line of the record form to indicate that the examinee gave a correct response.

## Spelling

Spelling is administered to examinees in kindergarten and beyond. Examinees write their responses in the Response Booklet using a pencil with an eraser (it is a good idea to have extras on hand in case of broken pencil points). The first three items require examinees to write a letter to complete a word, but the remaining items require the spelling of complete words. Watch the examinee on each item to make sure that they are writing their response on the correct line. You may ask the examinee to clarify what they wrote if their handwriting is unclear. Examinees are allowed to erase and correct a response. If an examinee does not respond immediately after you have said a word or if the examinee asks you to repeat something, you may repeat the word or sentence.

If the examinee you are testing has a motor disability or an inability to write for another reason, then you may permit the examinee to respond orally. If an examinee responds orally, then write their response on the record form as they spell it. However, this alternative procedure for responding should be used only after every attempt is made to have the student give a written response.

## Object Naming Facility

On the Object Naming Facility subtest, you first need to determine that the examinee knows the names of the objects. Thus, the practice items are administered to ensure that the examinee understands the task and knows the names of the objects. If the examinee uses a different name for one of the objects, tell them the correct name to use. As the examinee is responding, you should mark on the record form any stimulus that the examinee names incorrectly. Occasionally, examinees may lose their place or skip a row, and in such instances, you should immediately point to the appropriate place on the stimulus book to redirect him or her. If an examinee self-corrects (e.g., "ball ... I mean book"), then write "SC" next to the self-corrected item. When the examinee completes naming all of the stimuli for a trial, you should record the examinee's completion time.

### Reading Vocabulary

Select the correct Reading Vocabulary starting point based on the examinee's grade level by examining the Starting Point table on the stimulus book or the record form. Items 1 and 2 and Sample A and B are designed to teach the examinees the task demands for Reading Vocabulary. Items 1–12 require the examinee to read a word shown with a picture and pick the word from a list that is a synonym of the stimulus word. For items 13 and on, examinees read a question and pick a word in a sentence that has the same meaning as the target word in the question. Except on the sample items, examiners cannot read the words for the examinees. Examinees have the option of reading silently or aloud. If an examinee chooses to read aloud, you may find useful behavioral observations to record (e.g., mispronunciations, oral reading fluency, and so forth). However, accuracy of oral reading is not scored. Some examinees prefer to point to their response in the stimulus book, so examiners should be prepared to record pointing responses as well as oral responses. If an examinee responds with "I don't know" to an item, you may encourage them to "just try your best." If their final response it "I don't know," then record "DK" on the record form and circle a zero.

## CAUTION

..............................................

Prior to administering Letter Naming Facility, check to make sure that the examinee knows the names of the letters. However, do not administer the task if the student does not correctly name a letter during the Practice Items.

### Letter Naming Facility

Administration of Letter Naming Facility is very similar to Object Naming Facility subtest. During the Letter Naming Facility Practice Items, you first need to determine that the examinee knows the names of the letters. Occasionally, an examinee may say the letter sound rather than naming the letter, and in such instances, remind them during the practice item to *name* the letter. If the examinee misses one or more of the letters during the Practice Items, then discontinue testing. As the examinee is responding on each of the two trials, you should mark on the record form any letter that the examinee names incorrectly. Occasionally, examinees may lose their place or skip a row, and in such instances, you should immediately point to the appropriate place on the stimulus book to redirect him or her. If an examinee self-corrects (e.g., "D ... I mean P"), then write "SC" next to the self-corrected item. When the examinee completes naming all of the letters for a trial, you should record the examinee's completion time.

### Listening Comprehension

Listening Comprehension is administered via an audio player that has speakers or two sets of headphones (so that both you and the examinee can hear simultaneously). In an emergency or if you experience technical problems with your audio player, you can read the subtest's passages aloud yourself, as they are written in the test stimulus book. Similar to Reading Comprehension, Listening Comprehension items are grouped into item sets, and the examinee's grade level determines where to begin. Prior to beginning this subtest, you should check the volume on your audio player to ensure that the examinee will be able to hear adequately, and cue the audio player to the proper track. Before playing each passage, be sure that the examinee is ready to listen because examinees are not allowed to hear the passage more than once. Immediately after the passage has been played, pause the audio player and ask the questions about the story. Although the passage itself may not be replayed, you may repeat a test question at the student's request. The Don't Forget box reminds you of important points about administering Listening Comprehension.

## DON'T FORGET

### Reminders for Administering Listening Comprehension

Introduce the test before beginning the first passage.

Say, "You are going to hear a short story. Listen carefully, and then I will ask you some questions about the story. Ready? Listen."

Read the response choices for multiple-choice questions twice.

When administering multiple-choice questions, say the letter as well as the text of each answer choice, and then pause slightly after each choice. After completing the list of choices, say the list a second time as needed.

Prompt examinees for a second answer on questions with two-part answers.

If a question asks for a two-part answer and the student gives only one part, then say: "Yes, and what else?"

Play the passage only one time.

You may play the passage only once and may not answer any questions that the student asks about the story.

Test questions may be repeated.

You may repeat a test question if an examinee asks for repetition or if you suspect that the student did not hear the question the first time.

## Word Recognition Fluency

Prior to administering Word Recognition Fluency make sure that you have reviewed the pronunciation of these words on the audio file, because some of the words are quite challenging even to the most skilled examiners. The starting point for Word Recognition Fluency is based on an examinee's grade. If Set A is administered and the raw score for set A equals 48, then administer Set B. In contrast, if examinees who begin with Set B obtain a raw score of 2 or less, then you should drop back to Set A.

> # CAUTION
> ......................................................
> ### Order of Administration Reminder
>
> Do not administer Word Recognition Fluency before giving Letter & Word Recognition.

Introduce the test with the verbiage printed in the stimulus book. Once you say "Begin," then begin timing. After 15 seconds, say, "Stop." Examiners may find it useful to draw a line in the record form after the last word attempted. During administration of this subtest, examinees may hesitate or get stuck on a word. When such a pause occurs, encourage the examinee to keep going and move on to the next word. As examinees read the words, record any words that they misread or skip by circling zero for the item on the record form. However, do not penalize for articulation errors or variations due to regional speech patterns.

## Oral Expression

Oral Expression is administered in item sets and begins with the set determined by the examinee's grade (these starting points are listed in the stimulus book and record form). Because examinee's scores must be recorded verbatim for accurate scoring and error analysis, use of an audio recorder is recommended. Note that examiners may not ask examinees to repeat their response. Teaching is done on several items during the Oral Expression subtest (items A, 1, 2, 7, 8, 13, and 24). You may give additional instructional feedback to make sure that the examinee understands what to do for the task. During administration, you may repeat an item if the examinee requests or if you believe that he or she did not hear it. Some items require examinees to include particular words in their responses, and the record form includes a place to make if the target word was included.

## Decoding Fluency

Administration of Decoding Fluency is very similar to administration of Word Recognition Fluency. For administration, you need the stimulus book and a stopwatch or a watch that shows seconds. Prior to administration, you should listen to the audio file to hear examples of how to pronounce the nonsense words. To begin administration, you should introduce the subtest with the instructions printed in the stimulus book. After you say "Begin," immediately begin timing the examinee. After 15 seconds, say "Stop." Administer the second trial in the same manner as the first. Examiners may find it useful to make a slash on the record form after the last word that the examinee read. If an examinee pauses or hesitates during the task, encourage them to keep going or move onto the next one. As the examinee is reading the words, circle zero for any of the words that are mispronounced or skipped.

## HOW TO SCORE THE KTEA-3

The KTEA-3 yields several types of scores: raw scores, standard scores, grade equivalents, age equivalents, and percentile ranks. Raw scores reflect the number of points earned by the examinee on each subtest. These scores, by themselves, are meaningless because they are not norm-based. Converting raw scores to standard scores, which are norm-based, allows the examinee's performance to be compared to that of others. The KTEA-3 standard scores have a mean of 100 and an SD of 15. The theoretical range of standard scores for the subtests and composites is 40 to 160. An important theoretical assumption is that achievement-test performance is distributed on a normal curve, with the majority of examinees scoring within +/– 1 SD of the mean. Thus, about two-thirds (68%) of students score in the range of 85 to 115. Less than 3% of examinees score above 130 or below 70.

### Types of Scores

Each type of score in the KTEA-3 is described next.

#### *Raw Scores and Weighted Raw Scores*
Subtest raw scores are calculated in a variety of ways.

- For hand scoring, methods for calculating raw scores and weighted raw scores are summarized in Table 2.5.
- Using Q-global, fewer steps are required for calculating raw scores. For subtests that use weighted raw scores, enter the raw scores only. Q-global converts raw scores into weighted raw scores when calculating derived scores, although weighted raw scores are not provided in the score report. Methods for calculating raw scores using Q-global are summarized in Table 2.6.
- Using Q-interactive, raw score calculation is automatic for every subtest once items are scored by the examiner. Refer to Chapter 7 for information about Q-interactive.

**Table 2.5 Hand-Scoring Methods for Calculating Raw Scores**

| Subtest | Method |
|---|---|
| **Subtest with Basal/Discontinue Rules** | |
| Phonological Awareness<br>Letter & Word Recognition<br>Math Concepts & Applications<br>Math Computation<br>Nonsense Word Decoding<br>Spelling<br>Reading Vocabulary | Subtract the number of errors from the ceiling item. |
| **Speeded Subtest** | |
| Silent Reading Fluency | Use the scoring keys provided on the flash drive to score student responses. Subtract the number of incorrect responses from the number of correct responses. |
| Math Fluency | Use the scoring keys provided on the flash drive to score student responses. Sum the number of correct responses within the time limit. |
| Object Naming Facility<br>Letter Naming Facility | Across each trial, sum the completion time (in seconds) and sum the number of errors. Next, convert total time and total errors to a raw score. |
| Writing Fluency | Convert the number of words written within the time limit to a raw score. |
| Associational Fluency<br>Decoding Fluency | Sum correct responses provided within the time limit across items (AF) or trials (DF). |
| **Subtest with Item Sets** | |
| Reading Comprehension<br>Listening Comprehension<br>Written Expression | Sum the number of correct responses for items within the final level/set administered. Next, convert the raw score to a weighted raw score. |
| Oral Expression | Sum the Task and Grammar scores for items within the final set administered. Next, convert the raw score to a weighted raw score. |
| Word Recognition Fluency | Sum correct responses provided within the time limit across trials. Next, convert the raw score to a weighted raw score. |

When scoring subtests with item sets (i.e., Reading Comprehension, Listening Comprehension, Written Expression, Oral Expression, Word Recognition Fluency), the raw score must be converted to a *weighted raw score*. This is not a new type of score, although the terminology differed in the KTEA-II. For most of these subtests in the KTEA-II, the *total number of points* earned on the subtest (i.e., the raw score in the KTEA-3) was converted to a *raw score* (i.e., the weighted raw score in the KTEA-3), which was then converted to a derived score (e.g., standard score, growth scale value, etc.).

## Table 2.6  Methods for Calculating Raw Scores Using Q-global

| Subtest | Method |
|---|---|
| **Subtest with Basal/Discontinue Rules** | |
| Phonological Awareness Letter & Word Recognition Math Concepts & Applications Math Computation Nonsense Word Decoding Spelling Reading Vocabulary | Subtract the number of errors from the ceiling item. Enter this raw score. |
| **Speeded Subtest** | |
| Silent Reading Fluency | Option 1: Raw score entry. Use the scoring key provided on the flash drive to score responses. Subtract the number of incorrect responses from the number of correct responses. Option 2: Item entry. Enter the student's (Y, N) responses. |
| Math Fluency | Option 1: Raw score entry. Use the scoring key provided on the flash drive to score responses. Sum the number of correct responses within the time limit. Option 2: Item entry. Enter the student's numerical responses. |
| Object Naming Facility Letter Naming Facility | Enter the completion time (in seconds) and number of errors for each trial. |
| Writing Fluency | Enter the number of words written within the time limit. |
| Associational Fluency Decoding Fluency | Sum correct responses provided within the time limit across items (AF) or trials (DF). |
| **Subtest with Item Sets** | |
| Reading Comprehension Listening Comprehension Written Expression | Select set/level administered. Sum the number of correct responses for items within the final level/set administered. |
| Oral Expression | Select set administered. Sum the Task and Grammar scores for items within the final set administered. |
| Word Recognition Fluency | Select set administered. Sum correct responses provided within the time limit across trials. |

# DON'T FORGET

......................................................................................................

### How does a raw score differ from a weighted raw score?

A raw score is the number of points earned on the subtest.

A weighted raw score is used only on subtests with item sets to estimate the raw score that would be obtained if the entire subtest (every item set) had

*(continued)*

(Continued)

been administered. Psychometric methods were used to put item sets on a common scale, which enables scores obtained on different item sets to be directly compared.

## Are weighted raw scores really weighted?

No. Weights were not applied when norming the weighted raw scores. A more precise term for understanding weighted raw scores would be "adjusted" raw scores. However, it was desirable for the KTEA-3 and WIAT-III to use consistent terminology.

# DON'T FORGET

. . . . . . . . . . . . . . . . . . . . . . . . . . . . . . . . . . . . . . . . . . . . . . . . . . . . . . . . . . . . . . . . . . . . . . . . . . . . . . . . . . . . . . .

### Hand Scoring

Appendix C from the KTEA-3 Technical & Interpretive Manual contains all the tables needed for score conversions. Use the hyperlinks in the Table of Contents or the search function (e.g., Ctrl+F on PC or Command+F on Mac) to go directly to Appendix C.

Two types of conversion tables are provided: Raw score lookup tables and tables for converting raw scores to weighted raw scores.

Raw Score Lookup tables are used to obtain raw scores for the following subtests: Writing Fluency, Object Naming Facility, and Letter Naming Facility. Convert the number of words written, for Writing Fluency, and the completion time and number of errors, for ONF and LNF, to the subtest raw score. These raw score conversion tables do not differ by form (A or B) because performance across forms is so similar.

Tables are used to convert raw scores to weighted raw scores for the following subtests: Reading Comprehension, Listening Comprehension, Written Expression, Oral Expression, Word Recognition Fluency. Each of these tables includes separate columns for converting scores from Form A or Form B.

### Q-global Scoring

No score conversions or raw score look-ups are necessary when using Q-global. Enter raw scores, not weighted raw scores, for subtests with item sets. For subtests that convert raw data (i.e., completion time, number of errors, and number of words) to a raw score, simply enter the raw data. For Writing Fluency, enter the number of words written. For Object Naming Facility and Letter Naming Facility, enter the total completion time and total number of errors (summed across trials). Raw scores will calculate automatically for these three subtests. Figure 2.4 shows Q-global Raw Score Entry.

| | | | |
|---|---|---|---|
| **Nonsense Word Decoding** | Raw Score | 11 | (0 to 52) |
| **Writing Fluency** | Word Count | | |
| ⊞ **Silent Reading Fluency** | Raw Score | | (0 to 110) |
| ⊞ **Math Fluency** | Raw Score | | (0 to 96) |
| **Reading Comprehension** | Set | A ▼ | |
| | Raw Score | 14 | (0 to 20) |
| **Written Expression** | Level | Please Select... ▼ | |
| | Raw Score | | |
| **Associational Fluency** | Raw Score | 30 | |
| **Spelling** | Raw Score | 30 | (0 to 69) |
| ⊟ **Object Naming Facility** | | | Trial Entry |

Item Entry (Silent Reading Fluency)
Item Entry (Math Fluency)

Enter completion time in seconds.

| | Completion Time (sec.) | Errors |
|---|---|---|
| Trial 1 | 34 | 1 |
| Trial 2 | 32 | 0 |

**Figure 2.4  Q-global Raw Score Entry**

Source: Kaufman Test of Educational Achievement–Third Edition (KTEA-3). Copyright © 2014 NCS Pearson, Inc. Reproduced with permission. All rights reserved.

## Standard Scores

To be meaningfully interpreted, the raw scores or weighted raw scores of the KTEA-3 must be converted to standard scores. When converting from raw to standard scores, you must first decide whether to use age-based or grade-based norms. For examinees who have graduated high school, only age norms are provided. For all other examinees, the

> ### CAUTION
> ....................................................
> Many examiners find it helpful to compare a student's age-based scores with their grade-based scores. When reporting results, however, be consistent in using the same norms for all subtest and composite scores.

decision to use age or grade norms depends on whether you want to compare the student's test performance with that of same-age peers or same-grade peers. In most cases, the resulting standard scores will be similar. However, important differences can occur if the student has been retained or has received an accelerated grade placement, or if the student began school earlier or later in the year than is typical. In these cases, the grade-based norms are probably more relevant. However, if you plan to compare performance on the KTEA-3 with performance on an ability measure such as the KABC-II or a language measure such as the CELF-5 (Clinical Evaluation of Language Fundamentals, Fifth Edition; Wiig, Semel, & Secord, 2013), always use age-based norms because they are the basis for the standard scores on ability and language measures. The Caution and Don't Forget boxes provide further information about selecting and reporting age-based and grade-based standard scores.

# DON'T FORGET

## Grade Norms versus Age Norms

**Question:** I recently administered the KTEA-3 to a child age 8:11 who just completed third grade. I looked up her standard scores according to age norms (as is typically my practice), but then, out of curiosity, I also looked up her scores according to grade norms. The scores were quite different in some cases (e.g., both Reading Comprehension and Math Computation were 9 points lower when calculated according to the grade norms). Could you tell me why age and grade norms may yield different scores and give me your opinion about when each type of norm is most useful?

**Answer:** The explanation of the difference is pretty simple. Most children in the United States start kindergarten when they are 5 years old and start grade 3 when they are 8 years old. Therefore, virtually all children aged 8:11 are in grade 3. Children turn 8:11 at a steady rate throughout the grade 3 school year—about half of the students turn 8:11 in the fall, and about half in the spring. Thus, the norm sample for age 8:11 contains students from the beginning through the end of grade 3. This age norm sample performs lower, as a group, than the grade norm sample for the spring of grade 3.

Thus, for a student who turns 8:11 in the spring, the age norms will give higher standard scores than the grade norms. The reverse is true for a student who turns 8:11 in the fall. (The direction of the difference by time of year can't be generalized: It depends on what the "month" of age is. For a student aged 8:3 in the fall, age-based scores are higher than grade-based scores, because some students who turn 8:3 in the fall are in grade 2.)

In principle, there is no good, practical solution for taking curriculum exposure into account in age norms, and all of the achievement batteries have this problem. The ideal might be to have age-by-grade norm tables (e.g., age 8:6 in the fall of grade 3, age 8:6 in the spring of grade 3, age 8:6 in the spring of grade 2), but that is too complex. Simply subdividing age norms into fall and spring is flawed because at most "months" of age a student could be in either of two grades, which would be an even greater distortion for some students.

The bottom line is that the situation is complicated—the deeper you look into it, the messier it becomes. In these days when grade retention is rare, there might

(continued)

*(Continued)*

be a good argument to be made for using grade norms rather than age norms for clinical evaluations. The concern used to be that grade norms would make a student who had repeated a grade or two look "too good." These days, there would seem to be a better argument that age norms are problematic because they mix students with different amounts of curriculum exposure. However, examiners must follow requirements set forth by their state and school district based on IDEA. For some that will mean using age norms for special-ed classification and for others that will require using grade norms. Examiners should just be aware that occasionally differences do occur between them.

Using Q-global, selection of age or grade norms is simple. One of the report options is to select Norm Group: Age or Grade. The specific age or grade norm will be determined automatically based on the demographic/testing information you provided. If age is selected, the student's chronological age will be calculated based on the date of birth and date of testing previously entered in order to determine which age norm to use. If grade is selected, Q-global will use the date of testing to determine which semester (Fall, Winter, Spring) grade norm to use.

For hand scoring, you must determine the specific age or grade norm table to use. If testing occurred over multiple sessions, use the first test date to determine which age or grade norm to use. If using age norms, calculate the student's chronological age using the space provided on the cover of the record form. Disregard the number of days in the student's age. Age norms are based on years and months. If using grade norms, you must select from one of three norm groups: Fall (indicating that a student was assessed in August through November), Winter (indicating that a student was assessed in December through February), or Spring (indicating that a student was assessed in March through July). The cover of the record form has a box you can check to indicate whether the student is currently in the Fall, Winter, or Spring semester, and the corresponding months are provided next to each box for ease of reference.

In addition to separating each of the grade norms into Fall, Winter, and Spring, the *KTEA-3 Technical & Interpretive Manual* also has two columns for each subtest: one for Form A and one for Form B. Carefully select the correct column and the correct page of the norms book when you are determining the standard scores. The Don't Forget box reminds examiners about which tables to use to find various standard scores.

Because scores have error associated with them, it is wise to report standard scores with a band of error or within a confidence interval. The KTEA-3 allows you to choose 85%, 90%, or 95% confidence levels.

# DON'T FORGET

......................................................................................................

## Age Norm Bands

Age norms are provided in 3-month intervals for ages 4 and 5, 4-month intervals for ages 6 through 13, 1-year intervals for ages 14 through 16, and 2-year intervals for ages 17 through 20. Norms for ages 21 through 25 were combined into one 5-year interval. Norms with shorter time intervals are used for younger children because learning progresses very rapidly at these ages. As a result, each month of development or schooling greatly impacts achievement levels. On average, the academic skills of students who just turned 5, for example, are considerably less developed than those of students who are 5 and a half. The rate of learning becomes less steep with age, so the time interval of the norms is increasingly lengthened.

| Age | 4–5 | 6–13 | 14–16 | 17–20 | 21–25 |
|---|---|---|---|---|---|
| Norm Band | 3 months | 4 months | 1 year | 2 years | 5 years |
| Number of Age Norm Groups | 8 | 16 | 3 | 2 | 1 |

# DON'T FORGET

......................................................................................................

## Tips for Navigating the Digital Technical & Interpretive Manual

**Use the hypertext (text with hyperlinks).** All of the text included in the Quick Links and Table of Contents pages at the front of the manual contain hyperlinks, which means you can click a line of text with your cursor and the document will immediately advance to the page that includes the selected content. These hyperlinks are the fastest way to find a specific chapter, section, table, or figure. For example, in the following image, clicking "Table 1.2" will advance the document to page 24.

**List of Tables**

**Use the navigation bar.** In the KTEA-3 Brief Technical & Interpretive Manual, three navigation buttons appear at the bottom of every page: a left arrow, a home button, and a right arrow. Clicking the left or right arrow will move the document one page down or up, respectively. Clicking the home button will display the Quick Links page at the front of the manual. The navigation bar is designed to help the reader move through the manual quickly and efficiently.

(continued)

*(Continued)*

**Use the search function.** All PDF readers include a search function that is enabled by typing Ctrl+F (the Ctrl key and the F key at the same time on a PC or Command+F on a Mac). This box allows you to search for a word or phrase that appears anywhere in the manual. This is the best way to find specific content that may not be called out in the Table of Contents. For example, in the following image, searching "DSM-5" and then selecting "Next" or the left or right arrow will show each instance that the *DSM-5* is referenced in the manual.

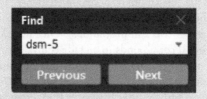

**Select a row of numbers.** When reading data tables on screen, some people find it difficult to visually track across a row of numbers without losing their place. One helpful tip is to select the row of numbers with your mouse to highlight the data on screen.

**Enlarge the font.** Remember that you can zoom in and out by clicking the plus or minus sign at the top of the navigational menu, making the size of the font bigger or smaller, when viewing the digital manual. You can also enlarge the font (zoom in) by selecting a larger percentage in the size box. Zoom in with keyboard shortcuts on a PC by using the Ctrl+equal sign (for Mac use Command+equal sign) and zoom out using Ctrl+hyphen on a PC or Command+hyphen on a Mac.

**Rotate the page.** Some PDF readers will automatically rotate the page to a portrait or landscape orientation, as needed. However, you can do this manually as well by typing the following three keys at the same time: Shift, Ctrl, +.

**Print.** You have the option to print the pages or tables in the digital manual that you use most frequently.

**Additional keyboard shortcuts.** Adobe Acrobat provides additional help on their keyboard shortcuts online at helpx.adobe.com/acrobat/using/keyboard-shortcuts .html.

### Grade and Age Equivalents

Grade and age equivalents may be found in Tables F.4 and F.5, respectively, in the *KTEA-3 Technical & Interpretive Manual*. However, we recommend that they be reported with caution, as they are frequently misunderstood. They are not precise like standard scores or percentile ranks and often suggest large differences in performance, when the differences are insignificant. On Math Concepts & Applications, for example, a raw score of 68 yields an age equivalent of 13.10, yet a raw score of 71 (just three points higher) corresponds to an age equivalent of 15.10. Using these same raw scores, an examinee age 15 would earn age-based standard scores of 96 (for a raw score of 68) and 101 (for a raw score of 71). Thus, when comparing scores based on the same raw scores, a 4-point standard score difference appears much smaller than the 2-year difference in age-equivalents. Consider also that both standard scores are well within the average range, so the age equivalent of 13.10 should not be interpreted as indicating underachievement or a skill deficit.

Grade and age equivalents correspond to the average raw score obtained by students at a particular grade or age level on a particular subtest. Grade and age equivalents do not indicate the curriculum or developmental level at which the student is functioning, nor do they indicate how much progress a student has made over time (if comparing scores across two administrations). On Phonological Processing, for example, a raw score of 40 corresponds to a grade equivalent of 7.0. If obtained by a student in the Fall of grade 5, these results might seem quite impressive at first glance. Is this fifth grader's phonological processing skills at a 7th grade level, 2 years more advanced than most fifth graders? Always refer to a standard score for this level of information. In this case, the student's grade-based standard score of 102 (95–109 with 90% confidence) is within the average range. So what then does the grade equivalent of 7.0 tell us? Two things: (1) the average student in grade 7.0 (the first month of grade 7) obtained the same raw score as our fifth grade student, and (2) phonological processing has a ceiling effect—the highest possible standard score is only 135 at grade 5. This ceiling effect is expected because the development of phonological processing skills naturally plateaus after the early elementary years.

## DON'T FORGET

Initially, to obtain grade equivalents using Q-global, users selected grade norms. To obtain age equivalents, users selected age norms. As of September 2016, users have the option to view both age and grade equivalents in the same report. Reports can be generated in Word format to facilitate copying and pasting data as needed.

More than anything else, age and grade equivalents are influenced by the content (the specific items and skills) of the particular subtest and the degree to which that content differentiates students at different grade levels. The slope of typical skill development will influence how well the KTEA-3 or any other test will be able to differentiate students at different age or grade levels. Age and grade equivalents are most informative for describing the norms of a test and the *average* performance of students across ages and grades; they are least informative (and often misleading) when used to describe an individual's achievement level or skill proficiency.

# CAUTION

Be careful when interpreting age equivalents and grade equivalents. Using age or grade equivalents to qualify a student for services, make educational placement decisions, select curricular or instructional materials, and/or describe the developmental level at which a student is functioning is considered a misuse of these scores.

Age/grade equivalents are *not* standard scores. Rather, equivalents indicate the average raw score obtained by students at a particular grade or age level on a particular subtest.

## *Percentile Ranks*

Percentile ranks are an excellent metric to communicate results to parents, teachers, and other nonpsychologists. They are often readily understood and interpreted. Regardless of whether age-based or grade-based standard scores are used, the percentile rank has the same meaning: It is the percentage of individuals that the examinee outperformed at his or her age (age norms) or grade level (grade norms). For example, a 12-year-old who scored at the 75th percentile on Nonsense Word Decoding performed better than 75% of 12-year-olds on that subtest. A first grader who scored at the 5th percentile on Phonological Awareness scored better than only 5% of first graders. Use caution when explaining percentile ranks to parents to avoid confusion with percent correct, and remember that percentile ranks are not equal interval (see Caution box).

Each standard score can be converted to a percentile rank by using Table F.3 of the *KTEA-3 Technical & Interpretive Manual* or Table F.9 in the *KTEA-3 Brief Technical & Interpretive Manual*.

# CAUTION

**Percentile Ranks Are Not Percent Correct**

Clearly communicate to parents that a percentile rank is the percent of children that an examinee scored better than. A percentile rank is not the percentage of items answered correctly.

**Percentile Ranks Are Not Equal Interval**

Percentile ranks differentiate performance better in the middle of the distribution, but provide less differentiation toward the extreme ends of the distribution. For this reason, percentile ranks cannot be manipulated statistically to measure progress over time (never add, subtract, multiply, divide, or average them).

# DON'T FORGET

......................................................

Q-global provides the option to choose the 15-point or the 10-point classification system when reporting KTEA-3 results.

## Descriptive Categories

Rapid Reference 2.5 presents the 10-point and 15-point classification systems that the test authors suggested for reporting KTEA-3 subtests and composites. Both systems divide the theoretical standard score range of 40 to 160 into seven categories, but one uses 10-point ranges and the other uses 15-point ranges. The suggested qualitative descriptors, which are the same across both classification systems, are intended to reflect in words the approximate distance of each range of scores from the group mean—a verbal translation of the normal curve. The classification systems and qualitative descriptors suggested in the KTEA-3 differ from those in the previous KTEA editions and those provided in the WIAT-III. Currently there is little consistency in the descriptive categories used across clinical assessments.

The KTEA-3 is the first clinical assessment, to our knowledge, to offer a choice between the two most commonly used classification systems. Providing a choice was intended to encourage flexibility and thoughtful consideration in the use of descriptive categories and to promote greater consistency in reporting results across similar instruments. Your decision to use the 15-point or the 10-point classification system and the qualitative descriptors you choose may be influenced by the examinee's score profile, the other tests you've administered, personal preference, and reporting requirements you've been given by outside agencies, among other things. When reporting similar standard scores across different instruments, consider using the classification system suggested by the cognitive measure. When reporting results from the KTEA-3 and the KABC-II, for example, it would be reasonable to use the 15-point scale described in the KABC-II manual to describe standard scores across both tests. However, when reporting results from the KTEA-3, WIAT-III, and WISC-V, for example, you might consider using the 10-point scale and qualitative descriptors described in the WISC-V manual to describe standard scores across all three tests.

When selecting qualitative descriptors, there is an increasing preference to avoid value-laden terms such as *superior* as well as vague or confusing terms such as *borderline*. Use of the term *borderline*, in particular, is not appropriate for describing low achievement scores. Whenever possible, use neutral terms that simply describe the score's distance from the mean (such as *low, average, high*).

The 10-point and 15-point classification systems each have advantages and disadvantages. An advantage of the 15-point system is that it provides more differentiation at the highest and lowest ends of the distribution. For this reason, some people prefer the 15-point scale for reporting very high or low scores. On the other hand, the 10-point system provides more differentiation within the middle of the distribution. The 10-point system defines the average range more narrowly as 90 to 109, which includes 50% of the sample, as compared to the 15-point system's average range of 85 to 115, which includes 68% of the sample. A student who obtains a standard score of 85 scored better than only 16% of his or her peers, and some would argue that the 16th percentile seems too low to be considered average. However, one concern with 10-point categories is that, when confidence intervals are used to provide a reasonable band of error, it is common for the confidence interval to span three different categories. Such a broad span of ability levels can be confusing when explaining an examinee's test performance to a parent, for example.

## DON'T FORGET

Avoid overwhelming readers of a case report by providing descriptive categories for each standard score. These labels serve best when they either summarize an individual's performance on all scales via a composite score or highlight significant discrepancies among the scales. Generally, the use of descriptive labels with subtests should be reserved for standard scores that are significantly above or below the examinee's own mean values or for standard scores that are high or low relative to other examinees of the same age.

## DON'T FORGET

### Descriptive Category Systems

**10-Point System**

| Range of Standard Scores | Name of Category | Percent of the Sample |
|---|---|---|
| 130–160 | Very high | 2.2% |
| 120–129 | High | 6.7% |
| 110–119 | Above average | 16.1% |
| 90–109 | Average range | 50% |
| 80–89 | Below average | 16.1% |
| 70–79 | Low | 6.7% |
| 40–69 | Very low | 2.2% |

Provides more differentiation in the middle of the distribution

(continued)

(Continued)

## 15-Point System

| Range of Standard Scores | Name of Category | Percent of the Sample | SDs from Mean |
|---|---|---|---|
| 146–160 | Very high | 0.13% | +3 to +4 |
| 131–145 | High | 2.14% | +2 to +3 |
| 116–130 | Above average | 13.59% | +1 to +2 |
| 85–115 | Average range | 68.26% | −1 to +1 |
| 70–84 | Below average | 13.59% | −1 to −2 |
| 55–69 | Low | 2.14% | −2 to −2 |
| 40–54 | Very low | 0.13% | −3 to −4 |

Provides more differentiation at the extremes of the distribution

### *Growth Scale Values*

Growth Scale Values (GSVs) are designed for measuring change and are based on the Item Response Theory (IRT) ability scale. In the same way that "inches" are an equal-interval scale of length, the GSV scale is an equal-interval scale of academic skill. Thus, GSVs can be used as a "yardstick" by which academic progress can be measured throughout the school years. GSVs reflect absolute performance rather than performance relative to a normative sample; however, the examinee's rate of progress may be compared to the typical growth rate in the normative sample using the GSV Chart Score Report in Q-global.

Key advantages of GSVs include the following:

- Sensitive to small increases and decreases in academic progress over time (see Don't Forget box).
- Allow direct comparison of GSVs obtained on alternate forms of a subtest. GSVs obtained from the Brief Form/Comprehensive Form B and Comprehensive Form A may be compared over time.

Limitations of GSVs include the following:

- The degree to which GSVs are able to measure academic learning is limited to the content and skill coverage of the subtest. The KTEA-3 is not designed to measure all aspects of a student's curriculum or provide in-depth coverage of all skill categories. Consider curriculum-based or criterion-referenced measures for more comprehensive content and skill coverage.

    Example: the LWR subtest includes items for naming consonant letter sounds, but only for a subset of consonant letters. To track a child's progress naming *all* consonant letters or letter sounds, consider administering the Letter Checklist (provided on the KTEA-3 flash drive) at regular intervals.

# DON'T FORGET

................................................................................................................

## Interpreting Growth Scale Values

For each KTEA-3 subtest, GSVs from one form may be directly compared with GSVs from the other form for measuring growth.

Unlike standard scores, GSVs will reflect even small amounts of academic improvement over time. If an examinee's skills are improving at a "typical" rate, the standard score will appear relatively unchanged over time but comparing the GSVs will indicate growth.

| | Age | Raw Score | GSV | Standard Score | |
|---|---|---|---|---|---|
| Over the course of one year | 8:0 | 26 | 155 | 80 | SS is the same |
| | 8:4 | 29 | 163 | 80 | |
| | 8:8 | 33 | 174 | 80 | |
| | 9:0 | 36 | 182 | 80 | |

GSV shows growth

## Stanines

Stanines (standard nines) provide a scale ranging from 1 to 9 with a mean of 5:

- Stanines 1, 2, and 3 represent the lowest 23% of the distribution of scores.
- Stanines 4, 5, and 6 represent the middle 54% of the distribution of scores, which some consider the average range.
- Stanines 7, 8, and 9 represent the highest 23% of test scores.

A stanine is not a single score. Similar to quartiles and deciles, each stanine represents a band of scores. Only stanines 2 through 8 span equal distances, each extending 0.5 standard deviation units. Stanines 1 and 9 extend through the tails of the distribution, including the lowest and highest 4% of scores, respectively. Stanines offer limited precision for describing an individual's performance and are not well suited for measuring change over time. Stanines are best suited to describing the performance of groups of students, such as categorizing schools or classrooms. Consider reporting stanines when exact scores are less important than identifying groups of students with similar performance.

## Normal Curve Equivalents

Normal curve equivalents (NCEs) were developed for the United States Department of Education by the RMC Research Corporation with program evaluation in mind

(Mertler, 2002). NCEs are an equal interval scale ranging from 1 to 99 with a mean of 50. NCEs are roughly equivalent to stanines to one decimal place (e.g., a NCE of 36 corresponds to a stanine of 3.6). In addition, NCEs align with percentile ranks only at 1, 50, and 99. At every other point on the scale, NCEs differ from percentile ranks because NCEs are an equal interval scale. For this reason, NCEs can be averaged and otherwise manipulated statistically, which makes them especially useful for analyzing the performance and progress of groups of students. For example, by comparing NCEs once per year, a zero difference in NCEs indicates 1 year's growth, a positive difference indicates more than 1 year's growth, and a negative difference indicates less than 1 year's growth. Remember, NCEs differ from growth scale values (GSVs) in that GSVs are sample-independent and offer greater precision and sensitivity in tracking individual progress over time.

### Subtest-by-Subtest Scoring Keys

Most of the items on the KTEA-3 have a simple dichotomous scoring system: 1 point (for correct) or 0 points (for incorrect). However, there are differences in how raw scores are calculated across the subtests. Regardless of how the raw score is calculated, you need to score the items (at least in a preliminary fashion) as you are testing. This score-as-you-go procedure is necessary so that you know when to discontinue a subtest or when you need to drop back to an earlier start point. We recommend that you double-check the accuracy of each item's score when you are completely done with the test administration, prior to calculating the raw score. The Caution box lists some common errors in hand scoring. Scoring keys for each of the subtests are listed in the following pages.

## CAUTION

### Common Errors in Hand Scoring

- Calculating the raw score incorrectly
- Transferring the raw score to the Subtest & Composite Score Computation form incorrectly
- Adding the subtest standard scores incorrectly when calculating the sum for the composite scores
- Using the wrong tables for standard score conversions
- Misreading the norms tables (e.g., using the wrong line or wrong column)
- Subtraction errors in comparing composites and subtest scores
- Errors in conducting the error analysis (e.g., totaling the error columns incorrectly)

## Phonological Awareness

Examiners should not penalize for variations in speech due to regional speech patterns or dialectal variations. For example, when scoring Section 5 (Segmenting), the segmentation of *lawnmower* may resemble *l-aw-n-m-ow-uh* in some regions (such as the south) where speakers tend to drop the ending -r from words. Hence, the student may provide a schwa sound for the last phoneme, rather than the -er phoneme. If this is consistent with the student's dialectal pronunciation, score the response as correct.

When scoring responses from students with articulation difficulties, an examiner must be knowledgeable about the student's difficulties, including which specific phonemes he or she has difficulty pronouncing and whether the student drops or substitutes phonemes. Score the student's responses accordingly, accepting dropped or substituted phonemes only where the mispronunciation is consistent with the student's speech patterns.

In the Rhyming section, a response should be scored as correct if it rhymes with the stimulus word, even if the response is a nonsense word (e.g., if an examinee says "*jook* rhymes with *book*"). In the Segmenting section, the student must make a noticeable pause between the word parts to score the response as correct. The Phonological Awareness total raw score is the sum of scores across all sections.

## Math Concepts & Applications

Correct responses are listed in the record form and stimulus book; however, numerically equivalent responses are also scored as correct. For example, the following three responses are all scored as correct: 3 hours, 15 minutes; 3 1/4 hours; 195 minutes. For most items, the record form lists the most common correct response (e.g., eight thirty), but the stimulus book may list additional, equivalent correct responses (e.g., eight thirty; half past eight). Refer to the stimulus book for additional responses to consider, but remember that these responses are not necessarily exhaustive. If a student provides yet another numerically equivalent response, score the response as correct (e.g., 30 minutes past eight). Improper fractions and responses that are not reduced to their lowest terms are generally acceptable.

Some items are problems requiring calculations with units of measure (e.g., inches, feet, pounds). For most items, omitting the unit of measurement from the response is acceptable. For such items, the fact that the unit of measurement is optional is indicated in the stimulus book by being printed in parentheses. For example, if the correct response is printed as "3 (inches)," then a response of "3" is acceptable. Items that require the unit of measurement will not use parentheses. For example, if the correct response is printed as "84 cents," then a response of "84" is incorrect.

Some items have multiple questions, and a correct response requires examinees to answer all parts of the question correctly (e.g., Item 28 on Form A).

To calculate the raw score, subtract the number of errors (0 scores) from the ceiling item. An error analysis may be conducted after the test is administered.

### Letter & Word Recognition

To properly score Letter & Word Recognition, you must have knowledge of the correct pronunciation(s) of each stimulus word. As you look at the pronunciations printed in the record form, listen to the correct pronunciations provided on the Audio files (for Q-interactive users, audio files are provided in the Support tab under Test Materials). Make notes to help you remember the pronunciations as needed. You also need to gain proficiency in recording responses phonetically (either with the phonetic key or sound-by-sound). A bright child or adolescent may rapidly read the six words listed on a stimulus page, and if you struggle with how to record what they say, you will undoubtedly run into trouble with scoring.

Audio recording is highly recommended. Even examiners who are proficient in recording responses phonetically can benefit from using an audio recording device. Whether the student reads fast or slow, it's helpful to listen to his or her responses again to verify your phonetic transcription and scoring. During subtest administration, the demands of listening, recording, and scoring simultaneously taxes our working memory capacity. Especially when processing demands are high, it's not uncommon for our sensory system to simplify information or "auto-correct" mistakes. Even when you feel confident in what you've recorded, it's often helpful to listen to the recorded responses to verify.

Some words have multiple correct pronunciations, and the various pronunciations are listed in the record form only (not in the stimulus book). For example, *elegant* may be pronounced "EL ih gunt" or "EL uh gent." Accented syllables are printed in all capital letters, and accenting the correct syllable is required to score the response as correct (e.g., "el uh GENT" would be scored as incorrect). Don't apply syllable breaks rigidly; for example, the correct pronunciation of *guarded* is listed as "GAR did," but "GARD id" would also be scored as correct (the difference between these pronunciations is very subtle).

Sometimes examinees will sound out a word two or three times (perhaps incorrectly) before they read it smoothly as their final response. Only score the final response, and award credit if the response is correctly pronounced in a relatively smooth manner with the accent properly placed.

A dysfluent or halting pronunciation (e.g., "pl..ease") should result in a prompt, but only prompt one time per item. If the student was prompted according to the administration instructions to "say it altogether," but the student still did not pronounce the word as a connected, smooth whole, score the response as incorrect.

If a student's dialect or regional speech pattern leads to a different pronunciation, give credit for an item if it is consistent with the student's dialect or speech pattern. For example, reading "car" with a Bostonian accent of "caw" would be an acceptable pronunciation in that region. Speakers from England, for example, may pronounce *united* as "yoo nye tid," whereas most American speakers say "yoo nye did." Students whose first language is not English may also have specific pronunciation differences. Make sure you are familiar with the student's English speech patterns and the specific articulation differences that he or she exhibits. Do not penalize for articulation differences that are consistent with the student's general English speech patterns. For example, a native Spanish speaker's pronunciation of the word *eleven* may resemble *eleben.*

To calculate the raw score, subtract the number of errors (0 scores) from the ceiling item. Skipped items (that could not be read) are scored as incorrect. If you allowed the student to finish reading all items on the stimulus page before discontinuing, as the instructions recommend, do not include items past the discontinue point when summing the total raw score. An error analysis may be conducted after the test is administered. Accurate verbatim transcription or audio recording of the examinee's responses is crucial if you intend to complete an error analysis.

## *Math Computation*

For most items, correct responses are listed in the record form only (correct responses for the earliest items only are printed in the stimulus book as well). Numerically equivalent responses are also scored as correct. For example, the most common correct response to an item may be 3/4, but .75 is also acceptable. The record form lists numerically equivalent responses that receive credit, but remember that these responses are not necessarily exhaustive. If a student provides yet another numerically equivalent response, score the response as correct (e.g., accept a response of 6/8 as equivalent to 3/4). Improper fractions and responses that are not reduced to their lowest terms are generally acceptable.

Numeral formation and reversal errors are penalized only on the earliest items (Items 6–9 on Form A), which are designed to assess numeral formation. When handwriting is unclear, you may ask the student to read his or her response to help you decipher what is written. Responses with transposition errors, such as 12 for 21, are scored as incorrect.

Math Computation has a discontinue rule of 4 consecutive 0s. Especially for young children, consider scoring their responses as they finish each problem so that you know when to discontinue the subtest. However, keep in mind that examinees with math anxiety and many older students may feel uncomfortable having someone watch them work. Some students may work better and show more persistence on difficult items if they are not being closely watched. If you believe this to be true, look at your own papers and busy yourself with other tasks while the students are working, glancing up only occasionally to check their progress and quickly score the items they've just completed to see if the discontinue rule has been met. For older students who may be able to complete some of the later items, consider giving them more physical space (perhaps move your chair away a bit) and ask them to tell you when they have completed all the items they know how to do. Try to observe a student's behaviors and strategies unobtrusively (for example, are they subvocalizing or counting on their fingers?).

# DON'T FORGET

## Scoring Math Computation

**Question:** I have a student who answered the first two Math Computation items correct verbally but could not recall how to write the numerals. Do I give credit for these responses?

**Answer:** In this case, no credit is given for oral responses. Math Computation was designed to assess written math computation skills. Only examinees with severe motor impairments are permitted to give responses orally. However, the fact that the student gave correct oral responses is a clinically relevant observation that ought to be reported when interpreting results.

Once the student has completed all the items he or she can do, or the discontinue point has been reached, don't forget to review all of the responses to ensure that you can decipher his or her writing.

Allowing students to work without being watched too closely may result in students attempting items past the discontinue point. If this occurs, simply disregard all responses after the discontinue point when calculating the subtest raw score. You may, however, consider these responses for qualitative purposes and testing the limits.

To calculate the raw score, subtract the number of errors (items with 0 scores) from the ceiling item. Skipped items (those that could not be completed) before the discontinue point are scored as incorrect. If the student completed items past the discontinue point, do not include those items when summing the total raw score. An error analysis may be conducted after the test is administered.

## Nonsense Word Decoding

*Do not penalize for misplacing the accent of a nonsense word.* This is an important difference from scoring Letter & Word Recognition. Even though the correct pronunciations printed in the stimulus book and record form include the accent information, a student is not required to place the accent correctly.

Aside from scoring syllable accents, the scoring rules resemble those described for Letter & Word Recognition (refer to the Letter & Word Recognition scoring information provided on an earlier page in this chapter for more explanation).

- Familiarize yourself with the correct pronunciation of the nonsense words on the Audio files (for Q-interactive users, audio files are provided in the Support tab under Test Materials). Don't apply syllable breaks rigidly; for example, the correct pronunciation of *dompest* is listed as DOMP ist, but "DOM pist" would also be scored as correct (the difference between these pronunciations is very subtle). Some words have more than one pronunciation, as shown in the record form.

- Record student responses phonetically using the phonetic key or sound-by-sound. Audio recording is highly recommended to confirm that the student's responses were recorded accurately.
- A dysfluent or halting pronunciation (e.g., gl..ux) should result in a prompt, but prompt only one time per item. If the student was prompted according to the administration instructions to "say it altogether," but the student still did not pronounce the word as a connected, smooth whole, score the response as incorrect.
- Articulation errors resulting from dialectal variations or nonnative English speech patterns are not penalized.
- Correct responses are those in which the student pronounces the word in a connected, relatively smooth whole–even if several attempts are made before pronouncing the word correctly.

To calculate the raw score, subtract the number of errors (items with 0 scores) from the ceiling item. Skipped items (that could not be read) are scored as incorrect. If you allowed the student to finish reading all items on the stimulus page before discontinuing, as the instructions recommend, do not include items past the discontinue point when summing the total raw score. An error analysis may be conducted after the test is administered. Accurate verbatim transcription or audio recording of the examinee's responses is crucial if you intend to complete an error analysis.

### *Writing Fluency*
The raw score for Writing Fluency is the number of recognizable (readable) words written by the student within the 5-minute time limit. Performance depends solely on productivity. Disregard errors in letter formation, spelling, capitalization, punctuation, grammar, and syntax. Skipping items is permitted. Count the number of words from the items attempted.

Recognizable words are counted even if they are misspelled or the letters are poorly formed or reversed. If the written response is difficult to read, you may ask the student read his or her response aloud. Listen to what the student reads aloud to help you decipher the written response. Do not score the student's oral response and do not permit the student to change his or her written response while reading. Scoring is based on the written response only. If the student "reads" something aloud that differs from what you see represented in writing, score only what you decipher in the written response.

Count the number of words used, regardless of word boundary or spacing errors. For example, if the student separated a word into two or more words, count only one word (e.g., She play ing in the gar den = 5 words). Similarly, if the student combined two or more words into one, count the number of words combined (e.g., *the dog drak out uvher bol* = 7 words, *uvher* is scored as *of her*).

# DON'T FORGET

## Scoring Writing Fluency

**Question:** Why would a written response that is nonsensical receive credit?

**Answer:** Writing Fluency was designed as a measure of contextual graphomotor speed and the orthographic loop of working memory. This subtest is not a measure of grammar, syntax, spelling or writing mechanics. Hence, credit may be given to a severely misspelled word or correctly spelled words that form a nonsensical sentence (e.g., cat cat and and). Writing nonsensical responses was extremely rare during standardization. When it occurred, the examinees were typically those with mild intellectual disability and may have known how to spell only a handful of words. Even under these circumstances, the Writing Fluency score provides useful information about graphomotor speed. Quality of response was positively related to writing speed, so examinees who wrote nonsensical sentences earned very low standard scores. If an examinee does not write meaningful sentences on the Writing Fluency subtest, it's reasonable to also administer a measure of Alphabet Writing Fluency, such as in the WIAT-III, and then compare the examinee's performance on the contextual and decontextualized task, respectively.

**Question:** What if the examinee writes incomplete sentences?

**Answer:** The sample and practice items are designed to encourage examinees to write simple, complete sentences in response to each picture. However, some students may not understand the concept of a sentence; other students may opt to use a strategy of writing fragments (e.g., cat sleeping; girl playing; etc.) in order to complete more items. The Writing Fluency subtest was not designed as a measure of grammar or syntax, so these errors are not penalized. Moreover, the scoring rules disregard the number of items completed, so the student who writes fragments to complete more items will receive a score comparable to that of a student of similar ability who writes complete sentences for fewer items.

## Silent Reading Fluency

The raw score for Silent Reading Fluency is the number of correct responses minus the number of incorrect responses given within the 2-minute time limit. Each item response is either *yes* or *no*, which provides a 50–50 chance of guessing the correct response. However, subtracting incorrect responses from the total correct provides a correction for guessing and random responding, and also results in a stiff penalty for incorrect responses due to reading errors or difficulties.

For hand scoring, use the scoring key provided in the flash drive. The scoring key is a reproducible page, so you can print it out on paper or on transparency film to create an overlay. Disregard any skipped or unattempted items—these are not scored as incorrect.

For scoring in Q-global, you don't need a scoring key. You may enter the student's responses as *y* or *n* into the entry fields for automatic scoring and raw score calculation. If the student skipped an item, leave the response blank.

### Math Fluency

The raw score for Math Fluency is the number of correct responses provided within the 1-minute time limit. Disregard any skipped or unattempted items—these are not scored as incorrect. Do not penalize for numeral formation and reversal errors. When handwriting is unclear, you may ask the student to read his or her response to help you decipher what is written. Responses with transposition errors, such as 12 for 21, are scored as incorrect.

For hand scoring, use the scoring key provided in the flash drive. The scoring key is reproducible, which means you are allowed to print out these pages for your personal use and ease of reference.

For scoring in Q-global, you don't need a scoring key. You may enter the student's numerical responses into the entry fields for automatic scoring and raw score calculation. If the student skipped an item, leave the response blank.

### Reading Comprehension and Listening Comprehension

Refer to the stimulus book for the most complete list of correct responses. For many items, specific criteria that a response must satisfy in order to be scored correct are listed along with examples. The record form lists abbreviated correct responses for all items except those that elicit lengthy or varied responses. Some responses have optional portions, which are shown in parentheses in the record form and stimulus book. When scoring, do not penalize for poorly worded responses, immature speech, articulation errors, or gross mispronunciations from the text (as long as the word is recognizable).

The early items of these subtests are fairly straightforward to score. The early Reading Comprehension items require a pointing or behavioral response, and the early Listening Comprehension items involve simple sentences and questions.

The later items of Reading Comprehension and Listening Comprehension require passage-level comprehension and involve answering multiple-choice and open-ended questions. The multiple-choice questions are straightforward to score. The open-ended questions generally are not difficult to score because the stimulus book has examples of correct and incorrect answers as well as the general criteria that is necessary for a response to receive credit. In most cases, the reasons behind the decisions regarding correct and incorrect responses are implicitly clear. However, for a handful of Reading Comprehension items (six items from Form A and 7 items from Form B), Chapter 1 of the *Scoring Manual* provides a helpful explanation for scoring decisions as well as additional examples of correct and incorrect responses. If the examinee's response includes extraneous information, simply disregard it when scoring. However, if the examinee's response includes factually incorrect information or information that suggests he or she misunderstood the text, score the response 0 (even if part of the examinee's response included a correct answer).

Sum the scores obtained within the final item set administered to obtain the raw score. A student who begins at set B and meets the decision point criteria to proceed to set C. If hand scoring, the raw score is then converted to a weighted raw score using a conversion table found in the *Technical & Interpretive Manual*. In Q-global, enter the final set administered and the raw score; the weighted raw score will be looked up automatically.

# CAUTION

## Computing the Raw Score for Reading Comprehension and Listening Comprehension

If a student is administered more than one item set, either because they reversed to an earlier item set or continued on to a more difficult item set after meeting the decision point criteria, use caution when computing the raw score. *Sum only scores from items within the final item set administered* (the item set for which the examinee met the criteria to discontinue or stop). Scores from items above or below the final item set are disregarded—they do not contribute to the final raw score.

The item sets overlap, so pay careful attention when summing scores. The items included in each set are printed next to the item set raw score boxes in the record form. The raw score entered in the box should be the sum of those item scores only.

### Which item set should be scored?

Question: A kindergartener answered 17 out of 20 questions correctly on Reading Comprehension set A. The decision point states that if there are three or fewer scores of 0 in a set, continue to the next set. So I started set B, and the student answered the next five questions incorrectly (which triggered the discontinue rule). Should I score the subtest using 0 points on Set B or 17 points on Set A? Set A seems to be a better representation of her ability.

Answer: The child's performance on Set A provides more information about her reading skills. When an examinee answers all items correctly or incorrectly, it's more difficult to estimate his or her ability level. The decision point is designed to help examiners find the most appropriate set, but in this case it's appropriate to use clinical judgment to score set A.

## DON'T FORGET

### FAQs: Scores Based on Out-of-Level Item Sets for Reading Comprehension, Listening Comprehension, and Written Expression

**Question:** When an examinee is administered an out-of-level item set (one that is higher or lower than the grade appropriate item set), do I use the same norms?

**Answer:** Yes, the same norms are used for all item sets administered because the subtest raw score is first converted to a "weighted raw score," which is then converted to a standard score. The weighted raw score adjusts the raw score based on the item set administered, so raw scores based on a more difficult item set are "worth more" than scores based on a less difficult item set.

---

**Question:** Is the examinee still compared with same age or grade peers when they take an out-of-level item set?

**Answer:** Essentially yes. A subset of examinees in the standardization sample were administered the item sets above and below the grade-appropriate item set to allow the item sets to be vertically scaled, or equated, using item response theory (IRT). In doing so, an examinee's performance on out-of-level item sets may be compared to the way same-age or same-grade peers would perform. However, the farther away the examinee moves from his/her grade-appropriate item set, the more estimation is required. While still considered reliable and valid, scores on item sets three or more levels above or below the grade appropriate item set are more challenging to interpret because the content and skill demands may be quite different from what is expected on grade level. For this reason, it's best to begin administration at the grade-appropriate item set and move up or down *one* item set at a time.

---

**Question:** If a standard score is based on an out-of-level item set, can I use it in an analysis to identify specific learning disabilities?

**Answer:** Yes, the score is a valid estimate of the examinee's skill level in that achievement domain and may be used in analyses to identify specific learning disabilities.

### *Written Expression*

Thorough scoring of the Written Expression subtest must be completed after the test is administered. Detailed item-by-item Written Expression scoring instructions are provided in the *Scoring Manual*. Each item of this subtest has one or more scoring categories that is scored 1 or 0. The most common categories include task, sentence structure, capitalization, punctuation, grammar, and other mechanical errors. In addition to the specific error categories, you should familiarize yourself with the general scoring guidelines for Written Expression (see the Don't Forget box for a review of these).

# DON'T FORGET

## Scoring Written Expression Form A Item 62 (Level 4)

For this item, the examinee is asked to write a sentence using the word *which*. However, the word *which* is not printed on the stimulus book page. Confusing *which/witch* among older examinees is very uncommon; however, if the examinee writes a sentence using the word to mean *witch* (regardless of how the word is spelled), then you may clarify the task by explaining that the sentence needs to use the other form of *which*. You may spell the word *which* for the examinee if needed, but do not use *which* in a sentence. If the examinee still cannot use *which* in a sentence, then move on and score the item as incorrect.

If the written response is difficult to read, you may ask the student to read his or her response aloud. Listen to what the student reads aloud to help you decipher the written response. Do not score the student's oral response and do not permit the student to change his or her written response while reading. Scoring is based on the written response only. If the student "reads" something aloud that differs from what you see represented in writing, score only what you decipher in the written response.

Once you have scored each of the categories 1 or 0, sum the scores obtained within the final level administered to obtain the raw score. If hand scoring, the raw score is then converted to a weighted raw score using a conversion table found in the *Technical & Interpretive Manual*. An error analysis may be conducted after the subtest is scored.

# DON'T FORGET

## General Scoring Guidelines for Written Expression

**Error categories are independent.** Score each error category independently of the others. Try not to let poor performance in one category influence the scores for other categories in that item.

**Structure and grammar errors should be obvious.** As a general guideline, score 0 for sentence structure and word form (grammar) if the error is obvious and would stand out in semi-formal writing such as a class paper.

**Use judgment to choose best-fitting category.** Sometimes a response is clearly erroneous, but it is not immediately evident which category should be scored 0. In those instances, choose the category that in your judgment best fits the error. The overall subtest score will not be affected.

**Most often, ignore extra writing.** If the task criterion specifies a limited product (e.g., one word or one sentence) and the student produces a response, part of which satisfies this criterion, ignore any additional material the student has written when scoring the task criterion. However, if the task criterion is open-ended (e.g., "one or more sentences"), score according to the entire response. For the

*(continued)*

(Continued)

sentence structure criterion, scoring usually is based on the student's entire response, except when the scoring rule for an item specifies otherwise.

**Give no credit for incomprehensible responses or no response.** If a student doesn't respond to an item, or if the response is incomprehensible (the meaning cannot be understood), score 0 on all categories for that item.

**Give no credit for task or sentence structure for misplaced sentence parts.** On later items, misplacement of a part of the sentence can cause failure on both the task criterion (because the sentence does not make sense or says something false) and the sentence structure criterion (because of the misplacement). In such cases, score 0 for both criteria.

**If a word is recognizable it is phonetically readable.** "Phonetically readable," a term used in Level 2 and 3 scoring, is not a technical term; it means that the word is recognizable.

**A letter is recognizable if it doesn't form another letter.** Penalize for letters that resemble or form another letter (b looks like a d, s looks like a z). Otherwise, as long as letters are recognizable, do not penalize if letters are poorly formed, upside-down, sideways, uppercase, lowercase, or a mix of upper/lowercase.

**Try not to penalize for poor handwriting or poor spelling.** If a response is difficult to read due to poor spelling or poor handwriting, score as much of it as possible.

Note: From Chapter 5 of the *KTEA-3 Scoring Manual* (Kaufman & Kaufman, 2014d).

## Associational Fluency

Scoring for the two Associational Fluency items is based on the number of different responses spoken by the examinee in 30 seconds that meet the scoring rules. Chapter 2 of the *Scoring Manual* lists the specific requirements for each of the Associational Fluency tasks. Key scoring guidelines to remember include the following:

> **CAUTION**
> ·········································
>
> ### Do not give credit for the sample words
>
> A common scoring mistake is to give credit for words given as samples in the prompt. The sample words for each item are printed in the *Scoring Manual* as a reminder.

- No credit is given for made-up words, words that were given as examples, or overly generic terms (such as *lunch* for a food or *mammal* for an animal).
- Responses in a language other than English generally do not receive credit; however, an exception is made for naming foods (Item 1 on Form A) to allow for various ethnic foods to be named.
- No additional credit is given for providing multiple responses that mean the same thing. For example, a response that includes *mouse* and *mice* would receive only 1 point. Similarly, a response that includes *chicken* and *hen* would receive only 1 point. A helpful rule of thumb is that the responses should bring to mind different visual images to receive credit.

## Spelling

Scoring Spelling is straightforward: Score 1 for correctly spelled words and 0 for misspelled words. Poorly formed letters, capitalization, and mixing print with cursive are not penalized.

The key to scoring Spelling is making sure that you know what the examinee intended to write during administration. During administration, carefully watch the examinee spell each item and ask him or her to name any letters that are unclear or ambiguous.

Avoid scoring the examinee's responses "by eye," reading through them and looking for misspelled words. This method of scoring is error prone—even if you are a good speller. Errors may include a correct spelling of the wrong word or may closely resemble the correct spelling. To prevent scoring errors, always compare each of the examinee's responses with the correct spelling printed in the record form.

To calculate the raw score, subtract the number of errors (items with 0 scores) from the ceiling item. Skipped items (those words that the examinee chose not to attempt) are scored as incorrect. An error analysis may be conducted after the subtest is scored.

## Object Naming Facility and Letter Naming Facility

For both Object Naming Facility (ONF) and Letter Naming Facility (LNF), the raw score is based on the examinee's completion time as well as the number of errors made. Scores cannot be obtained if the total number of errors for both trials exceeds 19, which would be extremely rare. Generally, examinees who make errors are still permitted to score this subtest in order to document a weakness in naming facility and/or retrieval accuracy. Nearly all examinees who lack familiarity with the stimuli will not pass the practice items, which is a prerequisite to administering the test items. However, examinees who have difficulty with retrieval, visual tracking, and/or self-monitoring may make errors even though they are familiar with the stimuli. Always consider both the speed and accuracy of performance when reporting and interpreting results.

Audio recording the ONF and LNF subtests is highly recommended to ensure accurate scoring. Examinees may lose their place and begin again, self-correct, or name very rapidly, all of which can make it difficult for an examiner to accurately track, record, and score the responses. For ONF, if an examinee says a synonym, such as *kitten* for *cat* or *home* for *house*, award credit for these items. For LNF, as a general rule, examinees provide letter names (not letter sounds) on the practice and test items. However, if the examinee mistakenly says the letter sound instead of the letter name for some of the test items, accept these responses as correct.

Naming facility, or rapid automatic naming, is not an academic area that improves with intervention. Rather, naming facility represents a basic processing ability that supports the development of literacy skills. Hence, ONF and LNF are the only subtests for which GSVs are not available. Similarly, because naming facility is not an area of academic achievement, ONF and LNF are the only subtests that cannot be selected as the achievement weakness in the Pattern of Strengths and Weaknesses analysis for the identification of a specific learning disability.

## Reading Vocabulary

A Reading Vocabulary item is scored as correct (1 point) if the examinee says or points to the correct synonym of the target word. Responses of two or more words are scored as incorrect, even if the correct answer is included as one of the words in the response. To calculate the raw score, subtract the number of errors (items with 0 scores) from the ceiling item. Skipped items (those words that the examinee chose not to attempt) are scored as incorrect.

## Word Recognition Fluency and Decoding Fluency

Scoring for both the Word Recognition Fluency and Decoding Fluency subtests involves calculating the number of correct items read within the time limit. To calculate the raw score, subtract the number of errors (items with 0 scores) from the ceiling item. Skipped items (those words that the examinee chose not to attempt) are scored as incorrect.

Remember, for the Decoding Fluency subtest only, *do not penalize for misplacing the accent of a nonsense word.*

---

## DON'T FORGET

### Raw Scores of 0 on Word Recognition Fluency and Decoding Fluency

Standard scores are not available for raw scores of 0 on WRF and DF, which is a change from the KTEA-II. Examinees who could not read any words correctly were excluded from the norm sample for the following reasons:

1. Improved construct validity: If the examinee's basic reading skills are not yet developed enough to read any words (or nonsense words), then the subtest score is not meaningful as a measure of fluency for that skill.
2. Improved psychometric properties: The norms for WRF were extended down to grade 1 (from grade 3 in the KTEA-II). A sizable percentage of young children (in grades 1 and 2 for WRF, in grade 3 for DF) earned raw scores of 0 during standardization because they had not yet mastered the basic skills required to recognize words or decode nonsense words, respectively. For WRF in particular, including children with raw scores of 0 in the norm would have lowered the average ability level of the norm group at these lower grades, so that even a low raw score would have resulted in an average or above average score. Including these children in the normative sample would have compared a first grade reader's performance with a norm group that included first graders who have not yet learned to read and did not perform the task.

By including only children who were able to read at least one word correctly, the WRF and DF norms have good floors and ceilings and reflect fluency skills among children who have acquired at least a very basic level of reading ability.

(continued)

(*Continued*)

**Question:** Why is a raw score of 0 possible for Silent Reading Fluency, but not WRF and DF?

**Answer:** Two administration and scoring rules differentiate raw scores of 0 obtained on Silent Reading Fluency (SRF) from either WRF or DF. (1) Examinees who respond incorrectly to three or more SRF teaching items are discontinued. This administration rule was designed to exclude those examinees from the norm sample who have not yet learned to read or who read very poorly. (2) Silent Reading Fluency is scored by subtracting the number of incorrect responses from the number of correct responses (in order to correct for guessing). A raw score of 0 may be obtained by examinees who read some items correctly, but also read the same (or more) number of items incorrectly. For any subtest, remember that the same raw score can be obtained for different reasons. We recommend documenting the number of correct and incorrect responses when reporting performance on SRF to indicate if the examinee was fast or slow, accurate or inaccurate.

## Oral Expression

General scoring guidelines are provided and summarized in the Don't Forget box.

Audio recording is highly recommended. Even examiners who are proficient in language transcription can benefit from using an audio recording device. Whether the examinee speaks fast or slow, it's helpful to listen to his or her responses again to verify your transcription and scoring. During subtest administration, the simultaneous demands of listening, recording, and scoring are taxing for an examiner's working memory capacity. To provide more efficient processing of information, it's not uncommon for our sensory system to simplify information or "auto-correct" grammatical and syntactic mistakes. You may feel confident in what you've recorded, but it's helpful to double-check your perceptions.

Sum the Task and Grammar scores across all items within the final item set administered to obtain the raw score. *Be careful: Don't include scores from items outside the final item set.* If hand scoring, the raw score is then converted to a weighted raw score using a conversion table found in the *Technical & Interpretive Manual*.

## DON'T FORGET

### General Scoring Guidelines for Oral Expression

*Error categories are independent.*

Score each error category independently of the others. Try not to let poor performance in one category influence the scores for other categories in that item.

(*continued*)

*(Continued)*

*Base scoring on commonly heard speech.*

Score 0 for sentence structure, word meaning, and word form (grammar) only if the error is obvious and would stand out in semi-formal speech such as speaking to the class.

*Use judgment to choose best-fitting category.*

Sometimes a response is clearly erroneous, but it is not immediately evident which category should be scored 0. In those instances, choose the category that in your judgment best fits the error. The overall subtest score will not be affected.

*Give no credit for incomprehensible responses or no response.*

If an examinee doesn't respond to an item, or if the response is incomprehensible (the meaning cannot be understood), score 0 on all categories for that item.

*Do not penalize false starts, self-corrections, or interjections.*

For example, give credit if an examinee says: "Before she went home—I want to go home—she went to the grocery store with her mom."

*Most often, ignore extraneous words or sentences.*

If the examinee says something that is not related to the task, but the examinee gives a correct response, ignore anything else he or she says.

Give no credit for task criterion and sentence structure for misplaced sentence parts.

On later items, misplacement of a part of the sentence can cause failure on both the task criterion (because the sentence does not make sense or says something false) and the sentence structure criterion (because of the misplacement). In such cases, score 0 for both criteria.

*Do not penalize for articulation errors.*

*Note: From Chapter 6 of KTEA-3 Scoring Manual (Kaufman & Kaufman, 2014d).*

## HOW TO INTERPRET THE KTEA-3

Once you have completed administration and scoring, then you may begin a systematic method of interpreting the scores yielded from the KTEA-3. The KTEA-3 yields a great deal of information: the Comprehensive Form yields scores from 19 possible subtests, three core composites, 10 supplemental composites, and an Academic Skills Battery (ASB) composite; the Brief Form yields scores from six possible subtest scores, three core composites, and two overall composites (BA-3 and ASB). Given the wealth of information provided by the KTEA-3, examiners need to methodically employ an efficient process of interpretation to glean the most from the data. A systematic and efficient procedure for interpreting the KTEA-3 is described in the following section, and key differences in the interpretation of the Comprehensive and Brief Forms will be explained.

## Introduction to Interpretation

The reason for referral typically dictates the battery of tests administered during an assessment. In the case of the KTEA-3, either the full battery may be administered or a partial battery may be administered to answer a question about a particular area of academic functioning. We present an approach to interpreting the comprehensive battery of the KTEA-3 and an alternative approach if only part of the KTEA-3 Comprehensive Form is administered. The interpretive approaches advocated in this book begin at the global level by looking at the Academic Skills Battery composite (ASB) and core composites, then interpreting subtest scores, and finally the specific patterns of errors. One goal of KTEA-3 interpretation is to identify and promote understanding of the examinee's strong and weak areas of academic functioning, from both *normative* (age-based or grade-based) and *ipsative* (person-based) perspectives. Similar to interpretive approaches presented for various cognitive instruments such as the KABC-II (Kaufman, Lichtenberger, Fletcher-Janzen, & Kaufman, 2005) and the WISC-V (Kaufman, Raiford, & Coalson, 2016), we support the notion of backing interpretive hypotheses with multiple pieces of supportive data. Such supportive data may be in the form of multiple test scores, behavioral observations, teacher reports, school records, or parent reports. In other words, test scores are not interpreted in isolation.

Interpretation of the complete KTEA-3 Comprehensive Form (and the KTEA-3 Brief Academic Skills Battery) involves five steps:

1. Interpret the Academic Skills Battery composite.
2. Interpret other composite and subtest scores.
3. Identify composite strengths and weaknesses.
4. Identify subtest strengths and weaknesses.
5. Determine the significance and unusualness of planned comparisons.

> ## DON'T FORGET
> ...................................................
>
> ### Interpretation of the Brief Form
>
> For the Academic Skill Battery composite, follow the same five-step procedure described for the Comprehensive Form.
>
> For the Brief Achievement (BA-3) composite, only four of the five steps described for the ASB procedure are necessary, but otherwise the steps are very similar:
> (1) Interpret the BA-3 composite.
> (2) Interpret subtest scores.
> (3) Identify subtest strengths and weaknesses.
> (4) Determine the significance and unusualness of planned comparisons.

When you administer only portions of the KTEA-3, the ASB and other composites will not be available for the interpretive analyses. For these cases, you may conduct an abbreviated interpretation. In the abbreviated interpretation of a partial battery you will conduct only two of the steps listed earlier:

2. Interpret composites and subtest scores.
5. Determine the significance and unusualness of planned comparisons.

When hand scoring, the data and calculations needed to conduct each of the interpretive steps outlined in this chapter are recorded on the KTEA-3 "Analysis and Comparisons" form on the Flash Drive.

After the interpretation of either the complete or the partial KTEA-3 Comprehensive Form battery, examiners may wish to obtain more detailed information by analyzing an examinee's errors. The final section on interpretation details a process of error analysis for each KTEA-3 subtest.

## Step 1: Interpret the Academic Skills Battery (ASB) Composite

The ASB is composed of three subtests for prekindergarteners, five subtests for kindergarteners, and six subtests for examinees in grades 1 and above. The ASB subtest structure is shown earlier in this chapter in Figure 2.1. If a partial KTEA-3 battery is administered, and all of the subtests that comprise the ASB are not obtained, then the ASB composite cannot be calculated, and this interpretive step can be skipped. The function of the ASB is to provide a global overview of an examinee's academic achievement across three domains: reading, math, and written language. The ASB composite standard score is also used in later interpretive steps as it represents an examinee's "average" academic ability or the "midpoint" of all his or her academic skills. Thus, in the later interpretive steps, the ASB composite is the basis of comparison for determining the examinee's relatively strong and weak areas of achievement.

When interpreting the ASB in written reports, you should report the ASB standard score, the confidence interval, percentile rank, and descriptive category. If the ASB's confidence interval spans more than one descriptive category, we suggest reporting the descriptive category as a range (e.g., if the confidence interval is 105 to 113, then write in the report: "Eliza's ASB composite was in the Average to Above Average range of academic functioning").

In addition to reporting the ASB composite standard score, confidence interval, percentile rank, and descriptive category, you should report whether the ASB is a Normative Strength or Normative Weakness. A Normative Strength (NStr) is defined as a standard score that is greater than 115 (or 110 in the 10-point scale) and a Normative Weakness (NWk) is defined as a standard score that is lower than 85 (or 90 in the 10-point scale). Thus, Normative Strengths and Weaknesses are those scores that fall outside of the Average range of academic functioning. The front page of the Analysis and Comparisons form has a place to record whether the ASB composite is a Normative Strength or Normative Weakness by circling the appropriate abbreviation. See Figure 2.5 for an excerpt from the Analysis & Comparisons Form, which is provided on the KTEA-3 Flash Drive for recording data for interpretive Step 1.

## Figure 2.5  Analysis of Academic Skills Battery Composite

*Source:* Kaufman Test of Educational Achievement–Third Edition (KTEA-3). Copyright © 2014 NCS Pearson, Inc. Reproduced with permission. All rights reserved.

Some examinee's ASB standard scores are comprised of scores that vary widely across the three academic domains. In such cases, the ASB should be interpreted with an appropriate explanation. For example, Tomás earned Reading Comprehension and Letter & Word Recognition standard scores of 74 and 75, respectively. He also earned much higher Math Computation and Math Concepts & Applications standard scores of 124 and 125, respectively. His ASB composite standard score was 100, which represents the midpoint of very diverse abilities. Because of the variability in the scores that comprise Tomás' ASB scores, a more meaningful understanding of his diverse academic abilities can be obtained by examining his performance on the separate academic domain composites.

Thus, the examiner's written report will communicate that, although Tomás earned an ASB composite score in the Average range, his academic skills are highly variable, ranging from Below Average to Above Average. The report will then go on to focus on those separate academic domains, as the Average ASB composite score does not provide as much useful and meaningful information as his scores on the separate academic domains.

### Step 2: Interpret Other Composite Scores and Subtest Scores

In the second interpretive step, a procedure similar to that of Step 1 is followed for interpreting the other composite scores and the subtest scores. Step 2 is conducted whether a complete or partial KTEA-3 battery was administered. For whichever subtests were administered, report the standard score, the confidence interval, and the percentile rank. We do not recommend reporting the descriptive categories for each of the subtests, as that amount of information (scores plus descriptive categories) is a bit overwhelming and unnecessary. However, we do recommend reporting the descriptive categories for the three Core composites, Oral Composites, Reading-Related composites, and Cross-Domain Composites in addition to the standard scores, the confidence intervals, and the percentile ranks.

The final part of Step 2 for each composite and subtest is to determine whether each is a Normative Strength or a Normative Weakness. Circle NWk (below average) and NStr (above average) on the front page of the Analysis and Comparisons form to indicate the Normative Weaknesses and Strengths (see Figure 2.6).

**Figure 2.6  Analysis of Domain Composites**

*Note:* Excerpt from front page of the *KTEA-3 Analysis & Comparisons Form.*
*Source:* Kaufman Test of Educational Achievement–Third Edition (KTEA-3). Copyright © 2014 NCS Pearson, Inc. Reproduced with permission. All rights reserved.

## Step 3: Identify Composite Strengths and Weaknesses

In Steps 1 and 2, you compare the examinee's abilities to that of the normative group (i.e., determining Normative Strengths and Weaknesses), but in Step 3 you compare the examinee's abilities to his or her own average level of academic performance (i.e., determining Personal Strengths and Weaknesses). The ASB standard score is used as the value that represents an examinee's "average level of performance," which is compared to the examinee's performance on the separate domain composites (Rapid Reference 2.6 gives the rationale for using the ASB to represent the examinee's "average" level of performance). Thus, for each of the Core composites (Reading, Math, and Written Language), two Oral Composites (Oral Language and Oral Fluency), the four Reading-Related composites (Sound Symbol, Decoding, Reading Fluency, and Reading Understanding), and the Cross-Domain Composites (Comprehension, Expression, Orthographic Processing, and Academic Fluency), subtract the composite standard score from the ASB standard score. Then record this difference on the front page of the Analysis and Comparisons form in the column labeled "Diff. from ASB." An examinee's composite that is significantly higher than the ASB is labeled a Personal Strength (PStr) and a domain composite that is significantly lower than the ASB is labeled a Personal Weakness (PWk). Tables in the *Technical & Interpretive Manual* provide the specific difference values necessary to be considered significant at the .05 level (refer to the "Significance" column of Table G.1 for grade norms or Table G.5 for age norms). If the difference between the ASB and a domain composite is equal to or greater than the value indicated in the table then that composite is deemed significantly different. A significant difference in which the domain composite is greater that the ASB is a Personal Strength and a significant difference in which the domain composite is less than the ASB is a Personal Weakness.

If a Personal Strength or Personal Weakness is found, you should refer to Table G.1 or G.5 to see how unusual the difference is in the normal sample. If the difference occurs in 10% or fewer of the norm sample cases, then it is considered unusually large. In such instances, record that the difference is "Infrequent (≤10%)" on the last column of the Analysis and Comparisons form.

---

## ≡ Rapid Reference 2.6

### Rationale for Using ASB as Examinee's Average Level of Performance

Interpretive Steps 3 and 4 suggest using the ASB composite as the midpoint or average level of examinee's academic performance when conducting comparisons with specific academic skill areas. The ASB includes one or two subtests from each of the academic domains, and it serves as an appropriate reference point for evaluating a broad range of individual composites and subtests.

Note: See page 106 of the KTEA-3 Technical & Interpretive Manual for additional information on the rationale.

---

Personal Strengths or Weaknesses that are also "Infrequent" and a Normative Strength or Weakness are especially noteworthy and demand special attention when translating scores to diagnostic and educational considerations. Personal Strengths and Weaknesses by definition are scores that are significantly different from an examinee's ASB—that is, the differences are very unlikely to have occurred by chance. Some significant differences may be quite common in the population. Thus, these significant differences, in and of themselves, may not be of particular clinical interest. However, if a difference is so large that it rarely occurs in the population (i.e., it is "Infrequent"), then it is usually worth investigating further.

### Step 4: Identify Subtest Strengths and Weaknesses

Step 4 is similar to Step 3 in that you are comparing an examinee's performance to his or her own average level of performance. However, Step 3 determined Personal Strengths and Weaknesses for composites and Step 4 determines them for subtest scores. To identify subtest strengths and weaknesses, follow the same procedure outlined in Step 3: Subtract each subtest standard score from the ASB standard score. Record the absolute difference between the scores on the front page of the Analysis and Comparisons form in the appropriate blank under "Diff. from ASB." Then refer to Table G.2 (grade norms) or G.6 (age norms) in the KTEA-3 Technical & Interpretive Manual to determine whether each difference is statistically significant at the .05 level. If a difference is large enough to be considered significant and the subtest score is higher than the ASB score, then that subtest is a Personal Strength (circle PStr on the form). If a difference is large enough to be considered significant and the subtest score is lower than the ASB score, then that subtest is a Personal Weakness (circle PWk on the form).

If a difference is statistically significant (deeming a subtest a Personal Strength or Personal Weakness), then determine how unusual it is in the norm sample. Refer to the columns labeled "Frequency" in Table G.2 (grade norms) or Table G.6 (age norms) in the *KTEA-3 Technical & Interpretive Manual*. If the value of the difference occurs in fewer than 10% of the norm sample cases, put a checkmark in the last column of the Analysis and Comparisons form in the "Infrequent" column. The subtests that are both a Personal Strength or Weakness and labeled "Infrequent" are worthy of further investigation, as they may provide useful diagnostic information or information related to educational considerations.

### Step 5: Determine the Significance and Unusualness of Planned Comparisons

Step 5 is useful for evaluating hypotheses about specific strong and weak areas of achievement or for evaluating a comparison between particular academic or reading-related skills. At times, specific planned comparisons of composites or subtests may provide useful information for diagnosis or instructional planning.

On the KTEA-3, there are numerous planned comparisons that can be made depending on the examiner's needs. However, the test authors recommend routinely making at least two comparisons in the Comprehensive Form: (1) Oral Expression subtest with Written Expression subtest, and (2) Reading Comprehension subtest with Listening Comprehension subtest. The Don't Forget box reminds readers what can be learned from these expression and comprehension comparisons as well as comparing other subtests.

## DON'T FORGET

### Which Subtest Comparisons Are Most Clinically Useful?

The most clinically useful subtest comparisons depend on the referral concerns as well as the examinee's unique profile of strengths and weaknesses; however, as a general guide, the following subtest comparisons may be considered for each academic area:

| Reading Concern | Writing Concern | Math Concern |
|---|---|---|
| RC vs. LC | WE vs. OE | MCA vs. MC |
| LWR vs. NWD, WRF, SRF | WE vs. SP | MC vs. MF |
| NWD vs. DF | SP vs. WF, LWR, NWD | |
| WRF vs. DF, SRF | AF vs. WF | |

(continued)

*(Continued)*

## What Can Be Learned From the Expression and Comprehension Comparisons?

If the Expression and Comprehension composites are unitary (the examinee performs similarly on OE and WE, and on RC and LC), then comparing these two composite scores may help identify a weakness in either receptive or expressive oral and written language.

| Oral Expression versus Written Expression | Reading Comprehension versus Listening Comprehension |
|---|---|
| OE and WE correlate .31 (K) to .54 (grade 12) | RC and LC correlate from .44 (PK) to .76 (grade 12) |
| These two expression subtests both require examinees to use expressive language in realistic situations. Both subtests are scored along similar dimensions: task (pragmatics), sentence structure (syntax), and word form (grammar). Thus, the comparison between these subtests may point to a particular difficulty in either written or spoken expression. | These two comprehension subtests both assess the literal and inferential comprehension of connected text, particularly the passage-reading tasks of Reading Comprehension and Listening Comprehension. Thus, the comparison between these subtests may help identify a problem specific to reading (that is distinct from a more general language problem). |

## What Can Be Learned From Comparing Associational Fluency and Object Naming Fluency?

ONF involves retrieving names of common objects (overlearned information). ONF is a relatively low-level processing task because it requires no categorizing, generation of ideas, or creativity; however, rapid naming requires linking a visual stimulus with an aural response, which is difficult for some individuals with LD. On the other hand, AF is a task that allows for more creativity, strategy, and flexibility in thought. AF is a higher-level processing task than ONF, and doesn't require linking the auditory and visual modalities. Comparing performance on AF and ONF (or LNF) may be clinically useful. For example, individuals with dyslexia tend to perform well on AF. In the KTEA-3 clinical validity study (Kaufman & Kaufman, 2014b), AF showed minimal difference between examinees with reading/writing disorders and their peers ($p = .04$, effect size was .37, the lowest effect size of any subtest).

The methods for evaluating planned comparisons between composites or subtests are very similar to those employed in Steps 3 and 4. Once you have determined which comparisons you would like to make, follow the substeps of Step 5 outlined in Rapid Reference 2.7. You will calculate the difference between the scores, and then determine the significance and frequency of that difference. The back page of the KTEA-3 Analysis and Comparisons form has places to record the data for these planned comparisons.

## ≡ Rapid Reference 2.7

### Substeps of Interpretive Step 5

A. Record the standard scores for the two composites or subtests of each comparison in the appropriate boxes of the back page of the KTEA-3 Analysis and Comparisons form.

B. Record the absolute value of the difference between them in the space between the boxes.

C. Determine whether the difference is statistically significant by referring to the appropriate table of the KTEA-3 Technical & Interpretive Manual (G.3 and G.4 for grade norms and G.7 and G.8 for age norms). Find the column for the smallest significance level in which the observed difference computed in Step B above is equal to or greater than the value in the table, and circle the appropriate number (<.05 or <.01) on the record form. Then draw a circle around the name of the composite or subtest having the higher score.

D. If the difference is statistically significant, refer again to the appropriate table in the manual (G.3 and G.4 for grade norms and G.7 and G.8 for age norms) to see whether the difference is also unusually large, meaning that it occurred infrequently in the norm sample. Find the column for the smallest percentage frequency in which the observed difference (computed in Step B) is equal to or greater than the value in the table, and circle the appropriate number (≤15%, ≤10%, or ≤5%) on the record form.

### Subtest Floors and Ceilings

When interpreting subtest standard scores, it is important to consider whether there are floor or ceiling limitations. The theoretical standard score range for all subtests is 40 to 160, but not all subtests reach the minimum and maximum standard score.

Floor effects occur when the lowest possible standard score is 71 or higher, which is less than 2 standard deviations below the mean. Floor effects may be inevitable for certain subtests due to a restricted score range with any of the subtests. The distributions of certain subtest scores are slightly skewed in the lower ages and grades due to the natural floor that exists before skills are acquired (see the Don't Forget box).

### DON'T FORGET

#### Subtests With Floor Effects

The lowest possible standard scores on both Forms A and B of the following subtests will be less than 2 standard deviations below the mean (>70) at the lower ages due to the natural floor that exists before skills are acquired:

Phonological Processing
(ages 4:0–4:2)

Letter & Word Recognition
(ages 4:0–4:5)

Nonsense Word Decoding
(ages 6:0–7:3)

Silent Reading Fluency (ages 6:0–7:3)

Reading Vocabulary (ages 6:0–6:7)

> ## DON'T FORGET
>
> ### Digital Resources
>
> Tables that summarize the minimum and maximum subtest standard scores available for each KTEA-3 subtest are included as digital resources with this book.

Ceiling effects occur when the highest possible standard score is 129 or lower, less than 2 standard deviations above the mean. Rapid Reference 3.9 reports the maximum possible subtest score by age. Refer to the Digital Resources for tables that report by age the lowest and highest possible score for each subtest.

## Interpretation of Composites

Information in the next section, including tables 2.7–2.19, provides an overview of the constructs measured in each composite, possible interpretation for high and low scores, as well as related areas of cognitive processing. As suggested earlier in this chapter, all interpretations of composites should be made in the context of multiple pieces of supportive data.

### Core Composites

**Table 2.7 Reading Composite**

| Subtests in Composite | Constructs Measured | Score Interpretation | Related Areas of Cognitive Processing |
|---|---|---|---|
| Letter & Word Recognition<br><br>Reading Comprehension | Overall reading ability, including skills in basic reading as well as reading comprehension. | High Score<br>Proficiency in reading achievement.<br><br>Low Score<br>Weaknesses in basic reading skills, language comprehension skills, or a combination of both. | Phonological processing, orthographic processing, grammatical (morphology and syntax) processing, receptive vocabulary, verbal or listening comprehension, verbal working memory, processing speed, naming facility, long-term storage and retrieval, and self-monitoring. |

**Table 2.8  Math Composite**

| Subtests in Composite | Constructs Measured | Score Interpretation | Related Areas of Cognitive Processing |
|---|---|---|---|
| Math Computation<br><br>Math Concepts & Applications | Achievement in math computation and problem solving. | High Score<br>Well-developed mathematical abilities.<br><br>Low Score<br>Difficulty in math computation and/or math problem solving. | Working memory, processing speed, quantitative reasoning, long-term storage and retrieval, and self-monitoring. |

**Table 2.9  Written Language Composite**

| Subtests in Composite | Constructs Measured | Score Interpretation | Related Areas of Cognitive Processing |
|---|---|---|---|
| Written Expression<br><br>Spelling | Achievement in *expressive* written language. | High Score<br>Proficiency in written expression and spelling.<br><br>Low Score<br>Difficulty written expression and spelling (see related areas of cognitive processing for possible underlying reasons). | Phonological processing, orthographic processing, grammatical (morphology and syntax) processing, receptive vocabulary, verbal working memory or the orthographic loop of working memory, processing speed, naming facility, long-term storage and retrieval, organization, and self-monitoring. |

### Reading-Related Composites

Comparing performance on oral and silent reading tasks provides relevant information for diagnosis and intervention planning. Some examinees may score higher on Silent Reading Fluency relative to Word Recognition Fluency and Decoding Fluency.

Silent Reading Fluency requires examinees to read well enough to understand the gist of what they read; however, it does not require the same level of articulation, precision, and accuracy that oral reading requires. As a result, examinees with good compensatory strategies may benefit from the contextual clues provided by reading connected text (as opposed to single words) and the reduced demands on precise and accurate articulation.

**Table 2.10 Sound-Symbol Composite**

| Subtests in Composite | Constructs Measured | Score Interpretation | Related Areas of Cognitive Processing |
|---|---|---|---|
| Phonological Processing<br><br>Nonsense Word Decoding | Phonological processing and decoding skills, which makes it particularly useful for documenting a phonological core deficit (a common underlying cause of dyslexia). | High Score<br>Strong phonological processing and decoding skills.<br><br>Low Score<br>Weaknesses in phonological, orthographic, and/or morphological awareness; and the phonological loop of working memory. | Phonological decoding (the process of using grapheme-to-phoneme conversion rules to sound out a word). |

**Table 2.11 Decoding Composite**

| Subtests in Composite | Constructs Measured | Score Interpretation | Related Areas of Cognitive Processing |
|---|---|---|---|
| Letter & Word Recognition<br><br>Nonsense Word Decoding | Broad basic reading skills. Recognizing and decoding real (regular and irregular) words as well as decoding novel words. | High Score<br>Well-developed basic reading skills.<br><br>Low Score<br>Weaknesses in phonological, orthographic, and/or morphological awareness; long-term storage and retrieval, receptive vocabulary, and the phonological loop of working memory. | Orthographic and phonological processing, morphological awareness; long-term storage and retrieval, receptive vocabulary, and the phonological loop of working memory. |

**Table 2.12 Reading Fluency Composite**

| Subtests in Composite | Constructs Measured | Score Interpretation | Related Areas of Cognitive Processing |
|---|---|---|---|
| Silent Reading Fluency<br><br>Word Recognition Fluency<br><br>Decoding Fluency | Reading automaticity across a range of conditions (all of which are speeded): reading real and novel words, reading words in isolation and in context, and reading with both oral and silent responses.[a] | High Score<br>Automaticity in basic reading skills.<br><br>Low Score<br>Weaknesses in phonological, orthographic, and/or morphological-syntactic processing, long-term storage and retrieval, processing speed, naming facility, and the phonological loop of working memory. | Orthographic and phonological processing, morphological awareness; long-term storage and retrieval, receptive vocabulary, and the phonological loop of working memory. |

[a]Pikulski and Chard (2005) described fluency as a bridge from word recognition accuracy to text comprehension. Reading with fluency does not simply mean reading fast; rather, it refers to the ability to read with automaticity and appropriate prosody—and prosody implies comprehension (Rasinski, 2012). Prosody is not directly measured by the KTEA-3; however, the Silent Reading Fluency subtest requires a basic level of comprehension to perform well.

**Table 2.13 Reading Understanding Composite**

| Subtests in Composite | Constructs Measured | Score Interpretation | Related Areas of Cognitive Processing |
|---|---|---|---|
| Reading Comprehension<br><br>Reading Vocabulary | Comprehension of literal and inferential information from written narrative and identifying or inferring the meaning of words that are read. | High Score<br>Strong vocabulary knowledge and ability to comprehend written passages.<br><br>Low Score<br>Weakness in vocabulary knowledge or weak ability to comprehend written passages or both. | Acquired knowledge and achievement: word recognition and decoding, vocabulary knowledge, language comprehension. Verbal working memory. |

## *Oral Composites*

**Table 2.14  Oral Language Composite**

| Subtests in Composite | Constructs Measured | Score Interpretation | Related Areas of Cognitive Processing |
|---|---|---|---|
| Oral Expression<br><br>Listening Comprehension<br><br>Associational Fluency | Ability to comprehend literal and inferential information from oral narratives, ability to orally describe a picture, and ability to fluently name words in a semantic category. | <u>High Score</u><br>Fluent and well-developed ability to comprehend formal speech and orally express oneself with appropriate pragmatics and grammar.<br><br><u>Low Score</u><br>Oral expression difficulties in areas of fluency, pragmatics, and grammar. Difficulty comprehending relatively formal speech. | Vocabulary knowledge, verbal working memory, discrimination of essential and nonessential details. |

**Table 2.15  Oral Fluency Composite**

| Subtests in Composite | Constructs Measured | Score Interpretation | Related Areas of Cognitive Processing |
|---|---|---|---|
| Associational Fluency<br><br>Object Naming Facility | Ability to fluently name words in a semantic category and name pictured object as quickly as possible (Rapid Automatic Naming). | <u>High Score</u><br>Strong rapid autonomic naming skills and fluent word naming.<br><br><u>Low Score</u><br>Weak word retrieval ability or inefficient retrieval of words from long-term memory. | Processing speed, verbal fluency, verbal working memory, cognitive flexibility, and vocabulary knowledge. |

*Note:* Substantial research supports Rapid Automatic Naming, a skill needed for Object Naming Facility, to identify children at risk for reading and spelling difficulties (Moats, 1993; Neuhaus & Swank, 2002; Savage Pillay, & Melidona, 2008; Stahl & Murray, 1994; Wolf, 1991).

## Cross-Domain Composites

According to the validity studies reported in the KTEA-3 and WISC-V manuals, the DAS-II and the WISC-V Processing Speed Indexes showed moderate correlations with the KTEA-3 Writing Fluency subtest (.34 and .44, respectively) and Math Fluency subtest (.50 and .42, respectively), but weaker correlations with the Decoding Fluency subtest (.22, .08, respectively). Academic fluency scores have been shown to predict the need for extended time among students with learning disabilities (Ofiesh, Mather, & Russell, 2005). When considering extended time, cross-validate performance on the KTEA-3 with information such as self-reports, teacher observations, and test scores to determine whether the student struggles to complete assignments and exams in the allotted time. Always consider whether interventions that improve automaticity and facilitate skill development would be helpful, either in conjunction with or instead of providing extended time (Lovett, 2011).

## Clinical Analysis of Errors

The KTEA-3 authors believe that understanding test performance by studying the student's incorrect responses is a profitable method of helping a student's progress, and that efforts to objectify and substantiate the value of various error analysis methods

### Table 2.16 Comprehension Composite

| Subtests in Composite | Constructs Measured | Score Interpretation | Clinical Information |
|---|---|---|---|
| Reading Comprehension<br><br>Listening Comprehension | Receptive language skills in both the written and oral modalities. | High Score<br><br>Well-developed receptive language skills in both reading and listening.<br><br>Low Score<br><br>Receptive language delay or impairment, low verbal working memory, inattention, and distractibility. | KTEA-3 clinical studies revealed the largest effect size for the Comprehension composite among the mild intellectual disability and language disorder groups, with large effect sizes also shown for the reading/writing disorder and math disorder groups. The academically gifted group showed a significant strength in Comprehension. |

*Note:* Compare performance on Reading Comprehension and Listening Comprehension to determine if receptive language weaknesses differentially affect one modality or the other. A student with a language delay or impairment or low verbal ability would be expected to perform poorly on this composite.

**Table 2.17 Expression Composite**

| Subtests in Composite | Constructs Measured | Score Interpretation | Clinical Information |
|---|---|---|---|
| Written Expression Oral Expression | Expressive language skills in both the written and oral modalities. | <u>High Score</u><br>Well-developed expressive language skills in both writing and speaking.<br><br><u>Low Score</u><br>Expressive language delay or impairment, weaknesses in grammar, low verbal working memory, and poor self-monitoring. | The KTEA-3 clinical studies revealed the largest effect size for the Expression composite among the mild intellectual disability and language disorder groups, with large effect sizes also shown for the reading/writing disorder and math disorder groups. The academically gifted group showed a significant strength in Expression. |

*Note:* Compare performance on Written Expression and Oral Expression to determine if expressive language weaknesses differentially affect one modality or the other. A student with a language delay or impairment or low verbal ability would be expected to perform poorly on this composite.

should be intensified (Kaufman & Kaufman, 2004a). Many good teachers intuitively apply error analysis skills in their everyday teaching. In today's schools, however, where psychologists, educational diagnosticians, special educators, and classroom teachers exchange information about students, a more formal systematic approach to error analysis, using a common language, is necessary for effective communication of information about students' academic functioning and teachers' instructional strategies (Kaufman & Kaufman, 2004a).

During development of the original K-TEA Comprehensive Form, its revision, the KTEA-II, and the current KTEA-3, the authors were aided by curriculum experts in reading, mathematics, spelling, writing, and oral language in defining the specific skills making up each subtest and examining the types of errors students are likely to make on subtest items. Based on the recommendations of these experts, a review of the literature on instructional theory and practice, discussions with many practicing school psychologists and educational diagnosticians, and the actual errors made by students participating in the standardization programs, the KTEA-3 error analysis method was developed (Kaufman & Kaufman, 2014a). It is built on the method used in the previous editions of the KTEA, but for some subtests it has been enhanced to provide a greater amount of detail. This procedure uses information documented during KTEA-3 administration to identify specific areas in which the student demonstrates strong, weak, or average skill development as defined by the performance of the standardization sample.

**Table 2.18 Orthographic Processing Composite**

| Subtests in Composite | Constructs Measured | Score Interpretation | Clinical Information |
|---|---|---|---|
| Spelling<br><br>Letter Naming Facility<br><br>Word Recognition Fluency | Forming, storing, and accessing orthographic representations. Spelling involves the retrieval of orthographic representations from long-term memory. Word Recognition Fluency involves recognizing the orthographic representations and their associated sounds. Letter Naming Facility also measures how automatically an examinee can name an array of letters. | High Score<br><br>Successful learning in both the receptive (reading/naming) and expressive (spelling) components of orthographic processing.<br><br>Low Score<br><br>Poor orthographic memory and difficulty learning phoneme-grapheme correspondences. May be due to weaknesses in phonological processing, auditory verbal working memory, and/or cognitive efficiency for manipulating and rapidly processing information. | A validity study with the WISC-V revealed that the Orthographic Processing composite correlated most highly (.60s) with Digit Span, the Auditory Working Memory Index, and the Cognitive Proficiency Index. The KTEA-3 clinical studies revealed large effect sizes for the Orthographic Processing composite among the mild intellectual disability, reading/writing disorder, language disorder, and math disorder. The academically gifted group showed a significant strength in Orthographic Processing. |

*Note:* Orthographic processing has been defined as "the ability to form, store, and access orthographic representations" (Stanovich & West, 1989, p. 404). In simple terms, it involves how we perceive and remember the visual look of words, letters, and numbers. Early orthographic processing tasks typically measure visual perception (e.g., visually matching letters, numbers, and symbols), or a person's sensitivity to the orthographic regularities in the language (e.g., Which looks like a word? ulpk or klup). Other tasks measure the outcomes of successful orthographic learning, such as fluent word recognition or orthographic choice tasks (e.g., Which is a word? rane or rain) (Castles & Nation, 2006).

The error analysis procedures provide examiners with more specific information about a student's performance than can be obtained from composite or subtest standard scores or comparisons. Some uses for the error analysis data are described by Kaufman and Kaufman (2014a) as:

- Obtaining a more precise level of diagnostic information than subtest standard scores
- Determining the concentration of skill problems

**Table 2.19 Academic Fluency Composite**

| Subtests in Composite | Constructs Measured | Score Interpretation | Clinical Information |
|---|---|---|---|
| Writing Fluency<br>Math Fluency<br>Decoding Fluency | Ability to perform rudimentary academic tasks quickly and maintain focused attention under a time pressure (Fry & Hale, 1996). The degree to which automaticity may be impacting academic performance. | **High Score**<br>Well-developed automaticity and processing speed. Academically gifted groups in KTEA-3 clinical studies showed a significant strength in Academic Fluency.<br><br>**Low Score**<br>Deficits in automaticity and processing speed may be present in all or some of the academic domains. KTEA-3 clinical studies revealed large effect sizes for the Academic Fluency composite among the reading/writing disorder, math disorder, and mild intellectual disability groups. | Efficient visual processing, working memory, long-term memory, and executive functioning all contribute to academic fluency (Berninger & Richards, 2002). Research suggests that academic fluency contributes to academic skills and enables the performance of more complex tasks (Nelson, Benner, Neill, & Stage, 2006). |

*Note:* Compare performance across the three subtests to determine whether automaticity differs by academic area. If performance is low on one or more subtests, attempt to rule out other explanations for slow performance such as anxiety and poor motivation. Compare performance on the timed subtest (e.g., Math Fluency) with an untimed subtest (e.g., Math Computation) to determine whether the student has a skill deficit and/or an automaticity problem.

- Determining the location of weak skills on a skill continuum
- Gauging the severity of skill deficiencies
- Identifying common sources of difficulty underlying several skill areas
- Integrating results from multiple subtests to help substantiate hypotheses about the sources of skill difficulties
- Contributing valuable data for interpreting subtest performance and planning intervention

Thus, the KTEA-3 Comprehensive Form offers detailed information beyond the examinee's subtest and composite scores that can provide important and specific information that becomes a basis for intervention. The details about an examinee's skills come from a system for analyzing specific errors made on 10 of the 19 subtests. The system of error analysis determines both strong and weak skill areas across global skills (such as reading and math) and more specific skills (such as Math Computation and Math Concepts & Applications).

# DON'T FORGET

## Skill Status Defined According to Number of Errors

| Skill Status Category | Definition | Implications for Obtaining Each Level of Skill Status |
|---|---|---|
| Strength | Average number of errors made by the top 25% of the national grade-level reference group. | A student's skill acquisition is considerably above that of typical students at that grade level. These areas require less instructional attention and may be used to teach to the student's strengths. |
| Average | Average number of errors made by the middle 50% of the national grade-level reference group (i.e., those between the 25th and 75th percentiles). | The student has demonstrated acquisition of that skill to a degree typical for pupils at that grade level. These areas require less instructional attention and may be used to teach to the student's strengths. |
| Weakness | Average number of errors made by the bottom 25% of the national grade-level reference group. | The student has a possible deficiency in that skill area, and further diagnostic evaluation is warranted. Appropriate remediation strategies may be needed to help the student with the deficiency. |

The KTEA-3 Comprehensive Form error analysis uses norm-referenced methodology to determine an examinee's relative mastery of specific skills that can then lead to effective remediation of skill deficiencies. Each student's performance across a range of skills is labeled: "strength," "average," or "weakness," compared to other students in the same grade level who took the same items on the same form. The Don't Forget box explains how each of these levels of skill status are defined and what the implications are for each. The Caution box highlights the limitations of the error analysis system and guidelines for use and interpretation.

*Use caution when interpreting error analysis results for students who perform above the mean.* The error analysis norms become less representative of the population the closer one gets to the ceiling of the subtest because only the higher achieving students reach the more difficult items (with the exception of Written Expression, for which all examinees complete the entire level). In such cases, the error analysis results may underrepresent skill proficiency relative to a stratified sample. Relative to a stratified sample, a skill status of "Strength" for a student who performed above the mean may actually reflect *exceptional* skill proficiency, "Average" may actually reflect *above average* skill proficiency, and "Weakness" may actually reflect *average* skill proficiency. See Caution box for further guidance.

---

## DON'T FORGET

### Information Gained from KTEA-3 Error Analysis

- The concentration of skill deficiencies: Within a subtest, are the weaknesses focused in just a few areas, or are they more pervasive in nature? When analyzing error results across subtests are there areas of common weakness that suggest possible sources of skill difficulties? For example, a common multiplication skill deficiency may be evident on Math Problem Solving and Math Computation, or difficulty with vowel digraph and diphthong patterns may be evident on both Nonsense Word Decoding and Letter & Word Recognition, or across these two reading subtests as well as the Spelling subtest.

- The location of skill deficiencies. Where on the skill continuum is the student experiencing the most difficulty? Are the weaknesses in earlier or later sections of the test? For example, math computation weaknesses in addition and subtraction are skills introduced early in the curriculum sequence, whereas weaknesses in multiplication and division might represent a higher-level skill deficiency for the student's grade level.

- The severity of skill deficiencies. Compare the number of errors made in a given error category with the number of opportunities (the number of items attempted). This provides an initial indication of how often the error was made. Next, use the error analysis norms to determine if the skill area is a strength, average, or a weakness as compared to the norm reference group.

---

## CAUTION

### Limitations of KTEA-3 Error Analysis

The KTEA-3 error analysis system has some important limitations to keep in mind.
- Error analysis is intended for use with examinees in grades Pre-K through 12 only. The reference groups do not include college students or adults.
- Error analysis is intended for use on subtests for which an examinee performs below the mean (standard score = less than 100). Interpreting error analysis results for higher achieving students may underrepresent skill proficiency.

*(continued)*

(Continued)

## Interpretation of Skill Status Based Upon Achievement Level

| Skill Status Category | Achievement Level | Interpretation |
|---|---|---|
| Strength | Above Average to Well Above Average | Strength relative to other high achieving students. May be an exceptional strength relative to the general population. |
| | Average | Strength |
| | Below Average to Well Below Average | Strength |
| Average | Above Average to Well Above Average | Average relative to other high achieving students. May be a strength relative to the general population. |
| | Average | Average |
| | Below Average to Well Below Average | Average |
| Weakness | Above Average to Well Above Average | Weakness relative to other high achieving students. May be average relative to the general population. |
| | Average | Weakness |
| | Below Average to Well Below Average | Weakness |

There are two basic types of error classification methods: item-level error classification and within-item classification. In the item-level error classification, each item is classified according to the process, concept, or skill that it assesses. If an item is incorrect, the error type is automatically assigned. For example, each of the Reading Comprehension and Listening Comprehension items are classified as either literal or inferential. Thus, if an incorrect response is given to Reading Comprehension Form A Item 29, it is automatically classified as a "literal error," whereas an incorrect response to Item 30 is automatically counted as an "inferential" error. Written Expression items are classified under the following item-level classifications: task, structure, word form, capitalization, and punctuation. Oral Expression items are classified along similar categories: task, structure, and word form. In contrast to item-level classification's automatic error assignment, within-item classification requires judgment on the part of the examiner to determine the error type. That is, the specific details of the student's response will lead examiners to select which types of errors were made. For example, on Letter & Word Recognition, examiners must evaluate the incorrect pronunciation of a word to determine if an error was made in categories such as *short vowel, long vowel, silent letter, prefix, suffix*, and more. Multiple error categories may be marked for a single item in the within-item classification. The Don't Forget box lists the types of error analysis that are used for the KTEA-3 subtests.

# DON'T FORGET

### How to Score "DK" or "NR" Responses for Error Analysis

Scoring "Don't Know" or "No Response" items, which are both scored 0 points, differs depending on whether item-level or within-item classification methods are used. For item-level classification, include DK or NR responses as an error within the relevant skill categories. For within-item classification, DK or NR responses are not included in the error analysis because no error information is available.

#### Types of Error Analysis Methods for KTEA-3 Subtests

| Subtests Using Item-Level Error Classification | Subtests Using Within-Item Error Classification |
|---|---|
| Reading Comprehension | Letter & Word Recognition |
| Listening Comprehension | Nonsense Word Decoding |
| Written Expression | Spelling |
| Oral Expression | Math Computation |
| Phonological Processing | |
| Math Concepts & Applications | |
| Math Computation | |

Subtests with errors categorized according to item-level error classifications are automatically assigned an error category when an item is incorrect. Subtests with errors categorized according to within-item error classification are assigned an error category or categories according to the examiner's qualitative analysis of the student's incorrect response.

Because within-item error analysis has a large number of error categories, the grids for classifying and counting errors on these four subtests are too large to be included in the record form. Thus, separate error analysis worksheets are provided on the KTEA-3 Flash Drive for tabulating errors on these subtests.

### General Procedures for Using the Error Analysis System

This section outlines the general procedures that must be followed in order to utilize the KTEA-3 error analysis methods. Error analysis may be scored using Q-global or hand scoring methods. As shown in Figure 2.7, after raw scores are entered, Q-global gives a preview of the subtest standard scores to allow the user to decide which subtests to include for error analysis. Subtests with a standard score below 85 are highlighted to indicate that error analysis is recommended. Figure 2.8 displays how within-item errors are entered in Q-global, using the Spelling subtest as an example. Rapid Reference 2.8 lists the procedures for hand scoring error analysis. The Caution box alerts examiners to the importance of utilizing "Items Attempted"

| Subtest | Age-Based Standard Score | Grade-Based Standard Score |
|---|:---:|:---:|
| ☐ Phonological Processing | 94 | 93 |
| ☐ Math Concepts & Applications | 92 | 87 |
| ☑ Letter & Word Recognition | 88 | 83 |
| ☑ Math Computation | 95 | 88 |
| ☑ Nonsense Word Decoding | 75 | 73 |
| ☐ Reading Comprehension | 92 | 85 |
| ☑ Written Expression | 90 | 85 |
| ☑ Spelling | 84 | 79 |
| ☐ Listening Comprehension | 108 | 104 |
| ☑ Oral Expression | 85 | 81 |

## Figure 2.7  Error Analysis in Q-global: Recommended Subtests

Source: Kaufman Test of Educational Achievement–Third Edition (KTEA-3). Copyright © 2014 NCS Pearson, Inc. Reproduced with permission. All rights reserved.

## Spelling

First Item Administered: 1 ▼          Last Item Administered: 10 ▼

If the student's highest item attempted falls in between two columns in the norms table, the lower item is used for normative comparisons. When this occurs, only items up to the lower item in the norms table are displayed here.

| ⊞ | Item Number 4 |
|---|---|
| ⊞ | Item Number 5 |
| ⊟ | Item Number 6 |

**Item: sun**

| Incorrect | Error | Error |
|---|---|---|
| ☐ | s | Single/Double Consonant |
| ☐ | n | Single/Double Consonant |
| ☑ | u | Short Vowel |
| ☐ | | Syllable Insertion/Omission |
| ☑ | | Nonphonetic |
| ☐ | | Whole Word Error |

## Figure 2.8  Within-Item Error Analysis Entry in Q-global

Source: Kaufman Test of Educational Achievement–Third Edition (KTEA-3). Copyright © 2014 NCS Pearson, Inc. Reproduced with permission. All rights reserved.

when interpreting error analysis results. In the next several Rapid References (2.9 through 2.15), specific information about conducting error analysis for each of the subtests is outlined. These Rapid References are grouped according to subtests with similar error analysis procedures.

## ≡ Rapid Reference 2.8

### Procedures for Hand Scoring Error Analysis

1. Tally errors. After test administration, place one or more check marks in the appropriate error category column for each item answered incorrectly.

    (a) For **item-level error analysis**, make a mark in every column with an open (unshaded) box if an item was incorrectly answered.

    (b) For **within-level error analysis**, make a mark in the open (unshaded) boxes in columns that apply to the student's incorrect responses.

2. Sum errors by skill category. After error categories have been checked for all incorrect items, sum the number of checks in each column and record the total number for each category.

3. Transfer the student's error totals to the *Error Analysis Summary Form*. This form is located on the KTEA-3 Flash Drive and may be printed. Transfer the error totals for the 10 subtests to the *Error Analysis Summary Form* under the column labeled "Student's # of Errors."

4. Determine the "Last Item Administered" or "Last Item in Scored Set." The *Last Item in Scored Set* is simply the last item administered for subtests with item sets. For subtests without item sets, the *Last Item Administered* is determined by comparing the student's highest item attempted with the *Last Item Administered* columns in the norms tables. (Refer to the error analysis norm tables in Appendix H of the *KTEA-3 Technical & Interpretive Manual*, located on the *KTEA-3 Flash Drive*.) If the student's highest item attempted falls in between two columns in the norms table, use the *lower* of the two. After selecting the appropriate *Last Item Administered* from the norms tables, record this number on the *Error Analysis Summary Form* in the space provided.

5. Transfer the "Average Number of Errors" for each error category from the norms table to the appropriate column in the *Error Analysis Summary Form*. Remember, this number represents the average number of errors for each error category made by students in the norm sample who are in the same grade and who attempted the same items on the same form. [1]

6. Determine "Items Attempted." *Items Attempted* refers to the number of items in each skill category that the student attempted up to and including the "Last Item Administered." Be careful: this is not necessarily the same as the number of items in each skill category that the student attempted. Include only the items attempted up to the "Last Item Administered" selected from the norms table. Do not include items attempted after this point. Referring to the record form,

*(continued)*

(Continued)

calculate this number by counting the number of white boxes in the skill column between item 1 and the "Last Item Administered," even if the examinee was not administered all of the earliest items.

7. Determine Skill Status. Compare the student's number of errors with the average number of errors and then circle the appropriate skill status (W for Weakness, A for Average, S for Strength). Use the following procedures:

If the examinee made more than the "Average Number of Errors," then mark that error category as a Weakness (circle W).

If the examinee made fewer than the "Average Number of Errors," then mark that error category as a Strength (circle S).

If the number of errors made by the examinee was equal to or within the range of the "Average Number of Errors," then mark that error category as Average (circle A).

[1] In the norms tables, the "average" is defined as the number of errors made by the middle 50% of students.

# CAUTION

........................................................................................

## How to Interpret and Report "Items Attempted"

A student's skill status is determined by comparing the number of errors made in a category to the normative average. So how is "Items Attempted" used or interpreted? *Items Attempted* refers to the number of opportunities a student had to demonstrate a specific skill. This number allows the examiner (and others) to interpret error analysis results within the context of the number of opportunities there were to demonstrate an error. The following statement exemplifies how error analysis data may be reported within the context of the number of *Items Attempted*: "Student A made six short vowel errors in 15 opportunities, whereas the average number of errors made by the reference group was 0." Without this information, it would be difficult to gauge the severity of the skill deficit, or the frequency with which the error is made.

## *Error Analysis in Reading Comprehension and Listening Comprehension*

Items from Reading Comprehension (with the exception of the early items) and Listening Comprehension are divided into literal and inferential comprehension, as well as narrative and expository comprehension. Literal versus inferential comprehension is an important distinction for describing the level of comprehension demands required to respond to an item correctly. Literal comprehension requires recognizing or recalling ideas, information, or events that are explicitly stated in an oral or written text. In contrast, inferential comprehension requires the generation of new ideas from those stated in the text. Students derive inferences from relating different concepts presented in the text or combining information with previously acquired knowledge. Sometimes inferences require students to evaluate the writer's or speaker's viewpoint. Literal questions do not require the student to go beyond the viewpoints of the writer or speaker and are usually paraphrased portions of the text.

New to the KTEA-3 is the addition of narrative and expository error categories. These error categories were provided to help examiners determine whether a student tends to have difficulty comprehending one passage type over the other, or both. In simple terms, narrative passages tell a story for the purpose of entertainment or enjoyment, whereas the primary purpose of expository passages is to convey information.

## ≡ Rapid Reference 2.9

### Using the Error Analysis System for Reading Comprehension and Listening Comprehension

**Types of Errors Recorded:** Each item is classified as either literal or inferential; and either narrative or expository.

**Items for Which Errors Are Recorded:** Error analysis is based on the final item set used for scoring.

### Error Analysis in Written Expression and Oral Expression

Students are required to communicate their ideas in words for both the Written Expression and Oral Expression subtests. The skills needed to communicate orally are similar to those needed to communicate in written form. However, oral communication is typically more spontaneous and natural, and writing is more deliberate and structured. Difficulty in both oral and written communication can be caused by a variety of errors, which the error analysis procedures attempt to quantify.

## ≡ Rapid Reference 2.10

### Using the Error Analysis System for Written Expression and Oral Expression

|  | Written Expression | Oral Expression |
|---|---|---|
| Types of Errors Recorded | Task<br>Structure<br>Word Form<br>Capitalization<br>Punctuation | Task<br>Structure<br>Word Form |
| Items for Which Errors Are Recorded | Error analysis is based on a level (or booklet) administered. | Error analysis is based on the final item set used for scoring the case. |

To quantify students' communication ability, error analysis examines several aspects of communication:

- How well the writing or speech adheres to the task demands to communicate in a comprehensible and functional manner (pragmatics)
- How well-constructed the student's sentences are (syntax)
- Appropriateness of the word forms (grammar)
- Correct use of words (semantics, scored under Word Form)
- Mechanics (capitalization and punctuation for written expression)

When contrasting the errors made in Written Expression with those from Oral Expression, examiners can differentiate language structure problems from writing problems. Some examinees have deficits in their basic knowledge or ability to express language, which will likely be evident in errors on both tests. Other examinees with intact oral language skills may exhibit deficits that are specific to written expression.

### Errors Analysis in Phonological Processing

The particular aspects of sound awareness and manipulation that a student has and has not mastered will be evident in the errors that are made on the Phonological Processing subtest. The development of skills tapped in this subtest—rhyming, sound matching, blending, segmenting, and deleting sounds—are important precursors to reading. Teachers can use information about deficits in certain areas of phonological awareness when trying to teach early reading skills.

Phonological processing involves skills that allow students to manipulate phonemes heard in spoken language. Examinees with poor phonological processing may be unable to identify sounds in words, manipulate sounds in words, perceive a word as a sequence of sounds, or isolate beginning, medial, or final sounds. These subskills are assessed using error analysis.

---

### ≡ Rapid Reference 2.11

.................................................................................................

**Using the Error Analysis System for Phonological Processing**

**Types of Errors Recorded:** Rhyming, sound matching, blending, segmenting, and deleting sounds

**Items for Which Errors Are Recorded:** Error analysis is based on the items administered within each section.

---

### Error Analysis in Math Concepts & Applications

This subtest contains two related sets of abilities: concepts and applications. Concepts are the basic ideas and relationships on which the system of mathematics is built.

Acquisition of math concepts is hierarchical, which requires students to master basic concepts before more advanced concepts can be learned. Applications involve using these concepts and skills to solve actual and hypothetical problems (e.g., reading graphs). If a student has not yet mastered a certain concept or skill, he or she will not be able to apply that concept to solve an actual or hypothetical problem.

## ≡ Rapid Reference 2.12

### Using the Error Analysis System for Math Concepts & Application

**Types of Errors Recorded:** Number concepts, addition, subtraction, multiplication, division, tables and graphs, time and money, geometry, measurement, fractions, decimals and percents, data investigation, algebra, multistep problems, word problems

**Items for Which Errors Are Recorded:** Error analysis is based on all administered items until the ceiling is reached.

Most Math Concepts & Applications items are associated with one primary skill, but a few items are associated with two primary skills (i.e., Geometry, Measurement). Many items are associated with one or two primary skills as well as a secondary skill: namely, Multistep Problems or Word Problems. Thus, if an examinee responds incorrectly to an item, then the item is marked as an error in one or two of the primary 13 categories (such as addition, multiplication, division, etc.). However, the final two skill categories (Multistep Problems, Word Problems) may be marked as an additional error along with the one or two primary error categories.

### Error Analysis in Math Computation

The error analysis system for Math Computation is unique in that it uses both item-level and within-item classifications. Error analysis for Math Computation provides information about nine skill areas (such as addition, multiplication, fractions) and about 10 specific processes (such as regrouping, converting to common denominators, or placing decimal points) in which the student has made errors. Useful information is gleaned from understanding students' skill deficits (item-level error analysis), but even more instructionally relevant information may be revealed from the process errors that students make (within-item error analysis). Understanding the reason that a student missed an item (e.g., because they added when they should have subtracted, because they made an error when regrouping) can help determine how and where to provide additional remedial instruction for that student.

≡ *Rapid Reference 2.13*

## Using the Error Analysis System for Math Computation

**Where Error Analysis Is Recorded (Hand Scoring):** Error Analysis Worksheet on Flash Drive

**Types of Errors Recorded:** Item-level errors: addition, subtraction, multiplication, division, fraction, decimal, exponent or root, algebra

Within-item errors: wrong operation, factor computation, regrouping addition, regrouping subtraction, subtract smaller from larger, add or subtract numerator and denominator, equivalent fraction/common denominator, multiply/divide fraction, mixed number, incorrect sign, uncodable

**Items for Which Errors Are Recorded:** Error analysis is based on all administered items until the ceiling is reached.

The first two error categories of the specific processes (listed under Within-Item Errors) are *Wrong Operation* and *Fact* or *Computation Error*. These two error categories can be applied to all items. However, if an error is better described by another type of error category, then the *Wrong Operation* category should not be marked. For example, if the examinee solves a problem involving division by a fraction by dividing the numerators and denominators instead of inverting and multiplying, then you should mark the *Multiply/Divide Fraction* category instead of the *Wrong Operation* category.

### Error Analysis in Letter & Word Recognition, Nonsense Word Decoding, and Spelling

The reading of words requires that students connect speech sounds to letter patterns. Three subtests tap this skill in slightly different ways. Nonsense Word Decoding assesses a student's ability to apply decoding and structural analysis skills to nonsense words composed of typically occurring letter patterns. Spelling requires students to relate speech sounds that they hear to letter patterns that they write. Letter & Word Recognition taps a student's ability to read words with both regular and irregular letter patterns.

The error analysis system for Letter & Word Recognition, Nonsense Word Decoding, and Spelling is made up of categories of predictable skill categories, which generalize across most words, and unpredictable skill categories, which are not generalizable to other words. A separate error category is provided for words with unpredictable patterns for two reasons. First, separating out errors on unpredictable patterns gives a clearer indication of the student's problem areas in the decoding or spelling of predictable patterns, and secondly, a weakness in the skill category of unpredictable patterns may suggest a deficit in orthographic processing.

# ≡ Rapid Reference 2.14

## Using the Error Analysis System for Letter & Word Recognition, Nonsense Word Decoding, and Spelling

**Where Error Analysis Is Recorded (Hand Scoring):** Error Analysis Worksheets on Flash Drive

**Types of Errors Recorded\*:** Single/double consonant; initial blend; consonant blend; medial/final blend; consonant digraph; wrong vowel; short vowel; long vowel; vowel team/diphthong; r-controlled vowel; silent letter; prefix/word beginning; suffix/inflection/hard or soft C, G, S; unpredictable pattern; initial/final sound; insertion/omission; nonphonetic; misordered sounds.

**Items for Which Errors Are Recorded:** Error analysis is based on all administered items until the ceiling is reached.

---

\*Errors for these subtests are defined and exemplified in the *KTEA-3 Scoring Manual* (Kaufman & Kaufman, 2014d). Some error categories are not scored for each of these subtests.

The error analysis system is set up in such a way that words are divided into parts based on orthographically predictable patterns. The Don't Forget box explains how words are divided within this system. Other error categories describe additional features of the error, such as incorrect initial or final sound or letter, wrong vowel, omitted or incorrectly inserted syllables, or, in Spelling, a nonphonetic misspelling. Although the categories are very similar for Letter & Word Recognition, Nonsense Word Decoding, and Spelling, some differences do exist, which are summarized in the Caution box.

## DON'T FORGET

### Dividing Words Into Parts Based on Orthographically Predictable Patterns for Error Analysis

| Number of Syllables | How Words Are Divided | Example |
|---|---|---|
| One-Syllable Words | Divided into vowel and consonant parts. | *what* is divided into:<br>*wh* (consonant digraph)<br>*a* (short vowel)<br>*t* (single consonant) |

(continued)

(Continued)

| Number of Syllables | How Words Are Divided | Example |
|---|---|---|
| Multisyllabic Words | Divided into words with roots and affixes, with the affixes as whole words and the roots further divided into vowel and consonant parts. | *roasted* is divided into:<br>*r* (single consonant)<br>*oa* (vowel team)<br>*st* (medial/final consonant blend)<br>*ed* (suffixes and inflections) |

# CAUTION

## Differences Between Skill Categories for Letter & Word Recognition, Nonsense Word Decoding, and Spelling

- All three subtests include a category for *Consonant Blends*, but in Nonsense Word Decoding and Spelling this category is divided into *Initial* and *Medial/Final* consonant blends because these subtests include a large number of instances of each subtype.

- Spelling error analysis does not contain the *Wrong Vowel* or *Misordered Sounds* categories. Writing a wrong vowel is categorized as a short or a long vowel error.

- All three subtests include *Prefixes and Word Beginnings* and *Suffixes and Inflections* categories. They are merged into one category in Nonsense Word Decoding because that subtest has few prefixes.

- In Spelling, if a student inserts a grapheme (smaller than a syllable) that is not in the sound of the word, count this is a *Nonphonetic* error.

*Note:* Adapted from the *KTEA-3 Scoring Manual* (Kaufman & Kaufman, 2014d, p. 47).

The last category in Letter & Word Recognition, Nonsense Word Decoding, and Spelling is *Whole Word Error*. Generally, if a student's response is significantly different from the stimulus word, then it is usually better to mark the item as a *Whole Word Error* rather than trying to identify numerous specific errors. There are several times when it is best to mark a student's response in the *Whole Word Error* category (Kaufman & Kaufman, 2004a, p. 50):

1. The response is unclassifiable, showing little or no correspondence to the stimulus. If the response contains several incorrect parts, mark Whole Word Error instead of trying to identify them. Record UN (unclassifiable) next to the word when recording errors.

2. The response is a different word, such as a real word that approximates the stimulus word. Record errors in the applicable error categories for each part of the word read incorrectly in addition to marking a Whole Word error. Write WS (word substitution) next to the word when recording errors.

3. In Letter & Word Recognition, if the mispronunciation contains a misplaced accent, write MPA (misplaced accent) next to the word when recording errors.

As we stressed in the administration and scoring sections, recording a student's exact responses is crucial for these subtests. In addition to being familiar with how to record students' responses phonetically, you should be familiar with the error categories before testing, which informs the most pertinent error information to record for error analysis scoring.

## Qualitative Observations

The KTEA-3 Comprehensive Form assists examiners in gathering and analyzing qualitative observations. Each observation statement may be answered Yes, No, or DK. Qualitative observations are not provided for Phonological Processing, Associational Fluency, Object Naming Facility, and Letter Naming Facility because these subtests measure cognitive processes rather than academic performance.

Q-global provides a qualitative observations tab that includes suggested observations—in general and for the 15 specific subtests. After responding to the qualitative observations by answering yes or no to each one, you may select Qualitative Observations as a report option. The Q-global standard report will display a table of areas of cognitive processing by achievement domain, as shown in Figure 2.9. An X indicates that one or more qualitative observations suggested a particular

| Domain | Graphomotor | Visual Processing | Phonological Processing | Orthographic Processing | Language | Executive Functioning | Processing Speed | RAN and Long-Term Memory | Working Memory |
|---|---|---|---|---|---|---|---|---|---|
| General Observations | | | | | | × | | | |
| Oral Expression | | | | | | | | | |
| Listening Comprehension | | | | | | | | | |
| Written Expression | × | × | | × | × | | | | × |
| Basic Reading | | | × | × | × | | | × | × |

**Figure 2.9 Qualitative Observations Analysis in Q-global Standard Report**

*Source:* Kaufman Test of Educational Achievement–Third Edition (KTEA-3). Copyright © 2014 NCS Pearson, Inc. Reproduced with permission. All rights reserved.

processing weakness in that domain. A shaded box indicates that no qualitative observations were applicable to that area/domain. These suggested areas of processing weaknesses must be cross-validated with other sources of information, including KTEA-3 scores, error analysis data, and tests of cognitive processing. Follow up testing to confirm or refute these hypotheses is recommended. This analysis of qualitative observations by cognitive processing areas is available only when using Q-global (not for hand scoring).

For those who choose not to use Q-global, the flash drive includes a Qualitative Observations Form for completing these same observations by hand. This form lists the qualitative observations in record form order, so the form may be completed easily during test administration.

## USING THE KTEA-3 ACROSS MULTIPLE ADMINISTRATIONS

### Repeated Administrations of the Same Form

Examiners with access to only one form of the KTEA-3 may readminister the same form to an examinee after enough time has passed. As a general rule, wait about 8 months to 1 year before readministering the same form to avoid an overestimation of achievement levels due to practice effects. This guideline may be reduced somewhat for young examinees, or increased somewhat for older examinees. Keep in mind that some subtests may elicit greater practice effects than others.

### Administering Alternate Forms

Examiners with access to both forms of the KTEA-3 Comprehensive, or the Brief Form and Comprehensive Form A, may alternate forms when evaluating an examinee across multiple points in time. Keep the following guidelines and considerations in mind when alternating forms:

- If a Form A subtest score was deemed invalid due to administration error, the Form B subtest may be administered in quick succession to obtain a valid subtest score (or vice versa).
- Administering an alternate form of the same subtest within a short time frame may result in scores that are slightly inflated due to

## CAUTION

- As a general guideline, wait 8 months to 1 year before readministering the same form of the KTEA-3.
- When readministering the same subtests less than 8–12 months (or so) later, alternate Comprehensive Form A with either the Brief Form or Comprehensive Form B.
- Use growth scale values (GSVs) for comparing performance across multiple administrations or assessing progress over time. Comparing any other type of score (i.e., raw scores, standard scores, percentiles, or age/grade equivalent scores) may be misleading for evaluating progress.

procedural learning effects (recent exposure to the same item type). However, these score differences tend to be small, as indicated by the effect sizes reported on the alternate-form reliability study in the *KTEA-3 Technical & Interpretive Manual* (Kaufman & Kaufman, 2014b).

## USING THE KTEA-3 BRIEF FORM

Two of the most common uses of the KTEA-3 Brief include progress monitoring and screening for a comprehensive evaluation. This section provides additional information about using the Brief Form for these purposes.

### Progress Monitoring

To monitor progress or response to intervention, KTEA-3 Brief Form results may supplement data provided by curriculum based and criterion-referenced measures, although the KTEA-3 Brief Form is not typically administered as frequently. As a general guideline, wait at least 8 months to 1 year before readministering the KTEA-3 Brief Form.

To reduce practice effects when reevaluating an examinee, the KTEA-3 Brief Form may be alternated with the KTEA-3 Comprehensive Form A.

Using growth scale values (GSVs) is highly recommended when comparing an examinee's performance across administrations. GSVs obtained from the Brief Form are comparable with those obtained by the same examinee on the Comprehensive Form.

### Screening for a Comprehensive Evaluation

Low performance on one or more KTEA-3 Brief Form subtests or significant score differences on the Brief Form may suggest the need for a comprehensive evaluation. The Brief Form includes score comparisons between the Brief Achievement (BA-3) composite and each of the three subtests in that battery (Letter & Word Recognition, Math Computation, Spelling) as well as score comparisons between the more comprehensive Academic Skills Battery (ASB) composite and each of the six subtests in that battery. These score comparisons identify academic strengths and weaknesses that are significantly different from the student's overall academic achievement level. Subtest score comparisons are also available for identifying discrepancies between reading, math, and written language domains.

The Brief Form subtests may be included in ability–achievement discrepancy (AAD) and Pattern of Strengths and Weaknesses (PSW) analyses when administered as part of a more comprehensive evaluation. Unlike the KTEA-II Brief Form, the KTEA-3 Brief Form subtests are identical to the core subtests in the Comprehensive

Form and have sufficient skill coverage, reliability, and validity to be used within AAD and PSW analyses.

AAD and PSW analyses are available only when the Brief Form is used in conjunction with a more comprehensive test battery because these analyses are not typically conducted when administering a brief achievement measure. Such analyses are more appropriate when conducting a comprehensive assessment with the Comprehensive Form.

When using the Brief Form as the only achievement measure, examiners may also administer a brief test of cognitive ability such as the Kaufman Brief Intelligence Test–Second Edition (KBIT-2; Kaufman & Kaufman, 2004c) in order to have an understanding of a person's general level of cognitive functioning.

Refer to the Caution box for additional information about using the Brief Form to screen for dyslexia or specific learning disabilities.

---

## CAUTION

### Limitations of Using the KTEA-3 Brief Form for Dyslexia or SLD Screening

Oral language measures are not included in the Brief Form. Hence, the Brief Form will not identify:
  (a) Weaknesses in oral language that may be hindering academic performance, or
  (b) Critical discrepancies between oral and written language areas (Listening Comprehension vs. Reading Comprehension, Oral Expression vs. Written Expression).

One key symptom of dyslexia/reading disorder is that reading comprehension skills are lower than listening comprehension skills (RC < LC). If both reading and listening comprehension skills are low, then either a language disorder or a global reading impairment (characterized by low overall ability) may be suspected.
  • Reading fluency, writing fluency, and math fluency subtests are not included in the Brief Form. Hence, specific fluency deficits may not be detected.
  • Subtests to identify processing deficits in phonological processing and naming facility are not included in the Brief Form.

---

### Using the Brief Form With the Comprehensive Form

Results from the Brief Form may warrant more in-depth testing using the Comprehensive Form. In such cases, the Brief Form and Comprehensive Form (A or B) may be integrated efficiently without readministering subtests.

Refer to Rapid Reference 2.15 for instructions on how to generate a Brief + Comprehensive Score Report in Q-global. The Don't Forget box summarizes scoring considerations when using the Brief Form with either Comprehensive Form A or B.

## ≋ Rapid Reference 2.15

### How to Generate a Brief + Comprehensive Score Report

**Step 1:** Enter score results from the KTEA-3 Brief Form in Q-global and generate the report. This assessment must be in Report Generated status.

**Step 2:** Enter score results from the KTEA-3 Comprehensive Form in Q-global and generate the report. This assessment must be in Report Generated status.

**Step 3:** On the Examinee page, select both the KTEA-3 Brief Form assessment and the KTEA-3 (Form A or Form B) Comprehensive Form assessment, and then select Generate Report. Q-global will ask you to select the report you want to generate. Select the KTEA-3 Brief + Comprehensive Report.

**Step 4:** Select the report options you want to use for this report.

## DON'T FORGET

### Using the Brief Form With the Comprehensive Form

Standard scores from the Brief and Comprehensive Forms (A or B) are comparable and derived from the same normative sample.

Scores from the Brief Form may be integrated or reported alongside scores from the Comprehensive Form if both forms were administered within a month or so. If more than a few months have passed, consider reporting the administrations separately.

Brief Form subtests may be included in AAD and PSW analyses when administered as part of a more comprehensive evaluation.

### Supplements to the Brief Form and Scoring Considerations

| Supplementing the Brief Form With | Q-global Scoring Considerations | Hand Scoring Considerations |
|---|---|---|
| Comprehensive Form A subtests | • Assign two assessments (Brief Form, Comprehensive Form A), and enter raw scores separately | • Score the Brief Form with the Brief norms. Score the Comprehensive Form with the Comprehensive norms. |
| | **Caution!** Entering Brief Form raw scores into the Comprehensive Form A assessment will yield inaccurate standard scores. | **Caution!** Converting Brief Form raw scores using the Comprehensive Form A norms will yield inaccurate standard scores. |

*(continued)*

(Continued)

| Supplementing the Brief Form With | Q-global Scoring Considerations | Hand Scoring Considerations |
|---|---|---|
| Comprehensive Form A subtests (continued) | • Create a Brief + Comprehensive Score Report to integrate the scores from the two assessments.<br><br>• The Brief + Comprehensive Score Report does not include AAD/PSW or error analysis capabilities. To access these features for a Brief Form subtest that was administered, use the Technical & Interpretive Manual from the Comprehensive Form to find the raw score from Form A that converts to the same standard score obtained from the Brief, and then enter that raw score into the Comprehensive Form A assessment. | • Brief Form standard scores may be used as if those scores had been obtained using Comprehensive Form A (for example, combine the LWR standard score from the Brief and the NWD standard score from the Comprehensive to obtain the Decoding composite score; use the LWR standard score from the Brief as part of an AAD/PSW analysis.)<br><br>• Error analysis may be conducted on Brief Form subtests by referring to the Form B error analysis norms. |
| Comprehensive Form B subtests<br><br>Reminder: The Brief Form is equivalent to the core subtests from Comprehensive Form B. | Option I<br><br>• Assign two assessments (Brief Form, Comprehensive Form B), and enter raw scores separately.<br><br>• Create a Brief + Comprehensive Score Report to integrate the scores from the two assessments.<br><br>If you want to utilize AAD/PSW or error analysis capabilities for Brief Form subtests, consider option 2. | • Using the Brief Form norms to score the Brief, and the Comprehensive Form norms to score the Comprehensive is recommended to avoid error.<br><br>Caution! It is acceptable to use the Comprehensive Form B norms to score the Brief Form only when the examinee's grade or chronological age (if using grade or age norms, respectively) is the same for both administrations. |

(continued)

(Continued)

| Supplementing the Brief Form With | Q-global Scoring Considerations | Hand Scoring Considerations |
|---|---|---|
| | **Option 2** <br> • Within the Comprehensive Form B assessment, enter raw scores from both the Brief Form and Comprehensive Form B. <br> **Caution!** If you use option 2, you lose documentation of which subtests were administered as part of the Brief Form, which may have been on a different administration date. <br> **Caution!** The examinee's chronological age may differ if the Brief Form and Comprehensive Form were administered on different days. If scoring using age norms, option 2 may yield inaccurate scores if the chronological age differs between the assessments. | • Brief Form standard scores may be used as if those scores had been obtained using Comprehensive Form B (for example, combine the LWR standard score from the Brief and the NWD standard score from the Comprehensive to obtain the Decoding composite score; use the LWR standard score from the Brief as part of an AAD/PSW analysis.) <br> • Error analysis may be conducted on Brief Form subtests by referring to the Form B error analysis norms. |

## KTEA-3 SCORE REPORTS

This section provides an overview and comparison of the KTEA-3 Brief and Comprehensive Form score reports that are currently available in Q-global. The Brief Form offers one standard report in Q-global. The Comprehensive Form offers three reports: a standard report, a parent report, and a GSV Charts report. For users who purchase both the Brief Form and Comprehensive Form assessments on Q-global, one additional standard report is available: the Brief + Comprehensive Score Report. The features included in each standard report are summarized in Rapid Reference 2.16.

## ≡ Rapid Reference 2.16

### Comparing KTEA-3 Brief Form, Comprehensive Form, and Brief + Comprehensive Score Reports

| Report Types | KTEA-3 Brief | KTEA-3 Comprehensive | Brief + Comprehensive |
|---|:---:|:---:|:---:|
| Standard Report | X | X | X |
| Parent Report | | X | |
| GSV Charts Report | | X | |
| **Standard Report Features** | **KTEA-3 Brief** | **KTEA-3 Comprehensive** | **Brief + Comprehensive** |
| Option to include GSV scores, age/grade equivalents, NCEs, stanines | X | X | X |
| Option of 85%, 90%, 95% confidence level | X | X | X |
| Age or Grade norms | X | X | X |
| Score summary with graphical profile | X | X | X |
| Subtest/composite score comparisons | X | X | X |
| Option of 10 or 15 pt. descriptive categories | X | X | X |
| AAD and PSW Analyses | | X | X |
| CHC Abilities Score Report | | X | X |
| Error Analysis (score summary, teaching objectives, interventions, word list, math problems) | | X | |
| Qualitative Observations | | X | |

Note: Score reports and their features may change over time. Refer to www.helloq.com for the most current information.

# 🖎 TEST YOURSELF 🖎

1. **In addition to the four Cross Domain composites (Comprehension, Expression, Orthographic Processing, Academic Fluency), which other composite is new to the KTEA-3?**
   (a) Oral Fluency
   (b) Reading Understanding
   (c) Oral Language
   (d) Decoding

2. **The KTEA-3 Academic Skills Battery composite includes the following subtests at every age/grade except**
   (a) Letter & Word Recognition
   (b) Math Concepts & Application
   (c) Listening Comprehension
   (d) Written Expression

3. **Which of the following should examiners consider when deciding whether to report KTEA-3 results using the 15-point or the 10-point classification system?**
   (a) The examinee's score profile
   (b) Consistency with the other tests administered to the examinee
   (c) Personal preference
   (d) Any or all of the above

4. **Students are not penalized for misspelled words on the Written Expression and Writing Fluency subtests.**
   (a) True
   (b) False

5. **All KTEA-3 subtests offer an error analysis.**
   (a) True
   (b) False

6. **Which value is used to represent a student's overall "average level of performance" on the KTEA-3 during the interpretive process?**
   (a) The mean of all core composites
   (b) The Academic Skills Battery (ASB) composite
   (c) The mean of only Reading and Math Composites
   (d) The mean of Reading, Math, and Writing Composites

7. **The suggested KTEA-3 interpretive steps base academic strengths on normative comparisons as well as ipsative (person-based) comparisons.**
   (a) True
   (b) False

8. **KTEA-3 error analysis is intended for use with students who perform well above the mean.**

   (a) True
   (b) False

9. **Pairs of KTEA-3 Comprehensive subtests (i.e., Reading Comprehension and Listening Comprehension, and Written Expression and Oral Expression) were developed specifically to have similar formats to enable useful comparisons that can help the examiner distinguish specific problems in reading or writing from more general language problems.**

   (a) True
   (b) False

10. **Which one of the following academic domains measured in the KTEA-3 Comprehensive Form is *not* measured by the KTEA-3 Brief Form?**

    (a) Reading
    (b) Mathematics
    (c) Written Language
    (d) Oral Language

*Answers:* 1. b; 2. c; 3. d; 4. a; 5. b; 6. b; 7. a; 8. b; 9. a; 10. d.

# Three

## WIAT®-III

The Wechsler Individual Achievement Test–Third Edition (WIAT-III; Pearson, 2009a) is a comprehensive, individually administered achievement test. It is designed for examinees who are in prekindergarten (Pre-K) through grade 12 or individuals ages 4:0 through 50:11 years. Adult norms for ages 20 through 50 years added to the WIAT-III in 2010. This test can be administered by special educators, school psychologists, educational diagnosticians, speech-language pathologists, and similar professionals who have formal training and experience in the administration and interpretation of individually administered, norm-referenced tests.

The WIAT-III includes 16 subtests for coverage of all eight specific learning disability areas identified in the Individuals with Disabilities Education Improvement Act of 2004 (IDEA, 2004), as shown in Table 3.1.

### HISTORY AND DEVELOPMENT

The first edition of the WIAT (Psychological Corporation, 1992) was designed as a measure of academic achievement for examinees in kindergarten through high school, ages 5:0 to 19:11, and contained eight subtests: Basic Reading, Mathematics Reasoning, Spelling, Reading Comprehension, Numerical Operations, Listening Comprehension, Oral Expression, and Written Expression. These subtests formed five composites: Reading, Mathematics, Language, Writing, and Total. These subtests corresponded to each of the areas of learning disability specified in the Education for All Handicapped Children Act of 1975 (PL 94-142). The WIAT was the only test of its kind to be linked with the Wechsler ability scales to facilitate the analysis of ability-achievement discrepancies.

The WIAT-II (Psychological Corporation, 2001) was originally published in 2001, with updated scoring and normative materials published in 2002 and 2005. The WIAT-II was designed for examinees in grades pre-kindergarten through 12, college examinees in 2-year and 4-year institutions, and adults, extending the age range to 4 through 85 years. The second edition included significant updates to the

**Table 3.1  IDEA 2004 and the WIAT-III**

| IDEA 2004 Area of Achievement | WIAT-III Composite | WIAT-III Subtest |
|---|---|---|
| Oral Expression | Oral Language Composite | Oral Expression |
| Listening Comprehension | | Listening Comprehension* |
| Written Expression | Written Expression Composite | Alphabet Writing Fluency |
| | | Sentence Composition |
| | | Essay Composition |
| | | Spelling |
| Basic Reading Skill | Basic Reading Composite | Early Reading Skills |
| | | Word Reading |
| | | Pseudoword Decoding |
| Reading Fluency Skills | Reading Comprehension and Fluency Composite | Oral Reading Fluency |
| Reading Comprehension | | Reading Comprehension |
| Mathematics Calculation | Mathematics Composite | Numerical Operations |
| Mathematics Problem Solving | | Math Problem Solving |
| *Not included in IDEA 2004* | Math Fluency Composite | Math Fluency—Addition |
| | | Math Fluency—Subtraction |
| | | Math Fluency—Multiplication |

eight subtests from the WIAT, changed the name of the Basic Reading subtest to Word Reading, and added one new subtest, Pseudoword Decoding. These subtests formed five composite scores: Reading, Mathematics, Written Language, Oral Language, and Total.

Planning and conceptual development of the WIAT-III began in 2005. Several key goals and primary considerations were identified for the revision of the WIAT-II and development of the WIAT-III, which are discussed in the following section. Pilot testing of new subtests and items was conducted in 2006 and then a national tryout of the full WIAT-III was conducted in 2007. The WIAT-III was standardized in the fall and spring of 2008.

## CHANGES FROM WIAT-II TO WIAT-III

The WIAT-III preserves and updates many of the same subtests included in the WIAT-II while expanding content coverage in the areas of listening, speaking, reading, writing, and mathematics. The primary goals for the third edition were to add new subtests to measure phonological awareness and early reading skills, reading fluency, and math fluency, improve ease of administration, simplify administration rules, minimize testing time, improve content coverage, floors, and ceilings in order to maximize diagnostic sensitivity, and provide a research-based, theoretically supported analysis for the identification of learning disabilities.

### Age Range

The WIAT-III age range of 4–50 years is narrower than the WIAT-II, which extended to 85 years. A more restricted age range allows the WIAT-III to focus primarily on the assessment needs of the school-age, adolescent, and college or young adult populations, with some extension of content appropriate for middle aged adults.

### New and Modified Subtests

Brief descriptions of the WIAT-III subtests are provided in Rapid Reference 3.1, which is organized by content area. Five subtests are new to the WIAT-III: Early Reading Skills, Oral Reading Fluency, Math Fluency–Addition, Math Fluency–Subtraction, and Math Fluency–Multiplication. The Early Reading Skills subtest items are adapted from the early items from the WIAT-II Word Reading and Reading Comprehension subtests. In addition, the components of the former Written Expression subtest now form distinct subtests: Alphabet Writing Fluency, Sentence Composition, and Essay Composition.

> ## DON'T FORGET
> ............................................................
> ### Pseudoword versus Nonsense word versus Nonword
>
> The WIAT-III includes a Pseudoword Decoding subtest, whereas the KTEA-3 includes Nonsense Word Decoding. For the purposes of these tests, a pseudoword and a nonsense word are synonymous. These terms refer to a unit of speech that follows the rules of English and resembles a real word but has no meaning in the lexicon (e.g., wug). In contrast, a nonword is not pronounceable and could not be a real word because it does not follow the rules of English (e.g., wgxu).

Several subtests retain the basic structure and administration format as in the WIAT-II but were updated with standard revisions, including new or modified items, art, and/or administration instructions. These subtests include Spelling, Numerical Operations, Math Problem Solving, Word Reading, and Pseudoword Decoding. The latter two subtests each include new supplemental scores.

Listening Comprehension and Reading Comprehension also feature new enhancements. Listening Comprehension now includes Receptive Vocabulary and Oral Discourse Comprehension. Receptive Vocabulary was modified to include updated art and a new ceiling item. Oral Discourse Comprehension was adapted from the Listening Comprehension subtest from the original WIAT and updated with new floor items and an audio CD administration of item stimuli to improve administration reliability. The Oral Discourse Comprehension component replaces Sentence Comprehension from the WIAT-II. The Expressive Vocabulary component was moved to the Oral Expression subtest. For Reading Comprehension, updates were made to many of the comprehension questions and scoring rules and one new passage was added. The subtest no longer includes the supplemental scores from the WIAT-II (target words, reading speed).

Oral Expression now includes Expressive Vocabulary, Oral Word Fluency, and Sentence Repetition. Expressive Vocabulary includes updated art, simplified item definitions, and new floor and ceiling items. Oral Word Fluency includes updated administration directions and scoring rules and one new item (naming colors). Sentence Repetition includes new items and updated administration directions and scoring rules. Sentence Repetition is now administered to all grade levels. Visual Passage Retell and Giving Directions from the WIAT-II subtest were dropped due to the time required to administer and score these components.

The Alphabet Writing Fluency, Sentence Composition, and Essay Composition subtests are each based upon components of the WIAT-II Written Expression subtest. These components were updated and expanded to form distinct subtests that yield separate scores, allowing for improved interpretation of performance strengths and weaknesses. New administration directions and scoring rules are provided for Alphabet Writing Fluency, Sentence Composition, and Essay Composition. Unlike the WIAT-II subtest, Essay Composition includes one essay prompt for examinees in grades 3 through 12, and the same scoring rules are used across grades.

## ≡ Rapid Reference 3.1

### Brief Description of WIAT-III Subtests

| Subtest | Description |
|---|---|
| **Oral Language Subtest** | |
| Listening Comprehension | Receptive Vocabulary: Measures listening vocabulary. The examinee points to the picture that best illustrates the meaning of each word he or she hears. |
| | Oral Discourse Comprehension: Measures literal and inferential listening comprehension. The examinee listens to sentences read aloud by the examiner (early items) and an audio recording of passages, and then orally responds to comprehension questions spoken by the examiner. |

*(continued)*

(Continued)

| Subtest | Description |
|---|---|
| **Oral Language Subtest** | |
| Oral Expression | Expressive Vocabulary: The examinee says the word that best corresponds to a given picture and definition.<br><br>Oral Word Fluency: Measures efficiency of word retrieval and flexibility of thought processes. The examinee names as many things as possible belonging to a given category (i.e., animals, colors) within 60 seconds.<br><br>Sentence Repetition: Measures oral syntactic knowledge and short-term memory. The examinee listens to sentences that increase in length and complexity and repeats each sentence verbatim. |
| **Reading Subtest** | |
| Early Reading Skills | The examinee provides oral and pointing responses to items that require rhyming, blending sounds, manipulation of sounds within words, letter and phonics knowledge, and word-reading comprehension. |
| Word Reading | Measures speed and accuracy of decontextualized word recognition. The examinee reads aloud from a list of words that increase in difficulty. The list of words is read without a time limit. The examiner records the examinee's progress after 30 seconds and continues administration until the discontinue rule is met or the last item is administered. |
| Pseudoword Decoding | Measures the ability to decode nonsense words. The examinee reads aloud from a list of pseudowords that increase in difficulty. The list of pseudowords is read without a time limit. The examiner records the examinee's progress after 30 seconds and continues administration until the discontinue rule is met or the last item is administered. |
| Reading Comprehension | Measures untimed reading comprehension of various types of text, including fictional stories, informational text, advertisements, and how-to passages. The examinee may read passages aloud or silently. After each passage, the examinee orally responds to literal and inferential comprehension questions that are read aloud by the examiner. |
| Oral Reading Fluency | Measures speed, accuracy, fluency, and prosody of contextualized oral reading. The examinee reads passages aloud, and then orally responds to comprehension questions after each passage. Fluency is calculated as the average number of words |

(Continued)

| Subtest | Description |
|---|---|
| **Reading Subtest** | |
| | read correctly per minute. A qualitative scale is completed by the examiner to assess the examinee's reading prosody. Comprehension questions are asked only to encourage reading for meaning; comprehension performance is not scored quantitatively. |
| **Writing Subtest** | |
| Alphabet Writing Fluency | Measures the ability to write letters of the alphabet within a 30-second time limit. The examinee may write letters in any order, in cursive or print, in uppercase or lowercase. |
| Spelling | Early items require examinees to write single letters that represent sounds. Later items involve spelling words from dictation. |
| Sentence Composition | Sentence Combining: Measures sentence formulation skills and written syntactic maturity. The examinee combines two or three sentences into one sentence that preserves the meaning of the original sentences. |
| | Sentence Building: Measures sentence formulation skills and written syntactic ability. For each item, the examinee writes one sentence that uses a target word with appropriate context. |
| Essay Composition | Measures spontaneous, compositional writing skills within a 10-minute time limit. |
| **Math Subtest** | |
| Math Problem Solving | The examinee provides oral and pointing responses to test items that focus on the (untimed) application of mathematical principles to real-life situations. |
| Numerical Operations | Measures untimed, written math calculation skills in the following domains: basic skills, basic operations with integers, geometry, algebra, and calculus |
| Math Fluency— Addition | The examinee writes the answers to as many addition problems as possible in 60 seconds. |
| Math Fluency— Subtraction | The examinee writes the answers to as many subtraction problems as possible in 60 seconds. |
| Math Fluency— Multiplication | The examinee writes the answers to as many multiplication problems as possible in 60 seconds. |

Note: Subtest descriptions were adapted from Table 1.1 of the *WIAT-III Examiner's Manual* (Pearson, 2009b, pp. 4–5).

## Composites

The WIAT-III includes eight composites. Total Achievement, Oral Language, Written Expression, and Mathematics are similar to their WIAT-II counterparts, whereas Total Reading, Basic Reading, Reading Comprehension and Fluency, and Math Fluency are new composites. WIAT-III core and supplemental composites are shown in Figures 3.1 and 3.2, respectively.

## Administration and Scoring Rules

Those WIAT-III subtests with multiple start points include the same reverse rule as in the previous edition: If the first three items administered are scored 0 points, administer items in reverse order until three consecutive scores of 1 are obtained (or item 1 is reached). However, the discontinue rule has been shortened to four consecutive scores of 0, and the discontinue rule is now the same for all applicable subtests.

New or modified scoring rules have been developed for all subjectively scored subtests (Reading Comprehension, Oral Expression, Alphabet Writing Fluency, Sentence Composition, and Essay Composition). The new scoring rules are designed to be valid, reliable, and clinically sensitive.

## Skills Analysis

# DON'T FORGET

........................................................

### Skills Analysis versus Error Analysis

The WIAT-III includes skills analysis (item level and within-item level), whereas the KTEA-3 includes error analysis (item level and within-item level). For the purposes of these tests, skills analysis and error analysis are synonymous. Consistent terminology will likely be used in future revisions of the tests.

The WIAT-III provides skills analysis capabilities at the item level or within-item level, depending on the subtest. Item-level skills analysis is provided for four subtests: Reading Comprehension, Early Reading Skills, Numerical Operations, and Math Problem Solving. Within-item level skills analysis is provided for three subtests: Word Reading, Pseudoword Decoding, and Spelling. Item-level skills analysis specifies the skill(s) measured by each item, whereas within-item skills analysis specifies the skill(s) measured by each part within the item and requires the examiner to select the specific parts within each item that were answered incorrectly.

## Intervention Goal Statements

For examiners who use Q-global or the WIAT-III Scoring Assistant, intervention goal statements are available for 10 of the 16 subtests: Reading Comprehension, Early Reading Skills, Numerical Operations, Math Problem Solving, Word Reading,

| Core Composites | Subtests | |
|---|---|---|
| Oral Language (PK-12+) | Listening Comprehension *(PK-12+)* | Total Achievement Composite |
| | Oral Expression *(PK-12+)* | |
| Total Reading (1-12+) | Word Reading *(1-12+)* | |
| | Pseudoword Decoding *(1-12+)* | |
| | Reading Comprehension *(1-12+)* | |
| | Oral Reading Fluency *(1-12+)* | |
| Written Expression (K-12+) | Alphabet Writing Fluency *(PK-3)* | |
| | Spelling *(K-12+)* | |
| | Sentence Composition *(1-12+)* | |
| | Essay Composition *(3-12+)* | |
| Mathematics (K-12+) | Math Problem Solving *(PK-12+)* | |
| | Numerical Operations *(K-12+)* | |

**Figure 3.1  Core Composite Structure of the WIAT-III**

*Source:* Figure is adapted from Figure 1.1 of the *WIAT-III Examiner's Manual* (Pearson, 2009b, p. 3).

| Supplemental Composites | Subtests | |
|---|---|---|
| Basic Reading (1-12+) | Word Reading (1-12+) | |
| | Pseudoword Decoding (1-12+) | |
| Reading Comprehension and Fluency (Grades 2-12) | Reading Comprehension (1-12+) | |
| | Oral Reading Fluency (1-12+) | |
| Math Fluency (1-12+) | Math Fluency - Addition (1-12+) | |
| | Math Fluency - Subtraction (1-12+) | |
| | Math Fluency - Multiplication (3-12+) | |

**Figure 3.2 Supplemental WIAT-III Composites**

Source: Figure is adapted from Figure 1.1 of the WIAT-III Examiner's Manual (Pearson, 2009b, p. 3).

Pseudoword Decoding, Spelling, Oral Reading Fluency, Sentence Composition, and Essay Composition.

### New Analyses

Federal regulations specify several criteria for identifying a specific learning disability (SLD), including underachievement in one or more areas, failure to make sufficient progress in response to targeted intervention, and a pattern of strengths and weaknesses in performance, achievement, or both (34 CFR §300.309[a]). The IDEA 2004 introduces greater flexibility in the assessment process for identifying learning disabilities and/or determining eligibility for special services. Similar to the WIAT-II, the WIAT-III provides the capability of conducting an ability-achievement discrepancy analysis using either the simple difference or predicted achievement method. The WIAT-III also includes the capability of conducting a pattern of strengths and weaknesses discrepancy analysis, which most closely resembles the Concordance-Discordance Model of SLD identification presented by Hale and Fiorello (2004).

## New Scores

Growth scale values (GSVs) are provided for tracking progress over time on each of the WIAT-III subtests. GSV Charts, or growth score curves, are also provided in Q-global and the Scoring Assistant to assist examiners in plotting a examinee's growth trend relative to the average growth trend.

Supplemental standard scores are available for Word Reading, Pseudoword Decoding, Essay Composition, and Oral Reading Fluency. Word Reading and Pseudoword Decoding each provide an optional measure of reading speed. This score is calculated by recording the item number reached at 30 seconds and converting that item number to a standard score. Essay Composition yields a supplemental standard score for Grammar and Mechanics, which requires the calculation of correct minus incorrect word sequences (CIWS). Finally, Oral Reading Fluency yields two supplemental scores, Oral Reading Accuracy and Oral Reading Rate.

New to the WIAT-III are standard scores for components of subtests. This new feature provides greater interpretability of subtest scores when the subtest is composed of two or three task components.

## Validity Studies

The WIAT-III provides linking (correlation) data with the Wechsler Preschool and Primary Scale of Intelligence–Third Edition (WPPSI-III; Wechsler, 2002), the Wechsler Intelligence Scale for Children–Fourth Edition (WISC-IV; Wechsler, 2003), the Wechsler Adult Intelligence Scale–Fourth Edition (WAIS-IV; Wechsler, 2008), the Wechsler Nonverbal Scale of Ability (WNV; Wechsler & Naglieri, 2006), and the Differential Ability Scales–Second Edition (DAS-II; Elliott, 2007). In addition, WIAT-III linking data with the WPPSI-IV is provided in the WPPSI-IV *Technical and Interpretive Manual* (Wechsler, 2012b) and linking data with the WISC-V is provided in the WISC-V *Technical and Interpretive Manual* (Wechsler, 2014b).

## Materials

The WIAT-III kit components differ from the WIAT-II in three important ways: (1) Only one stimulus book is required to administer the WIAT-III, and the stimulus book contains stimuli on both sides of the pages. During administration, both examiner and examinee view the same side of the stimulus book. (2) All administration directions are included in the record form rather than the stimulus book. (3) Two new components are included: the Oral Reading Fluency booklet and the Audio CD.

## Scoring and Reporting

Automated scoring of the WIAT-III is currently available on Q-global, Pearson's web-based scoring and reporting platform. Q-global is automatically updated as new editions of tests release and new features become available. When the WIAT-III originally published in 2009, the kit included a Scoring Assistant CD for automated scoring and reporting. The original Scoring Assistant may still be used by customers, although it is no longer commercially available and will not be updated to include AAD and PSW analyses with new editions of cognitive ability tests.

## DESCRIPTION OF THE WIAT-III

The WIAT-III subtests combine to form eight composites, as shown in Figures 3.1 and 3.2. The *WIAT-III Examiner's Manual* (2009b) does not differentiate composites as part of a core or supplemental battery because examiners are encouraged to utilize the WIAT-III within a flexible, customized approach to assessment. For examiners who prefer to design a comprehensive assessment around a core academic battery, four of the WIAT-III composites are typically used as the core battery (Oral Language, Total Reading, Written Expression, and Mathematics) while the remaining three may be considered supplemental (Basic Reading, Reading Comprehension and Fluency, and Math Fluency).

As a broad measure of overall achievement, the Total Achievement composite is typically used as an indicator of an examinee's level of achievement in all academic areas relative to his or her age- or grade-matched peers. The 13 subtests that correspond to the 8 IDEA areas of achievement (as shown in Table 3.1) also contribute to the Total Achievement composite, although not at every administration grade level. With the exception of the three Math Fluency subtests, every subtest contributes to the Total Achievement composite. Also, notice that the subtest administration grade levels do not always correspond to the composite grade levels. For example, Alphabet Writing Fluency is administered at grades Pre-K through 3 but contributes only to the Written Expression composite for grades K through 2 and contributes only to the Total Achievement composite for grades Pre-K through 1. Rapid Reference 3.2 displays the Total Achievement composite subtests by grade level.

## ≡ *Rapid Reference 3.2*

A total of 13 subtests contribute to the Total Achievement composite, but at any given grade level this composite includes between five and 11 subtests. Three subtests are included in the Total Achievement composite at every grade/age: Listening Comprehension, Oral Expression, and Math Problem Solving. The other 10 subtests are restricted to younger or older examinees due to developmental or curricular limitations.

### Total Achievement Composite by Grade

| Total Achievement Composite Subtest | Grade | Total Achievement Composite Subtest | Grade |
|---|---|---|---|
| Listening Comprehension | PK–adult | Reading Comprehension | 1–adult |
| Oral Expression | PK–adult | Sentence Composition | 1–adult |
| Math Problem Solving | PK–adult | Word Reading           · | 1–adult |
| Numerical Operations | K–adult | Pseudoword Decoding | 1–adult |
| Early Reading Skills | PK–1 | Oral Reading Fluency | 2–adult |
| Alphabet Writing Fluency | PK–1 | Essay Composition | 3–adult |
| Spelling | K–2 | | |

## DON'T FORGET

The biggest difference between the WIAT-III and KTEA-3 overall achievement composites is that the WIAT-III Total Achievement composite includes oral language subtests, whereas the KTEA-3 Academic Skills Battery composite does not. The correlation between the WIAT-III Total Achievement composite and the KTEA-3 Academic Skills Battery composite range is .95 (Pearson, 2014b). The number of subtests and approximate administration times for each overall composite is included in the table below.

### Comparing Overall Achievement Composites

| WIAT-III TA Composite | KTEA-3 ASB Composite |
|---|---|
| 5–11 subtests | 3–6 subtests |
| Includes oral language, reading, math, and writing subtests | Includes reading, math, and writing subtests |
| 30 min to 1.5 hrs | 15 min to 1.5 hrs |

# DON'T FORGET

## When to Use the Reading Comprehension and Fluency Composite

Most of the WIAT-III composites refer to one primary achievement area. However, the Reading Comprehension and Fluency composite is different in that it combines two reading domains into one composite score. This composite score indicates how well an examinee reads with fluency and comprehension. For some examinees, comprehension and fluency performance are positively related. The Reading Comprehension and Fluency composite is most useful for estimating these reading skills when an examinee performs similarly across the Reading Comprehension and Oral Reading Fluency subtests.

### Subtests With Component Scores

Four of the WIAT-III subtests are made up of two or three subtest components, as shown in Table 3.2. These subtests include Listening Comprehension, Oral Expression, Sentence Composition, and Essay Composition. In addition to the overall subtest standard score, standard scores are provided for each component of the subtest. Subtest component standard scores allow practitioners to evaluate strengths and weaknesses within each of these subtests.

### Mapping WIAT-III to Common Core State Standards

The WIAT-III was not designed as a measure of Common Core State Standards (CCSS; National Governors Association Center for Best Practices & Council of Chief State School Officers, 2010). Rather, the WIAT-III is intended for use in all 50 states, regardless of whether a state has adopted or rejected CCSS.

For practitioners interested in mapping the WIAT-III to CCSS, the tables in Rapid Reference 3.3 show that the WIAT-III measures many of the skills identified by the CCSS as important for meeting grade level expectations. The WIAT-III was primarily

**Table 3.2 WIAT-III Subtests With Component Scores**

| Subtest | Subtest Component |
|---------|-------------------|
| Listening Comprehension | Receptive Vocabulary |
|  | Oral Discourse Comprehension |
| Oral Expression | Expressive Vocabulary |
|  | Oral Word Fluency |
|  | Sentence Repetition |
| Sentence Composition | Sentence Combining |
|  | Sentence Building |
| Essay Composition | Theme Development and Text Organization |
|  | Word Count |

designed to measure skills that are clinically sensitive, some of which may also correspond to CCSS. Certain CCSS are not measured by the WIAT-III because the standards are not relevant to the purpose and intended use of the WIAT-III, or the skill would be difficult to measure with a norm-referenced clinical assessment.

## ≡ Rapid Reference 3.3

### WIAT-III and the Common Core State Standards

**WIAT-III Content Map to English Language Arts CCSS**

| Subtest | Grade | | | | | | | | | | |
|---|---|---|---|---|---|---|---|---|---|---|---|
| CCSS Domain | K | 1 | 2 | 3 | 4 | 5 | 6 | 7 | 8 | 9–10 | 11–12 |
| **Listening Comprehension** | | | | | | | | | | | |
| Comprehension and Collaboration | • | • | • | • | • | • | • | — | — | — | — |
| Vocabulary Acquisition and Use | • | • | • | • | • | • | • | • | • | • | • |
| **Early Reading Skills** | | | | | | | | | | | |
| Phonological Awareness | • | • | | | | | | | | | |
| Print Concepts | • | — | | | | | | | | | |
| **Reading Comprehension** | | | | | | | | | | | |
| Craft and Structure | — | • | • | • | • | • | • | • | • | — | — |
| Key Ideas and Details | • | • | • | • | • | • | • | • | — | — | — |
| Phonics and Word Recognition | • | • | • | • | • | • | | | | | |
| Vocabulary Acquisition and Use | • | • | • | • | • | • | • | • | • | — | — |
| **Alphabet Writing Fluency** | | | | | | | | | | | |
| Print Concepts | • | • | | | | | | | | | |
| **Sentence Composition** | | | | | | | | | | | |
| Conventions of Standard English | • | • | • | • | • | • | • | • | — | — | — |
| Print Concepts | • | • | | | | | | | | | |
| **Word Reading** | | | | | | | | | | | |
| Print Concepts | • | — | | | | | | | | | |
| Phonics and Word Recognition | • | • | • | • | • | • | | | | | |
| **Essay Composition** | | | | | | | | | | | |
| Conventions of Standard English | • | • | • | • | • | • | • | • | • | • | • |
| Print Concepts | • | • | | | | | | | | | |
| Production and Distribution of Writing | — | — | — | • | • | • | — | — | — | — | — |
| Text Types and Purposes | — | • | • | • | • | • | • | • | • | — | — |

(continued)

(Continued)

| Subtest | Grade | | | | | | | | | | |
|---|---|---|---|---|---|---|---|---|---|---|---|
| CCSS Domain | K | 1 | 2 | 3 | 4 | 5 | 6 | 7 | 8 | 9–10 | 11–12 |
| **Pseudoword Decoding** | | | | | | | | | | | |
| Phonics and Word Recognition | • | • | • | • | • | • | | | | | |
| **Oral Expression** | | | | | | | | | | | |
| Conventions of Standard English | • | • | • | • | • | • | • | • | • | — | — |
| Presentation of Knowledge and Ideas | • | • | • | • | — | — | — | — | — | — | — |
| Vocabulary Acquisition and Use | • | • | • | • | • | • | • | • | • | • | • |
| **Oral Reading Fluency** | | | | | | | | | | | |
| Fluency | • | • | • | • | • | • | | | | | |
| Key Ideas and Details | • | • | • | • | • | • | — | — | — | — | — |
| Phonics and Word Recognition | • | • | • | • | • | • | | | | | |
| Vocabulary Acquisition and Use | • | • | • | • | • | • | • | • | • | — | — |
| **Spelling** | | | | | | | | | | | |
| Conventions of Standard English | • | • | • | • | • | • | • | • | • | • | • |

Note: If a cell is shaded, no Common Core State Standard is available for that domain at that grade level.

## WIAT-III Content Map to Mathematics CCSS

| Subtest | Grade | | | | | | | | | |
|---|---|---|---|---|---|---|---|---|---|---|
| CCSS Domain | K | 1 | 2 | 3 | 4 | 5 | 6 | 7 | 8 | High School |
| **Numerical Operations** | | | | | | | | | | |
| Building Functions | | | | | | | | | | • |
| Counting and Cardinality | • | | | | | | | | | |
| Expressions and Equations | | | | | | | • | • | • | |
| Interpreting Functions | | | | | | | | | | • |
| Measurement and Data | • | — | — | • | • | — | | | | |
| Number and Operations in Base Ten | — | • | • | • | • | • | | | | |
| Number and Operations—Fractions | | | | — | • | • | | | | |
| The Number System | | | | | | | • | • | • | |
| Operations and Algebraic Thinking | • | • | • | • | — | • | | | | |

(continued)

(*Continued*)

| Subtest | Grade | | | | | | | | | |
|---|---|---|---|---|---|---|---|---|---|---|
| CCSS Domain | K | 1 | 2 | 3 | 4 | 5 | 6 | 7 | 8 | High School |
| The Real Number System | | | | | | | | | | • |
| Reasoning with Equations & Inequalities | | | | | | | | | | • |
| Seeing Structure in Expressions | | | | | | | | | | • |
| Similarity, Right Triangles, & Trigonometry | | | | | | | | | | • |
| **Math Problem Solving** | | | | | | | | | | |
| Conditional Probability & the Rules of Probability | | | | | | | | | | • |
| Congruence | | | | | | | | | | • |
| Counting and Cardinality | • | | | | | | | | | |
| Expressions and Equations | | | | | | | • | • | • | |
| Geometry | • | • | • | • | — | • | • | • | • | |
| Measurement and Data | • | • | • | • | • | — | | | | |
| Number and Operations in Base Ten | — | • | • | • | • | • | | | | |
| Number and Operations—Fractions | | | | • | • | • | | | | |
| The Number System | | | | | | | • | • | • | |
| Operations and Algebraic Thinking | • | • | • | • | • | • | | | | |
| Ratios and Proportional Relationships | | | | | | | • | — | | |
| Statistics & Probability | | | | | | | • | • | — | |
| **Math Fluency** | | | | | | | | | | |
| Number and Operations in Base Ten | — | • | • | • | • | — | | | | |
| Operations and Algebraic Thinking | • | • | • | • | — | — | | | | |

Note: If a cell is shaded, no Common Core State Standard is available for that domain at that grade level.

## STANDARDIZATION AND PSYCHOMETRIC PROPERTIES OF THE WIAT-III

This section of the chapter describes the standardization sample and provides reliability and validity information for the WIAT-III.

## Standardization

The WIAT-III was standardized with a grade-based sample of 2,775 examinees in pre-kindergarten through grade 12 and two age-based samples: 1,826 examinees ages 4 through 19 (overlaps with the grade-based sample), and 225 examinees ages 20 through 50. For each grade level, the sample size ranged from 150-200 examinees (with half of the examinees tested in the Fall and the other half in the Spring). For each age level, most sample sizes included 128 examinees, except age 4 with a sample size of 100, ages 17–19 with a sample size of 190, and ages 20–25, 26–35, and 36–50, each with a sample of 75.

> **DON'T FORGET**
> ....................................................
> The 2009 WIAT-III *Technical Manual* includes normative data for grades Pre-K–12 and ages 4–19. The 2010 updated *Technical Manual* includes a new Appendix L with norms for ages 20–50.

The standardization sample was stratified to closely match the U.S. population. Thus, on the variables of gender, ethnicity, parental education, geographic region, and special education or gifted placement, the standardization sample closely corresponded to data from the American Community Survey of the U.S. Census Bureau for 2005 and 2008. The 2008 Census data were used for the adult norms, ages 20–50, which published in 2010; all other samples were stratified using the 2005 Census data. Self-education was used instead of parent education for examinees ages 26–50.

To establish a normative sample that is representative of the national school-age population, 4% of the normative sample consisted of examinees who met established criteria for a learning disorder in reading, writing, and/or mathematics; 1.9% of the sample consisted of examinees with expressive language disorder; and 1.8% of the sample included examinees with mild intellectual disability. A maximum of 1% of the sample at each grade level was permitted a diagnosis of attention-deficit/hyperactivity disorder (ADD/ADHD). In addition, 1.8% of the sample included examinees who qualified as academically gifted and talented. Separate norms are provided for fall, winter, and spring for grades Pre-K through 12, enabling the examiner greater precision by measuring an examinee's performance against the normative sample at a specific semester of the school year.

## Reliability

The internal-consistency and test-retest reliability coefficients for the WIAT-III are shown in Table 3.3 for subtests and composites. The average internal-consistency reliability values are in the .90s for the WIAT-III composite scores and for Math Problem Solving, Word Reading, Pseudoword Decoding, Numerical Operations, Oral Reading Fluency, Oral Reading Rate, and Spelling. The average reliability coefficients are predominantly in the .80s and .90s for Listening Comprehension, Early Reading Skills, Reading Comprehension, Sentence Composition, Essay Composition, Essay Composition: Grammar and Mechanics, Oral Expression, and the

**Table 3.3 Average Grade-Based Reliability Coefficients for Subtests and Composites**

| Subtests | Split-Half | | Test-Retest (Corrected R2) |
|---|---|---|---|
| | **Fall** | **Spring** | |
| Listening Comprehension | .84 | .83 | .75 |
| Early Reading Skills | .90 | .87 | .82 |
| Reading Comprehension | .88 | .86 | .90 |
| Math Problem Solving | .92 | .91 | .85 |
| Alphabet Writing Fluency | | | .69 |
| Sentence Composition | .90 | .87 | .79 |
| Word Reading | .97 | .97 | .94 |
| Essay Composition | .87 | .87 | .84 |
| Essay Composition: Grammar and Mechanics | .84 | .84 | .84 |
| Pseudoword Decoding | .96 | .96 | .94 |
| Numerical Operations | .93 | .92 | .89 |
| Oral Expression | .87 | .87 | .89 |
| Oral Reading Fluency | | | .94 |
| Oral Reading Accuracy | | | .83 |
| Oral Reading Rate | | | .94 |
| Spelling | .95 | .95 | .92 |
| Math Fluency—Addition | | | .86 |
| Math Fluency—Subtraction | | | .89 |
| Math Fluency—Multiplication | | | .89 |
| **Subtest Components** | | | |
| Receptive Vocabulary | .70 | .69 | .67 |
| Oral Discourse Comprehension | .83 | .82 | .77 |
| Sentence Building | .87 | .82 | .74 |
| Sentence Combining | .81 | .80 | .76 |
| Expressive Vocabulary | .71 | .72 | .82 |
| Sentence Repetition | .85 | .83 | .83 |
| Oral Word Fluency | .73 | .73 | .73 |
| Theme Development and Text Organization | .79 | .79 | .79 |
| Word Count | .80 | .80 | .80 |
| **Composites** | | | |
| Oral Language | .91 | .91 | .87 |
| Total Reading | .98 | .97 | .96 |
| Basic Reading | .98 | .98 | .95 |
| Reading Comprehension and Fluency | .93 | .93 | .94 |
| Written Expression | .95 | .94 | .91 |
| Mathematics | .96 | .95 | .93 |
| Math Fluency | .95 | .95 | .93 |
| Total Achievement | .98 | .98 | .96 |

*Note:* Subtest and composite reliability data are from Tables 3.1, 3.2, and 3.9 of the *WIAT-III Technical Manual* (Pearson, 2010a). Subtest component reliability data are from the *WIAT-III Technical Report #2* (pearsonclinical.com). Mean grade-level values were calculated using Fisher's *z* transformation.

Math Fluency subtests. Generally, reliabilities of .90 or higher support the use of a score for making educational decisions; however, scores with reliabilities between .80 and .90 may also be suitable for educational decision making in some settings or circumstances.

As shown in Table 3.3, the WIAT-III subtest and composite scores possess adequate stability over time. Test-retest stability coefficients were used as the primary reliability estimates for subtests without item-level data (i.e., Essay Composition, Sentence Composition, Alphabet Writing Fluency, and Oral Reading Fluency) and subtests that are speeded (i.e., Alphabet Writing Fluency and Math Fluency subtests). The average corrected stability coefficients range from 0.87 to 0.96 for the composite scores, and most coefficients are in the .80s and .90s for subtest scores. The lowest average stability coefficient (0.69) is for Alphabet Writing Fluency due to the speeded nature of this subtest and the restricted raw score range.

In general, average test-retest gains are more pronounced for the Oral Language subtests (4–7 points) and the Reading Comprehension subtests (4 points) and are less pronounced for the Written Expression subtests (3–7 points) than for the other subtests. For the Written Expression subtests, the diminished performance of the second testing may be explained by the relatively greater amount of time and/or effort involved in completing these subtests, which may lead to reduced motivation with subsequent testing sessions that follow closely in time.

## Validity

The validity of the WIAT-III was demonstrated via multiple methods. First, intercorrelations between the subtests and composites were calculated to test for expected relationships and discriminant evidence of validity. Correlations with other instruments were also conducted to evaluate the construct validity of the test. Finally, special population studies were conducted to show the efficacy of applying the WIAT-III to the assessment of examinees with learning disabilities, language disorder, mild intellectual disability, and academic giftedness. The results of these special studies are detailed in the Clinical Applications chapter in this book.

The subtest intercorrelations confirm expected relations between the subtests within composites. The subtests that comprise each composite are generally moderately correlated with one another. Correlations among the composites range from 0.45 to 0.93, with stronger correlations among the Reading composites and weaker correlations between the Math Fluency composite and other composites. The intercorrelations also provide discriminant evidence of validity. For example, the Mathematics subtests correlate more highly with each other than with other subtests. Some examples of strong correlations across achievement domains are evident, such as the strong correlation between Word Reading and Spelling, which reflects the interrelatedness of some skills utilized across domains.

Correlations with other instruments were conducted to evaluate construct validity. Correlations with the WIAT-II suggest that the two instruments are measuring similar constructs. The corrected correlations between the composite scores for the two instruments ranged from 0.76 (Oral Language) to 0.93 (Total Achievement), and correlations between the common subtests ranged from 0.62 (Oral Expression) to 0.86 (Spelling). Consistent with expectations, the corrected correlations were high (.80s) for subtests that are highly similar in content and structure to the WIAT-II subtests, but were lower (.40s to .60s) for subtests in which content and structure changed considerably, including Reading Comprehension (0.69), Listening Comprehension (0.64), Oral Expression (0.62), and the Written Expression measures: Sentence Composition (0.56), Essay Composition (0.45), and Essay Composition: Grammar and Mechanics (0.59). A summary of the WIAT-III correlational studies with the WIAT-II and KTEA-3 are provided in Table 3.4. Most correlations between like-named composites were in the .80s and .90s, and correlations between the total achievement scores were in the .90s. Correlations between measures of oral language tend to be lower (.70s) due to greater content variations between measures.

> **DON'T FORGET**
>
> The WIAT-III shows moderate to strong correlations with the WIAT-II in many achievement areas. For this reason, most of the validity evidence reported in previous research related to the WIAT-II is still relevant and should be considered.

When the WIAT-III was published in 2009, correlations were reported with the most recent version of the Wechsler scales at that time (WPPSI-III, WISC-IV, WAIS-IV, and WNV) and with the DAS-II. Since then, the WISC-V was published, and correlations between the WIAT-III and WISC-V were reported in the WISC-V manual. Correlations between the KABC-II and WIAT-III are not available. The correlations between the WIAT-III and the overall cognitive ability scores (full scale IQ [FSIQ] or general conceptual ability) from these measures range from 0.60 to 0.82. Generally, the WIAT-III core composites correlate highest with measures of crystallized ability and fluid reasoning.

**Table 3.4 Correlations of WIAT-III With Other Achievement Test Composites**

| WIAT-III Composite | WIAT-II | KTEA-3 |
|---|---|---|
| Oral Language | .76 | .73 |
| Total Reading | .89 | .86 |
| Mathematics | .91 | .90 |
| Written Expression | .83 | .91 |
| Total Achievement | .93 | .95 |

*Note:* Data are from Table 3.11 in the *WIAT-III Technical Manual* (Pearson, 2010a) and Table 2.11 of the *KTEA-3 Technical & Interpretive Manual* (Kaufman & Kaufman, 2014a). Sample sizes were $N = 73$ for the KTEA-3 study and $N = 140$ for the WIAT-II study.

**Table 3.5 WIAT-III Composites Correlations With DAS-II and WISC-V Global Scales**

| WIAT-III Composite | DAS-II GCA | DAS-II SNC | WISC-V FSIQ | WISC-V NVI |
|---|---|---|---|---|
| Oral Language | .61 | .47 | .74 | .53 |
| Total Reading | .65 | .60 | .70 | .46 |
| Written Expression | .51 | .54 | .68 | .53 |
| Mathematics | .71 | .76 | .71 | .59 |
| Total | .67 | .64 | .81 | .61 |

*Note:* GCA = General Conceptual Ability; SNC = Special Nonverbal Composite; FSIQ = Full Scale Intelligence Quotient; NVI = Nonverbal Index. Data for the DAS-II GCA are from Table J.1 of the *WIAT-III Technical Manual* (Pearson, 2010a). Data for the WISC-V are adapted from Table 5.13 of the *WISC-V Technical and Interpretive Manual* (Wechsler, 2014b). Data for the DAS–II SNC were not published but requested post-publication (Jianjun Zhu, personal communication, May 16, 2011).

Table 3.5 shows correlations between the WIAT-III core composites and the overall cognitive ability and nonverbal index scores from the DAS-II and WISC-V. As expected, GCA and FSIQ scores correlate most strongly with the Total Achievement composite, and the nonverbal indexes from the DAS-II and WISC-V correlate most strongly with the Mathematics and Total Achievement composites. Such correlations provide divergent evidence of validity, suggesting that different constructs are being measured by the WIAT-III than those measured by each cognitive ability test, and indicate varying degrees of overlap in the cognitive skills required.

# DON'T FORGET

......................................................

## WIAT-III Administration Materials

**Provided in Kit**

Stimulus Book

Record Form

Response Booklet

Oral Reading Fluency Booklet

Word Card

Pseudoword Card

Audio files

**Provided by Examiner**

Audio playback device

Audio recorder

Stopwatch

Blank scratch paper

Pencils without erasers

## HOW TO ADMINISTER THE WIAT-III

The WIAT-III can be used to assess only in the area(s) of concern or to comprehensively assess all areas of achievement. Examiners have the flexibility to select which subtests to administer and the order of administration; however, the preferred subtest order is the order of subtests in the record form because this order was used to standardize the test. Subtest selection is often determined by the referral question (or the hypothesis being tested), the educational data available, and local and state regulation require-ments. For example, some school districts and educational agencies require the use of composite scores rather than subtest-level scores when making placement or eligibil-ity decisions. For this reason, an examiner may select to administer the subtests that are necessary to yield a composite score in the area(s) of interest.

As with any standardized test, the WIAT-III should be administered according to its administration instructions. The *Examiner's Manual* reviews the general administration procedures, and the record form lists the specific administration directions. The essential materials required to administer the WIAT-III are provided in the Don't Forget box. Since 2010, the WIAT-III record forms and response booklets have been marked "Enhanced" and packaged together. Information about these enhancements is provided in the Caution box.

# CAUTION
........................................................................................................

## Enhanced Content and Scoring Modifications

It's best to use WIAT-III record forms and response booklets marked "Enhanced" in the upper right hand corner of the front cover. However, you may continue to use the original versions of the record form and response booklet, as long as they are used in combination with each other. For example, do not use a record form marked Enhanced with an original response booklet. Both should be the original version or the Enhanced version.

The Enhanced materials include the following content and scoring modifications, none of which affect the reliability, validity, or integrity of the norms (adapted from Pearson, April 22, 2010):

- Written Expression comma usage (*Examiner's Manual*, p. 128): The scoring rule has been amended to permit a comma after a coordinating conjunction if the coor-dinating conjunction is followed immediately by a word or phrase that is set off by commas. For example: He found the book challenging, but, he enjoyed it. This change did not affect the norms because standardization cases were not penalized for this usage of commas.

- An alternate pronunciation option has been added to Pseudoword Decoding Items 51 and 52.

- Math Problem Solving Item 71: the range of correct responses was increased to include the responses 16.77 and 16.82 minutes, which are defensible as correct answers. This extension of the range of correct answers has no measurable effect on the difficulty of this item or on the norms. Item 71 was already very difficult, with only about 5% of the standardization examinees who attempted it giving the original correct answer (16.65). Fewer than 1% gave a response between 16.66 and 16.82 minutes.

(continued)

(Continued)

- Revisions of Numerical Operations Items 49 and 56: Each of these items depicts a triangle with sides of indicated lengths. However, in the original version of the Response Booklet, the lengths do not represent logically possible conditions. In Item 49, the length of one side is greater than the sum of the lengths of the other two sides; and in Item 56, the lengths are not consistent with a right triangle. Replacement items were developed for these items and tested in a special study.

## Starting and Discontinuing Subtests

The WIAT-III provides four indicators that examiners must use in order to administer subtests correctly. These include start and stop points, as well as reverse and discontinue rules.

### Start and Stop Points

Start points are provided for every subtest on the WIAT-III. Some subtests have one start point for all grades (item 1), and other subtests have multiple start points, depending upon the grade level of the examinee. An examinee who has completed a grade but not yet started the next grade should begin at the level of the completed grade. Generally, if the examiner is relatively certain that the grade-appropriate start point is much too easy or difficult for a particular examinee, then the examinee may begin a subtest at an earlier or later start point. In most cases, do not begin more than one start point up or down from the grade-appropriate start point.

A stop point indicates the completion of an item set; hence, the only subtests containing stop points are those with item sets (i.e., Reading Comprehension and Oral Reading Fluency). Stop points are labeled according to the grade level(s) associated with each item set. If the item set reverse rule is applied and the examinee is administered an item set other than his or her grade-appropriate item set, the examiner administers items up to the stop point for that particular item set—not the stop point for the examinee's grade level.

> ### CAUTION
>
> #### Beginning Earlier Than the Grade-Appropriate Start Point
>
> When testing an examinee who demonstrates significant limitations on grade-level material, an examiner may choose to begin earlier than the grade-appropriate start point. Use caution, however, if the examinee later responds correctly to the grade-appropriate start point item and the next two items (meets basal criteria). In this case, award full credit for items that precede the examinee's grade-appropriate start point—even if the examinee answered one or more items incorrectly. The earlier items must be scored as if the examinee had begun at the grade-appropriate start point.

### Reverse and Discontinue Rules

A reverse rule applies only when administration does not begin with item 1. The purpose of a reverse rule is to ensure that the easiest items administered are not above that examinee's proficiency level. There are two types of reverse rules in the WIAT-III: (1) the standard reverse rule and (2) the item set reverse rule.

The standard reverse rule specifies that if the examinee scores 0 points on any of the first three items given, the examiner administers earlier items in reverse order from the start point until three consecutive items are answered correctly (or until item 1 is administered). Alternatively, if the examinee receives credit for the first three items administered, the reverse rule is not applied, and the examiner awards credit for all preceding, unadministered items.

As shown in the Don't Forget box, the item set reverse rule applies only to the two subtests containing item sets (Reading Comprehension and Oral Reading Fluency). The purpose of an item set reverse rule is to better ensure that the examinee is administered the most appropriate item set for his or her ability level. Item set start points are determined by an examinee grade of enrollment; however, the content within each item set may range from below grade level to slightly above grade level. For this reason, examiners are discouraged from beginning at an item set other than the examinee's grade-appropriate item set. It is preferable to always begin at the grade-appropriate item set and follow the reverse rule to the most appropriate item set. However, if you believe that the examinee would perform poorly at the grade-appropriate item set and that beginning at that item set would discourage the examinee, it is permissible to begin one item set below the grade-appropriate item set.

## DON'T FORGET

### WIAT-III Reverse Rules by Subtest

| No Reverse Rule | Standard Reverse Rule | Item Set Reverse Rule |
|---|---|---|
| Receptive Vocabulary | Oral Discourse Comprehension | Reading Comprehension |
| Early Reading Skills | Math Problem Solving | Oral Reading Fluency |
| Alphabet Writing Fluency | Numerical Operations | |
| Sentence Composition | Spelling | |
| Word Reading | | |
| Essay Composition | | |
| Pseudoword Decoding | | |
| Oral Expression | | |
| Math Fluency | | |

The discontinue rule is applied only to subtests with items of increasing difficulty. To minimize testing time and to help prevent the examinee from becoming frustrated or discouraged, the examiner stops administration of a subtest when the item difficulty exceeds the examinee's skill level. The WIAT-III uses the same discontinue rule across all applicable subtests: Discontinue administration of a subtest if the examinee receives 0 points on five consecutive items. If the examinee never receives 0 points on five consecutive items, continue administration until the last item of the subtest is administered.

## Sample, Teaching, and Practice Items

Sample, teaching, and practice items are intended to communicate the nature of the task by showing how to respond correctly to an item (sample), giving feedback to explain why a response was incorrect (teaching), or presenting an unscored item that gives the examinee an opportunity to practice and receive feedback (practice). Most WIAT-III subtests do not require instructional feedback because they resemble familiar academic tasks. However, five subtests include sample, teaching, or practice items: the Receptive Vocabulary component of Listening Comprehension (teaching item), Early Reading Skills (teaching item), Sentence Composition (sample items), Pseudoword Decoding (practice items), and the Expressive Vocabulary and Sentence Repetition components of Oral Expression (teaching items). Instructions for administering the sample, teaching, and practice items are printed on the record form.

## Recording Responses

Recording demands for the examiner range from minimal to very extensive, depending on the subtest (see Don't Forget box for an overview). Accurately recording responses during administration of WIAT-III subtests is very important—especially if you intend to conduct skills analysis after scoring the subtests is complete. On eight of the 16 subtests, the examinees write their responses, requiring minimal recording on the examiner's part until scoring is conducted. Receptive Vocabulary, Expressive Vocabulary, Early Reading Skills, and Math Problem Solving require simple recording of either a zero for incorrect or a one for correct, or recording a one-word response. Reading Comprehension and Oral Discourse Comprehension require that the gist of the examinee's responses are recorded with as much detail as possible, but the Oral Word Fluency and Sentence Repetition components of Oral Expression and Oral Reading Fluency (ORF) require that an examinee's response (or errors, for Sentence Repetition and ORF) are recorded verbatim. Word Reading and Pseudoword Decoding require careful listening in order to correctly record the examinee's responses. Mispronunciations on these two subtests should be recorded using the phoneme key provided on the record form or by writing the examinee's response phonetically. Recording responses either by the phonetic key or by phonetically spelling the examinee's response takes some practice. Chapter 3 of the *WIAT-III Examiner's Manual* (Pearson, 2009b) describes in more detail how to record responses for use with the skills analysis system.

# DON'T FORGET

## Subtest Recording Demands

| Recording Demands | Subtest | Audio Recording |
|---|---|---|
| Minimal. Examinees write their responses. | Alphabet Writing Fluency<br>Sentence Composition<br>Essay Composition<br>Numerical Operations<br>Spelling<br>Math Fluency subtests (Addition, Subtraction, and Multiplication) | No |
| Score 0 or 1, record a brief response | Receptive Vocabulary (LC subtest)<br>Expressive Vocabulary (OE subtest)<br>Early Reading Skills<br>Math Problem Solving | No |
| Record the gist of the examinee's response, including key details | Reading Comprehension<br>Oral Discourse Comprehension (LC subtest) | Helpful, but not typically needed |
| Verbatim recording of entire response | Oral Word Fluency (OE subtest) | Yes, strongly recommended |
| Verbatim recording of errors or incorrect responses | Letter & Word Recognition<br>Nonsense Word Decoding<br>Sentence Repetition (OE subtest)<br>Oral Reading Fluency | Yes, strongly recommended |

## Timing

Nine of the 16 WIAT-III subtests require timing with a stopwatch. The following subtests/components have strict time limits: Alphabet Writing Fluency, Essay Composition, Oral Word Fluency, Math Fluency—Addition, Subtraction, and Multiplication. In these speeded tasks, the examinee's performance within the specified time is the basis of the score. Word Reading (Speed Score) and Pseudoword Decoding (Speed Score) require timing to determine the item reached at 30 seconds, although the overall subtest score is based on accuracy rather than speed. Oral Reading Fluency requires examiners to record completion time, the time taken by the examinee to read each passage.

## Queries and Prompts

Occasionally, examinees' responses may be missing an essential detail or qualifier to be 100% correct. These responses will most commonly occur during Reading

Comprehension and Oral Discourse Comprehension, and will require you to query the examinee to clarify his or her response. Specific queries are listed in the record form. When querying is done, a notation such as "Q" should be made on the record form.

Prompts are used to encourage examinees or request clarification. For example, an examinee may give multiple responses and it is unclear which response is the final answer. In such instances you should ask the examinee which is the intended response. Unclear written responses are prompted sparingly. During standardization, most examiners did not clarify illegible responses, so written responses were scored based on what could be deciphered. Refer to the Don't Forget box for a summary of the recommended prompts to use in various circumstances.

---

# DON'T FORGET

## Recommended Prompts

| Circumstance | Prompt |
|---|---|
| Reluctant to respond | Just try your best. <br> Do the best you can. |
| Confusing response | What do you mean? <br> Tell me more. |
| Unclear response on Word Reading or Pseudoword Decoding | I did not hear you clearly. <br> [Wait until last item is administered, then give prompt and ask examinee to reread the line of words containing the unclear response.] |
| Unclear written response | I cannot read what this says. <br> [Use sparingly. If much of the examinee's writing is illegible, then decipher as best you can for scoring.] |

---

## SUBTEST-BY-SUBTEST NOTES ON ADMINISTRATION

This section highlights pertinent information for administering each of the WIAT-III subtests and points out common errors in administration. Generally subtests are listed in record form order, although subtests with very similar administration considerations have been grouped together.

### Listening Comprehension

Listening Comprehension has two components: Receptive Vocabulary and Oral Discourse Comprehension. Prior to administering Receptive Vocabulary, you should become familiar with how to pronounce each item correctly by listening to the audio file/CD (track 22) and referring to the pronunciation guide in the Examiners Manual. Administration of Receptive Vocabulary requires use of the stimulus book. The subtest always begins with item 1 and continues until the examinee answers four consecutive items incorrectly.

The stimulus book is used to administer Oral Discourse Comprehension; however, administration of Oral Discourse Comprehension also requires the audio files/CD. The audio files can be played using a smart phone, CD player, MP3 player, computer, or any other device that plays media files. Prior to administering Oral Discourse Comprehension, you should listen to the audio file to adjust the volume of your media player and become familiar with when to push pause and how to change tracks in forward and reverse direction. To improve the reliability of administration and maintain standard procedure, use of the audio file is highly recommended. However, the examinee may be administered without use of the audio file by reading the item passages from the record form. If the audio file is not used, the item passages should be read aloud at a natural, conversational pace with a clear speaking voice. Ensure that the examinee is paying attention prior to starting each passage because passages cannot be repeated.

The reverse rule should not be applied too rigidly on Oral Discourse Comprehension. If the examinee has answered three consecutive items incorrectly and there is one additional item remaining that pertains to a given passage, do not reverse immediately to the preceding passage. Rather, administer the remaining question that pertains to the passage before reversing, and then reverse to the preceding passage.

### Early Reading Skills

For the Early Reading Skills subtest, some items share a stimulus book page, so pay close attention to the record form and the item numbers printed on the stimulus book pages to ensure that you present the correct page for each item. All items must be administered. This subtest does not use a discontinue rule because items are not ordered by difficulty. Rather, items are grouped by the type of skill being measured, and item difficulty varies within and across skills. Recording the examinee's verbatim response is recommended.

> **DON'T FORGET**
>
> **Tips for Administering Oral Discourse Comprehension**
>
> Passages may *not* be repeated, but comprehension questions may be repeated as needed.
>
> Administer all questions that pertain to a given passage before applying the reverse rule.

> **DON'T FORGET**
>
> **Tips for Administering Early Reading Skills**
>
> When reading item prompts to the examinee, if a letter is shown within slash marks (e.g., \a\), say the letter sound, not the letter name.

## Reading Comprehension

The stimulus book contains the passages necessary to administer the Reading Comprehension subtest. Allow the examinee to review each passage while answering questions, and encourage the examinee to look back at the passage if he or she is hesitant to do so. Recording the examinee's verbatim response is recommended for later reference, particularly when the examinee's response is scored less than 2 points.

### DON'T FORGET

#### Applying the Reading Comprehension Item Set Reverse Rule

You may reverse up to 3 item sets if the examinee meets the reverse criterion each time. After three reversals from the grade-appropriate item set, you must administer the full item set. The most appropriate item set is the one closest to the grade-appropriate item set in which the examinee meets the basal criterion.

Applying the item set reverse rule correctly is necessary for properly administering the Reading Comprehension subtest. The item set reverse rule requires the examinee to reverse one start point if the sum of scores on all reversal items is 2, 1, or 0 points. Beginning at the examinee's grade-appropriate start point is preferred because it helps to ensure the most appropriate item set is used. The most appropriate item set is the one closest to the grade-appropriate item set in which the examinee scores 3 or more points on the first passage. If you are certain that the examinee will not be able to read the passage and you believe that starting at the grade-appropriate start point would be detrimental to the examinee's subsequent motivation and performance, you may begin one start point below the grade-appropriate start point.

### CAUTION

#### Testing Academically Gifted or Advanced Readers on Reading Comprehension

Question: I have a first grader, age 7 years 4 months, who took the Grade 1 item set and obtained a raw score of 23 (weighted raw score of 48), which converts to an age-based standard score of 98. Later cognitive testing and classroom observation indicated that this child is gifted with an IQ in the very superior range. Six months later, she was tested again on the Reading Comprehension subtest outside of the limits. The examiner realized that the child could read the sixth-grade passages (Items 38–59) and still receive a raw score of 16 (weighted raw score of 48),

*(continued)*

(*Continued*)

which converts to an age-based score of 98–still using the norms for age 7 years 4 months. How can this be? A 7-year-old student reading at a first grade level is vastly different from a 7-year-old reading at a sixth grade level.

**Answer:** Administering the Grade 6 item set to a first grader is considered "testing the limits" and is not permitted according to standard administration procedures. The Reading Comprehension item sets are vertically scaled (put on the same scale to estimate ability on any item set), but the estimate is going to be less accurate the farther away you get from the grade-appropriate item set. No first graders took the Grade 6 item set in standardization, so using the Grade 6 item set to assess a first grader's reading comprehension ability will not yield as precise an estimate. This subtest estimates reading ability very well at the grade-appropriate item set and it was specifically designed to estimate reading level one to two item sets below the grade-appropriate set for struggling readers.

**Question:** If an examinee obtains full credit on their grade-appropriate item set, can the examinee take the next highest item set?

**Answer:** If the examinee earns full credit, or only nearly full credit, on the grade-appropriate item set and the examiner would like to test the limits, then it would be appropriate to administer one item set higher. Starting at the grade-appropriate item set and moving up or down one item set at a time is preferred. Moving up or down more than one or two item sets is not recommended.

### *Math Problem Solving*

Some Math Problem Solving items share a stimulus book page, so pay close attention to the record form and the item numbers printed on the stimulus book pages to ensure that you present the correct page for each item. The examinee is not permitted to use a calculator; however, for qualitative evaluation purposes, you may indicate those items for which the examinee used paper and pencil to solve the problem by circling "Y" (for "yes") under the "Paper and Pencil Used" column. This information may be used to assist in evaluating errors

## DON'T FORGET

### Reminder to Use Paper and Pencil

If an examinee appears to struggle on one of the later items without attempting to work the problem on paper, you may remind the examinee that using paper and pencil is permitted. Administer the prompt by saying, "You may use this paper and pencil at any time to help work a problem."

on individual items and for summing the percentage of items for which the examinee used paper and pencil.

## DON'T FORGET

### Alphabet Writing Fluency Prompts

If the examinee begins writing the same letter in both upper- and lowercase or in both print and cursive, say, "Write each letter only once."

If the examinee asks for clarification of the directions or does not respond after you start timing, say, "You can write the letters of the alphabet in order, starting with a-b-c, or you can write any letters you know, like the letters in your name."

## DON'T FORGET

### Sentence Composition Prompts

If the examinee's response contains an abbreviation, texting language, or a symbol (e.g., lol, btw, @, &), say, "Please write out the words instead of using symbols or abbreviations."

On Sentence Building, if the examinee's response uses the target word within a title or as the subject or object of the sentence, say, "Please write a new sentence that uses this word in a different way."

### Alphabet Writing Fluency

The Alphabet Writing Fluency subtest has a 30-second time limit in which the examinee is asked to write as many letters of the alphabet as he or she can. This subtest requires the use of a stopwatch or clock with a second hand in order to discontinue after exactly 30 seconds. The examinee can write the letters in upper- or lowercase, in print or in cursive, and in any order. Each letter should be written only once. If the examinee needs encouragement, you may occasionally prompt him or her to keep working until the time limit is reached. Two specific prompts for this subtest are provided in the Don't Forget box. Do not pause the stopwatch when providing additional explanation or encouragement.

### Sentence Composition

Sentence Composition includes two components: Sentence Combining and Sentence Building. It is preferable to administer the components in this order because this is the order in which examinees in the standardization sample were administered the subtest.

Administration of Sentence Combining and Sentence Building each begin with item 1. If the examinee scores 0 points on the first two items of Sentence Combining, discontinue administration and proceed to Sentence Building. Sentence Building follows the same discontinue rule: If the examinee scores 0 points on the first two items, discontinue administration. Otherwise, administer all items.

On Sentence Building, a prompt is administered if the examinee's response uses the target word within a title or as the subject or object of the sentence (e.g., for the target word "as": "*As* is a word"; "I just said *as*"; "As *the World Turns* is a show"). If he or she does not write a new sentence, proceed to the next item. The purpose of this prompt is to discourage examinees from writing sentences that fail to use the target word with meaningful context. Use this prompt only under the conditions specified, and do not give the prompt simply because the examinee used the target word incorrectly. Both prompts may be administered once per item.

Some examinees may get "stuck" and have difficulty thinking of a sentence that uses a particular word. The target words were chosen specifically because they tend to be challenging for examinees with learning disabilities and language disorders. Aside from encouraging examinees to try their best, no additional help should be offered on this subtest.

### Word Reading and Pseudoword Decoding

Recording responses accurately is essential, particularly if you plan to conduct a skills analysis, and use of an audio recorder is highly recommended. Many examinees provide responses at a rapid pace, making it difficult to score and record errors accurately. Always begin administration with item 1 and continue administration until the discontinue rule is met.

To obtain a supplemental Word Reading Speed or Pseudoword Decoding Speed score, record the item completed at 30 seconds. This information is not required to obtain the Word Reading subtest standard score. Simply mark the item reached at 30 seconds and then continue administration until the discontinue rule is reached. If this information was not captured during administration, it helps to have an audio recording of the administration to obtain the item reached at 30 seconds by listening to the recording.

If the examinee skips a word or row, redirect the examinee immediately. If the examinee does not say a word clearly, circle or star the item, and after administration is complete, point to the row containing the item in question and say, "I did not hear you clearly. Please read these words again." Asking the examinee to repeat a row rather than a single item is done to avoid the implication that a particular word was read incorrectly and should be read differently the second time. If the examinee reads a word slowly or in parts, prompt the examinee once per item to "say it all together." For qualitative evaluation purposes, you may record which items took the examinee longer than

## DON'T FORGET

### Tips for Word Reading and Pseudoword Decoding

The most common error made on these subtests is an early discontinue. Do not discontinue administration after the item completed at 30 seconds is recorded. Continue administration until the discontinue rule is met.

Recording responses accurately is essential, particularly if you plan to conduct a skills analysis. Use of an audio recorder is highly recommended.

3 seconds to complete and which items elicited a self-correction from the examinee by recording check marks in the columns provided in the record form.

### Essay Composition

The Essay Composition subtest has a 10-minute time limit in which the examinee is asked to write an essay. This subtest requires the use of a stopwatch or clock with a second hand in order to discontinue after exactly 600 seconds. Prompt the examinee as directed at 5 minutes and 1 minute before the time limit expires to help the examinee pace his or her work and avoid running out of time. If the examinee finishes early, you should stop timing and verify that the examinee has written at least 30 words; if not, prompt the examinee to "try to write a full page." If the examinee finishes early and has written more than 30 words, record the elapsed time and discontinue the subtest.

"Favorite game" is defined very broadly in the manual as any enjoyable, rule-governed activity. Some examinees may not enjoy sports or traditional games. Other examinees may not be permitted to play games due to cultural or religious beliefs. In these cases, you may encourage the examinee to write about a hobby or activity that he or she enjoys, such as arts and crafts, schoolwork, chores, or cooking.

### Numerical Operations

If the examinee needs help reading any of the words printed in the Response Booklet, such as "Simplify," you may read the words aloud to the examinee. In order to apply the discontinue rule for Numerical Operations, you may choose to allow the examinee to complete as many problems as he or she can and then score the responses later, or you may score the examinee's responses during administration and discontinue the subtest after the examinee receives four consecutive scores of 0. If you score during administration, it is important to avoid making an examinee feel uncomfortable or nervous by watching him or her work each problem. Instead, it may be helpful to allow the examinee to work without feeling watched and then review the responses after he or she is finished. However, if the child is comfortable, valuable behavioral observations may be obtained by observing the examinee at work. The examinee is not permitted to use a calculator.

### Oral Expression

Oral Expression includes three components: Expressive Vocabulary, Oral Word Fluency, and Sentence Repetition. It is preferable to administer the components in this order because this is the order in which examinees in the standardization sample were administered the subtest.

The stimulus book is required to administer Expressive Vocabulary, and administration always begins with item 1. Item prompts may be repeated if the examinee requests a repetition or does not respond within a reasonable amount of time. The examinee must provide a one-word response. If more than one word is given, prompt the examinee by saying, "Tell me one word." If the examinee gives a slang term or closely related term (e.g., "cape" for "peninsula"), say, "Tell me another word."

However, do not prompt the examinee after an incorrect response. Certain responses are insufficient to earn credit but warrant a query. These responses and associated queries are printed in the record form.

Oral Word Fluency is a timed subtest that requires the use of a stopwatch or clock with a second hand. Discontinue each item after exactly 60 seconds. Both items must be administered in the order presented in the record form. If an examinee gives up before the time limit is reached, ask him or her to keep trying and repeat the item prompt as needed. Many examinees provide responses at a rapid pace, making it difficult to write all responses accurately. If you use an audio recorder, you can play back the recording after administration is complete to record the responses in the record form.

Administration of Sentence Repetition always begins with item 1. You may choose to administer all 15 items and apply the discontinue rule after administration and scoring are completed, or you may score responses during administration and discontinue administration after four consecutive scores of 0. This subtest requires careful recording of three error types: Additions, Substitutions/Omissions, and Transpositions. Prior to administration, review the recording and scoring directions carefully. Recording errors incorrectly could result in an early discontinue; for this reason, it is a good idea to administer additional items past the discontinue rule if you are unsure about whether you have recorded or scored the responses correctly.

### Oral Reading Fluency

The Oral Reading Fluency subtest is administered by item sets that use grade-based start and stop points. The examinee reads passages aloud from the Oral Reading Fluency booklet and is allowed to review each passage while answering the comprehension question. The comprehension questions are for qualitative evaluation purposes only and do not contribute to the subtest score. However, the comprehension questions are not optional and must be administered according to the directions in the record form. The purpose of the comprehension questions is to structure the subtest in a way that encourages the examinee to read for meaning. After all passages and comprehension questions have been administered for the examinee's item set, complete the Prosody Scale at the end of this subtest for qualitative evaluation purposes.

Prior to administration, review the recording and scoring directions carefully. This subtest requires careful recording of four error types: Supplied Words, Additions, Substitutions/Omissions, and Transpositions. Supplied Words are words that the examiner provides to the examinee after the examinee spends 5 seconds attempting to read a word. Record a "G" (for "given")

### DON'T FORGET

#### Timing Oral Reading Fluency

After reading the instructions and saying, "Start here. Begin," start timing as soon as the examinee begins reading the first word.

# DON'T FORGET

## Redirection on Oral Reading Fluency

If the examinee skips a line of text, redirect the examinee to the appropriate line, but do not stop timing, and do not score as an error. When examinees lose their place, the overall fluency and rate scores will be affected by the time it takes to redirect them. There is no additional standardized process for deducting points based on the number of skipped words or lines. If the examinee skips a word, simply record the omitted word as an error (no redirection is needed).

# DON'T FORGET

## Applying the Oral Reading Fluency Item Set Reverse Rule

You may reverse up to two item sets if the examinee meets the reverse criterion each time. After two reversals from the grade-appropriate item set, you must administer the full item set. Remember, the most appropriate item set is the one closest to the grade-appropriate item set in which the examinee meets the basal criterion.

above each word supplied to the examinee. Recording and scoring Additions, Substitutions/Omissions, and Transpositions follow similar rules as described for Sentence Repetition. You may choose to record errors as the examinee is reading, or you may create an audio recording of the subtest administration and review the recording after administration is complete to record reading errors. Use of an audio recorder is recommended to ensure accurate recording and scoring. A stopwatch is recommended to time how long it takes the examinee to read each passage. Record the elapsed time in seconds.

Applying the item set reverse rule correctly is necessary for properly administering this subtest. This subtest includes an item set reverse rule that requires the examinee to reverse one start point if the reading time on the first passage of the item set exceeds the specified time limit. If so, you may choose to interrupt the examinee's reading to reverse to the preceding item set, or you may allow the examinee to finish reading the passage before reversing. Use your clinical judgment to determine the best way to maintain rapport, sustain the examinee's motivation, and avoid causing the examinee undue frustration. The reverse rule may be applied a maximum of two times from the grade-appropriate item set if the examinee meets the reverse rule criterion each time. After two reversals, the full item set must be administered.

It is recommended that you begin at the examinee's grade-appropriate start point whenever possible because it is important to find the most appropriate item set for the examinee. The most appropriate item set is the one closest to the grade-appropriate item set in which the examinee reads the passage within the given time limit. If you believe that the examinee will not be able to read the passage and that starting at the grade-appropriate start point would be detrimental to the examinee's subsequent motivation and performance, you may begin one start point below the grade-appropriate start point.

## Spelling

Prior to administering the Spelling subtest, you should become familiar with how to pronounce each item correctly by listening to the audio file (track 25) and referring to the pronunciation guide in the *Examiner's Manual*. Read each item prompt at a natural, conversational pace, and pronounce each spelling word according to the pronunciation guide. Do not pronounce the target word slowly or with unusual emphasis, because this may help or hinder the examinee's performance. For words with more than one pronunciation, choose the one you think is most familiar to the examinee. You may provide an alternate pronunciation as needed. Item prompts may be repeated if the examinee requests a repetition or has not responded in an appropriate time frame.

In order to apply the discontinue rule, you must be able to score the examinee's responses during administration. However, it is important to avoid making the examinee feel uncomfortable or nervous by watching him or her spell each word. Instead, it may be helpful to allow the examinee to work on an item without feeling watched and then review the response after he or she is finished.

## Math Fluency—Addition, Subtraction, and Multiplication

The Math Fluency subtests may be administered individually or together. If all three Math Fluency subtests are administered, it is preferable to administer the subtests in the order presented in the record form because this is the order in which examinees in the standardization sample were administered the subtests. As specified in the record form, the full administration instructions must be read before administering Math Fluency—Addition and before each subsequent Math Fluency subtest if there is a delay between subtest administrations. If more than one Math Fluency subtest is administered and there is no delay between subtest administrations, the brief (abbreviated) administration instructions may be read before administering each of the following: Math Fluency—Subtraction and/or Math Fluency—Multiplication.

For each Math Fluency subtest, make sure the examinee completes the problems in the specified order. If this requires redirection, do not stop timing, but immediately redirect the examinee by pointing to the appropriate item and reminding the examinee to solve the problems in that order. If the examinee

> ## DON'T FORGET
> ......................................................
> ### Redirect Examinees on Math Fluency
>
> Items must be completed in the following order: left to right, row by row, down the first page and then from left to right, row by row, down the second page.
>
> If an examinee skips items or works in a different order, redirect him or her as needed to complete items in the specified order but do not stop timing.

solves the problems in a different order than the instructions specify but does not complete all items in the subtest, the validity of the results may be compromised and should be interpreted with caution. Order of administration is important, because item difficulty varies within each subtest, so following a different order may result in exposure to a subset of items before the time limit is reached that differs in difficulty from the subset of items that would have been administered according to the standard order. If the examinee solves the problems in a different order than the instructions specify but completes all items in the subtest before the time limit, the validity of the results should not be affected.

## HOW TO SCORE THE WIAT-III

The WIAT-III yields several types of scores: raw scores, standard scores, grade equivalents, age equivalents, and percentile ranks. Raw scores reflect the number of points earned by the examinee on each subtest. These scores, by themselves, are meaningless because they are not norm-based. Converting raw scores to standard scores, which are norm-based, allows the examinee's performance to be compared to that of others.

The WIAT-III standard scores have a mean of 100 and a SD of 15. The theoretical range of standard scores for the subtests and composites is 40 to 160, although the actual standard score ranges for certain subtests do not span the full theoretical range due to floor or ceiling limitations (refer to the Min & Max WIAT-III Subtest Scores file in the online Digital Resources for actual score ranges by subtest). An important theoretical assumption is that achievement test performance is distributed on a normal curve, with the majority of examinees scoring within +/– 1 SD of the mean. Thus, about two-thirds (68%) of examinees score in the range of 85 to 115. Less than 3% of examinees score above 130 or below 70. Generally, standard scores or percentile ranks should be used when comparing performance on one WIAT-III subtest with another, one composite to another, and when comparing WIAT-III results to performance on another norm-referenced test.

Items are objectively scored as correct (1 point) or incorrect (0 points) for a majority of the WIAT-III subtests: Listening Comprehension, Early Reading Skills, Math Problem Solving, Word Reading, Pseudoword Decoding, Numerical Operations, the Expressive Vocabulary component of Oral Expression, Spelling, and each of the Math Fluency subtests. A set of scoring rules, which employ subjective judgment, must be applied to score the remaining subtests.

### Types of Scores

Considerations for calculating and using each type of score in the WIAT-III are provided in this section. Each of the subtest raw scores is converted to age-based or grade-based derived scores, including standard scores, percentile ranks, age or grade equivalents, normal curve equivalents, and stanines. Growth scale values are also available. An overview of each type of score included in the WIAT-III is provided in Rapid Reference 3.4.

## ≡ *Rapid Reference 3.4*

### Types of Scores in the WIAT-III

| Type of Score | Description |
| --- | --- |
| Raw Score | The raw score is the sum of points awarded for each subtest or subtest component. Raw scores should not be used to compare performance between tests, subtests, or composites. |
| Weighted Raw Score | For Reading Comprehension and Oral Reading Fluency, the raw score is converted to a weighted raw score prior to conversion to a standard score or other derived score. |
| | When examinees of the same age or grade take different item sets, weighted scores are necessary in order to make the scores comparable. Weighted raw scores are not "weighted" in the traditional sense. This term is used to differentiate these vertically scaled scores from traditional raw scores. |
| Standard Score | Age-based and grade-based standard scores are reported for WIAT-III subtests and composites. The standard scores form a normal distribution, ranging from 40 to 160, with a mean of 100 and a standard deviation of 15. As an equal-interval measure, these standard scores can easily be compared across subtests and with other standardized test scores. A standard score is not sensitive to small changes in performance, so GSVs are preferred for measuring growth over time. |
| Percentile Rank | Percentile ranks, ranging from <0.1 to 99.9, indicate the percentage of individuals of the same age or grade who scored at or below the performance of the examinee. Percentiles are not on an equal-interval scale, so they differentiate performance better towards the middle of the distribution and are less precise in describing very high or low performance. Percentile ranks should not be averaged or used to demonstrate growth. Avoid confusing percentile rank with percent correct. |
| Age or Grade Equivalent | Age or grade equivalents indicate the age or grade level for which the examinee's score is typical (i.e., the median score of the age or grade group). Age equivalents are expressed in years and months; for example, an age equivalent of 10:3 refers to 10 years, 3 months. Grade equivalents are expressed in tenths of a grade; for example, a grade equivalent of 1.2 refers to the second month of first grade. |

*(continued)*

(Continued)

| Type of Score | Description |
| --- | --- |
| | For subtests with two or more components, the equivalents of the components are averaged. Averaging age and grade equivalents is prone to error. Instructions are provided in the *Examiner's Manual*, but using Q-global to obtain these scores is highly recommended. |
| | Age and grade equivalents do not reflect local curricula or classroom expectations. These scores are on a rank-order scale and do not increase at equal intervals. For these reasons, age/grade equivalents are not comparable across subtests or tests and are not suitable for making diagnostic, placement, or instructional decisions. **Interpret with caution.** |
| Growth Scale Values (GSVs) | GSVs are sample-independent scores on an equal-interval scale and are used to track an individual's achievement growth over time. The average GSVs of third graders on the WIAT-III is anchored at 500. |

The following scores are commonly used for group reporting but are rarely used for individual assessments.

## Common Group Reporting Scores

| Type of Score | Description |
| --- | --- |
| Normal Curve Equivalent (NCE) | NCEs have a mean of 50, a standard deviation of 21.06, and a range of <1 to >99. NCEs reflect examinees' percentile rankings along a bell curve. Unlike percentile ranks, NCEs are on an equal-interval scale, allowing the scores to be averaged. These scores are typically used for evaluating and comparing the performance of groups of individuals. |
| Stanine | A stanine (standard nine) is a single-digit, normalized score between 1 and 9, with a mean of 5 and a standard deviation of 2. Stanines are not scaled at equal intervals. Stanines are most useful for evaluating group performance. Due to the scale's limited range and unequal scaling, stanines are not sensitive to small differences in scores and offer limited precision for describing the performance of examinees with very high or low scores. |

### *Raw Scores and Weighted Raw Scores*
Subtest raw scores are calculated in a variety of ways.

- For hand scoring, methods for calculating raw scores and weighted raw scores are summarized in Table 3.6.
- Using Q-global or the Scoring Assistant, fewer steps are required for calculating raw scores. For subtests that use weighted raw scores, enter the raw scores only. The raw score entry screen for Q-global is shown in Figure 3.3. Raw scores will be automatically converted into weighted raw scores when calculating derived scores. Methods for calculating raw scores using Q-global are summarized in Table 3.7.
- Using Q-interactive, raw score calculation is automatic for every subtest once items are scored by the examiner. Refer to Chapter 7 for information about Q-interactive.

### *Standard Scores*
To be meaningfully interpreted, the raw scores or weighted raw scores of the WIAT-III must be converted to standard scores. The norms are reported within various age or grade bands, as shown in the Don't Forget box.

# DON'T FORGET
................................................................................................................

Norms are grouped into larger age or grade bands for older examinees and adults for whom academic growth progresses at a slower rate. If grade-based scores are selected, the scores are based upon semester (fall, winter, or spring) norms for grades Pre-K through 12.

If age-based scores are selected, the scores for ages 4 to 13 years are reported in 4-month intervals. The scores for ages 14 to 16 years are reported in 12-month (annual) intervals. The scores for high school examinees aged 17 to 19 years are based upon one 3-year age band norm. The age bands increase up to age 50.

### Age and Grade Norm Bands

| Age | 4–13 | 14–16 | 17–19 | 20–25 | 26–35 | 36–50 |
|---|---|---|---|---|---|---|
| Norm Band | 4 months | 1 year | 3 years | 6 years | 10 years | 15 years |
| Number of Age Norm Groups | 29 | 3 | 1 | 1 | 1 | 1 |

When converting from raw to standard scores, you must first decide whether to use age-based or grade-based norms. For examinees who have graduated high school, only age norms are provided. Selecting age-based or grade-based scores determines the peer group with which the examinee's performance is compared, and the decision is influenced by a number of different factors, such as whether a particular skill develops

## Listening Comprehension

| | | |
|---|---|---|
| Receptive Vocabulary | 0 - 19 | 12 |
| Oral Discourse Comprehension | 0 - 27 | 18 |

## Reading Comprehension

| | | |
|---|---|---|
| Item Set | Grades 9-12+ ▼ | |
| Total Raw Score (Do not enter weighted score) | 0 - 50 | 40 |

## Math Problem Solving

| | | |
|---|---|---|
| Total Raw Score | 0 - 72 | 40 |

## Sentence Composition

**Sentence Combining**

| | | |
|---|---|---|
| A: Semantics and Grammar | 0 - 10 | 8 |
| B: Mechanics | 0 - 10 | 6 |
| C: Extra Credit | 0 - 5 | 3 |
| Raw Score (0 to 25) | | 17 |

**Sentence Building**

| | | |
|---|---|---|
| A: Semantics and Grammar | 0 - 14 | 5 |
| B: Mechanics | 0 - 14 | 7 |
| Raw Score (0 to 28) | | 12 |

## Word Reading

| | | |
|---|---|---|
| Total Raw Score | 0 - 75 | 50 |
| Speed | 0 - 75 | 44 |

## Essay Composition

**Content and Organization**

| | | |
|---|---|---|
| Word Count Raw Score | 0 - 9999 | 57 |
| Introduction | 0 - 2 | 1 |
| Conclusion | 0 - 2 | 1 |
| Paragraphs | 0 - 5 | 3 |
| Transitions | 0 - 5 | 2 |
| Reasons Why | 0 - 3 | 2 |
| Elaborations | 0 - 3 | 0 |
| Theme Development and Text Organization | | |
| Raw Score (0 to 20) | | 9 |

**Grammar and Mechanics**

| | | |
|---|---|---|
| Correct Word Sequences | 0 - 999 | |
| Incorrect Word Sequences | 0 - 999 | |
| Total Raw Score (CIWS) | | |

## Pseudoword Decoding

| | | |
|---|---|---|
| Total Raw Score | 0 - 52 | 34 |
| Speed | 0 - 52 | 41 |

## Numerical Operations

| | | |
|---|---|---|
| Total Raw Score | 0 - 61 | 30 |

## Oral Expression

| | | |
|---|---|---|
| Expressive Vocabulary | 0 - 17 | |
| Oral Word Fluency | 0 - 999 | |
| Sentence Repetition | 0 - 30 | |

## Oral Reading Fluency

| | | |
|---|---|---|
| Item Set | Please select.. ▼ | |

**Passage 1**

| | | |
|---|---|---|
| Completion Time (in seconds) | 1 - 1500 | |
| Addition Errors | 0 - 498 | |
| Other Errors | 0 - 498 | |

**Passage 2**

| | | |
|---|---|---|
| Completion Time (in seconds) | 1 - 1500 | |
| Addition Errors | 0 - 498 | |
| Other Errors | 0 - 498 | |

| |
|---|
| Fluency Total Raw Score |
| Accuracy Total Raw Score |
| Rate Total Raw Score |

## Spelling

| | | |
|---|---|---|
| Total Raw Score | 0 - 63 | 40 |

## Math Fluency - Addition

| | | |
|---|---|---|
| Total Raw Score | 0 - 48 | |

## Math Fluency - Subtraction

| | | |
|---|---|---|
| Total Raw Score | 0 - 48 | |

## Math Fluency - Multiplication

| | | |
|---|---|---|
| Total Raw Score | 0 - 40 | |

**Figure 3.3 WIAT-III Raw Score Entry in Q-global**

Source: Wechsler Individual Achievement Test–Third Edition (WIAT-III). Copyright © 2009 NCS Pearson, Inc. Reproduced with permission. All rights reserved.

**Table 3.6 Hand Scoring Methods for Calculating Raw Scores**

| Subtest | Method |
|---|---|
| **Subtest With Basal/Discontinue Rules** | |
| Early Reading Skills<br>Math Problem Solving<br>Word Reading<br>Pseudoword Decoding<br>Numerical Operations<br>Spelling<br>Expressive Vocabulary (Oral Expression) | Subtract the number of errors from the ceiling item. |
| Listening Comprehension | A total raw score is not calculated for the subtest. Calculate raw scores for Receptive Vocabulary and Oral Discourse Comprehension. For each, subtract the number of errors from the ceiling item. |
| Sentence Composition | A total raw score is not calculated for the subtest. Calculate raw scores for Sentence Combining and Sentence Building.<br><br>To calculate the Sentence Combining raw score, sum the scores for *Semantics & Grammar*, *Mechanics*, and *Extra Credit*. To calculate the Sentence Building raw score, sum the scores for *Semantics & Grammar* and *Mechanics*. |
| Sentence Repetition (Oral Expression) | Score each item 2-1-0 and then sum the scores of all items up to the discontinue point. |
| **Timed/Speeded Subtest** | |
| Word Reading Speed<br>Pseudoword Decoding Speed | The item number completed at 30 seconds is the raw score. |
| Math Fluency (Addition, Subtraction, and Multiplication) | Use the scoring keys provided in Appendix C of the *Examiner's Manual* to score responses. Sum the number of correct responses within the time limit. |
| Alphabet Writing Fluency | Sum the letters written within the time limit that receive credit. |
| Oral Word Fluency (Oral Expression) | Sum correct responses provided within the time limit across both items. |
| Essay Composition | A total raw score is not calculated for the subtest. Calculate raw scores for Word Count and Theme Development and Text Organization (TDTO). The Word Count raw score is the number of words written within the time limit. The TDTO raw score is the sum of scores for each of the six elements of the scoring rubric. |

*(continued)*

**Table 3.6** (*Continued*)

| Subtest | Method |
|---|---|
| **Timed/Speeded Subtest** | |
| | To calculate the supplemental *Grammar and Mechanics* raw score, enter the number of Correct Word Sequences and the number of Incorrect Word Sequences. Subtract the number of Incorrect Word Sequences from the number of Correct Word Sequences. Negative values are possible. |
| **Subtest With Item Sets** | |
| Reading Comprehension Oral Reading Fluency | Sum the number of correct responses for items within the final set administered. Next, convert the raw score to a weighted raw score. |

**Table 3.7 Methods for Calculating Raw Scores Using Q-global**

| Subtest | Method |
|---|---|
| **Subtest With Basal/Discontinue Rules** | |
| Listening Comprehension Early Reading Skills Math Problem Solving Word Reading Pseudoword Decoding Numerical Operations Spelling | Subtract the number of errors from the ceiling item. Enter the raw score. |
| Sentence Composition | Raw scores will be calculated automatically for Sentence Combining and Sentence Building. Enter scores for *Semantics and Grammar*, *Mechanics*, and *Extra Credit* (the latter for Sentence Combining only). |
| Listening Comprehension Oral Expression | Enter raw scores for each component of the subtest. |
| **Speeded Subtest** | |
| Word Reading Speed Pseudoword Decoding Speed Math Fluency (Addition, Subtraction, and Multiplication) | Enter the item number completed at 30 seconds as the raw score. Use the scoring keys provided in Appendix C of the *Examiner's Manual* to score responses. Sum the number of correct responses within the time limit. Enter the raw score. |

(*continued*)

**Table 3.7** (*Continued*)

| Subtest | Method |
|---|---|
| **Speeded Subtest** | |
| Alphabet Writing Fluency | Sum the letters written within the time limit that receive credit. Enter the raw score. |
| Essay Composition | Enter the raw score for Word Count. You may either enter the raw scores for each component of Theme Development and Text Organization, or use the interactive Scoring Guide to score each component and calculate the raw score automatically. |
|  | For the supplemental *Grammar and Mechanics* score, enter the number of Correct Word Sequences and Incorrect Word Sequences. The raw score will be calculated automatically. |
| **Subtest With Item Sets** | |
| Reading Comprehension | Sum the number of correct responses for items within the final set administered. Select the item set administered, then enter the raw score. (Do not convert raw score to a weighted raw score.) |
| Oral Reading Fluency | Sum the number of correct responses for items within the final set administered. For each passage, enter Completion time (in seconds) and the number of Addition errors and Other errors. The raw scores (and weighted raw score) for Fluency, Accuracy, and Rate will be calculated automatically. |

according to age (i.e., developmental skills) or grade (i.e., curriculum-based skills), whether an examinee is outside of the typical age range for his or her grade level, and district/agency/state requirements. For example, some settings may require the use of age-based scores when evaluating for a specific learning disability. Many examiners compute both age-based and grade-based scores in order to compare them.

# DON'T FORGET

## Tips for Navigating the Digital Technical Manual

Use the hypertext (text with hyperlinks). All of the text included in the Quick Links and Table of Contents pages at the front of the manual contain hyperlinks, which means you can click a line of text with your cursor and the document will

(continued)

*(Continued)*

immediately advance to the page that includes the selected content. These hyperlinks are the fastest way to find a specific chapter, section, table, or figure. For example, in the following image, clicking "Table 1.2" will advance the document to page 15.

**Tables**

**Use the Main TOC button.** A button appears in the bottom right corner of every page that reads "MAIN TOC." This is a home button that will move the document back to the Table of Contents at the beginning of the manual. This button is designed to help the reader move through the manual quickly and efficiently.

**Use the search function.** PDF readers include a search function that is enabled by typing Ctrl+F (the Ctrl key and the F key at the same time on a PC or Command+F on a Mac). This box allows you to search for a word or phrase that appears anywhere in the manual. This is the best way to find specific content that may not be called out in the Table of Contents. For example, in the following image, searching "test-retest" and then selecting "Next" or the left or right arrow will show each instance that test-retest is referenced in the manual.

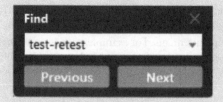

**Select a row of numbers.** When reading data tables on screen, some people find it difficult to visually track across a row of numbers without losing their place.

*(continued)*

*(Continued)*

One helpful tip is to select the row of numbers with your mouse to highlight the data on screen.

**Enlarge the font.** Remember that you can zoom in and out by clicking the plus or minus sign at the top of the navigational menu, making the size of the font bigger or smaller, when viewing the digital manual. You can also enlarge the font (zoom in) by selecting a larger percentage in the size box. Zoom in with keyboard shortcuts on a PC by using the Ctrl+equal sign (for Mac use Command+equal sign) and zoom out using Ctrl+hyphen on a PC or Command+hyphen on a Mac.

**Rotate the page.** Some PDF readers will automatically rotate the page to a portrait or landscape orientation, as needed. However, you can do this manually as well by typing the following three keys at the same time: Shift, Ctrl, +.

**Print.** You have the option to print the pages or tables in the digital manual that you use most frequently.

**Additional Keyboard Shortcuts.** Adobe Acrobat provides additional help on their keyboard shortcuts online at helpx.adobe.com/acrobat/using/keyboard-shortcuts .html.

In most cases, age and grade based standard scores will be similar. However, important differences can occur if the student has been retained or has received an accelerated grade placement, or if the student began school earlier or later in the year than is typical. In these cases, the grade-based norms are probably more relevant. The Don't Forget box provides further information about selecting and reporting age-based and grade-based standard scores.

When achievement scores are compared with scores on ability or language tests, age-based norms are recommended to quantify examinee performance on the achievement measure. However, with the WIAT-III as well as other measures of academic achievement, there are times when age-based scores can be misleading. For example, when an examinee has been retained in a grade, comparing him or her to age-mates assumes that the equivalent instructional opportunity has been provided. In such a case, the individual might have lower scores because some skills have not been taught. For this reason, grade-based scores are typically preferred for examinees who have repeated or skipped grades. Especially when communicating results to teachers and parents, discussing how the examinee is performing academically in relation to others in the same grade is typically easier to interpret.

# CAUTION

## Students Who Are Young or Old for Grade

Grade norms must be used to obtain scores for certain subtests and composites when an examinee's age is out of level. If an examinee is unusually young or old for his or her grade, age norms may not be available for all subtests or composites. For example, age norms are not available for a 7-year-old third grader who is administered the Essay Composition subtest (administered to grades 3–12), because this examinee's age is considered unusually young (out of level) for third grade. However, it is possible to yield age norms for this examinee for subtests such as Listening Comprehension and Oral Expression, because these subtests are administered at every age and grade.

## Descriptive Categories

When the WIAT-III was published in 2009, a 15-point classification system for reporting scores was suggested. When the KTEA-3 published in 2014, a choice between a 10-point and 15-point classification system was offered. Both systems divide the theoretical standard score range of 40 to 160 into seven categories, but one uses 10-point ranges and the other uses 15-point ranges. The same classification systems and descriptive categories suggested for the KTEA-3 may be considered for the WIAT-III. These options are summarized in the Don't Forget box. The same considerations described in the KTEA-3 chapter for choosing between the classification systems are applicable to the WIAT-III as well.

As shown in the Don't Forget box, the qualitative descriptors suggested for the WIAT-III at the time of its publication include the terms *superior* and *very superior*, which are now considered to be value-laden terms that are best avoided. Using neutral terms that simply describe the score's distance from the mean (such as *low, average, high*) are currently preferred for all clinical assessment instruments.

Your decision to use the 15-point or the 10-point classification system and the qualitative descriptors you choose may be influenced by the examinee's score profile, the other tests you've administered, personal preference, and reporting requirements you've been given by outside agencies, among other things. When reporting similar standard scores across different instruments, consider using the classification system suggested by the cognitive measure. When reporting results from the WIAT-III and the WISC-V, for example, it would be reasonable to use the 10-point scale described in the WISC-V manual (shown in the Don't Forget box) to describe standard scores across both tests.

# DON'T FORGET

## Options for Descriptive Category Systems

### 10-Point System

| Range of Standard Scores | KTEA-3 Suggested Name of Category | WISC-V Suggested Name of Category |
| --- | --- | --- |
| 130–160 | Very High | Extremely High |
| 120–129 | High | Very High |
| 110–119 | Above Average | High Average |
| 90–109 | Average | Average |
| 80–89 | Below Average | Low Average |
| 70–79 | Low | Very Low |
| 40–69 | Very Low | Extremely Low |

### 15-Point System

| Range of Standard Scores | New Suggested Name of Category | Previously Suggested Name of Category |
| --- | --- | --- |
| 146–160 | Very High | Very Superior |
| 131–145 | High | Superior |
| 116–130 | Above Average | Above Average |
| 85–115 | Average Range | Average |
| 70–84 | Below Average | Below Average |
| 55–69 | Low | Low |
| 40–54 | Very Low | Very Low |

# DON'T FORGET

## Qualitative Descriptors Are Suggestions

Qualitative descriptors are only suggestions and are not evidence-based. You may use alternate terms as appropriate.

## Growth Scale Values

Growth Scale Values (GSVs) are designed for measuring change and are based on the Item Response Theory (IRT) ability scale. In the same way that "inches" are an equal-interval scale of length, the GSV scale is an equal-interval scale of academic skill. Thus, GSVs can be used as a "yardstick" by which academic progress can be measured throughout the school years. GSVs reflect absolute performance rather than performance relative to a normative sample, although the examinee's rate of progress may be compared to the typical growth rate in the normative sample using the GSV Charts report in Q-global.

The degree to which GSVs are able to measure academic learning is limited to the content and skill coverage of the test or subtest. The WIAT-III is not designed to measure all aspects of a student's curriculum or provide in-depth coverage of all skill categories. Consider curriculum-based or criterion-referenced measures for more comprehensive content and skill coverage.

# DON'T FORGET

## Using Growth Scale Values

- GSVs are sensitive to small changes in performance across time.
- Comparing, subtracting, and averaging GSVs from the same subtest is encouraged but *not* across different subtests.
- Three or more months between testing sessions is recommended to avoid practice effects.
- Three or more GSV scores are recommended to form a reliable growth trend.

### Interpreting GSVs and Standard Scores

| GSV Change | Standard Score Change | Interpretation |
|---|---|---|
| Increase | Increase | The increase in the GSVs suggests that the student's achievement skills have improved. The increase in standard scores across testing sessions suggests that the student's achievement skills improved at a faster rate than his or her peers'. |
| Increase | No Change | The increase in the GSVs suggests that the student's achievement skills have improved. The consistency of standard scores across testing sessions suggests that the student's achievement skills improved at the same rate relative to his or her peers'. |

*(continued)*

(Continued)

| GSV Change | Standard Score Change | Interpretation |
|---|---|---|
| Increase | Decrease | The increase in the GSVs suggests that the student's achievement skills have improved. The decrease in standard scores indicates that the student's peers improved even more during the same time period. In other words, the student improved but at a slower rate than his or her peers. |
| No Change | Decrease | The consistency of GSVs across testing sessions indicates that the student has not shown growth or decline in the achievement area. The decrease in standard scores suggests that during the same time period, his or her peers' skills improved. |

Note: This table includes the most likely combination patterns of change for GSVs and standard scores. Less likely combinations (e.g., GSV scores decrease, standard scores increase) are intentionally omitted.

## Score Reports

Three score reports are available: the standard score report, the parent report, and the GSV Charts report. A summary of the score report options for each report type is included in Rapid Reference 3.5. With the exception of GSV charts, the standard score report includes all of the reporting capabilities discussed in this section. The parent score report is a simplified report that provides subtest descriptions and summarizes subtest and composite performance. The parent report is intended to facilitate a discussion of assessment results between examiners and parents/guardians. The GSV Charts report only includes GSV charts and tables. The only way to access the GSV Charts report option is to select two or more WIAT-III assessments for an examinee and then select Generate Report.

Q-global (as well as the original Scoring Assistant) performs all of the basic scoring conversions and calculations and provides tables and graphs of the examinee's performance. Raw scores are converted into various derived scores (e.g., standard scores, percentiles) for subtest scores, supplemental subtest scores, and composite scores. There is no need to look up weighted raw scores when using Q-global. Always enter raw scores for Reading Comprehension and Oral Reading Fluency. The raw scores will be automatically converted into the weighted raw scores before calculating the derived scores.

## ≣ Rapid Reference 3.5

### WIAT-III Report Options and Report Types

| Report Feature | Description | Score Report | Parent Report | GSV Charts |
|---|---|---|---|---|
| **Tables and Graphs** | | | | |
| Subtest Score Summary | Includes all subtests administered and the corresponding raw scores, standard scores, confidence intervals, percentile ranks, NCEs, stanines, age and grade equivalents, and, if selected, growth scores (GSVs). | X | | |
| Subtest Standard Score Profile | Plots standard scores and confidence intervals for all subtests administered, organized by achievement area. | X | | |
| Supplemental Subtest Score Summary | Provides the same types of scores as the "Subtest Score Summary" for Oral Reading Accuracy and Oral Reading Rate. | X | | |
| Cumulative Percentages | Provides the cumulative percentages (base rates) and interpretive statements (statements that describe the examinee's performance) for Word Reading Speed and Pseudoword Decoding Speed. | X | | |
| Subtest Component Score Summary | Provides raw scores, standard scores, percentile ranks, NCEs, stanines, and qualitative descriptions of performance for subtest components. | X | | |
| Composite Score Summary | Provides sums of standard scores, confidence intervals, percentile ranks, NCEs, stanines, and qualitative descriptions for each of the composites. | X | | |
| Composite Score Profile | Plots standard scores and confidence intervals for all available composites. | X | | |

(continued)

(Continued)

| Report Feature | Description | Score Report | Parent Report | GSV Charts |
|---|---|---|---|---|
| Composite Standard Score Differences | Lists composite comparisons, standard score differences, critical values, whether the differences are significant, and the base rates. | X | | |
| Pattern of Strengths and Weaknesses Model | Provides a table with the score comparisons, standard scores, standard score differences, critical values, whether the differences are significant, and whether the result supports the hypothesis of SLD. A graph shows the comparisons, and indicates whether each comparison was discrepant. | X | | |
| Skills Analysis | Summarizes the total number of errors by skill, the maximum possible number of errors per skill, and the percent correct by skill and broad feature, if applicable. | X | | |
| Goal Statements | Provides annual goals and short-term objectives for each subtest by skill area, and the items answered incorrectly for each skill. | X | | |
| Subtest Descriptions | Includes a brief description of each subtest administered. | | X | |
| Graph of Performance by Composite | Displays the examinee's performance on each composite beneath a bell curve delineated by qualitative descriptions. | | X | |
| Graph of Performance by Subtest | Displays the examinee's performance on each subtest beneath a bell curve delineated by qualitative descriptions. | | X | |
| GSV Charts | Charts GSV score across two or more administrations. Compares rate of progress to average rate of peers. | | | X |

(continued)

(Continued)

| Report Feature | Description | Score Report | Parent Report | GSV Charts |
|---|---|---|---|---|
| **Score Options** | | | | |
| Include Growth Scores | Indicates whether to include growth scores (GSVs) in the "Subtest Score Summary" and the "Supplemental Subtest Score Summary" tables. | X | | |
| Age-Based or Grade-Based Norms | Indicates whether to report age-based or grade-based derived scores. For GSV Charts, this option determines whether progress is shown by age or grade. GSV scores are the same whether age or grade is selected. | X | X | X |
| **Significance Levels** | | | | |
| Confidence Intervals (95% or 90%) | Indicates whether to report 95% or 90% standard score confidence intervals. | X | | |
| Composite Level Differences (0.01 or 0.05) | Indicates whether to use critical values at the 0.01 or 0.05 significance level when comparing composite standard scores. | X | | |
| Pattern of Strengths and Weaknesses Discrepancy (0.01 or 0.05) | Indicates whether to use critical values at the 0.01 or 0.05 significance level in the "Pattern of Strengths and Weaknesses Model." | X | | |

The WIAT-III Scoring Assistant can be used alone or in combination with other ability tests that use the same software platform, such as the DAS-II and WAIS-IV. Provision is made for comparing ability and achievement and conducting ability-achievement discrepancy (AAD) analyses so that results from both the WIAT-III and an ability test can be included in a single report.

## SUBTEST-BY-SUBTEST SCORING KEYS

This section highlights pertinent information for scoring each of the WIAT-III subtests and points out common errors in scoring. Generally subtests are listed in record form order, although subtests with very similar administration considerations are grouped together.

## Listening Comprehension

Scoring the Receptive Vocabulary component of Listening Comprehension is straightforward and requires very little judgment. Only the responses listed in the record form may be scored as correct.

For scoring Oral Discourse Comprehension, if the examinee paraphrases a correct response by conveying the same meaning using different words, score the response as correct. Disregard item scores after the discontinue point of four consecutive scores of 0. For example, after the examine scored two consecutive scores of 0 on a passage, the examiner administered one additional item for that passage before reversing to an earlier passage then discontinuing after all items for the earlier passage were scored 0. The additional item that was administered would not be included in the subtest raw score because the item is after the discontinue point of four consecutive scores of 0.

> ## CAUTION
> ·············································
>
> ### Scoring Receptive Vocabulary Item 19
>
> Item 19 (ponderous) bears no relationship to the verb *to ponder*, although one of the distractors suggests this as a possibility. Many examiners have mistakenly believed that the scoring key for this item is incorrect.

## Early Reading Skills

Correct responses are included in the record form and specify the expected mode of response: (O) for oral, (P) for pointing, and (P or O) when either a pointing response or an oral response is acceptable. Encourage the examinee to respond in the expected manner. For example, if the student responds orally when the response indicates that he or she should point, encourage the student to point to the answer.

## Reading Comprehension

Sample 2-point and 1-point responses are included in the record form. These sample responses were collected from a national sample of examinees. The 2-point answers listed include only high-quality responses that capture the most salient and pertinent features of the text. The Don't Forget box offers additional explanation for certain items that may be challenging to score.

> ## CAUTION
> ·············································
>
> ### Scoring Reading Comprehension Items
>
> The following items tend to raise questions for examiners about how the scoring rules were determined. Additional explanation is provided here.
>
> Item 73 requires the examinee to explain what caused whales to begin to make a recovery, and two specific answers are necessary to obtain full credit. Only two of the
>
> *(continued)*

*(Continued)*

three 1-point responses are acceptable in the 2-point response. A 1-point response is "Placed on endangered species list," which requires a query by the examiner of "Tell me more." However, "Placed on endangered species list" does not qualify as one of the necessary 2-point responses. This response is queried to encourage the examinee to elaborate and possibly provide a 2-point response.

Item 76: Identify the three consequences that would result if zoo prices are not raised. The answers that receive credit (i.e., zoo closes, animals sold off, children lose learning experiences, families lose entertainment) are the most salient consequences listed in the passage, because the passage clearly states that the zoo would close if zoo prices are not raised, and these are the consequences of the zoo closing. There are alternative responses that could be derived from the passage, such as the employees not receiving raises or the facilities not being kept up; however, these are not the most salient consequences because none of these would be relevant if the zoo were no longer open.

---

# CAUTION

····································

## Reporting Reading Comprehension Scores From Out-of-Level Item Sets

When reporting scores for an examinee who reversed to a preceding item set, explain the ways in which the WIAT-III Reading Comprehension score differs from scores on many other reading achievement tests. You may wish to include this information in the description of the subtest in the report and in the presentation and discussion of the test results. Otherwise, persons reading the report are likely to assume that the score reflects reading comprehension of grade-level passages. When interpreting the subtest standard score, emphasize that the examinee's performance on an out-of-level item set is still compared with same-age or same-grade peers.

Understanding the design of this subtest and the purpose of the item set reverse rule is essential for correctly interpreting the subtest results when an examinee reverses to a preceding item set (see Caution box). Interpreting the results can be challenging when, for example, a examinee reverses to a preceding item set and receives a standard score in the average—or even above average—range. Initially, it may seem inaccurate that an examinee who was unsuccessful in completing his or her grade-appropriate item set could receive such a strong score; however, examinees with comprehension weaknesses that are primarily due to word recognition weaknesses may demonstrate intact comprehension skills at their reading level. For these examinees, comprehension is not a primary area of weakness.

Many standardized achievement tests or curriculum-based measures assess only reading comprehension of grade-level passages. These tests assess basic reading skills as well as comprehension skills. As a diagnostic achievement test, the WIAT-III is designed to home in on skill strengths and weaknesses. When an examinee performs poorly on reading comprehension items with grade-level passages, it must be determined whether the examinee has a weakness in word identification skills, reading vocabulary, reading comprehension skills, or some combination of these. By reversing to an item set, examinees have the opportunity to demonstrate reading comprehension skills on passages at a lower readability level, placing fewer demands on word identification and vocabulary skills. If the examinee performs poorly on the preceding (lower) item set, then it is likely that the examinee has a weakness in the area of reading comprehension, and further assessment, error analysis, and intervention in this area should be pursued. On the other hand, if the examinee performs well on the preceding item set, the examiner may rule out reading comprehension as the area of weakness. It is important for the examiner to complete an error analysis to identify how word identification and vocabulary difficulties may have affected the examinee's ability to comprehend written material at the grade-appropriate start point. The examinee's performance on the Word Reading and the Listening Comprehension (Receptive Vocabulary) subtests should be evaluated in conjunction with the error analysis results to determine if intervention should include work in one or both of these areas.

# DON'T FORGET

## Constructs Measured by the WIAT-III Reading Comprehension Subtest

### For Readers Who Complete the Grade-Appropriate Item Set

For examinees who do not need to reverse to a preceding item set, this subtest measures reading comprehension of passages that are generally appropriate for the examinee's grade level. It is important to keep in mind that the passages within an item set generally cover a range of reading difficulty, from slightly below to slightly above grade level; as a result, all passages in the first-grade item set, for example, may not be precisely at a first-grade reading level.

### For Struggling Readers Who Reverse to a Preceding Item Set

The item set reverse rule allows reading comprehension of *below*-grade-level material relative to be compared with the performance of *same-age* or *same-grade* peers. Each passage (and item set) is composed of questions designed to measure a variety of comprehension skills. Each item set includes several types of factual and inferential questions, which simulate comprehension questions that teachers ask to test students' understanding of reading materials. As a result, the types of questions included in each item set do not uniformly increase in difficulty, nor do comprehension questions

*(continued)*

*(Continued)*

measure increasingly complex skills from one item set to the next. A sampling of the same literal and inferential comprehension skills are distributed within and across item sets. This design enables an examinee to demonstrate reading comprehension skills on passages at a lower readability level and controls for potentially confounding weaknesses in word identification and vocabulary knowledge. Consequently, the Reading Comprehension subtest becomes a "purer" measure of reading comprehension for struggling readers.

# CAUTION

## Scoring Math Problem Solving Item 13

Item 13 asks the examinee to count aloud and tell how many chips there are in total. The child may count the chips incorrectly but provide the correct total. The item should be scored correctly in this case, but the examiner should discuss this behavioral observation when reporting the results. Items like this one are designed to yield valuable qualitative information about how the child arrived at the answer.

## Math Problem Solving

If the examinee provides an answer that is equivalent to the correct answer listed in the record form, award credit for the response. If the examinee provides a response in a different response modality (i.e., oral or pointing) than the one listed beside the correct answer in the record form, query the examinee to tell you their answer or point to their answer as appropriate.

### Alphabet Writing Fluency

The raw score for Alphabet Writing Fluency is the number of letters written within the time limit that meets the scoring criteria listed in Appendix B.1 of the *Examiner's Manual*. Helpful scoring examples are provided in Appendix B.1 as well as in the WIAT-III Scoring Workbook. Score responses after administration is complete. Use the score box provided in the record form to record which letters received credit, whether the letters were upper- or lowercase, and the types of errors made.

Alphabet Writing Fluency is not a handwriting test, so scoring is lenient when it comes to letter formation. Letters are typically easier to recognize in the context of a word. When written in isolation, letters may resemble each other (e.g., h and n). When trying to decipher the examinee's handwriting, use the following tips:

**Use Context Cues** Use the letter's position or order relative to other letters on the page and the student's writing style as context cues to help you determine which letter it is. If a letter does not resemble the letter it should be, given its order, do not award credit.

**Compare With Other Letters** If a student does not write the letters in order, compare similar looking letters with one another.

---

## CAUTION

### Scoring Alphabet Writing Fluency

The maximum possible raw score is 25 because no credit is given for the letter A, which is already provided as an example in the response booklet.

Do not give credit for repetitions of letters, overwriting (letters written on top of other letters), letter reversals, transpositions, or upside-down letters.

Do not penalize for letter form/case, poor/improper letter formation, stray marks, reformation (attempts to correct letter formation issues), or placement on the line.

---

## DON'T FORGET

### Alphabet Writing Fluency Scoring FAQ

**Question:** A child wrote six perfectly formed letters, but the child provided incorrect names for the letters. For example, the child wrote a U but orally identified it as a P, and wrote a B but called it a G. Do these letters receive credit?

**Answer:** Yes, this subtest measures letter formation fluency, not knowledge of letter names/sounds.

---

### Sentence Composition

Sentence Composition is scored post-administration using the scoring rules provided in the *Examiner's Manual*. Before scoring, refer to the "Basic Rules of Written Grammar and Mechanics" in Appendix B of the *Examiner's Manual* for guidance in

# DON'T FORGET

## Tip for Identifying Word Boundary (Mechanics) Errors

Look at the overall writing style of the examinee to identify word boundary errors. If a child habitually writes sentences without any spaces between the words, for example: "Catsarepetsanddogsarealsopets," do not penalize for word boundary errors. This writing style indicates a more pervasive spacing concern, rather than word boundary errors.

identifying grammar and mechanics errors. Errors that could be attributed to dialect or slang are penalized, except when oral language is being quoted or explicitly referenced.

For Sentence Combining, three areas are scored: (1) Syntax and Semantics, (2) Mechanics, and (3) Extra Credit. For Sentence Building, two skill areas are scored: (1) Mechanics and (2) Syntax and Semantics. Sentence Building does not include a score for extra credit.

For both Sentence Combining and Sentence Building, use the score boxes provided in the record form to record errors and scores. Examples of scored responses are included in the Scoring Workbook.

# DON'T FORGET

## Sentence Combining "Extra Credit" Score

Award 1 extra point for each item in which the examinee (a) combined the original sentences into one sentence that means the same thing, (b) did not use poor sentence structure, and (c) did not use the word "and" to join two independent clauses/sentences.

Meeting these criteria indicates a level of syntactic maturity and efficiency that was characteristic of high-achieving examinees in the standardization sample.

Item: Cats are pets. Dogs are pets.

Response example that receives extra credit:
Cats and dogs are pets.

Response examples that do not receive extra credit:
Cats are pets and dogs are pets.
Cats and birds are pets.

## Word Reading and Pseudoword Decoding

Prior to administering the Word Reading and Pseudoword Decoding subtests, become familiar with the acceptable pronunciation(s) of each item by listening to the audio files and referring to the pronunciation guides in the *Examiner's Manual*.

This will prepare you to score the examinee's responses quickly and efficiently during administration. Pronunciations that are not read fluently are scored 0 points. If the examinee makes multiple attempts to read a word, score only the last attempt.

### Essay Composition

The Essay Composition subtest standard score is computed by summing the standard score for Word Count

> **DON'T FORGET**
> ...............................................................
>
> **Acceptable Pseudoword Pronunciations**
>
> Only the pronunciations listed in the record form may be scored as correct. Correct responses were determined by reviewing the tryout and standardization data and consulting with speech and language experts.

(the number of words written) and the standard score for Theme Development and Text Organization. A supplemental (optional) Grammar and Mechanics standard score is also available.

Word Count and Theme Development and Text Organization (TDTO) are weighted equally when producing the standard score for Essay Composition. The subtest score is essentially a composite of these two scores. Therefore, anytime the subtest score is nonunitary (comprised of discrepant scores between Word Count and TDTO), the overall subtest score should be interpreted cautiously. Research supports a high correlation between word count and writing quality (Gregg, Coleman, Davis, & Chalk, 2007), meaning that good writers tend to write more and poor writers tend to write fewer words. However, there are exceptions to this general trend. For example, an examinee may score high on Word Count but lower on TDTO. When this occurs, report the separate standard scores for Word Count and TDTO in addition to the subtest standard score to explain performance and plan intervention.

All scoring for this subtest occurs after administration is complete. To begin scoring, read through the examinee's essay to become familiar with its content and structure. Consider making a photocopy of the essay to write on for scoring purposes.

Scoring Theme Development and Text Organization is easiest using the Scoring Guide provided in Q-global (see Rapid Reference 3.6). For hand scoring, a Quick Score Guide (Pearson, 2010b) is available on the WIAT-III website (www .pearsonclinical.com) under the Resources tab. Excellent interscorer reliabilities are reported in the *Technical Manual* for Essay Composition as a whole (0.92–0.99) and for Theme Development and Text Organization specifically (0.92). To acquire this level of proficiency, practice scoring using the Scoring Workbook and then score using the Scoring Guide or Quick Score Guide. The Scoring Guide may be used to score every section of the Theme Development and Text Organization scoring rubric or just specific sections as needed.

To obtain the supplemental Grammar and Mechanics standard score, refer to the scoring rules in the *Examiner's Manual* to count the number of Correct Word

Sequences and Incorrect Word Sequences. Essentially, a Correct Word Sequence (CWS) is two adjacent words that are correctly spelled, capitalized, and punctuated, and grammatically and semantically acceptable within the context of the sentence. A caret (^) is used to mark each CWS (on a photocopy of the examinee's essay). If the first word of a sentence is capitalized, always mark a CWS in front of the word. If correct ending punctuation follows the last word of a sentence, always mark a CWS after the word. An Incorrect Word Sequence (IWS) is two adjacent words that do not qualify as a CWS. A dot (•) is used to mark each IWS. To calculate the CIWS score, sum CWS and IWS separately, and subtract IWS from CWS. Refer to the WIAT-III website under the Resources tab for a study called "Assessing Writing Skills Using Correct-Incorrect Word Sequences." This research supports the reliability and clinical validity of this scoring method.

## DON'T FORGET

### How to Score Essays That Do Not Respond to the Prompt

Some examinees write essays that do not directly respond to the prompt, which may be a clinically relevant observation. These essays may still be scored. However, if you believe the examinee did not understand the task and would perform much differently if the instructions were clarified, you may readminister the subtest at a later time.

Examples of essays that do not respond directly to the prompt include the following. The essay

- Focuses exclusively on explaining the rules or how to play.

- Describes two or more games.

- Gives reasons for liking two or more games.

- Gives reasons for *not* liking or doing something.

## DON'T FORGET

### Scoring Tips

*Word Count*
Do not count crossed-out words.

Incomplete words can be counted if they are understandable as a spelling error or abbreviation.

Illegible handwriting can be counted as a word. It is appropriate to ask the examinee to read his or her writing to confirm the number of words.

(continued)

(Continued)

*Theme Development and Text Organization*

Do not penalize for spelling, capitalization, or punctuation errors.

*Grammar and Mechanics*

Errors that could be attributed to dialect or slang are penalized, except when oral
language is being quoted or explicitly referenced.

---

# ≡ Rapid Reference 3.6

## Using the Scoring Guide for Theme Development and Text Organization

In Q-global, the Scoring Guide is accessible by clicking the pencil icon beside each criterion, as shown in the figure below. A Scoring Guide window will open and guide you
through the scoring of that criterion. Respond to each question and then click next or
save (when complete). When you complete the Scoring Guide, the raw score for that
criterion will be entered automatically.

| Essay Composition | | |
|---|---|---|
| **Content and Organization** | | |
| Word Count Raw Score | 0 - 9999 | 57 |
| Introduction | 0 - 2 | 1 |
| Conclusion | 0 - 2 | 1 |
| Paragraphs | 0 - 5 | 3 |
| Transitions | 0 - 5 | 2 |
| Reasons Why | 0 - 3 | 2 |
| Elaborations | 0 - 3 | 0 |
| Theme Development and Text Organization | | |
| Raw Score (0 to 20) | | 9 |

(continued)

(Continued)

*Scoring Guide Tips*

- Reasons Why and Elaborations are scored concurrently, so selecting the Scoring Guide for either Reasons Why *or* Elaborations will result in scores for both criteria.

- If you already know the raw scores for one or more criteria, you may enter those scores manually rather than using the Scoring Guide.

- To review or rescore a section, reopen the scoring guide by selecting the icon next to the criterion that was previously scored. A warning message will appear to verify that you want to override the previous score. Select "Yes," and the scoring guide will open. You may review your previous responses or change them as needed.

# DON'T FORGET

Many of the following tips were adapted from the WIAT-III Scoring Guide (Pearson, 2009b):

*Scoring Reasons Why*

- Reasons Why and Elaborations are separate scores, but they are scored concurrently.

- If you reach the maximum score for Reasons Why but have not yet reached the maximum score for Elaborations, continue highlighting additional reasons as instructed.

- Do not highlight or score a thesis statement in the introduction or conclusion as a reason.

- Do not highlight or score a restatement of the thesis statement as a reason.

- A statement can count as only one reason.

- If a reason is repeated, it can count only as one reason (i.e., 1 point).

- A statement must be an independent clause or complete sentence to receive credit as a reason.

- Fragments and incomplete thoughts do not receive credit as reasons.

- A response that uses "cuz" instead of because may still count as a reason (misspelling is not penalized when scoring Reasons Why).

## Numerical Operations

All acceptable correct responses for the Numerical Operations items are printed in the record form. For early items, the mode of response for correct answers is designated as (W) for written, (O) for oral, and (P) for pointing. Encourage the examinee to respond accordingly. On later items, if you allow the examinee to attempt all items or work beyond the discontinue point to gather additional qualitative information, do not award credit for any items completed after the first four consecutive scores of 0.

---

# DON'T FORGET

## Scoring Numerical Operations Items

The following items tend to raise questions for examiners about how the scoring rules were determined. Additional explanation is provided here.

**Item 1:** Item 1 asks the examinee to count the number of balls and tell how many there are, and then Item 2 asks the examinee to write the number of balls counted. If the examinee miscounted the number of balls for Item 1 (e.g., says 4 instead of 5), which would be scored 0, and then writes that number for Item 2 (writes "4"), Item 2 is also scored 0. Why is the response for Item 2 incorrect even though the examinee followed the directions correctly? Numerical Operations is primarily a test of *written* math computation, so writing the correct answer is required on Item 2; however, these early items were designed to provide additional information about how the examinee arrived at his or her answer by asking the examinee to provide an oral response first.

**Item 52:** The answer is 5.375. If the examinee wrote 5.3, is it scored as correct? No, the answer must be 5.375 because the purpose of this item is division of a number with a decimal point.

**Item 53:** The answer is 17. If the examinee wrote the square root of 289, is it scored as correct? Yes, this is an equivalent answer that reflects an understanding of how to work the problem.

---

## Oral Expression

All acceptable correct responses for the Expressive Vocabulary items are printed in the record form. Queries that result in a correct response are scored 1 point. If the examinee mispronounces a correct response, such as "cestenarian" for centenarian, score 0 points. Providing a similar sounding, related, or mispronounced word may indicate difficulties with word retrieval and should be described when reporting results.

For Oral Word Fluency, scoring rules are detailed in Appendix B.8 of the *Examiner's Manual*. To calculate the raw score, count the responses that receive credit for Items 1 and 2, and then sum the scores from Items 1 and 2.

# CAUTION

·······································

## Scoring Oral Word Fluency

The most common scoring error for Oral Word Fluency is giving credit for the sample responses. As a first step, go through all responses to look for instances where the examinee provided one of the sample responses and mark these as incorrect (no credit).

For Sentence Repetition, count one error for each addition and one error for each transposition—regardless of the number of words added or transposed. However, for omitted or substituted words, count one error for each word omitted. The following deviations from print are not scored as errors: repetitions of words, forming or separating correct contractions, and self-corrections. The most common scoring errors are illustrated in the following text and are organized by scoring rule:

1. Scoring rule: Forming or separating contractions are not scored as errors.
   (a) *Example*: Saying "you're" for "you are" is not an error. It is acceptable to either record "you're" in parentheses above the item, as in the following example, or to not record it at all.
   *(You're)*
   you are not
2. Scoring Rule: Changing verb form/tense is scored as one error.
   *Example*: Changing the verb "wanted" to "had hoped" is one error.
   *(had hoped)*
   man ~~wanted~~ to keep
3. Scoring Rule: Adding two or more words is scored as one error.
   (a) *Example*: Adding the words "from the" is scored as one error.
   *(from the)*
   stop her ^ crying
4. Scoring Rule: Each omitted/substituted word is scored as one error.
   *Example*: If the examinee says, "I don't remember the rest" or "something about a bus" or "they couldn't move" instead of "when the bus got stuck," simply count the number of words omitted from the item. In this case, "when the bus got stuck" is five words, so this would be scored as five errors.

## Oral Reading Fluency

The scoring rules for Oral Reading Fluency are very similar to the scoring rules for Sentence Repetition. When counting errors, count one error for each addition and one error for each transposition—regardless of the number of words added or transposed. However, for omitted, substituted, or given (supplied) words, count one error for each word omitted or given. The following deviations from print are not scored as errors: repetitions of words, forming or separating correct contractions, and self-corrections.

Using Q-global or the Scoring Assistant is helpful for scoring Oral Reading Fluency. Simply enter the following information for each passage in the item set: Elapsed time (in seconds), the number of Addition errors, and the number of Other errors (which includes Supplied Words and Substitution/ Omission and Transposition errors). If scoring by hand, you must incorporate the preceding information into the formulas provided in the record form in order to calculate the Fluency and Accuracy raw scores.

## CAUTION

### Hand Scoring Oral Reading Fluency

Calculate the three total raw scores using the formulas in the record form, and then round to the nearest whole number. Preserve all decimal places in each step of the calculation and round only the final raw score. A calculator is recommended to avoid calculation error.

## DON'T FORGET

### Qualitative Data From Oral Reading Fluency

The comprehension questions and the prosody scale are for qualitative evaluation purposes only and do not contribute to the subtest score.

## CAUTION

### Scoring Oral Reading Fluency Passage "The Moon"

The comprehension question asks, "What does the author like to do by moonlight?" The first sentence of the passage reads, "I like to watch the moon as it shines at night." "Watch the moon" is not listed as a correct response (and was not given as a response during tryout or standardization); however, this response is well supported by the first sentence of the passage and should be considered as an alternate correct response. Since the comprehension questions are for qualitative purposes only, accepting this alternate response will not alter standardized procedures or affect the validity of the scores.

## Spelling

Scoring Spelling is straightforward: score 1 for correctly spelled words and 0 for misspelled words. Poorly formed letters, capitalization, and mixing print with cursive are not penalized. Responses that contain letter reversals are scored 0 points unless the examinee is in Kindergarten or first grade. If the examinee is in Kindergarten or first grade, letter reversals are not penalized as long as the reversal does not form a different letter. During administration, carefully watch the examinee spell each item and ask him or her to name any letters that are unclear or ambiguous.

Avoid scoring the examinee's responses "by eye," reading through them and looking for misspelled words. This method of scoring is error prone—even if you are a good speller. Errors may include a correct spelling of the wrong word or may closely resemble the correct spelling. To prevent scoring errors, always compare each of the examinee's responses with the correct spelling printed in the record form.

To calculate the raw score, subtract the number of incorrect items from the ceiling item. Skipped items (those words that the student chose not to attempt) are scored as incorrect. An error analysis may be conducted after the subtest is scored.

### Math Fluency—Addition, Subtraction, and Multiplication

The raw score for each of the three Math Fluency subtests is the number of correct responses provided within the 1-minute time limit. Disregard any skipped or unattempted items—these are not scored as incorrect. Do not penalize for numeral formation and numeral reversal errors. When handwriting is unclear, you may ask the examinee to read his or her response to help you decipher what is written. Responses with transposition errors, such as 12 for 21, are scored as incorrect.

**DON'T FORGET**

........................................................

**Scoring Math Fluency**

Numeral reversals are not penalized.

For hand scoring and Q-global scoring, use the scoring key provided in Appendix C of the *Examiner's Manual*. The scoring keys are reproducible, which means you are allowed to make copies of these pages for your personal use and ease of reference.

## HOW TO INTERPRET THE WIAT-III

Interpretation of the WIAT-III results should be purposeful by responding to the original referral question(s) and testing one or more hypotheses. The score comparisons and subsequent analyses should be evaluated according to these purposes. The WIAT-III yields a great deal of information: scores from 16 possible subtests, seven domain composites, and a Total Achievement composite. Given the wealth of information provided by the WIAT-III, examiners need to methodically employ an efficient process of interpretation to glean the most from the data. A systematic and efficient procedure for interpreting the WIAT-III is described in the following section.

## Introduction to Interpretation

The reason for referral typically dictates the battery of tests administered during an assessment. In the case of the WIAT-III, either the full battery may be administered or a partial battery may be administered to answer a question about a particular area of academic functioning. The recommended interpretive approach for the WIAT-III begins at the global level by looking at the available composite scores, then interpreting subtest scores, and then drilling down further by analyzing skills analysis and qualitative data, and conducting additional analyses as needed. Interpretation of the WIAT-III involves the following five basic steps:

1. Interpret the composite scores.
2. Interpret the subtest scores.
3. Identify composite strengths and weaknesses.
4. Identify subtest strengths and weaknesses.
5. Determine the significance and unusualness of planned comparisons.

After these five interpretive steps, examiners may wish to obtain more detailed information by conducting a skills analysis and considering qualitative information. The final sections on interpretation detail the skills analysis process and how to best utilize qualitative observations.

# CAUTION

••••••••••••••••••••••••••••••••••••••••••••••••••••••••••••••••••••••••••••••••••••••

## Use Confidence Intervals

Every score has a margin of error. When interpreting and reporting standard scores for subtests and composites, use the confidence interval for reporting scores within a range.

When using confidence intervals, you must first select the degree of confidence you want to report: 85%, 90%, or 95%. Generally, the higher the degree of confidence, the larger the score range. Many examiners prefer 90% because the score range is not so large yet the level of confidence is still quite high.

For example, if a 13-year-old examinee obtained a Word Reading age-based standard score of 100, the examiner can be 90% confident that the examinee's true score is in the range of 95 to 105 ($100 \pm 5$) and 95% confident that the examinee's true score is in the range of 94 to 106 ($100 \pm 6$). When reporting results using 90%, you might say: Marie's word reading skills were estimated in the average range (95–105), or Marie's word reading skills were estimated in the 37th–63rd percentile range.

## Step 1: Interpret the Composite Scores

Most examiners do not administer all the WIAT-III subtests available at a given age/grade due to time limitations or the need for a more targeted assessment. The WIAT-III is designed to be comprehensive enough to provide the measures most often needed for a diagnostic assessment, but flexible enough to allow examiners to select only the subtests or composites that are most relevant to addressing the referral concern. For this reason, the first step in the interpretation process does not assume the Total Achievement composite was obtained.

If the Total Achievement (TA) composite was obtained, interpretation begins by evaluating the TA composite score and its component subtest scores. The TA composite provides a global overview of an examinee's academic achievement across four domains: oral language, reading, writing, and math. Review the TA standard score, confidence interval, percentile rank, and corresponding descriptive category. If the TA composite confidence interval spans more than one descriptive category, we suggest reporting the descriptive category as a range (e.g., if the confidence interval is 105 to 113, it would be appropriate to report that "Lena's TA composite was in the Average to Above Average range of academic functioning").

> ## CAUTION
> ......................................................
>
> ### Total Achievement Composite Varies by Grade
>
> The subtests included in the Total Achievement composite vary by grade level, so the composite score must be interpreted accordingly. A Total Achievement score at Kindergarten reflects proficiency across a different combination of skill domains than a Total Achievement score at Grade 3. Refer to Rapid Reference 3.2 for an overview of the TA composite structure.

Use the graphical profile to easily visualize the examinee's profile of subtest scores on a normal distribution and compare scores with each other. The TA composite score indicates an examinee's "average" or overall academic functioning, which is useful on its own for general screening, educational placement, or research purposes. For clinical and diagnostic purposes, valuable information is obtained from interpreting the degree of variability in performance across the subtest scores that comprise the Total achievement composite. Some examinees exhibit similar performance (a low degree of scatter) across subtest standard scores; however, it is generally more common to see at least a moderate degree of scatter with one or more subtest scores that are considerably higher or lower than the TA composite score. A large degree of scatter is easy to spot. If the confidence intervals of two scores do not overlap, the scores are significantly different (see Don't Forget box). Areas of strength and weakness suggested by the examinee's TA profile of scores may be explored further in subsequent interpretive steps.

If a partial WIAT-III battery was administered and the Total Achievement (TA) composite was not obtained, then the first interpretive step is to interpret the composites scores that were obtained. For each composite, review the standard score, confidence interval, percentile rank, and corresponding descriptive category. If the composite confidence interval spans more than one descriptive category, we suggest reporting the descriptive category as a range (e.g., performance was in the Average to Above Average range). Evaluate the consistency of subtest scores within each composite. A composite score is not unitary if it includes subtests with significant score differences (see Don't Forget box). Nonunitary composite scores may still be considered valid and useful for certain purposes but need to be reported and interpreted cautiously.

### Step 2: Interpret the Subtest Scores

Subtest scores are often interpreted within the context of a composite, but a subtest score may also be interpreted in isolation. First, determine whether each subtest score is a normative strength (standard scores above 115) or a normative weakness (standard scores below 85). Review the standard score, confidence interval, percentile rank, and corresponding descriptive category. If the subtest confidence interval spans more than one descriptive category, we suggest reporting the descriptive category as a range (e.g., performance was in the Average to Above Average range).

## Step 3: Identify Composite Strengths and Weaknesses

After interpreting composite scores relative to the normative sample, consider the examinee's relative or personal strengths and weaknesses by evaluating composite scores relative to the examinee's own level of performance. Consider whether each composite score is consistent with the level of achievement across composite areas or if there is variation in performance across composite areas. Possible areas of relative strength or weakness are the highest or lowest composite scores, which are easy to spot on the graphical profile. Evaluate whether the differences between pairs of composite standard scores are statistically significant at the desired level of confidence. For any statistically significant differences, determine if the differences are typical or rare by looking up the cumulative percentages of the standardization sample that obtained the same or similar composite score discrepancies.

## Step 4: Identify Subtest Strengths and Weaknesses

Step 4 uses a procedure similar to the one described in Step 3. Consider the examinee's relative or personal strengths and weaknesses at the subtest level by evaluating subtest scores relative to the examinee's own level of performance. Consider whether each subtest score is consistent with the level of achievement across subtests or if there is variation in performance across subtest areas. Possible areas of relative strength or weakness are the highest or lowest subtest scores, which are easy to spot on the graphical profile. Evaluate whether the differences between pairs of subtest standard scores are statistically significant at the desired level of confidence. For any statistically significant differences, determine if the differences are typical or rare by looking up the cumulative percentages of the standardization sample that obtained the same or similar subtest score discrepancies.

## Step 5: Determine the Significance and Unusualness of Planned Comparisons

Step 5 is useful for evaluating hypotheses about specific strong and weak areas of achievement or for evaluating a comparison between particular academic or reading-related skills. Specific planned comparisons of composite scores or subtest scores may provide useful information for diagnosis or instructional planning. Numerous planned comparisons can be made depending on the examiner's needs. However, specific score comparisons are recommended for reading, writing, and math referral concerns, as shown in Rapid Reference 3.7. Subtest and composite score comparisons can be evaluated using Q-global or by completing the tables provided in the record form.

# ≡ *Rapid Reference 3.7*

## Recommended Score Comparisons

The most clinically useful subtest comparisons depend on the referral concerns as well as the examinee's unique profile of strengths and weaknesses; however, as a general guide, the following subtest comparisons may be considered for each academic area:

| Reading Concern | Writing/Spelling Concern | Math Concern |
|---|---|---|
| Reading Comprehension vs. Listening Comprehension | Oral Expression vs. Sentence Composition | Math Problem Solving vs. Numerical Operations, Math Fluency |
| Word Reading vs. Pseudoword Decoding, Oral Reading Fluency | Spelling vs. Alphabet Writing Fluency (K–3), Sentence Composition, Word Reading, Pseudoword Decoding | Numerical Operations vs. Math Fluency |
| Word Reading Speed vs. Pseudoword Decoding Speed (compare base rates) | Essay Composition: Theme Development & Text Organization vs. Grammar & Mechanics | |

## What can be learned from comparing reading and listening comprehension subtests, and oral and written expression subtests?

| Oral Expression vs. Sentence Composition | Reading Comprehension vs. Listening Comprehension |
|---|---|
| OE and SC correlate .49 (grade 1) to .67 (grade 5). | RC and LC correlate from .42 (K) to .66 (grade 10). |
| These two expression subtests measure different aspects of expressive language. A comparison between these subtests may point to a particular difficulty in either written or spoken expression. | These two comprehension subtests both assess the literal and inferential comprehension of connected text. Thus, the comparison between these subtests may help identify a problem specific to reading (that is distinct from a more general language problem). However, LC measures receptive vocabulary, but RC does not measure reading vocabulary. |
| OE < SC may suggest weaknesses in vocabulary, verbal fluency, or auditory working memory. | RC < LC may suggest weaknesses in one or more reading skills. |
| SC < OE may suggest weaknesses in grammar, written mechanics, or the orthographic loop of working memory. | LC < RC may suggest weaknesses in vocabulary, language comprehension (if both LC and RC are weak), or auditory verbal working memory. |

For example, examinees with certain types of reading disorders have trouble with both encoding (spelling) and decoding (Lyon, Shaywitz, & Shaywitz, 2003). Compare performance on the Word Reading and Pseudoword Decoding subtests to performance on the Spelling subtest. Evaluate skills analysis results to determine if similar types of errors occur across these subtests. For example, does the individual show a pattern of errors with a particular letter-sound relationship? Are there similar morphological errors (e.g., omission of word suffixes)? In the area of mathematics, for example, comparing an examinee's performance on the Numerical Operations and the Math Problem Solving subtests helps identify whether difficulties in math are specific to calculation or the application of math skills to solve problems.

In the area of oral language, two comparisons are important:

1. Compare Listening Comprehension performance to Oral Expression performance. Evaluate whether weaknesses are specific to certain tasks (e.g., expressive vocabulary but not receptive vocabulary) and whether difficulties are demonstrated on receptive tasks, expressive tasks, or both.
2. Compare performance in the area of oral language with performance in the area of written language (reading and writing subtests). For example, a student with weaknesses in Reading Comprehension and Listening Comprehension (Oral Discourse Comprehension) requires instruction in language comprehension. In contrast, a student who performs poorly on Reading Comprehension, Oral Reading Fluency, and Word Reading but demonstrates average performance on Listening Comprehension would likely benefit from instruction in word identification and reading fluency rather than language comprehension. On the other hand, a student who performs poorly on Word Reading may have underlying oral language weaknesses in word retrieval (measured by Oral Word Fluency and Expressive Vocabulary) and vocabulary (measured by Receptive Vocabulary and Expressive Vocabulary) that contribute to a weakness in word identification.

## Subtest Floors and Ceilings

When interpreting subtest standard scores, it is important to consider whether there are floor or ceiling limitations. The theoretical standard score range for all subtests is 40 to 160, but not all subtests reach the minimum and maximum standard score.

Floor effects occur when the lowest possible standard score is 71 or higher, which is less than 2 standard deviations below the mean. Floor effects may be inevitable for certain subtests due to a restricted score range with any of the subtests. The distributions of certain subtest scores are slightly skewed in the lower ages and grades due to the natural floor that exists before skills are acquired (see the Don't Forget box). Ceiling effects occur when the highest possible standard score is 129 or lower, less than 2 standard deviations above the mean. Refer to this book's online Digital Resources for tables that report by age the lowest and highest possible score for each subtest.

# DON'T FORGET

## Subtests With Floor Effects

The lowest possible standard score for the following subtests will be less than 2 standard deviations below the mean (>70) at the lower ages due to the natural floor that exists before skills are acquired:

| | | |
|---|---|---|
| Early Reading Skills | Alphabet Writing Fluency | Numerical Operations |
| Reading Comprehension | Sentence Composition | Math Fluency (all 3 subtests) |
| Word Reading | | |
| Pseudoword Decoding | | |

For example, many examinees in first grade (age 6) are not yet able to write sentences; hence, 6-year-olds who earn a raw score of 0 on the Sentence Composition subtest earn a score of 88, which is less than 1 standard deviation below the mean. This score indicates that 21% of 6-year-olds during standardization also scored 0 on this subtest, so a raw score of 0 is not far below average relative to same-age peers.

# DON'T FORGET

## Digital Resources

Tables that summarize the minimum and maximum subtest standard scores available for each WIAT-III subtest are accessible online as digital resources with this book.

## Skills Analysis

The WIAT-III provides skills analysis to help practitioners evaluate an examinee's specific skill strengths and weaknesses and plan targeted interventions. Skills analysis is most useful for evaluating performance on subtests that are normative or relative weaknesses for the examinee, but the WIAT-III skills analysis may also be used to identify skill strengths.

To evaluate a student's skill strengths and weaknesses on seven of the 16 subtests, the WIAT-III provides both item-level and within-item level skills analysis capabilities. Table 3.8 lists the seven subtests according to the skills analysis method used. For the four subtests with item-level skill classifications, each item is associated with a skill category. When an item is scored as incorrect, an error is marked for the associated skill category. The three subtests that use within-item error classification are assigned one or more error categories according to the examiner's qualitative analysis of the examinee's response.

**Table 3.8  Skills Analysis Methods for WIAT-III Subtests**

| Subtests Using Item-Level Error Classification | Subtests Using Within-Item Error Classification |
| --- | --- |
| Early Reading Skills | Word Reading |
| Reading Comprehension | Pseudoword Decoding |
| Numerical Operations | Spelling |
| Math Problem Solving | |

**DON'T FORGET**

**How to Score "DK" or "NR" Responses for Skills Analysis**

Scoring "Don't Know" or "No Response" items, which are both scored 0 points, differs depending on whether item-level or within-item classification methods are used. For item-level classification, include DK or NR responses as an error within the relevant skill categories. For within-item classification, DK or NR responses are not included in the error analysis because no error information is available.

To conduct a skills analysis using Q-global, follow the steps outlined in Rapid Reference 3.8. The skills analysis report includes the specific skills that are measured by each subtest, the item number(s) that correspond to each skill, and, within each skill, the item numbers answered incorrectly and the percentage of items answered correctly.

For hand scoring, separate skills analysis worksheets are provided in Appendix A of the *Examiner's Manual* for tabulating errors on all seven subtests with skills analysis capabilities. These worksheets are reproducible, which allows them to be copied for repeated use.

*≡ Rapid Reference 3.8*

**Q-global Steps for Conducting Skills Analysis or Obtaining Intervention Goal Statements**

1. Enter the subtest raw scores under the "Raw Scores" tab.
2. Select the "Skills Analysis" tab.
3. On the Summary page, select the subtests that you want to include for skills analysis and/or goal statements based upon the standard scores shown for each. Consider selecting subtests that are highlighted in yellow, which indicates below-average performance relative to the normative sample. The following image shows the subtest selection section of the Summary page.

*(continued)*

(Continued)

| Subtest | Age-Based Standard Score (AB) | Grade-Based Standard Score (GB) |
|---------|------------------------------|--------------------------------|
| ☐ Reading Comprehension | 106 | 101 |
| ☑ Math Problem Solving | 93 | 83 |
| ☑ Sentence Composition | 96 | 88 |
| ☑ Word Reading | 111 | 98 |
| ☐ Essay Composition | 95 | 87 |
| ☑ Pseudoword Decoding | 99 | 90 |
| ☑ Numerical Operations | 86 | 79 |
| ☐ Spelling | 108 | 92 |

4. For each selected subtest, either enter skills analysis information or select component areas for providing goal statements, as appropriate. The following image shows the entry screen for Pseudoword Decoding within-item skills analysis.

▼ Item Number 1

| Incorrect | Item | Error | Skill |
|-----------|------|-------|-------|
| ☑ | ik | i | Single Short Vowels |
| ☐ | ik | k | Single Consonants |
| ☐ | ik | Other | Insertions |
| ☐ | ik | Other | Mis-Sequence of Sounds |
| ☐ | ik | Other | Whole Word Error |

▶ Item Number 2
▶ Item Number 3

5. Select Save and Close, then Generate Report.
6. Select Skills Analysis and/or Goal Statements, and create the score report. After the score report is created, scroll to the end of the report to view the skills analysis summary table and the goal statements. The following image shows an excerpt from the skills analysis summary table for Math Problem Solving.

## Math Problem Solving

| Feature | Skill | Total Errors by Skill | Max. Errors by Skill | % Correct By Skill | % Correct By Feature |
|---------|-------|-----------------------|----------------------|--------------------|----------------------|
| Basic Concepts | One-to-One Counting | 0 | 5 | 100% | 81% |
| | Recognizing Shapes | 0 | 2 | 100% | |
| | Recognizing Numerals | 0 | 2 | 100% | |
| | Basic Concepts | 0 | 5 | 100% | |
| | Counting On | 0 | 1 | 100% | |
| | Naming Numerals (<11) | 0 | 3 | 100% | |
| | Comparing Numerals | 2 | 3 | 33% | |
| | Ordering Numerals | 2 | 3 | 33% | |
| | Addition and Subtraction of Objects | 1 | 2 | 50% | |

(continued)

(Continued)

| Feature | Skill | Total Errors by Skill | Max. Errors by Skill | % Correct By Skill | % Correct By Feature |
|---------|-------|----------------------|----------------------|--------------------|----------------------|
| Everyday Applications | Interpreting Graphs | I | I | 0% | 25% |
| | Measuring an Object | 0 | I | 100% | |
| | Interpreting a Number Line | I | I | 0% | |
| | Interpreting a Calendar | I | I | 0% | |
| | Completing Number Patterns | - | - | - | |
| | Money | - | - | - | |
| | Time | - | - | - | |
| | Identifying Place Value | - | - | - | |
| | Single-Operation Word Problems: General | - | - | - | |
| | Single-Operation Word Problems: Time | - | - | - | |
| | Mixed-Operations Word Problems: Money | - | - | - | |

# DON'T FORGET

## Information Gained From WIAT-III Error Analysis

**The concentration of skill deficiencies.** Within a subtest, are the weaknesses focused in just a few areas, or are they more pervasive in nature? When analyzing error results across subtests are there areas of common weakness that suggest possible sources of skill difficulties?

**The location of skill deficiencies.** Where on the skill continuum is the student experiencing the most difficulty? Are the weaknesses in earlier or later sections of the test? For example, math computation weaknesses in addition and subtraction are skills introduced early in the curriculum sequence, whereas weaknesses in multiplication and division might represent a higher-level skill deficiency for the student's grade level.

**The severity of skill deficiencies.** Compare the number of errors made in a given skill category with the number of opportunities to make that error type. The percentage of errors made by skill category suggests the severity of skill deficiency.

# CAUTION

## Limitations of WIAT-III Skills Analysis

Unlike the KTEA-3 error analysis, the WIAT-III skills analysis may be used with high-performing students who perform above the mean because the skill results are provided as percent correct (rather than as a normative strength, average, or weakness). However, the WIAT-III skills analysis system has some important limitations to keep in mind:

- The WIAT-III was not designed to provide broad coverage of each skill category at each grade level. As a result, the student may have attempted only a few items that measured a particular skill. Follow-up testing with a larger pool of items is recommended to confirm skill strengths and weaknesses.

- Results are reported as percentages. Percentages may exaggerate perceived skill strengths and weaknesses when based on small numbers of items. Use caution when the percentage is based on just a few opportunities to demonstrate the skill.

- Norm-referenced data are not provided, so it may be difficult to determine the percentage of items in a given skill category that a student would be expected to answer correctly for their grade level. Combining skills analysis results with classroom performance and input from teachers is helpful for determining skill weaknesses that warrant intervention.

## Skills Analysis in Reading Comprehension

Items from Reading Comprehension are divided into literal and inferential comprehension. Literal versus inferential comprehension is an important distinction for describing the level of comprehension demands required to respond to an item correctly. Literal comprehension requires recognizing or recalling ideas, information, or events that are explicitly stated in an oral or written text. In contrast, inferential comprehension requires the generation of new ideas from those stated in the text. Students derive inferences from relating different concepts presented in the text or combining information with previously acquired knowledge. Sometimes inferences require students to evaluate the writer's or speaker's viewpoint. Literal questions do not require the student to go beyond the viewpoints of the writer or speaker and are usually paraphrased portions of the text.

## Skills Analysis in Early Reading Skills

Items from Early Reading Skills were designed to measure four skill domains and 12 skill categories, as shown in Rapid Reference 3.9. These skills include naming letters, letter-sound correspondence (phonics), phonological awareness skills such as rhyming, sound matching, and blending, and early reading comprehension skills for matching words with pictures. These skills are important precursors to reading, and teachers can use information about skill weaknesses on the Early Reading Skills subtest to tailor early reading instruction.

## ≋ Rapid Reference 3.9

### Skill Domains and Categories for Early Reading Skills

| Skill Domain | Skill Category |
|---|---|
| Naming Letters | Naming Letters: Vowels<br>Naming Letters: Consonants |
| Letter-Sound Correspondence | Matching Single Letters and Sounds<br>Consonant Digraphs<br>Consonant Blends |
| Phonological Awareness | Recognizing Rhyming Words<br>Producing Rhyming Words<br>Recognizing Initial Sounds in Words<br>Recognizing Initial Two Sounds in Words<br>Recognizing Ending Sounds in Words<br>Blending Sounds |
| Word Reading Comprehension | Matching Words with Pictures |

### Skills Analysis in Math Problem Solving and Numerical Operations

All items from Math Problem Solving and nearly all items from Numerical Operations are associated with one skill category. The only exceptions are items that involve regrouping on Numerical Operations. These items are classified under Regrouping and one other skill category. Math skills are acquired in a mostly hierarchical order, which requires students to master basic concepts before more advanced concepts can be learned. The skills are also listed in the Skills Analysis Worksheets and the score report in a hierarchical order, so it is possible to determine where a student's skill level falls along a continuum of skill acquisition, or whether the student's skill acquisition is uneven or spotty across the continuum (Pearson, 2009b, p. 90). The skill domains for both math subtests include Basic Concepts, Algebra, and Geometry, but Numerical Operations also includes Basic Math Operations and Advanced Math whereas Math Problem Solving includes Everyday Applications. However, the specific skills differ across subtests—even for skill domains with the same name.

Numerical Operations assesses math computation ability with a total of 39 skill categories, which are listed in Rapid Reference 3.10. Math Problem Solving assesses computation and problem solving abilities with a total of 36 skill categories. Performance on Math Problem Solving depends on math computation skill and the ability to apply math skills to solve actual and hypothetical problems. The examinee must discriminate relevant from irrelevant information, identify the correct procedure or operation, and set up the problem correctly.

## ≡ Rapid Reference 3.10

### Skill Domains and Categories for Math Problem Solving

| Skill Domain | Skill Category |
|---|---|
| Basic Concepts | Counting |
| | Recognizing Shapes |
| | Recognizing Numerals |
| | Basic Concepts |
| | Counting On |
| | Naming Numerals (<11) |
| | Comparing Numerals |
| | Ordering Numerals |
| | Addition & Subtraction of Objects |
| Everyday Applications | Interpreting Graphs |
| | Measuring an Object |
| | Interpreting a Number Line |
| | Interpreting a Calendar |
| | Completing Number Patterns |
| | Money |
| | Time |
| | Identifying Place Value |
| | Single-Operation Word Problems: General |
| | Single-Operation Word Problems: Time |
| | Mixed-Operations Word Problems: Money |
| Geometry | Interpreting Transformation of Figures |
| | Finding Perimeter |
| | Finding Angles and Sides/Distances |
| | Finding Circumference |
| | Geometry Word Problems |

(continued)

(Continued)

| Skill Domain | Skill Category |
| --- | --- |
| Algebra | Making Fractions (Less Than Whole)<br>Ordering Fractions<br>Converting Fractions to Decimals<br>Fraction Word Problems<br>Algebra Word Problems<br>Solving Simultaneous Equations<br>Recognizing Prime Numbers<br>Solving Probability Problems<br>Solving Combination Problems<br>Mean, Median, Mode<br>Finding Slope and y-Intercept |

## Skill Domains and Categories for Numerical Operations

| Skill Domain | Skill Category |
| --- | --- |
| Basic Concepts | One-to-One Counting<br>Numeral Formation<br>Discriminating Numbers From Letters<br>Number Formation and Order<br>Identifying Mathematical Symbols |
| Basic Math Operations | Addition With Single-Digit Numbers<br>Addition With 2-Digit Numbers<br>Addition With 3-Digit Numbers<br>Subtraction With Single-Digit Numbers<br>Subtraction With 2-Digit Numbers<br>Subtraction With 3-Digit Numbers<br>Multiplication With Single-Digit Numbers<br>Multiplication With 2-Digit Numbers<br>Multiplication With 3-Digit Numbers<br>Division<br>Long Division<br>Order of Operations<br>Calculating the Percent of an Integer<br>Adding Negative Integers |

(continued)

(Continued)

| Skill Domain | Skill Category |
|---|---|
| Algebra | Addition of Fractions |
| | Multiplication of Fractions |
| | Division of Fractions |
| | Simplifying Fractions |
| | Solving 2-Step Equations |
| | Solving 3-Step Equations |
| | Solving Simplified Quadratic Equations (Finding Roots) |
| | Solving Simultaneous Equations |
| | Finding Functions |
| | Factoring |
| | Simplifying Exponents and Radicals |
| | Logarithms |
| Geometry | Numerical Value of pi |
| | Finding Area |
| | Finding Sides of Triangle |
| Advanced Math | Trigonometry |
| | Limits |
| | Differentiation |
| | Integration |
| Other (used as a secondary classification) | Regrouping |

### Skills Analysis in Word Reading, Pseudoword Decoding, and Spelling

The reading of words requires that students connect speech sounds to letter patterns. Three subtests tap this skill in slightly different ways. Pseudoword Decoding assesses a student's ability to apply decoding and structural analysis skills to pseudowords composed of typically occurring letter patterns. Spelling requires students to relate speech sounds that they hear to letter patterns that they write. Word Reading taps a student's ability to read words with both consistent and inconsistent letter-sound patterns. The skill domains and categories for these three subtests are listed in Rapid Reference 3.11. Although the categories are very similar across these three subtests, a few skill categories differ. Only Spelling includes a *Homophone* skill category, *C-le syllables* is used only in Pseudoword Decoding, and *C as \sh\* is included only in Word Reading and Pseudoword Decoding.

Recording verbatim responses is essential for Word Reading and Pseudoword Decoding. In addition to being familiar with how to record students' responses phonetically, you should be familiar with the error categories before testing, which informs the most pertinent error information to record for error analysis scoring.

# ☰ Rapid Reference 3.11

## Skill Domains and Categories for Word Reading and Pseudoword Decoding Subtests

| Skill Domain | Skill Category |
|---|---|
| Morphology Types | Common Prefixes/Word Beginnings |
| | Common Suffixes/Word Endings |
| Vowel Types | VCE Syllables |
| | C–le Syllables (Pseudoword Decoding only) |
| | Irregular Vowels |
| | Single Short Vowels |
| | Single Long Vowels |
| | Schwa Vowel Sounds |
| | Vowel Digraphs |
| | Diphthongs |
| | R-Controlled Vowels |
| | Silent Vowels |
| Consonant Types | Consonant Digraphs |
| | Single Consonants |
| | Double Consonants |
| | S as \z\ or \zh\ |
| | T as \sh\ or \ch\ |
| | C as \sh\ (not included in Spelling) |
| | R-Family Blends |
| | L-Family Blends |
| | S-Family Blends |
| | Consonant Blends/Clusters |
| | Silent Consonants |
| Other | Insertions |
| | Mis-Sequence of Sounds |
| | Whole Word Error |
| Word Types | Homophones |

(continued)

(Continued)

## Skill Domains and Categories for Spelling Subtests

| Skill Domain | Skill Category |
|---|---|
| Morphology Types | Common Prefixes/Word Beginnings |
| | Common Suffixes/Word Endings |
| Vowel Types | VCE Syllables |
| | Irregular Vowels |
| | Single Short Vowels |
| | Single Long Vowels |
| | Schwa Vowel Sounds |
| | Vowel Digraphs |
| | Diphthongs |
| | R-Controlled Vowels |
| | Silent Vowels |
| Consonant Types | Consonant Digraphs |
| | Single Consonants |
| | Double Consonants |
| | S as \z\ or \zh\ |
| | T as \sh\ or \ch\ |
| | R-Family Blends |
| | L-Family Blends |
| | S-Family Blends |
| | Consonant Blends/Clusters |
| | Silent Consonants |
| Other | Insertions |
| | Mis-Sequence of Sounds |
| | Whole Word Error |

# DON'T FORGET

## Unpredictable Patterns

The KTEA-3 error analysis systems for Letter & Word Recognition, Nonsense Word Decoding, and Spelling include an error category called Unpredictable Patterns, which includes words for which there is inconsistent letter-sound correspondence. These words cannot be read or spelled using a purely phonetic, "sound-it-out" strategy.

(continued)

*(Continued)*

The Unpredictable Patterns category is beneficial for identifying students with weaknesses in orthographic coding.

WIAT-III includes 7 skill categories for Word Reading, Pseudoword Decoding, and Spelling that may be considered unpredictable patterns, as summarized in the following table. If a student tends to have difficulty with several of these skill categories, a processing weakness in orthographic coding may be contributing to reading and spelling difficulties.

*Unpredictable Pattern Skill Categories*

Irregular Vowels

Schwa Vowel Sounds

Silent Vowels

S as \z\ or \zh\

T as \sh\ or \ch\

C as \sh\ (*not included in Spelling*)

Silent Consonants

## Intervention Goal Statements

The WIAT-III provides intervention goal statements that were written and reviewed by experts in the field of special education. These goal statements are available only when using Q-global (or the original Scoring Assistant). To obtain intervention goal statements using Q-global, follow the steps outlined previously in Rapid Reference 3.8 for conducting skills analysis and then select "Goal Statements" as a report option.

The goal statements are displayed at the end of the score report and include recommended intervention tasks and activities. The statements include multiple choice options and spaces to fill in the blank to assist examiners in writing goals that are specific, measurable, and customizable for a student's individualized education plan. A sample of a completed annual goal and short-term objective for the Word Reading subtest is shown in Figure 3.4.

The ability to customize the goal statements allows the examiner to adjust the difficulty level of the goal based upon the needs of a particular examinee. In addition, it allows the examiner to formulate goal statements that meet various school district or institutional standards and preferences. For example, some practitioners may generally prefer using goals that require a percent accuracy of at least 70% but may require a higher percent accuracy from a high-ability, low-achieving examinee who is likely to respond well to instruction.

If a subtest is selected that includes skills analysis, such as the Word Reading subtest, goal statements will be provided for each skill area in which the examinee made one or more errors. Certain subtests such as Essay Composition have the option to include goal statements even though skills analysis is not an option. For these

## Word Reading

### VCE Syllables

**Items with Errors:** 31

**Annual Goal**

Given a list of _30_ (circle/enter one) two, three, _____) - syllable words containing one VCE syllable, the student will read the list aloud with no more than _3_ errors.

List examples: face, pace, lace; lake, bake, take; like, bike, hike; mine, wine, fine

**Short-Term Objectives**

Given a list of _20_ one-syllable word pairs, each pair including one VCE syllable word and the same word without the silent e, the student will pronounce the word pairs with no more than _4_ errors.

Word pair examples: win, wine; fin, fine; tap, tape; mop, mope; wip, wipe

**Figure 3.4 Sample of WIAT-III Intervention Goal Statements**

Source: Wechsler Individual Achievement Test–Third Edition (WIAT-III). Copyright © 2009 NCS Pearson, Inc. Reproduced with permission. All rights reserved.

subtests, the same goal statements are provided regardless of the examinee's performance on specific items or scoring criteria.

Use only the goal statements that are most appropriate for the student. For example, the examiner may decide not to use the Essay Composition intervention goal statement regarding essay planning because the examinee demonstrated above average planning skills by using a graphic organizer prior to writing the essay but may focus instead on the paragraph-writing goal statements. Similarly, the examiner may determine that missing one item in a particular skill area is not sufficient to justify an annual goal statement and may decide to administer supplemental curriculum-based measures to test the hypothesis that instruction is needed in that skill area.

### Qualitative Data

Both quantitative and qualitative information should be considered when interpreting test results. Qualitative information can be obtained by recording behavioral observations during testing and conducting a skills analysis. A qualitative analysis helps clarify why an individual might achieve a set of scores. Qualitative observations are especially important for the following purposes:

- To provide information that can serve as a cross-check on the validity of the examinee's scores, and
- To provide valuable information for linking assessment results to instructional planning.

When recording behavioral observations, pay close attention to the examinee's performance on each subtest. Observe how the examinee approaches a task and responds to perceived success or failure. Review the examinee's responses to determine where the problem-solving process may break down. Because examinees are required to write their responses using a pencil without an eraser, you can more easily identify how errors were made on written responses. Understanding why an error occurs or under what conditions an examinee achieves success can lead to a more tailored instructional approach. The Don't Forget box lists additional qualitative considerations to consider during WIAT-III administration.

# DON'T FORGET

## Qualitative Considerations

*General*
- Are test behaviors typical of the examinee's performance? Cross-validate results with reports from teachers, parents, and others who are familiar with the examinee.
- Are there mitigating circumstances such as illness or anxiety that might have affected test performance?
- How does the examinee perceive their own strengths and weaknesses, and are their self-perceptions accurate?
- Does the examinee seek out your encouragement and approval? Does the examinee seem concerned about whether responses are right or wrong?

*Strategy Use*
- Record the use of problem-solving strategies, such as subvocalization or thinking out loud, counting on fingers, and sounding out words letter by letter. Strategies have implications for how the examinee processes information. For example, an examinee who uses subvocalization when spelling a word may be relying on phonological cues or using rehearsal to keep the word in working memory. An examinee who misspells a word, says, "That doesn't look right," and then tries a different spelling may be relying on orthographic memory to identify the correct spelling.

*Executive Function*
- Does the examinee self-monitor his or her work, rereading what was written, verifying an answer, or rechecking a passage prior to answering a comprehension question? Are some errors seemingly due to lack of attention to detail or lack of self-monitoring, rather than a knowledge gap?
- Is the examinee attentive and alert during the test session? Note signs of distractibility, inattention, or fatigue.
- Does the examinee tend to respond thoughtfully or impulsively? Does the examinee wait to respond until the instructions are finished?

*(continued)*

(*Continued*)

- Differentiating *can't* versus *won't*. Does the examinee seem to give his or her best effort? When the examinee says "Don't Know," are they unable or unwilling to perform that skill? Does frustration set in once errors begin to occur? Is the examinee quick to give up?

*Task Analysis*
- Compare the examinee's performance across subtests, and observe how task demands affect performance. For example, observe how the examinee decodes unfamiliar words when reading from a list (on Word Reading and Pseudoword Decoding) in comparison to reading unfamiliar words in context (on Oral Reading Fluency).

## USING THE WIAT-III ACROSS MULTIPLE ADMINISTRATIONS

The WIAT-III may be readministered to the same examinee by following the guidelines provided in the Caution box. With only one form, practice effects become a concern if subtests are readministered too frequently or after too short a time. The WIAT-III and KTEA-3 may be alternated across administrations; however, growth scale values are not comparable across tests (see Don't Forget box).

## CAUTION
••••••••••••••••••••••••••••••••••••••••••••••••••••••••••••••••••••••••••••••••••••••

- As a general guideline, wait 8 months to 1 year before readministering the same subtests from the WIAT-III.
- Use growth scale values (GSVs) for comparing performance across multiple administrations or assessing progress over time. Comparing standard scores may be misleading for evaluating progress.

## DON'T FORGET
••••••••••••••••••••••••••••••••••••••••••••••••••••••••••••••••••••••••••••••••••••••

**Question:** Are the WIAT-III and KTEA-3 growth scale values (GSVs) comparable? If a student was administered the WIAT-III Pseudoword Decoding subtest and one year later was administered the KTEA-3 Nonsense Word Decoding subtest, can I compare the GSVs to measure progress?

**Answer:** No. Even though the WIAT-III and KTEA-3 GSVs were developed and scaled similarly, GSVs are never comparable across different tests or subtests. GSVs reflect the content and raw score distribution of the specific subtest.

## 🖋 TEST YOURSELF 🖋

1. **The WIAT-III normative sample includes representative proportions of students with clinical diagnoses and a representative proportion of students identified as academically gifted.**

   (a) True
   (b) False

2. **Average test-retest gains are least pronounced for subtests in which of the following achievement area?**

   (a) Oral Language
   (b) Basic Reading
   (c) Reading Comprehension
   (d) Reading Fluency
   (e) Written Expression
   (f) Mathematics

3. **Average test-retest gains are most pronounced for subtests in which of the following two achievement areas?**

   (a) Oral Language
   (b) Basic Reading
   (c) Reading Comprehension
   (d) Reading Fluency
   (e) Written Expression
   (f) Mathematics

4. **The WIAT-III skills analysis may be used with all students—even those who perform well above the mean.**

   (a) True
   (b) False

5. **As a general guideline, how much time should pass before readministering a WIAT-III to the same examinee?**

   (a) 3 to 7 months
   (b) 8 to 12 months
   (c) Over 12 months

6. **If an examiner obtains a grade-based standard score for a ninth-grade student who reversed to the eighth-grade item set on the Reading Comprehension or Oral Reading Fluency subtest, which comparison group is used to derive that standard score?**

   (a) Ninth graders' performance on the eighth-grade item set
   (b) Ninth graders' performance on the ninth-grade item set
   (c) Eighth graders' performance on the eighth-grade item set
   (d) Eighth graders' performance on the ninth-grade item set

7. **Grade-based norms are generally preferred when interpreting assessment results from a student who is unusually young or old for his/her grade.**
   (a) True
   (b) False

8. **Use of an audio recorder to record student responses is highly recommended when administering which of the following subtests?**
   (a) Oral Expression
   (b) Word Reading
   (c) Pseudoword Decoding
   (d) Oral Reading Fluency
   (e) All of the above

9. **Audio files are provided for administering the items for which of the following subtest components?**
   (a) Oral Discourse Comprehension
   (b) Receptive Vocabulary
   (c) Sentence Repetition
   (d) Oral Word Fluency

10. **Which type of score should be used when comparing an examinee's performance across two or more WIAT-III administrations to determine how much progress has been made?**
    (a) Standard scores
    (b) Percentile ranks
    (c) Age or grade equivalents
    (d) Growth scale values

*Answers:* 1. a; 2. e; 3. a, c; 4. a; 5. b; 6. a; 7. a; 8. e; 9. a; 10. d.

# Four

## CLINICAL APPLICATIONS

This chapter focuses on some key clinical applications of the KTEA-3 and WIAT-III, which are organized into two parts:

*Part One: Using the KTEA-3 and WIAT-III With Cognitive Ability Tests*
- Linking studies
- Overview of the WISC-V, WISC-V Integrated, and KABC-II
- Using a Cattell-Horn-Carroll (CHC) framework to integrate assessment results
- Using a neuropsychological approach to integrate assessment results
- Qualitative-behavioral analysis of assessment results
- Identification of specific learning disabilities

*Part Two: New Composite Scores, Special Considerations, and Ongoing Research*
- Interpretation and use of three new composite scores: KTEA-3 Dyslexia Index, WIAT-III Dyslexia Index, and KTEA-3 Oral Reading Fluency composite.
- Considerations for testing special populations, including accessibility and accommodation concerns.
- Ongoing research on gender differences in writing.

In the first half of this chapter, we discuss topics related to utilizing the relationship between measures of achievement and cognitive ability. The KTEA-3 and WIAT-III were designed to work in tandem with specific cognitive instruments to identify strengths and weaknesses in academic skills as well as cognitive processing areas. For this reason, the KTEA-3 and WIAT-III included linking studies with tests of cognitive ability. When the KTEA-3 or WIAT-III are paired with a cognitive ability instrument (e.g., WISC-V, DAS-II, KABC-II), examiners can develop a more comprehensive understanding of the reasons for academic difficulties and how to bridge assessment to intervention. Two approaches to integrating achievement and cognitive ability are outlined in this first half of the chapter, including a CHC-framework and a neuropsychological approach. In addition, considerations for how to integrate behavioral and qualitative data in the interpretation of assessment results are provided.

In the final section of Part One, we review some of the data on the clinical application of the KTEA-3 and WIAT-III in special populations and how these data may inform intervention. We describe how the results from the KTEA-3 and WIAT-III may be used within contemporary models for identifying specific learning disabilities, and provide information about a newly available intervention guide.

In Part Two, we discuss new composite scores, special considerations for testing individuals with special needs, and ongoing research on gender differences. Examiners who assess students with dyslexia will be particularly interested in the new composite scores that are presented, which include the KTEA-3 Dyslexia Index, WIAT-III Dyslexia Index, and KTEA-3 Oral Reading Fluency composite. Before testing individuals who have visual impairment, who are hard of hearing, or who have motor impairment, clinicians will benefit from reviewing the section on accessibility and accommodation concerns. Part Two culminates with a discussion of research findings on gender differences in achievement tests.

## PART ONE: USING THE KTEA-3 AND WIAT-III WITH COGNITIVE ABILITY TESTS

Part One reviews the essential information needed to pair the KTEA-3 or WIAT-III with a cognitive ability test, including a review of the cognitive validity linking data available for the KTEA-3 and WIAT-III, and the key features of the WISC-V, WISC-V Integrated, and KABC-II.

Helpful guidance is also provided for integrating test results using a CHC framework or a neuropsychological approach, and conducting a qualitative/behavioral analysis of assessment data. There are many approaches to integrating the results of the KTEA-3 and WIAT-III with a cognitive ability instrument, and no single approach will match the needs of all examiners. Each examiner brings a wealth of experience, internal norms, and beliefs to the use of these tests. Additionally, every examiner has areas of diagnostic specialties and special populations with whom he or she works, and different needs and wants. We recommend acquiring a flexible interpretive approach that allows you to utilize different theoretical and procedural frameworks for different circumstances.

For examiners involved in identifying specific learning disabilities (SLD), Part One also reviews the key clinical studies that have been conducted, describes several models for identifying SLD, and provides guidance for analyzing subtypes of SLD for intervention planning.

### Linking Studies

A linking study is conducted by administering an achievement test (KTEA-3 or WIAT-III) and a cognitive ability test to the same group of examinees for the purpose of reporting correlations between their scores. The varying strengths of these

**Table 4.1 KTEA-3 and WIAT-III Cognitive Ability Linking Studies**

| Cognitive Ability Test | KTEA-3 | WIAT-III |
|---|:---:|:---:|
| DAS-II | X | X |
| KABC-II | X | |
| WPPSI-III | | X |
| WPPSI-IV | | X |
| WISC-IV | | X |
| WISC-V | X | X |
| WAIS-IV | | X |
| WNV | | X |

*Notes:* DAS-II = Differential Ability Scales–Second Edition (Elliott, 2007); KABC-II = Kaufman Assessment Battery for Children–Second Edition (Kaufman & Kaufman, 2004b); WPPSI-III and WPPSI-IV = Wechsler Preschool and Primary Scale of Intelligence–Third Edition (WPPSI-III; Wechsler, 2002) and Fourth Edition (WPPSI-IV; Wechsler, 2012a); WISC-IV = Wechsler Intelligence Scale for Children–Fourth Edition (Wechsler, 2003); WISC-V = Wechsler Intelligence Scale for Children–Fifth Edition (Wechsler, 2014a); WAIS-IV = Wechsler Adult Intelligence Scale–Fourth Edition (Wechsler, 2008); WNV = Wechsler Nonverbal Scale of Ability (Wechsler & Naglieri, 2006).

correlations provide evidence to support the construct validity of each test. A linking study is also conducted to provide the necessary data (e.g., critical values, base rates) for conducting an ability-achievement discrepancy (AAD) or a pattern of strengths and weaknesses (PSW) analysis for the identification of a specific learning disability.

Table 4.1 lists the linking studies available (at the time of this book's publication) between the KTEA-3 or WIAT-III and various cognitive ability tests. As shown in the table, the KTEA-3 and WIAT-III both have linking data with the DAS-II and WISC-V. However, only the KTEA-3 is linked with the KABC-II, and only the WIAT-III is linked with the WPPSI-IV, WPPSI-V, WISC-IV, WAIS-IV, and WNV.

For linking studies data with the KTEA-3, refer to the KTEA-3 *Technical & Interpretive Manual* for data with the DAS-II and KABC-II, and refer to the *WISC-V Technical and Interpretive Manual* (Wechsler, 2014a) for data with the WISC-V.

For linking studies data with the WIAT-III, refer to the *WIAT-III Technical Manual* (Pearson, 2010a) for data with the WPPSI-III, WISC-IV, WAIS-IV, WNV, and DAS-II. Refer to the *WPPSI-IV Technical and Interpretive Manual* (Wechsler, 2012b) for data with the WPPSI-IV, and refer to the *WISC-V Technical and Interpretive Manual* for data with the WISC-V.

This chapter focuses on using the KTEA-3 and WIAT-III with the new WISC-V, WISC-V Integrated, and KABC-II because these tests are commonly used when assessing school age children.

## Overview of the WISC-V, WISC-V Integrated, and KABC-II

A brief review of the WISC-V and KABC-II is provided here prior to discussing how to integrate these cognitive tests with the achievement tests within a CHC Framework and a neuropsychological approach, as well as linking them with behavioral and qualitative analysis. For the interested reader, in-depth information on each of these cognitive tests can be found elsewhere (e.g., Kaufman, Lichtenberger, Fletcher-Jansen, & Kaufman, 2005; Kaufman, Raiford, & Coalson, 2015). Note that the general principles of integrating the KTEA-3 and WIAT-III through a CHC-framework or a neuropsychological approach can be applied to integration with other cognitive instruments, but the WISC-V and KABC-II are highlighted here because of their frequent use by clinicians.

### *Description of the WISC-V*

Because the WISC-V can be used together with the KTEA-3 or WIAT-III, it is important to understand the structure of the WISC-V and the WISC-V Integrated (Wechsler, 2014ab, Wechsler & Kaplan, 2015), and to identify the cognitive abilities measured by each index. Correlational studies between the achievement instruments and the WISC-V and the WISC-V Integrated are discussed. Clinical studies, which are addressed later in this chapter, reveal unique patterns of performance between achievement and the WISC-V and WISC-V Integrated.

Rapid Reference 4.1 presents the five-domain structure of the WISC-V. The subtests were designed to measure a broad range of cognitive abilities. The new framework of the WISC-V is based on theory and supported by clinical research and factor-analytic results (see a discussion in Chapter 4 of the *WISC-V Technical and Interpretive Manual*). Subtests are grouped into three categories: primary (recommended for comprehensive evaluation of ability), secondary (yield further information for clinical decision making), or complementary (giving further information about other cognitive abilities). An individual's performance can be evaluated using the five Primary index scores: Verbal Comprehension Index (VCI), Visual Spatial Index (VSI), Fluid Reasoning Index (FRI), Working Memory Index (WMI), and Processing Speed Index (PSI). The WISC-V also yields five Ancillary Index Scales and three Complementary Index Scales (see Rapid Reference 4.1). Each subtest yields a scaled score ($M = 10$; $SD = 3$) and each index produces a derived standard score ($M = 100$; $SD = 15$). In addition to the WISC-V subtest and composite scores, 10 scaled or standard *process* scores on four subtests (i.e., Block Design No Time Bonus, Block Design Partial Score, Digit Span Forward, Digit Span Backward, Digit Span Sequencing, Cancellation Random, and Cancellation Structured, Naming Speed Color-Object, Naming Speed Letter-Number, Naming Speed Letter-Number) can be obtained for the purpose of providing more in-depth information about an examinee's performance.

# ≡ Rapid Reference 4.1

## Structure of the WISC–V

| Full Scale[1] | | | | |
|---|---|---|---|---|
| Verbal Comprehension | Visual Spatial | Fluid Reasoning | Working Memory | Processing Speed |
| Similarities | Block Design | Matrix Reasoning | Digit Span | Coding |
| Vocabulary | *Visual Puzzles* | Figure Weights | *Picture Span* | *Symbol Search* |
| *Information* | | *Picture Concepts* | *Letter-Number Sequencing* | *Cancellation* |
| *Comprehension* | | *Arithmetic* | | |

| Primary Index Scales | | | | |
|---|---|---|---|---|
| Verbal Comprehension | Visual Spatial | Fluid Reasoning | Working Memory | Processing Speed |
| Similarities | Block Design | Matrix Reasoning | Digit Span | Coding |
| Vocabulary | Visual Puzzles | Figure Weights | Picture Span | Symbol Search |

| Ancillary Index Scales | | | | |
|---|---|---|---|---|
| Quantitative Reasoning | Auditory Working Memory | Nonverbal | General Ability | Cognitive Proficiency |
| Figure Weights | Digit Span | Block Design | Similarities | Digit Span |
| Arithmetic | Letter-Number Sequencing | Visual Puzzles | Vocabulary | Picture Span |
| | | Matrix Reasoning | Block Design | Coding |
| | | Figure Weights | Matrix Reasoning | Symbol Search |
| | | Picture Span | Figure Weights | |
| | | Coding | | |

| Complementary Index Scales | | |
|---|---|---|
| Naming Speed | Symbol Translation | Storage and Retrieval |
| Naming Speed Literacy | Immediate Symbol Translation | Naming Speed Index |
| Naming Speed Quantity | Delayed Symbol Translation | Symbol Translation Index |
| | Recognition Symbol Translation | |

[1] The subtests that may be used for substitutes at the Full Scale level are shown in italics.

The WISC-V introduced new subtests to improve the measurement of fluid reasoning, working memory, and visual spatial ability. The importance of fluid reasoning is emphasized in many theories of cognitive functioning (Carroll, 1997; Cattell, 1943, 1963; Cattell & Horn, 1978; Sternberg, 1995). Tasks that require *fluid reasoning* involve the process of "manipulating abstractions, rules, generalizations, and logical relationships" (Carroll, 1993, p. 583). The measurement of fluid reasoning is incorporated in the new subtest, Figure Weights (paired with the old subtest Matrix Reasoning). *Working memory* is the ability to actively maintain information in conscious awareness, perform some operation or manipulation with it, and produce a result. Working memory is an essential component of fluid reasoning and other higher-order cognitive processes and is closely related to achievement (Fry & Hale, 1996; Perlow, Jattuso, & Moore, 1997; Swanson, 1996). Working memory is assessed with the new Picture Span subtest and by the former Digit Span subtest. Because research indicates greater demands on working memory occur for Digit Span Backward than Digit Span Forward, separate process scores were developed for this subtest. The third new subtest Visual Puzzles was added to measure *visual spatial ability* alongside the familiar Block Design subtest. Visual Puzzles measures spatial relations, visual processing, nonverbal reasoning, and analysis of whole-part relationships.

If clinically necessary, the WISC-V also has five complementary subtests that can be administered to provide information about other cognitive abilities. These complementary subtests are used only to derive the three complementary index scores (see Rapid Reference 4.1) and are not used in any other composite scores. The complementary subtests are designed to measuring naming speed and visual-verbal associative memory, which are cognitive processes associated with reading, math, and writing.

### Description of the WISC-V Integrated

Rapid Reference 4.2 shows the structure of the WISC-V Integrated 2015, which adds 14 process subtests to the WISC-V battery. Six of the process subtests are *multiple-choice adaptations* of the WISC-V subtests (i.e., Similarities Multiple Choice, Vocabulary Multiple Choice, Picture Vocabulary Multiple Choice, Comprehension Multiple Choice, Information Multiple Choice, Block Design Multiple Choice). These subtests contain the same item content as their corresponding core or supplemental subtests, but they contain modifications to the mode of presentation or response format. Figure Weights Process Approach is a new subtest that gives additional time for the examinee to respond. Arithmetic Process Approach is an adaptation of the WISC-V Arithmetic subtests that presents the items in multiple modalities. Written Arithmetic presents the WISC-V Arithmetic items in a paper-and pencil format. Spatial Span is a visual analog of Digit Span that requires the child to reproduce a sequence of tapped blocks forward and backward. Sentence Recall is an auditory working memory task that has the child recall the last word of questions that are asked. Coding Recall and Coding Copy provide information about performance on the WISC-V Coding subtest, including recognition memory, visual recall, learning ability, and graphomotor speed. Finally, Cancellation Abstract has a child scan a random and a structured

# ≡ Rapid Reference 4.2

## Structure of the WISC-V Integrated

|  | WISC-V | WISC-V Integrated | Index Score |
|---|---|---|---|
| Verbal Comprehension | Similarities | Similarities Multiple Choice | Multiple Choice Verbal Comprehension Index |
|  | Vocabulary | Vocabulary Multiple Choice |  |
|  |  | Picture Vocabulary Multiple Choice |  |
|  | Information | Information Multiple Choice |  |
|  | Comprehension | Comprehension Multiple Choice |  |
| Visual Spatial | Block Design | Block Design Multiple Choice |  |
| Fluid Reasoning | Figure Weights | Figure Weights Process Approach |  |
|  | Arithmetic | Arithmetic Process Approach Written Arithmetic |  |
| Working Memory | Picture Span | Spatial Span | Visual Working Memory Index |
|  |  | Sentence Recall |  |
| Processing Speed | Coding | Coding Recall Coding Copy |  |
|  | Cancellation | Cancellation Abstract |  |

arrangement of shapes within a specified time limit to tap rate of test taking, speed of visual perceptual processing, and decision making. Overall, the process subtests provide additional measures of cognitive abilities and may be used to test specific hypotheses regarding underlying cognitive processes and test-taking behaviors that contribute to performance on the core and supplemental subtests. On occasion, a process subtest may not measure the same construct as the primary subtest within a cognitive domain. For example, if a child performs poorly on Coding B (a measure of processing speed), the examiner may elect to administer Coding Recall (a measure of incidental learning) to see if the child remembers the pairings of numbers and symbols on Coding B. Although it is not a measure of processing speed, Coding Recall is included in the Processing Speed domain because it provides additional information about the cognitive processes contributing to performance on Coding B.

One of the primary benefits of adding select subtests from the WISC-V Integrated to a psychoeducational battery that includes the WIAT-III or KTEA-3 is to delve more deeply into the role played by executive functions, working memory, and processing speed in learning. For example, empirical data gathered from clinical populations suggest that working memory may be affected differentially by neurodevelopmental problems or brain injury. Studies have identified distinct neuroanatomical locations for verbal, visuospatial, and executive working memory functions (Gathercole et al., 2004). The WISC-V Integrated measures both the auditory-verbal (e.g., Digit-Span and Letter-Number Sequencing Process Approach) and the visuospatial (i.e., Visual Digit Span and Spatial Span) components. Further, several of the WISC-V subtest process scores (e.g., Block Design and Block Design No Time Bonus) provide scaled scores that are derived from total raw scores with and without time-bonus points. This type of information is especially helpful when making recommendations for instruction and accommodations in the classroom.

### Quantitative Analyses With the WISC-V

For comparing ability and achievement performance, WIAT-III or KTEA-3 subtest or composite standard scores may be compared with index scores from the WISC-V. With some achievement tests it is necessary to use the composite scores to identify ability-achievement discrepancies because of the lower reliability scores on the individual achievement subtests. This is not the case with the WIAT-III or KTEA-3 because of strong reliability scores. On the WIAT-III nearly all average subtest reliabilities across the fall, spring, and age samples range from good (.83–.89) to excellent (.90–.97). KTEA-3 mean subtest reliabilities are also in the good to excellent range (with the exception of Object Naming Facility, Letter Naming Facility, Associational Fluency, and Writing Fluency, which have reliabilities of <.80). Reliabilities of .90 or higher provide strong support for the use of a subtest score for making educational decisions. Subtest scores with reliabilities between .80 and .90 are also suitable for making educational decisions in most settings. In fact, there are times when a discrepancy among subtests contributing to a composite exists, and individual subtest scores should be used because the composite score could mask important weaknesses and be misleading.

Correlation coefficients between WIAT-III or KTEA-3 scores and WISC-V scores demonstrate the strong relationship between the tests. The WISC-V and the WIAT-III were administered to 211 children aged 6–16 years with a testing interval between 0 and 59 days. The WISC-V and the KTEA-3 were administered to 207 children aged 6–16 years with a testing interval between 0 and 52 days. The correlations between the KTEA-3 and WISC-V are highest at the composite level. Correlations between the WISC-V FSIQ and KTEA-3 composite scores are moderate to high, with the strongest correlation between the Academic Skills Battery and FSIQ (.82). The FSIQ correlations between KTEA-3 Reading, Math and Written Language composites were .75, .79, and .69, respectively. WISC-V VCI also shared the highest correlations with KTEA-3 Reading (.77), Reading Understanding (.76), ASB (.76), and Comprehension (.78) composites. See Table 5.11 in the *WISC-V Technical and Interpretive Manual* (Wechsler et al., 2014b) for the complete correlation data. Similar to findings with the KTEA-3, the WIAT-III and WISC-V show the strongest correlation between Total Achievement and WISC-V FSIQ (.81). The FSIQ correlations between WIAT-III Total Reading, Mathematics, and Oral Language composites were .70, .71, and .74, respectively. The WISC-V VCI additionally shared the highest correlations with Total Achievement (.74).

Conceptually and psychometrically, the WISC-V and WISC-V Integrated paired with the either the KTEA-3 or WIAT-III have enhanced clinical utility, especially in the assessment of children with various types of learning disabilities, children with ADHD, children with language disorders, children with open or closed head injury, children with Autistic Disorder, and children with Asperger's Disorder. Later in this chapter, information related to some of these clinical groups will be presented.

### Description of the KABC-II

The KTEA-II and the KABC-II were conormed tests that allowed a similar and cohesive theoretical basis for these tests.[1] Although neither the KTEA-3 nor the WIAT-III was conormed with the KABC-II, each achievement test can enhance the diagnostic "reach" of the cognitive battery; and the combination of tests provides a cohesive and large portion of a comprehensive assessment, especially when interpreted within a theoretical framework.

This section introduces the reader to the design and make-up of the KABC-II and the Cattell-Horn-Carroll (CHC) broad and narrow abilities that the KABC-II was designed to assess. Different aspects of the integration of the KTEA-3, WIAT-III, and the KABC-II are explored by examining theoretical, quantitative, clinical, qualitative, and procedural points of view.

The KABC-II is a measure of the processing and cognitive abilities of children and adolescents between the ages of 3 years 0 months and 18 years 11 months. The KABC-II is founded in two theoretical models: Luria's (1966, 1970, 1973) neuropsychological model, featuring three Blocks, and the Cattell-Horn-Carroll (CHC) approach to categorizing specific cognitive abilities (Carroll, 1997; Flanagan, McGrew, & Ortiz, 2000). The KABC-II yields a separate global score for each of these two theoretical models: the global score measuring general mental processing ability from the Luria perspective is the Mental Processing Index (MPI), and global score measuring general cognitive ability from the Cattell-Horn-Carroll perspective is the Fluid-Crystallized Index (FCI). The key difference between these two global

---

1. The section titled "Description of the KABC-II" is adapted with permission from Chapter 6 of *Essentials of KABC-II Assessment* (Kaufman, Lichtenberger, Fletcher-Janzen, & Kaufman, 2005).

scores is that the MPI (Luria's theory) *excludes* measures of acquired knowledge, whereas the FCI (CHC theory) *includes* measures of acquired knowledge. Only one of these two global scores is computed for any examinee. Prior to testing a client, examiners choose the interpretive system (i.e., Luria or CHC) that best fits with both their personal orientation and the reason for referral.

In addition to the MPI and FCI, the KABC-II offers from one to five scales depending on the age level of the child and the interpretive approach that the clinician chooses to take. At age 3, there is only one scale, a global measure of ability, composed of either five subtests (Mental Processing Index [MPI]) or seven subtests (Fluid-Crystallized Index [FCI]). For ages 4–6, subtests are organized into either three scales (Luria model) or four scales (CHC model): Sequential/*Gsm*, Simultaneous/*Gv*, and Learning/*Glr* are in both models, and Verbal/*Gc* is only in the CHC model. For ages 7–18, four scales (Luria) or five scales (CHC) are available, with the Planning/ *Gf* scale joining the aforementioned KABC-II scales. The KABC-II scales for each age level are shown in Rapid Reference 4.3.

## ≡ *Rapid Reference 4.3*

### KABC-II Scales at Each Age Level

| Age 3 | Ages 4–6 | Ages 7–18 |
|---|---|---|
| MPI, FCI, or NVI | MPI, FCI, or NVI | MPI, FCI, or NVI |
| *(no additional scales are obtained at age 3)* | Learning/Glr | Learning/Glr |
| Sequential/Gsm | Sequential/Gsm | Sequential/Gsm |
| Simultaneous/Gv | Simultaneous/Gv | Simultaneous/Gv |
| | Knowledge/Gc | Planning/Gf |
| | | Knowledge/Gc |

Note: The MPI from the Luria system excludes Knowledge/Gc subtests (age 3) and scale (ages 4–18). The FCI of the CHC system includes the Knowledge/Gc subtests (age 3) and scale (ages 4–18).

From the Luria perspective, the KABC-II scales correspond to learning ability, sequential processing, simultaneous processing, and planning ability. From the vantage point of the CHC model, as applied to the KABC-II, the scales measure the following Broad Abilities: Short-term memory, visualization, long-term memory, fluid reasoning, and crystallized ability (Rapid Reference 4.4 describes how the scales are conceptualized by each theoretical perspective). The names of the KABC-II scales reflect both the Luria process it is believed to measure and its CHC Broad Ability, as indicated in Rapid Reference 4.4: Learning/*Glr*, Sequential/*Gsm*, Simultaneous/*Gv*, and Planning/*Gf*. However, the Verbal/*Gc* scale that measures crystallized ability reflects only CHC theory, as it is specifically excluded from the Luria system.

## ≡ Rapid Reference 4.4

### Definitions of Luria and CHC Terms

| Luria Term | CHC Term |
|---|---|
| Learning Ability | Long-Term Storage & Retrieval (*Glr*) |
| Reflects an integration of the processes associated with all three Blocks, placing a premium on the attention-concentration processes that are in the domain of Block 1, but also requiring Block 2 coding processes and Block 3 strategy generation to learn and retain the new information with efficiency. Sequential and simultaneous processing are associated primarily with Luria's Block 2 and pertain to either a step-by-step (sequential) or holistic (simultaneous) processing of information. | Storing and efficiently retrieving newly learned or previously learned information |
| Sequential Processing | Short-Term Memory (*Gsm*) |
| Measures the kind of coding function that Luria labeled "successive" and involves arranging input in sequential or serial order to solve a problem, where each idea is linearly and temporally related to the preceding one. | Taking in and holding information and then using it within a few seconds |
| Simultaneous Processing | Visual Processing (*Gv*) |
| Measures the second type, or simultaneous, coding function associated with Block 2. For its tasks, the input has to be integrated and synthesized simultaneously (holistically), usually spatially, to produce the appropriate solution. As mentioned earlier, the KABC-II measure of simultaneous processing deliberately blends Luria's Block 2 and Block 3 to enhance the complexity of the simultaneous syntheses that are required. | Perceiving, storing, manipulating, and thinking with visual patterns |
| Planning Ability | Fluid Reasoning (*Gf*) |
| Measures the high-level, decision-making, executive processes associated with Block 3. However, as Reitan (1988) states, "Block 3 is involved in no sensory, motor, perceptual, or speech functions and is devoted exclusively to analysis, planning, and organization of programs for behavior" (p. 335). Because any cognitive task involves perception of sensory input and either a motor or verbal response, the KABC-II measure of planning ability necessarily requires functions associated with the other two Blocks as well. | Solving novel problems by using reasoning abilities such as induction and deduction |

*(continued)*

(Continued)

| Luria Term | CHC Term |
|---|---|
| (Crystallized ability does not have an analogous ability that is included in the Luria model.) | Crystallized Ability (Gc) |
| | Demonstrat I 0ng the breadth and depth of knowledge acquired from one's culture |

Note: The names of the KABC-II scales were chosen to reflect both their Luria and CHC underpinnings. Verbal/Gc is included in the CHC system for the computation of the FCI, but it is excluded from the Luria system for the computation of the Mental Processing Index (MPI). The Planning/Gf scale is for ages 7–18 only. All other scales are for ages 4–18. Only the MPI and FCI are offered for 3-year-olds.

In addition to the MPI and FCI, and the five scales, the KABC-II has a Nonverbal Scale, composed of subtests that may be administered in pantomime and responded to motorically. The Nonverbal Scale permits valid assessment of children who are hearing impaired, have limited English proficiency, have moderate to severe speech or language impairments, and other disabilities that make the Core battery unsuitable. This special scale comprises a mixture of Core and supplementary subtests for all age groups. The interested reader can find more information about this scale in *Essentials of KABC-II Assessment* (Kaufman, Lichtenberger, Fletcher-Janzen, & Kaufman, 2005).

The KABC-II includes 18 subtests (described in Rapid Reference 4.5), which comprise a Core battery and an Expanded battery. The Expanded battery offers supplementary subtests to increase the breadth of the constructs that are measured by the Core battery, to follow up hypotheses, and to provide a comparison of the child's initial learning and delayed recall of new learning. The scale structure for each age group varies slightly, and is described in detail in the *KABC-II Manual* (Kaufman & Kaufman, 2004b).

## ≡ Rapid Reference 4.5

### Description of KABC-II Subtests

| Subtests | Description |
|---|---|
| Sequential/Gsm | |
| Word Order | The child touches a series of silhouettes of common objects in the same order as the examiner said the names of the objects; more difficult items include an interference task (color naming) between the stimulus and response. |

(continued)

(Continued)

| Subtests | Description |
|---|---|
| **Sequential/*Gsm* (continued)** | |
| Number Recall | The child repeats a series of numbers in the same sequence as the examiner said them, with series ranging in length from two to nine numbers; the numbers are single digits, except that 10 is used instead of 7 to ensure that all numbers are one syllable. |
| Hand Movements | The child copies the examiner's precise sequence of taps on the table with the fist, palm, or side of the hand. |
| **Simultaneous/*Gv* Subtests** | |
| Rover | The child moves a toy dog to a bone on a checkerboard-like grid that contains obstacles (rocks and weeds) and tries to find the "quickest" path—the one that takes the fewest moves. |
| Triangles | For most items, the child assembles several identical rubber triangles (blue on one side, yellow on the other) to match a picture of an abstract design; for easier items, the child assembles a different set of colorful rubber shapes to match a model constructed by the examiner. |
| Conceptual Thinking | The child views a set of four or five pictures and identifies the one picture that does not belong with the others; some items present meaningful stimuli, and others use abstract stimuli. |
| Face Recognition | The child attends closely to photographs of one or two faces that are exposed briefly and then selects the correct face or faces, shown in a different pose, from a group photograph. |
| Gestalt Closure | The child mentally "fills in the gaps" in a partially completed "inkblot" drawing and names (or describes) the object or action depicted in the drawing. |
| Block Counting | The child counts the exact number of blocks in various pictures of stacks of blocks; the stacks are configured such that one or more blocks is hidden or partially hidden from view. |
| **Planning/*Gf* Subtests** | |
| Pattern Reasoning | The child is shown a series of stimuli that form a logical, linear pattern, but one stimulus is missing; the child completes the pattern by selecting the correct stimulus from an array of four to six options at the bottom of the page. (Most stimuli are abstract, geometric shapes, but some easy items use meaningful stimuli.) |
| Story Completion | The child is shown a row of pictures that tell a story, but some of the pictures are missing. The child is given a set of pictures, selects only the ones that are needed to complete the story, and places the missing pictures in their correct locations. |

(continued)

(Continued)

| Subtests | Description |
|---|---|
| **Learning/Glr Subtests** | |
| Atlantis | The examiner teaches the child the nonsense names for fanciful pictures of fish, plants, and shells; the child demonstrates learning by pointing to each picture (out of an array of pictures) when it is named. |
| Atlantis—Delayed | The child demonstrates delayed recall of paired associations learned about 15–25 minutes earlier during Atlantis by pointing to the picture of the fish, plant, or shell that is named by the examiner. |
| Rebus Learning | The examiner teaches the child the word or concept associated with each particular rebus (drawing) and the child then "reads" aloud phrases and sentences composed of these rebuses. |
| Rebus Learning—Delayed | The child demonstrates delayed recall of paired associations learned about 15–25 minutes earlier during Rebus Learning by "reading" phrases and sentences composed of those same rebuses. |
| **Knowledge/Gc Subtests** | |
| Riddles | The examiner provides several characteristics of a concrete or abstract verbal concept and the child has to point to it (early items) or name it (later items). |
| Expressive Vocabulary | The child provides the name of a pictured object. |
| Verbal Knowledge | The child selects from an array of six pictures the one that corresponds to a vocabulary word or answers a general information question. |

(a) At ages 5–6, Pattern Reasoning and Story Completion are categorized as Simultaneous/Gv subtests.
Note: Descriptions are adapted from the KABC-II Manual (Kaufman & Kaufman, 2004b).

## Quantitative Analyses With the KABC-II

Correlation coefficients between KTEA-3 global scores and scores on cognitive tests were presented and discussed in the validity section of Chapter 2 in this book. (Correlations between the WIAT-III and KABC-II are not available.) Overall, the KABC-3 FCI and MPI correlated substantially (mean $r = .71–.75$) with the KTEA-3 Academic Skills Battery. The KTEA-3 Comprehensive Form Written Language and Math composites also strongly correlated with the KABC-II FCI and MPI (ranging from .67–.71). The KTEA-3 Reading and Oral Language composites had slightly lower correlations with the KABC-II (e.g., ranging from .54 to .60).

To further examine the cognitive-achievement relationships we can study how each KABC-II Scale Index correlates with major KTEA-3 composites. Rapid Reference 4.6 shows these correlations and asterisks are used to indicate the KABC-II Index that correlates highest (**) and second highest (*) with each KTEA-3 composite.

## ≡ Rapid Reference 4.6

### KABC-II Scale Index Correlations With KTEA-3 Composites (Ages 4–18 Years)

| KABC-II Scale | KTEA-3 Composite | | | |
|---|---|---|---|---|
| | Academic Skills Battery | Reading | Math | Written Language |
| Sequential/Gsm | .44 | .25 | .44 | .40 |
| Simultaneous/Gv | .52 | .39 | .59** | .42 |
| Learning/Glr | .55 | .48 | .46 | .65** |
| Planning/Gf | .58* | .50* | .57* | .49 |
| Knowledge/Gc | .63** | .57** | .50 | .61* |

*Second-highest correlate of each KTEA-3 composite.
**Highest correlate of each KTEA-3 composite.
Note: Total = N = 99. Data are adapted from Table 2.15 of KTEA-3 Technical & Interpretive Manual (Kaufman and Kaufman, 2014a).

Knowledge/Gc scale was the strongest correlate for the KTEA-3 Reading composite (.63), Simultaneous/Gv was the strongest correlate for the KTEA-3 Math composite (.59), and Learning/Glr was the strongest correlate for the KTEA-3 Written Language composite (.65). The second-best correlate was Planning/Gf (r's of .50 and .57 for Reading and Math, respectively), although Knowledge/Gc was the second-best correlate of Written Language (.61). The poorest relationships with all areas of academic achievement was Sequential/Gsm (r's of .25–.44).

Given that the KABC-II's Knowledge/Gc Index is designed to measure the depth and breadth of knowledge acquired from one's culture (including schooling), the strong relationship between it and reading was not surprising. The good correlations with achievement for the KABC-II scales—Planning/Gf and Learning/Glr—attest to the importance in the classroom of the ability to solve problems and learn new material during a clinical evaluation of general cognitive ability. Math tends to be more strongly related to visual-spatial abilities than other areas, hence the relationship demonstrated between KABC-II Simultaneous/Gv and KTEA-3 Math composite.

## USING A CHC FRAMEWORK TO INTEGRATE ASSESSMENT RESULTS

The integration of both the WIAT-III and KTEA-3 with cognitive ability tests like the WISC-V and KABC-II allows examiners to sample the spectrum of Broad and Narrow Abilities defined by the Cattell-Horn-Carroll (CHC) model. The most recent derivation of the CHC model which was detailed in the WJ IV Manual (Schrank, McGrew, & Mather, 2014a) includes 10 Broad Abilities and about 35 Narrow Abilities. However, prior to that refinement of the theory in 2014, scholars such as Flanagan and her colleagues created interpretive models based on CHC theory's list of 16 broad abilities and about 80 narrow abilities (Flanagan, Ortiz, & Alfonso, 2013). In their CHC-based Cross-Battery approach to interpretation, Flanagan, Ortiz, and Alfonso (2013) note that approximately 9 broad abilities and 35 to 40 narrow abilities are measured by popular cognitive and achievement instruments. Some nomenclature changes to CHC theory were presented in the WJ IV Manual, but most will not significantly impact CHC-based approaches to interpretation (Kaufman, Raiford, & Coalson, 2015). Both the WISC-V and the KABC-II address five or six of the CHC broad abilities: Short-Term Memory ($Gsm$) [sometimes referred to as Short-term Working Memory ($Gwm$)], Visual Processing ($Gv$), Fluid Reasoning ($Gf$), Crystallized Ability ($Gc$), and Long-Term Storage and Retrieval ($Glr$) (V. Alfonso, personal communication, October 26, 2015; Flanagan, Ortiz, & Alfonso, 2013). Processing Speed ($Gs$) is also measured by the WISC-V. The WIAT-III and the KTEA-3 Comprehensive Form measure three additional broad abilities: Auditory Processing ($Ga$), Reading and Writing ($Grw$), and Quantitative Knowledge/$Gq$ ability. These achievement tests also measure $Glr$ Narrow Abilities that increase the breadth of the $Glr$ Narrow Abilities measured by the WISC-V and KABC-II when the achievement batteries are administered together with a test of cognitive ability. The WISC-V and KABC-II also provide measures of $Gq$ Narrow Abilities. WISC-V Arithmetic taps Mathematical Achievement. The KABC-II also indirectly measures one of the $Gq$ Narrow Abilities (i.e., Mathematical Achievement, by virtue of the fact that Rover and Block Counting each require the child to count).

The WISC-V Symbol Search, Coding, Cancellation, and Naming Speed Quantity subtests as well as the KTEA-3 and WIAT-III Math Fluency subtests provide measures of Processing Speed ($Gs$). KTEA-3 Decoding Fluency and Word Recognition Fluency also tap the $Gs$ narrow ability of Rate of Test Taking. However, neither $Gs$ nor Decision Speed/Reaction Time ($Gt$) are measured by the KABC-II. These two Broad Abilities were purposefully excluded from the KABC-II because these abilities are only concerned with speed, not quality, of processing; they lack the requisite complexity for inclusion; and they are weak measures of $g$ in Carroll's (1993) factor-analytic survey (Kaufman & Kaufman, 2004b). $Gt$ is not measured by any major test battery.

Rapid Reference 4.7 through Rapid Reference 4.15 provide specific information regarding the precise WISC-V, WIAT-III, KABC-II, and KTEA-3 subtests that are believed to measure specific Narrow Abilities based on categorizations by Flanagan and colleagues (V. Alfonso, personal communication, October 26, 2015; Flanagan, Ortiz, & Alfonso, 2013). The Rapid References are organized by Broad Ability (e.g., Rapid Reference 4.7 covers the subtests that measure *Glr* Narrow Abilities, Rapid Reference 4.8 is confined to *Gsm* Narrow Abilities, and so forth). The Broad Abilities of *Glr, Gsm, Gv, Gf,* and *Gc* were defined earlier in Rapid Reference 4.4. The Broad Ability of *Gs* plus remaining three Broad Abilities, which are measured only by the WIAT-III and KTEA-3, are defined as follows (Schneider & McGrew, 2012):

*Processing Speed (Gs):* The ability to perform simple, repetitive cognitive tasks quickly and fluently.

*Quantitative Knowledge (Gq):* The depth and breadth of knowledge related to mathematics.

*Auditory Processing (Ga):* The ability to detect and process meaningful nonverbal information in sound.

*Reading/Writing Ability (Grw):* The depth and breadth of knowledge and skills related to written language.

One of the most important expectations that you may have about using CHC theory for interpretation of the WISC-V or KABC-II with the WIAT-III or KTEA-3 is that there is a cohesive theoretical umbrella over the pairs of tests. When using a CHC framework, the explanation for what is cognitive processing and what is achievement on the WISC-V, WIAT-III, KABC-II, and KTEA-3 is theoretically based and evidence-based, and the results of combining the test batteries will give the examiner a comprehensive and fruitful examination of the child's cognitive abilities and how they translate into academic skills.

That is not to say that the achievement and cognitive batteries do not overlap in Broad or Narrow Abilities. As is evident from Rapid Reference 4.10–Rapid Reference 4.15, there is some overlap. However, there is minimal redundancy overall. For example, both the KABC-II and KTEA-3 measure *Glr* and *Gc* Narrow Abilities, but each measures a separate set. When they do measure the same Narrow Ability, they do it in quite different ways: Mathematical Achievement is a minor aspect of two KABC-II subtests, but this *Gq* ability is the major thrust of Mathematics Computation; in contrast, the *Gf* Narrow Ability of Induction is a key component of the KABC-II Planning/*Gf* subtests. Similarly, the WISC-V and WIAT-III both provide measures of *Gsm, Gf, Gc, Gs,* and *Gq,* but each measures unique Narrow Abilities with minimal overlap. The WISC-V and WIAT-III overlap in the measurement of some Narrow Abilities (i.e., Memory Span, Quantitative Reasoning, Lexical Knowledge, and Mathematical Achievement); however, each measures these Narrow Abilities very differently. For example, WISC-V Arithmetic and WIAT-III Math Problem Solving both measure Mathematical Achievement. However, Math Problem Solving was designed primarily as a measure of Mathematical Achievement, whereas Working Memory Capacity is the primary Narrow Ability measured by WISC-V's Arithmetic and Mathematical Achievement is a secondary aspect.

Flanagan and colleagues (Flanagan & Ortiz, 2001; Flanagan, Ortiz, & Alfonso, 2007, 2013) suggest that you need at least two different primary Narrow Ability measures to adequately measure a Broad Ability from a cross-battery perspective. Examiners who integrate the WISC-V with the WIAT-III or the KABC-II with the KTEA-3 should easily be able to achieve adequate measurement of eight Broad Abilities: *Glr, Gsm, Gv, Gf, Gc, Gs* (excluded from KABC-II), *Gq*, and *Grw*. However, assessment of *Ga* (Phonetic Coding) depends on a single KTEA-3 subtest (Phonological Awareness) that is normed for grades pre-K–12 (ages 4–25) or a single WIAT-III subtest (Early Reading Skills) that is normed for grades pre-K–3 (ages 4–9).

Of course, no one battery can cover the CHC model in its entirety, but the WISC-IV or KABC-II with the WIAT-III or KTEA-3—like the WJ III Cognitive and Achievement Batteries—provide a substantially positive start for the clinician to examine a child's performance from a CHC perspective. To supplement the WISC-V, WIAT-III, KABC-II, and KTEA-3 via Cross Battery Assessment, using CHC theory as a foundation, consult publications by Flanagan and her colleagues (Flanagan & Kaufman, 2004; Flanagan, McGrew, & Ortiz, 2000; Flanagan & Ortiz, 2001; Flanagan, Ortiz, & Alfonso, 2007, 2013, 2015; Flanagan, Ortiz, Alfonso, & Mascolo, 2002; McGrew & Flanagan, 1998). These works provide an in-depth study of CHC theory and the Cross Battery Assessment approach, which is valuable for linking the Wechsler and Kaufman batteries with each other and with other instruments.

### Long-Term Storage and Retrieval (Glr)

Long-term storage and retrieval requires an individual to engage in activities that measure the efficiency of how well information is stored and retrieved. Examiners can obtain a rich measurement of *Glr* by administering a variety of KTEA-3, WISC-V, and KABC-II subtests. The WISC-V subtests (Delayed Symbol Translation, Immediate Symbol Translation, Naming Speed Literacy, and Recognition Symbol Translation) measure *Glr* Narrow Abilities including Associative Memory and Naming Facility. The KTEA-3 subtests that measure *Glr* include Associational Fluency, Letter Naming Facility, Listening Comprehension, and Object Naming Facility. The KABC-II Core Battery measures a single *Glr* Narrow Ability (Associative Memory); an additional Narrow Ability is assessed when examiners administer the supplementary Delayed Recall scale (Atlantis Delayed and Rebus Delayed each measure Associative Memory).

KTEA-3 Listening Comprehension demands that the child listens to and encodes a story and then manipulates the information to answer questions about the story. Although "long-term storage and retrieval" implies that there is a long time between encoding and retrieval, this is not necessarily the case because the information has to be retrieved by association for whatever time interval has lapsed. The CHC model calls the Narrow Ability measured by KTEA-3 Listening Comprehension subtests "Meaningful Memory."

The KTEA-3 Letter Naming Facility and Object Naming Facility measure the CHC Narrow Ability, Naming Facility. The KTEA-3 Associational Fluency measures the Narrow Ability of Ideational Fluency items (e.g., name as many colors or foods as you can). See Rapid Reference 4.7 for an outline of the Long-Term Storage and Retrieval (*Glr*) Narrow Abilities.

---

## ≣ Rapid Reference 4.7

### CHC Analysis: Long-Term Storage & Retrieval (*Glr*) Narrow CHC Abilities Measured by WISC-V, KTEA-3, and KABC-II Subtests

**Glr Narrow Ability**

*Associative Memory*
    KABC-II Atlantis
    KABC-II Rebus
    KABC-II Atlantis Delayed
    KABC-II Rebus Delayed
    WISC-V Delayed Symbol Translation
    WISC-V Immediate Symbol Translation
    WISC-V Recognition Symbol Translation

*Naming Facility*
    KTEA-3 Letter Naming Facility
    KTEA-3 Object Naming Facility
    WISC-V Naming Speed Literacy

*Ideational Fluency*
    KTEA-3 Associational Fluency

*Meaningful Memory*
    KTEA-3 Listening Comprehension

---

### Short-Term Memory (Gsm) (Also Referred to as Short-Term Working Memory [Gwm])

Short-term memory is required by the WIAT-III Sentence Repetition component of the Oral Expression subtest. This subtest is primarily designed to measure oral syntactic knowledge using a task that is constrained by auditory short-term memory. The student is required to listen to sentences of increasing length and syntactic complexity, and then repeat each sentence verbatim.

The WISC-V Digit Span Forward and Picture Span subtests measure *Gsm* Narrow Ability of Memory Span. Digit Span Forward provides a measure of Memory Span (auditory short-term memory) by requiring the child to repeat numbers in the same order as presented aloud by the examiner, and Picture Span measures this narrow ability (visual short-term memory) by selecting pictures that were viewed in sequential order. Four WISC-V subtests measure Working Memory Capacity: Arithmetic, Digit

Span Backward, Digit Span Sequencing, and Letter-Number Sequencing (all tasks require auditory processing).

The primary subtest that measures auditory short-term memory on the KABC-II is Number Recall. The CHC model mostly mentions auditory short-term memory tests for *Gsm*, but visual and haptic activities such as Hand Movements also measure *Gsm*. The three subtests together measure different modalities of short-term memory and also how short-term memory can evolve into working memory.

All three KABC-II *Gsm* subtests (Number Recall, Word Order, and Hand Movements) measure Memory Span. In addition, Word Order has a color interference task that puts some demands on the Narrow Ability of Working Memory Capacity. Consequently, for young children (ages 3 to 5 or 6), who are not likely to reach the color interference items in Word Order, the KABC-II measures only a single CHC Narrow Ability—Memory Span. However, for children 6–7 years or older, the KABC-II measures Memory Span, but will require some Working Memory for success. See Rapid Reference 4.8 for an outline of the Short-Term Memory (*Gsm*) Narrow Abilities.

---

## ≡ *Rapid Reference 4.8*

### CHC Analysis: Short-Term Memory (*Gsm*) Narrow CHC Abilities Measured by WIAT-III, WISC-IV, and KABC-II (KTEA-3 Subtests Do Not Measure Any *Gsm* Narrow Abilities)

#### *Gsm* **Narrow Ability**

*Memory Span*
> WIAT-III Oral Expression (Sentence Repetition component)
> WISC-V Digit Span Forward
> WISC-V Picture Span
> KABC-II Word Order (without color interference)
> KABC-II Number Recall
> KABC-II Hand Movements

*Working Memory Capacity*
> WISC-V Digit Span Backward
> WISC-V Digit Span Sequencing
> WISC-V Arithmetic
> WISC-V Letter-Number Sequencing

Note: The Broad Ability of Short-Term Memory (*Gsm*) is also referred to as Short-Term Working Memory (*Gwm*) (Schrank, McGrew, & Mather, 2014b). Success on WIAT-III Early Reading Skills and the Oral Discourse Comprehension component of Listening Comprehension and KTEA-3 Phonological Awareness and Listening Comprehension is also dependent, to some extent, on *Gsm*. When color interference is introduced to older children on KABC-II's Word Order, the task demands include Working Memory.

## Visual Processing (Gv)

The WISC-V measures the *Gv* Narrow Ability of Visualization with Block Design and Visual Puzzles. The KABC-II provides measurement of four *Gv* Narrow Abilities, although examiners need to administer supplementary subtests such as Gestalt Closure (Closure Speed) and Hand Movements (Visual Memory) to measure all. See Rapid Reference 4.9 for an outline of the Visual Processing (*Gv*) narrow abilities.

≡ *Rapid Reference 4.9*

### CHC Analysis: Visual Processing (*Gv*) Narrow CHC Abilities Measured by WISC-V and KABC-II (WIAT-III and KTEA-II Subtests Do Not Measure Any *Gv* Narrow Abilities)

**Gv Narrow Ability**

*Visual Memory*
  KABC-II Face Recognition
  KABC-II Hand Movements

*Visualization*
  WISC-V Block Design
  WISC-V Visual Puzzles
  KABC-II Triangles
  KABC-II Conceptual Thinking
  KABC-II Block Counting
  KABC-II Pattern Reasoning

*Spatial Scanning*
  KABC-II Rover

*Closure Speed*
  KABC-II Gestalt Closure

Note: Success on WIAT-III Numerical Operations and KTEA-3 Written Expression is also dependent, to some extent, on Visual Processing.

## Fluid Reasoning (Gf)

Fluid reasoning is measured by the WISC-V Figure Weights, Matrix Reasoning, Picture Concepts, and Similarities subtests. Matrix Reasoning and Picture Concepts both measure Induction, but Similarities also measures the narrow *Gc* ability of Lexical Knowledge. Matrix Reasoning, Picture Concepts, and Similarities measure the narrow ability of Induction. General Sequential Reasoning is measured by Figure Weights.

Fluid reasoning is specifically measured by the subtests that constitute the KABC-II Planning/*Gf* scale (Pattern Reasoning, Story Completion). On the Planning/*Gf* scale, Pattern Reasoning primarily measures the Narrow Ability of Induction whereas Story Completion measures *both* Induction (figuring out what the story is about) and General Verbal Information (a *Gc* ability).

KTEA-3 Math Concepts & Applications and WIAT-III Math Problem Solving are primarily *Gq* tasks, but each also requires considerable *Gf* for success, specifically the Narrow Ability Quantitative Reasoning. See Rapid Reference 4.10 for an outline of the Fluid Reasoning (*Gf*) Narrow Abilities.

## ≡ Rapid Reference 4.10

### CHC Analysis: Fluid Reasoning (*Gf*) Narrow CHC Abilities Measured by WISC-V, WIAT-III, KTEA-3, and KABC-II Subtests

**Gf Narrow Ability**

*Induction*
  WISC-V Matrix Reasoning
  WISC-V Picture Concepts
  WISC-V Similarities
  KABC-II Conceptual Thinking
  KABC-II Pattern Reasoning
  KABC-II Story Completion

*General Sequential Reasoning*
  WISC-V Figure Weights
  KABC-II Story Completion

*Quantitative Reasoning*
  WIAT-III Math Problem Solving
  KTEA-3 Math Concepts & Applications

*Note:* Success on WIAT-III Listening Comprehension (Oral Discourse Comprehension component), Reading Comprehension, and Essay Composition; KABC-II Rebus; and four KTEA-3 subtests (Reading Comprehension, Listening Comprehension, Oral Expression, and Written Expression) is also dependent, to some extent, on Fluid Reasoning.

### *Crystallized Ability (Gc)*

The WISC-V measures two *Gc* Narrow Abilities: (1) Lexical Knowledge, measured by Vocabulary and Similarities subtests; and (2) General Verbal Information, measured by the Information and Comprehension subtests. The Narrow Ability of Lexical Knowledge is also measured by three KABC-II Knowledge/*Gc* subtests: Riddles, Expressive Vocabulary, and Verbal Knowledge. WIAT-III's Listening Comprehension and Oral Expression lend added measures of Lexical Knowledge.

KTEA-3 subtests tap two more narrow *Gc* abilities, including Communication ability (with Oral Expression subtest) and Listening Ability (with Listening

Comprehension Subtest). Hence, administering a combination of these various subtests together provides greater breadth of coverage of this *Gc* Broad Ability. See Rapid Reference 4.11 for an outline of Crystallized Ability (*Gc*) Narrow Abilities.

---

## ≡ Rapid Reference 4.11

**CHC Analysis: Crystallized Ability (*Gc*) Narrow CHC Abilities Measured by WISC-V, WIAT-III, KTEA-3, and KABC-II Subtests**

### Gc Narrow Ability

*Lexical Knowledge*
- WISC-V Vocabulary
- WISC-V Similarities
- WIAT-III Listening Comprehension (Receptive Vocabulary component)
- KTEA-3 Reading Vocabulary
- KABC-II Riddles
- KABC-II Verbal Knowledge (items that measure vocabulary)
- KABC-II Expressive Vocabulary

*General Verbal Information*
- WISC-V Information
- WISC-V Comprehension
- KABC-II Story Completion

*Communication Ability*
- KTEA-3 Oral Expression

*Listening Ability*
- WIAT-III Listening Comprehension (Oral Discourse Comprehension component)
- KTEA-3 Listening Comprehension

---

### Processing Speed (Gs)

*Gs* measures the ability to fluently and automatically perform relatively simple cognitive tasks under timed conditions (Flanagan, McGrew, & Ortiz, 2000). The WISC-V measures three *Gs* Narrow Abilities: Number Facility, Perceptual Speed, and Rate of Test Taking. Perceptual Speed is the ability to rapidly search, identify, and compare visual information, and this Narrow Ability is measured by the WISC-V Symbol Search and Cancellation subtests. Rate of Test Taking, the ability to perform tests quickly and accurately, is measured by WISC-V Coding subtest.

Number Facility is the speed at which basic arithmetic operations are performed accurately, and this ability is measured by WISC-V Naming Speed Quantity. The

WIAT-III also measures Number Facility, with three Math Fluency subtests: Math Fluency–Addition, Math Fluency–Subtraction, and Math Fluency–Multiplication, as does KTEA-3 Math Fluency. See Rapid Reference 4.12 for an outline of Processing Speed (*Gs*) Narrow Abilities.

## ≋ *Rapid Reference 4.12*

### CHC Analysis: Processing Speed (*Gs*) Narrow CHC Abilities Measured by WIAT-III, WISC–V, and KTEA-3 Subtests (KABC-II Subtests Do Not Measure Any *Gs* Narrow Abilities)

**Gs Narrow Ability**

*Perceptual Speed*
    WISC-V Symbol Search
    WISC-V Cancellation

*Rate of Test Taking*
    WISC-V Coding

*Number Facility*
    WISC-V Naming Speed Quantity
    WIAT-III Math Fluency–Addition
    WIAT-III Math Fluency–Subtraction
    WIAT-III Math Fluency–Multiplication
    KTEA-3 Math Fluency

### Quantitative Knowledge (Gq)

*Gq* measures the individual's store of accumulated mathematical knowledge (Flanagan & Ortiz, 2001). It is different from the *Gf* Narrow Ability of Quantitative Reasoning because *Gq* is more about what the child knows than how the child reasons with quantitative information. WIAT-III Math Problem Solving and KTEA-3 Math Concepts & Applications each measure Quantitative Reasoning to some extent but primarily measure *Gq*. WIAT-III Numerical Operations and KTEA-3 Math Computation also provide measures of *Gq*. Both WIAT-III subtests that comprise the Mathematics composite and KTEA-3 subtests that make up the Math composite measure the *Gq* Narrow Ability of Mathematical Achievement, but none provide measurement of the *Gq* Narrow Ability of Mathematical Knowledge. Note that because of their speed component, the math fluency tasks on both WIAT-III and KTEA-3 measure primarily Number Facility (a *Gs* narrow ability). WISC-V Arithmetic primarily measures the *Gsm* Narrow Ability of Working Memory Capacity, but secondarily measures the *Gq* Narrow Ability of Mathematical Achievement. See Rapid Reference 4.13 for an outline of Quantitative Knowledge (*Gq*) narrow abilities.

## ≡ Rapid Reference 4.13

....................................................................................................

### CHC Analysis: Quantitative Knowledge (*Gq*) Narrow CHC Abilities Measured by WIAT-III, KTEA-II, and WISC-V Subtests

**Gq Narrow Ability**

*Mathematical Achievement*
    WIAT-III Math Problem Solving
    WIAT-III Numerical Operations
    KTEA-3 Math Concepts & Applications
    KTEA-3 Math Computation
    WISC-V Arithmetic

### *Auditory Processing (Ga)*

*Ga* "requires the perception, analysis, and synthesis of patterns among auditory stimuli as well as the discrimination of subtle differences in patterns of sound" (Flanagan & Ortiz, 2001, p. 18). Both the analytic and synthetic Narrow Abilities associated with the *Ga* Broad Ability are measured by WIAT-III Early Reading Skills and by KTEA-3 Phonological Processing.

The WIAT-III subtest is normed for young children (Pre-K–grade 3) and does not provide separate scores for performance on analytic and synthetic items; however, skills analysis capabilities allow the examiner to evaluate performance at the item level and compare performance on items measuring analytic and synthetic Phonetic Coding.

Similarly, the KTEA-3 subtest is of appropriate difficulty primarily for young children (Pre-K–grade 6), but standardized through grade 12+. It yields an overall score rather than separate scores for its Narrow Abilities. Nonetheless, the KTEA-3 Error Analysis procedure for Phonological Processing permits examiners to determine whether the child performed at a "Strong," "Average," or "Weak" level on the separate sections of the subtest (see Chapter 2 of this book). Hence, the error analysis allows examiners to compare the child's ability on the sections of the subtest (Rhyming, sound matching, blending, segmenting, and deleting sounds) that measure *Ga* Narrow Abilities. See Rapid Reference 4.14 for an outline of Auditory Processing (*Ga*) Narrow Abilities.

## ≡ Rapid Reference 4.14

**CHC Analysis: Auditory Processing (*Ga*) Narrow CHC Abilities Measured by WIAT-III and KTEA-3 (WISC-V and KABC-II Subtests Do Not Measure Any *Ga* Narrow Abilities)**

### *Ga* Narrow Ability

*Phonetic Coding*
    WIAT-III Early Reading Skills
    KTEA-3 Phonological Processing

*Note:* Deficits in certain *Ga* Narrow Abilities like Speech Sound Discrimination (US) may impact performance negatively on such tests as WIAT-III Listening Comprehension; KABC-II Riddles, Word Order, and Number Recall; WISC-V Digit Span and Letter-Number Sequencing, and KTEA-3 Listening Comprehension.

### *Reading and Writing (Grw)*

*Grw* is measured by achievement tests (Flanagan & Ortiz, 2001). The WIAT-III and KTEA-3 provide measurement of six *Grw* Narrow Abilities: Reading Decoding, Reading Comprehension, Reading Speed, Spelling Ability, Writing Ability, and Writing Speed. The fluency-type tasks also measure *Gs* ability of Rate of Test Taking. Seven *Grw* Narrow Abilities are measured by WIAT-III subtests: Word Reading, Pseudoword Decoding, Reading Comprehension, Sentence Composition, Essay Composition, Oral Reading Fluency, Spelling, and Alphabet Writing Fluency. Several of the new subtests added to the KTEA-3 Comprehensive Form greatly enriched the measurement of *Grw* Narrow Abilities relative to the prior versions of the test, which now tap six different *Grw* Narrow Abilities. See Rapid Reference 4.15 for an outline of Reading and Writing (*Grw*) Narrow Abilities.

## ≡ Rapid Reference 4.15

**CHC Analysis: Reading & Writing (*Grw*) Narrow CHC Abilities Measured by WIAT-III and KTEA-II (WISC-V and KABC-II Subtests Do Not Measure Any *Grw* Narrow Abilities)**

### *Grw* Narrow Ability

*Reading Decoding*
    WIAT-III Word Reading
    WIAT-III Pseudoword Decoding
    KTEA-3 Decoding Fluency

*(continued)*

(Continued)

KTEA-3 Letter & Word Recognition
KTEA-3 Nonsense Word Decoding
KTEA-3 Word Recognition Fluency

*Reading Comprehension*
WIAT-III Reading Comprehension
KTEA-3 Reading Comprehension
KTEA-3 Reading Vocabulary

*Spelling Ability*
WIAT-III Spelling
KTEA-3 Spelling

*Writing Speed (fluency)*
WIAT-III Alphabet Writing Fluency

*Writing Ability*
WIAT-III Sentence Composition
WIAT-III Essay Composition
KTEA-3 Written Expression

*English Usage Knowledge*
WIAT-III Sentence Composition
WIAT-III Essay Composition
KTEA-3 Written Expression

*Reading Speed*
WIAT-III Oral Reading Fluency
KTEA-3 Silent Reading Fluency

## Using a Neuropsychological Approach to Integrate Assessment Results

CHC theory and quantitative analyses (which can be conducted by using software like Flanagan Ortiz and Alfonso's 2015 "X-bass") provide valuable ways of integrating cognitive instruments like the WISC-V and KABC-II with achievement instruments like the WIAT-III and KTEA-3. However, it is important to remember that (a) the KABC-II is built on and can be interpreted from a dual theoretical foundation (Luria's neuropsychological approach as well as CHC psychometric theory), (b) the WISC-V can be interpreted from multiple theoretical perspectives (Wechsler, 2014b), and (c) the WISC-V, WIAT-III, KABC-II, and KTEA-3 are individually administered, clinical instruments that afford examiners rich opportunities for qualitative observations. We cannot envision the examiner obtaining the full benefit of an analysis of these instruments without including the important *process and qualitative* information. This information comes from observing an examinee in a standardized setting that minimizes unnecessary interactions (e.g., wording in instructions) *and* maximizes opportunities to actively engage learning processes (e.g., dynamic subtests like Atlantis and Rebus) with the child.

This section on clinical analysis fully takes into account the neuropsychological processing model developed by Luria and addresses brain functions/processes involved in cognitive *and* achievement tests. For example, the Phonological Processing subtest on the KTEA-3 is a subtest that requires the child to remem-

> # DON'T FORGET
>
> For detailed information on the demands of each of the KTEA-3 subtests, see Table 1.5 of the KTEA-3 *Administration Manual.*

ber and manipulate sounds and words. Similarly, on WIAT-III Early Reading Skills, the general content domains of Naming Letters, Letter-Sound Correspondence, Phonological Awareness, and Word Reading Comprehension are assessed. These two subtests are wonderful measures of auditory skills (*Ga*). However, the KTEA-3 Phonological Processing subtest also taps working memory and cognitive sequencing. These latter skills are specifically measured by the KABC-II Sequential/ *Gsm* scale and the WISC-V WMI, indicating that a complete understanding of the young child's performance on KTEA-3 Phonological Processing or WIAT-III Early Reading Skills requires examiners to compare that performance to the child's success (or lack of it) on KABC-II Sequential/*Gsm* or WISC-V WMI subtests.

It is not a coincidence that these kinds of tasks reflect years of research based on auditory/sequential skills and the phonemic awareness skills needed for reading (e.g., Hooper & Hynd, 1982; Kamphaus & Reynolds, 1987; Lichtenberger, Broadbooks, & Kaufman, 2000; Lichtenberger, 2001) and associated with left-hemispheric processing (James & Selz, 1997; Lyon, Fletcher, & Barnes, 2003; Reynolds, Kamphaus, Rosenthal, & Hiemenz, 1997).

For each section that follows, discussion emphasizes functional processing abilities that will hopefully help examiners with construct and skill analyses. Both the CHC and Luria theoretical approaches reflect an aspect of comprehensive assessment that needs to be buttressed by qualitative/process information. Furthermore, all cognitive and achievement test data must be interpreted in the context of other important information such as history, medical status, medications, family involvement, quality of teaching, developmental stage, social and emotional functioning, visual-motor functioning, and responses to prior interventions.

### Sequential Processing, Short-Term Memory, Phonological Awareness, and Listening Comprehension

As indicated in Rapid Reference 4.8, we believe that WIAT-III Early Reading Skills and Listening Comprehension, and KTEA-3 Phonological Processing and Listening Comprehension are each dependent, to some extent, on the CHC *Gsm* Broad Ability. The process rationale for each subtest follows.

*Process Rationale for WIAT-III Early Reading Skills and KTEA-3 Phonological Processing*

It is important to understand both the Lurian and CHC ways of interpreting the Sequential/*Gsm* scale because there is a great deal of research literature that combines sequential processing and auditory short-term memory with the type of phonological processing skills that are measured by the KTEA-3 Phonological Processing subtest and the WIAT-III Early Reading Skills subtest (Siegal, 1997; Teeter, 1997). The combination of these phonological awareness tasks and the KABC-II Sequential/*Gsm* subtests or the WISC-V WMI subtests provides a large window of opportunity for evaluating reading problems and the more phonologically based subtypes of learning disabilities (see the section of this chapter on "Identification of Specific Learning Disabilities").

As a primary measure of auditory short-term memory, the KABC-II Sequential/*Gsm* Core subtests and WISC-V WMI subtests help the examiner evaluate the critical listening skills that children need in the classroom. The phonological awareness tasks on the achievement tests measure sound-symbol connections, but because of the way they are designed, they also measure auditory short-term memory and sequencing skills. These are interactive tasks where the child has to listen very closely to the examiner and then reproduce sounds, and manipulate word syllables and sounds.

A skilled examiner can retrieve a lot of information by assessing behavioral clues about how well the child can remember sounds and use working memory. Does the child attempt to reproduce the sound? Does the child miss the examiner's cues and ask for repetitions? Is the child shy and too embarrassed to verbalize? Does the child get the sounds right but in the wrong order? When you move to a part of the phonological awareness tasks that needs working memory does the child's behavior shift dramatically? Does the child pay attention or do you have to cue each item?

The reading research literature indicates that many early reading problems stem from a learning disability subtype called "auditory-linguistic or phonological form of dyslexia" (Spreen, 2001; Teeter, 1997). This is not to say that visual and other processing deficits are not important subtypes of reading problems, but for the moment, let us explore the relationship between the processing and production of phonology in young readers.

Phonological processing is basically the ability to understand and use the sound components of language. The KTEA-3 Phonological Processing subtest and the WIAT-III Early Reading Skills subtest include five different activities that correspond to Adams's (1990) five levels of phonemic awareness tasks in ascending order of difficulty: rhyming, sound matching, blending, segmenting, and manipulating phonemes.

Phonological processing is closely related to problems in speech perception, naming and vocabulary ability, and auditory short-term memory with sounds. When phonological awareness deficits are present, reading comprehension suffers because the cognitive processes that are required for comprehension are tied up in decoding and word recognition (Stanovich, 1992). This leaves the child with a myopic focus on the elements of the text and few resources for fluid reading and comprehension.

Young children who have reading problems can be helped by evaluating their ability to understand the phonetic/linguistic parts of reading. If we know which parts are problematic, then we will be able to better describe interventions that are targeted to the child's specific deficit. There is evidence to support interventions in phonemic awareness with young elementary-aged children not only from an academic outcome perspective, but also from neuropsychological growth perspective in that neural networks that support reading can be enhanced with the appropriate instruction (Lyon, Fletcher, & Barnes, 2003).

As indicated, the WISC-V and KABC-II scales that have an important part in the assessment of phonological awareness skills, especially in younger readers, are the WMI and Sequential/*Gsm* scales, respectively. The primary task of the WMI and Sequential/*Gsm* scales is to measure how the child processes information in a linear, step-by-step fashion. How a child performs on the WMI or Sequential/*Gsm* scale can illuminate whether the child has the prerequisite auditory sequencing and short-term memory skills to be able to put sounds together with symbols while he or she is decoding a word (Das, Naglieri, & Kirby, 1994; Kirby & Williams, 1991; Naglieri, 2001).

*Process Rationale for Listening Comprehension*

The KTEA-3 Listening Comprehension subtest and the Oral Discourse Comprehension portion of the WIAT-III Listening Comprehension subtest also support the WMI and Sequential/*Gsm* scales because they straddle auditory short-term memory, auditory working memory, and auditory long-term encoding. The tasks are presented in a pure auditory form and therefore should be compared with Phonological Awareness and the WMI and Sequential/*Gsm* subtests. Does the child remember well on Phonological Processing with small, short-term auditory segments and then do very poorly on Listening Comprehension that requires a much higher auditory memory load? Or, the opposite, where the child does not do well with small, pure auditory segments but when the task is put in story form on Listening Comprehension the child performs quite well? Answers to these types of processing questions will help with differential diagnosis later on.

## *The WISC-V VSI and PSI, KABC-II Simultaneous/Gv Scale and Written Expression*

You may wish to compare performance on the WISC-V Visual Spatial Index and Processing Speed Index scales and the KABC-II Simultaneous/*Gv* scale with achievement tasks that involve visual-motor ability. For example, examine the visual-motor aspects of KTEA-3 Written Expression, WIAT-III Sentence Composition, WIAT-III Alphabet Writing Fluency, and WIAT-III Essay Composition and how they relate to some of the visual-motor activities on the WISC-V subtests like Block Design, Symbol Search, and Coding or KABC-II subtests like Rover or Triangles. These comparisons may help you figure out why a child has poor handwriting or poor visual organization on writing tasks. Remember when you were administering the achievement tests that involved writing. Did you observe the child having trouble holding the pencil? Did the child lose his or her place a lot? Did the child write a lot of words or letters in a reversed way? Were there multiple erasures? Did the child have trouble figuring out where he or she should write the responses even though you were pointing to the correct starting point?

If you do suspect that achievement in writing is partly due to visual-motor issues then it would be appropriate to pursue this hypothesis further by administering tests designed specifically for assessing visual-motor problems. We believe that the WIAT-III subtests, Alphabet Writing Fluency, Sentence Composition, and Essay Composition, and the KTEA-3 Written Expression are dependent, to some extent, on the CHC *Gv* Broad Ability (see Rapid Reference 4.9).

### *Planning, Reasoning, and Executive Functions*

Rapid Reference 4.10 indicates that the *Gf* Narrow Abilities of Induction are measured by WISC-V's Matrix Reasoning and Picture Concepts and the *Gf* Narrow Ability of General Sequential Reasoning (deduction) is measured by WISC-V's Figure Weights and KABC-II's Rover. Other subtests (three WIAT-III subtests, KABC-II Rebus, four KTEA-3 subtests) are mentioned in the "Note" to that Rapid Reference as being dependent, to some extent, on the *Gf* Broad Ability. The process rationale for each of these subtests follows.

### *Process Rationale for Matrix Reasoning and Picture Concepts*

Matrix Reasoning requires the child to reason with nonverbal visual stimuli. The child must complete the missing portion of a $2 \times 2$ or $3 \times 3$ visual matrix by selecting one of five response choices. This subtest also requires secondary cognitive abilities, such as visual acuity, visual discrimination, visualization and working memory, and so on. Picture Concepts requires a child to view two or three rows of pictures and select one picture from each row to form a group with a common characteristic. Like Matrix Reasoning, this subtest also requires secondary cognitive abilities including visual-perceptual recognition, conceptual thinking visual scanning, and working memory. It is important to first evaluate the role of secondary cognitive capacities to determine whether poor performance on Matrix Reasoning or Picture Concepts is the result of a weakness in (nonverbal) fluid reasoning.

When you are evaluating the Planning/*Gf* scale, consider the child's performance on Matrix Reasoning and Picture Concepts. Did the child talk through the items, relying to some extent on verbal reasoning skills? Observe the child's eye movements when solving the problems: Does the child's approach appear systematic or random? Did the child carefully evaluate each problem before answering, or did the child appear to respond impulsively? How easily frustrated is the child? Is the child quick to give a "Don't Know" response? If you note executive function-type weaknesses during Matrix Reasoning, see if these weaknesses were evident on Picture Concepts as well. Make qualitative observations of the child's strategy use and approach to reasoning tasks and then administer other tests of executive functions to support or refute your hypotheses.

*Process Rationale for Rover and Figure Weights*

Rover was designed to explore the child's ability to create numerous ways to solve a problem and then choose the best plan. Like the game of chess, however, Rover also has a visual-spatial component that is just as essential as planning ability to efficiently navigate the game board. When Rover was initially developed, it was intended as a measure of Planning/*Gf*. However, confirmatory factor analyses of National Tryout clearly pinpointed Rover as a measure of simultaneous and visual processing. Because the child has to look for different ways a dog can get to a bone on a map-like game board containing rocks, weeds, and grass, it is ultimately the child's visual mapping ability that plays the most important part in solving the problems.

Nonetheless, Rover was included in the KABC-II because regardless of its scale membership, the task presented an interesting challenge to children and adolescents, measures *both Gf* and *Gv* Narrow Abilities, and demands intact executive functions for success. If a child has poor planning or executive functions, performance on this subtest is severely impacted. Even though the child's visual-spatial mapping abilities lead the way, the child still has to figure out several plans, hold them in working memory, and then determine the value of the best plan. The latter is, most definitely, an executive functioning task.

Indeed, in a KABC-II study of 56 children with attention deficit/hyperactivity disorder (ADHD), a group that is notorious for having deficits in executive functions (Barkley, 2003), the ADHD children had significantly lower scores ($p < .001$) on Rover than their nonclinical peers (Kaufman & Kaufman, 2004a). They also had significantly lower scores on more pure measures of executive functions such as the Planning/*Gf* Pattern Reasoning and Story Completion subtests ($p < .01$).

Also tapping the *Gf* narrow ability of General Sequential Reasoning is WISC-V's Figure Weights, which requires the child to view a scale with missing weights, and the child must select a response that keeps the scale balanced. The child must use the quantitative concept of equality and apply concepts of addition or multiplication to select the correct response. This is a time-limited task that is primarily nonverbal.

When you are evaluating a student's planning, reasoning, and executive functions abilities, therefore, consider the child's process and their performance on Rover or Figure Weights. Was the child organized? Did he/she take the time to look for all of the possible solutions, or did he/she just blurt out the first answer? Also look at the style of processing. Did the child take time and think about the routes on Rover or weights on Figure Weights and then determine the solution (reflective style), or did the child charge right in and then have to self-correct (impulsive style)? Rover can help you look at the differences in subtest scores and including the processing and qualitative aspects of how the child obtained the scores. If you note executive function-type deficits during Rover or Figure Weights, see if these deficits were evident on Pattern Reasoning and Story Completion. Also, examine your qualitative observations of the child's strategy generation and then administer other tests of executive functions to test your hypotheses.

### Process Rationale for Rebus and Symbol Translation

The CHC model places Rebus and the three WISC-V Symbol Translation tasks (Immediate, Delayed, and Recognition Symbol Translation) in the *Glr* Narrow Ability category of Associative Memory (MA) because the examinee is required to learn the word associated with a particular rebus drawing and then read phrases and sentences composed of these drawings. Although Rebus and the Symbol Translation tasks primarily measure a *Glr* Narrow Ability they still require a great deal of organization, not just retrieval.

Rebus and Symbol Translation also measure the process of how an examinee responds to the teaching/learning situation. Unlike with other subtests (except KABC-II Atlantis), the examinee has to learn more and more information and then apply the information. These subtest task demands are similar to a classroom situation except that the subtests are strictly controlled and measurable because the examiner gives standardized teaching prompts. These are subtests where the examiner feeds information and rehearsal to the child step-by-step. The examiner is constrained by only being able to teach in a standardized fashion; however, this constraint also frees the examiner to look at how the child responds to teaching. This is a dynamic and controlled process and provides key qualitative data to the KABC-II and WISC-V examiner.

The reason why tasks like Rebus and Symbol Translation are considered to depend on *Gf* to some extent is because during administration these tests demand executive functions to be at maximum alert. Many researchers (e.g., Goldberg & Bougakov, 2000) liken the executive functions to an orchestra conductor. The first and second functional areas of the brain, if you will, are the actual musicians in the orchestra and are directed to play certain instruments at certain times. The orchestra conductor is the third functional area of the brain (frontal lobe area), which has to direct complex cognitive functions that require input, processing, prioritizing, organizing, planning, and output.

Rebus and Symbol Translation tax the orchestra conductor because there are many first and second functional unit tasks like paying attention to each tiny word/picture, processing the visual information, processing the auditory information, melding the symbol and sound, only learning exactly what the examiner is teaching at paced intervals, organizing the reading of symbols and their sounds into coherent and meaningful sentences, and checking for mistakes and comprehension. It takes quite a conductor to direct the symphony during Rebus and Symbol Translation!

There are many qualitative or behavioral indicators during Rebus and Symbol Translation that can give the examiner clues as to problems with attention or executive functions. Many young children on these tasks will try very hard to learn the words and their matching symbols and then be completely oblivious to the fact that they are reading meaningful sentences. Therefore, if they make a mistake on a word and the meaning of the sentence disappears they do not mentally register the lack of meaning, they simply just continue to read isolated symbols. On the other hand, children who do have developing executive or metacognitive functions will notice the break in comprehension and skip back to where they think they went wrong and try to figure out the mistaken symbol. This behavior is indicative of the orchestra conductor checking where lower functions went wrong, and it also makes for a difference in scores because the child self-corrects.

An alert examiner will know by the presence or absence of self-corrective behaviors if the child has problems with organization. A low score on Rebus or Symbol Translation could mean that there is a problem with transferring information from short/recent memory to long-term memory (as the *Glr* classification implies), but a low score could also mean that there is trouble with planning/executive functions. Hence, a comparison with the strong planning subtests like KABC-II Pattern Reasoning and KABC-II Story Completion or WISC-V Matrix Reasoning and WISC-V Picture Concepts is appropriate. Therefore, while Rebus and the Symbol Translation tasks clearly tap *Glr* abilities, these tasks can also assist in the exploration of the child's fluid reasoning abilities.

### Process Rationale for KTEA-3 and WIAT-III Subtests

There are three subtests on the WIAT-III and four subtests on the KTEA-3 that require not only academic knowledge, but organizational, deductive, inductive, and planning skills: WIAT-III Listening Comprehension (Oral Discourse Comprehension component), Reading Comprehension, and Essay Composition, and KTEA-3 Written Expression, Reading Comprehension, Oral Expression, and Listening Comprehension. These subtests all require "higher levels of cognition" (Sattler, 2001), "cognitive load" (Raney, 1993), or "higher-complex abilities" (Mather, Wendling, & Woodcock, 2001). Sattler and Mather and colleagues describe primary academic tasks in a hierarchy ranging from ones requiring low levels of cognition, such as letter identification, to those that require higher levels, such as reading comprehension and the construction of written text. Figure 4.1 illustrates the hierarchical relationship among achievement areas and subtests on the WIAT-III and KTEA-3 Comprehensive Form with respect to their level of cognitive processing.

Informally interpreting these subtest scores alongside the subtests that truly measure *Gf* Narrow Abilities acknowledges that the more sophisticated skills needed for these upper-level academic tasks should be assessed in a cognitive processing way. Again, the skilled and observant examiner watches how the child takes these achievement tests and looks for behavioral clues to see if the child has the organization and planning skills to do a good job.

For example, during the WIAT-III or KTEA-3 Reading Comprehension subtest, the child has to pick the best of several responses to answer the question about comprehension correctly. Watch for processing style here. Does the child read the passage quickly and impulsively pick an answer (impulsive, inattentive style), or does the child

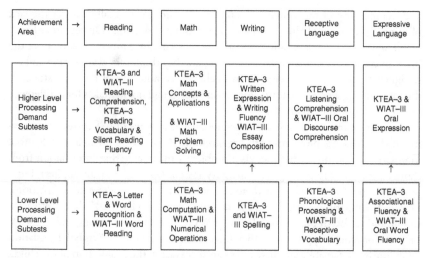

| Achievement Area → | Reading | Math | Writing | Receptive Language | Expressive Language |
|---|---|---|---|---|---|
| Higher Level Processing Demand Subtests → | KTEA–3 and WIAT–III Reading Comprehension, KTEA–3 Reading Vocabulary & Silent Reading Fluency | KTEA–3 Math Concepts & Applications & WIAT–III Math Problem Solving | KTEA–3 Written Expression & Writing Fluency WIAT–III Essay Composition | KTEA–3 Listening Comprehension & WIAT–III Oral Discourse Comprehension | KTEA–3 & WIAT–III Oral Expression |
| | ↑ | ↑ | ↑ | ↑ | ↑ |
| Lower Level Processing Demand Subtests → | KTEA–3 Letter & Word Recognition & WIAT–III Word Reading | KTEA–3 Math Computation & WIAT–III Numerical Operations | KTEA–3 and WIAT–III Spelling | KTEA–3 Phonological Processing & WIAT–III Receptive Vocabulary | KTEA–3 Associational Fluency & WIAT–III Oral Word Fluency |

**Figure 4.1  Hierarchy of Cognitive Processing Load by Achievement Area**

read the passage and then spend quite a bit of time reading the possible answers and deliberating on the correctness of a response (reflective style)? Does the child have so many problems decoding the reading passage that he or she misses the overall story? Observe the child's eye movements. Does the child read from left to right with occasional loops back to check for comprehension (fluid movements), or do the child's eyes flicker back and forth, lose place, skip lines, or other nonfluid movements (poor eye tracking/nonfluid movements)? These types of observations can give valuable clues as to what factors bring about a low score on reading comprehension.

Comparing these kinds of observations with other subtests that require organization, executive functions, and fluid reasoning may give the examiner some keys as to why reading comprehension performance is problematic for a child. Perhaps the problem is not that the child does not know math facts, perhaps it is because he or she cannot *organize* the math facts to be able to apply them to a problem. If the child does have problems with organization and other *Gf* subtests, then the remediation plan calls for including prescriptions about organization (not necessarily drilling of math facts).

Similar observations need to be made by the examiner about WIAT-III Listening Comprehension (Oral Discourse Comprehension component) and Essay Composition and KTEA-3 Written Expression, Oral Expression, and Listening Comprehension because all of these subtests require the child to have good *Gf* skills. The beauty of comparing these scores with subtests on the KABC-II Planning/*Gf* scale or WISC-V Fluid Reasoning Scale is that the process of how a child utilizes upper-level cognitive skills to perform academic tasks is being compared, not just the concrete details that the teacher probably already knows about (e.g., reading and math levels).

There is also a quantitative method for examining the child's reasoning ability on the WIAT-III and KTEA-3 via its Skills Analysis or Error Analysis procedures, respectively. WIAT-III Reading Comprehension and KTEA-3 Reading Comprehension and Listening Comprehension deliberately include items that measure inferential thinking (*Gf*) as well as literal recall of facts. The items on each WIAT-III and KTEA-3 subtest have been preclassified as either "Literal" or "Inferential." The KTEA-3 Error Analysis determines whether the child performed at a "Strong," "Average," or "Weak" level on each type of item (Kaufman & Kaufman, 2004b). Hence, if the child's category on the Inferential items of Reading Comprehension and/or Listening Comprehension is classified as "Weak" or "Strong," that classification can be used to corroborate other quantitative and qualitative data about the child's reasoning ability.

From a process point of view, information and data gleaned from the WIAT-III and KTEA-3 "high-level" subtests can help the examiner look at how well the "orchestra conductor" organizes complex tasks and large bodies of information. If you do suspect that the child might have executive function deficits, then it is appropriate to test further with tests that are specifically designed to measure this area. If you do not feel comfortable incorporating measures of executive functions into the Comprehensive Assessment, then a referral to a colleague who is familiar with these measures is an appropriate course of action.

### Auditory Processing (Ga) and Several Auditory Tasks on the WISC-V, KABC-II, WIAT-III, and KTEA-3

The Listening Comprehension subtest on both the WIAT-III and KTEA-3, the WIAT-III Sentence Repetition Portion of Oral Expression, two WISC-V subtests (Digit Span, Letter-Number Sequencing), and three KABC-II subtests (Riddles, Number Recall, Word Order) are dependent, to some extent, on the CHC *Ga* Broad Ability (see note in Rapid Reference 4.14). The process rationale for these subtests follows.

*Process Rationale for WIAT-III and KTEA-3 Listening Comprehension, WIAT-III Sentence Repetition, WISC-V Digit Span, WISC-V Letter-Number Sequencing, KABC-II Riddles, KABC-II Number Recall, and KABC-II Word Order*

These subtests do not measure the CHC defined auditory processing/*Ga* because they are more to do with auditory memory and the keeping of auditory input long enough to come up with an answer. The primary subtests that measure *Ga*—like KTEA-3 Phonological Processing and WIAT-III Early Reading Skills—are more concerned with the discrimination of sounds and with phonemic analysis and synthesis. Nonetheless, Listening Comprehension, WIAT-III Sentence Repetition, WISC-V Digit Span, WISC-V Letter-Number Sequencing, KABC-II Riddles, KABC-II Number Recall, and KABC-II Word Order still all use auditory input as the main processing vehicle and that, by nature, is serial and sequential. Because most of these auditory processes take place in similar places in the brain, and have resultant brain-behavior similarities (e.g., language problems, reading problems) the examiner should make an effort to distinguish auditory memory from auditory discrimination. Both processes require different intervention strategies and have different influences on academic performance.

Listening Comprehension on both the WIAT-III and KTEA-3, in particular, is a supportive subtest for *Ga* because it measures the kind of listening comprehension that students must do in school—that is, comprehension of relatively formal speech, rather than casual or naturalistic speech. This would serve the purpose of enhancing the relevance of the test score to a school-based evaluation. The Listening Comprehension measures on the WIAT-III and KTEA-3 also have a second, important design objective: To parallel the passage items of the respective Reading Comprehension subtests. The primary difference between the listening and reading comprehension subtests from each test is that the listening comprehension measure requires the student to listen to prerecorded passages and then answer questions spoken by the examiner. Because students perform similar tasks in Listening Comprehension and Reading Comprehension, a significantly lower score on the latter subtest may suggest the presence of a reading problem rather than a more general deficit in language development (Stanovich, 1992).

## Qualitative/Behavioral Analyses of Assessment Results

By comparing behavioral observations during both cognitive and achievement testing, you can see how a child behaviorally responds to different types of tests. (Qualitative Observations on the KTEA-3 and the KABC-II are described in detail in the KABC-II and the KTEA-3 manuals.) On the KTEA-3 Flash Drive, examiners can download a "Qualitative Observations Hand Scoring Form" that outlines general observations as well as observations to note for each subtest (Q-Global can also be used to record these observations). Examine the following scenarios to determine if there are any differences in performance for each battery.

### Look for Differences With Affect and Motivation
Does the child enjoy the novel game-like activities on the WISC-V or KABC-II but then become quiet, sullen, or bored on the WIAT-III or KTEA-3? Or vice versa? Does he act nervous and unsure on the WISC-V or KABC-II but cheers up with familiar tasks on the WIAT-III or KTEA-3? Look for changes in behavior going from novel process tasks to familiar academic tasks.

### Look for Differences With Self-Confidence
Does the child try hard on the WISC-V or KABC-II subtests and knows when she performed well? Does she verbalize self-confidence with statements like "I'm good at this!" "This is easy!" Do these self-confident statements reach over into the WIAT-III or KTEA-3 test performance? Or does she falter, say self-deprecating statements, or act unsure? Look for changes in behavior (verbalization about the self) when tasks change from process oriented to academic.

### *Look for Differences Between Modalities*

Some children have specific and preferred processing styles. Many times their behavior will reflect these visual, auditory, haptic, and verbal strengths and weaknesses. Look for changes in behavior when the modality of the task changes. Does he pay attention better when he has tasks that are visual and gets fidgety when the tasks are auditory with no visual stimulus? Does he chatter on verbal subtests and act unsure on visual-spatial tasks?

### *Look for Differences in Behavior With Cognitive Load*

Both the WISC-V and the KABC-II change cognitive load from subtest to subtest and especially from basal to ceiling items on each subtest. The WIAT-III and KTEA-3 each have four or five specific subtests that have a higher cognitive load because they require complex skills (see Figure 4.3). Look for changes in behavior when the load level changes or items go from easy to difficult. Does she do well on simple tasks and then get confused on ones where she has to organize? What strategies does she employ on both batteries when she starts to approach ceiling items? Gives up? Gets impulsive? Acts like it is an enjoyable challenge? Gets frustrated, angry, or oppositional?

### *Look for How the Child Responds When You Teach on the Learning Scale of the KABC-II and Interactive Subtests on the WISC-V, KTEA-3, and WIAT-III*

Note any changes in behavior when you administer the Atlantis and KABC-II Rebus subtests or the WISC-V Symbol Translation subtest. These subtests are different from the others because they are interactive, and the examiner basically teaches the child each item and then requests retrieval of the information. It is important to note how a child responds to the interactive and regimented pace. Symbol Translation, Atlantis, and Rebus are dynamic subtests where there is a more intense social dependency between the examiner and the examinee and the behaviors and social strategies that the child uses in this type of teaching/learning arrangement are valuable information.

You may also want to compare the behavioral observations from tasks that involve actively engaging with the examiner such as on Reading Comprehension, Sentence Composition, Early Reading Skills, Listening Comprehension, and Oral Expression from the WIAT-III, and Written Expression, Phonological Processing, Listening Comprehension, and Oral Expression subtests from the KTEA-3. They also are interactive subtests where the examiner engages the child throughout the test. Does the child enjoy engaging with you? Is the child nervous about being so interactive with you? Does the child act dependent and need you to lead them? Or is the child defiant, impatient, or oppositional? It would be interesting to mention these types of behaviors to the child's teacher and see if the child's responses are similar in the classroom.

Qualitative observations need to be supported by other data. If you observe behaviors that you believe are disruptive and that hurt the child's performance on the WISC-V, KABC-II, WIAT-III, or the KTEA-3, check your observations out with staff and teachers to see if these types of behaviors are present in other settings and not only in the testing situation. Also, look at the scores for these subtests. If you believe that the behaviors lowered the child's scores, then interventions for those behaviors may help the child perform better in the classroom. Remember, qualitative observations are not just about negative behaviors. Qualitative observations can provide valuable information about how a child gets around a disability or weakness. Watching how a child naturally compensates for learning or behavioral deficits is very valuable information, and it should be included in any prescriptive recommendations.

## Identification of Specific Learning Disabilities

Clinical studies have been conducted using the KTEA-3, WIAT-III, WISC-V, and KABC-II with samples of children with learning disabilities primarily in reading, math, or written expression. The clinical studies will be reviewed with the goal of understanding how these data may inform test selection and interpretation of assessment results.

For the KABC-II learning disability clinical studies, the subjects were diagnosed with learning disabilities based upon a severe discrepancy between performance on an achievement measure and a measure of intellectual ability (the most prevalent definition of a learning disability at the time that the research took place). For the KTEA-3, WIAT-III, and WISC-V learning disability clinical studies, the students were previously classified as having a specific learning disability, and were drawn from a variety of clinical settings, so the samples were composed of children identified using various criteria. Students were classified based upon meeting either traditional ability-achievement discrepancy criteria and/or interachievement discrepancy criteria. The Individuals with Disabilities Education Improvement Act (IDEA, 2004) allows for multiple approaches to identify children for the category of specific learning disability.

### Reading Disability
#### WIAT-III Study

A sample of 108 individuals in grades 2–12, aged 7–19 ($M = 12{:}1$ years), diagnosed with learning disability in reading (LD-R) were administered the WIAT-III (Pearson, 2009a, 2010). Their performance was compared to a non-LD control group matched based on sex, age and grade/semester, ethnicity/race, parent education level, and geographic region. Rapid Reference 4.16 reports the mean performance of the two groups. The LD-R group scored significantly lower than the control group ($p < .01$) on every subtest and composite with the exception of the Alphabet Writing Fluency subtest. The lowest mean scores for the LD group were on the reading subtests (i.e., $M = 75.7$ on Word Reading; $M = 83.7$ on Reading Comprehension; $M = 78.1$ on Pseudoword Decoding; and 77.5 on Oral Reading Fluency). The highest scores for the LD-R group were on Alphabet Writing Fluency ($M = 92.6$) and Essay Composition ($M = 92.5$). At the composite level, the lowest scores for the LD-R group were in Total Reading ($M = 76.0$), Basic Reading ($M = 76.7$), and Reading Comprehension and Fluency ($M = 77.4$) compared to the non-LD sample ($M = 98.8, 99.2, 98.9$, respectively). The next lowest composite score for the LD-R group was Written Expression ($M = 83.2$) in comparison to the control sample ($M = 100.4$). This is not surprising given that approximately 10 percent of the LD-R students had a comorbid diagnosis of Disorder of Written Expression. Individuals with reading disorders presented a distinct pattern of scores and overall performance on WIAT-III.

## ≡ Rapid Reference 4.16

### Notable Findings on WIAT-III for Students With Specific Learning Disabilities

**Highest and Lowest Mean Scores**

| ↑ or ↓ | Reading Disability Group | Math Disability Group | Writing Disability Group |
|---|---|---|---|
| Lowest Mean Scores | Word Reading (75.7) Total Reading (76) Basic Reading Composite (76.7) Oral Reading Accuracy[a] (76.8) | Math Problem Solving (80.5) Mathematics Composite (80.6) Math Fluency– Subtraction (81.6) | Word Reading (77.3) Spelling (78.3) Total Reading (78.5) Basic Reading (78.5) |
| Highest Mean Scores | Listening Comprehension (89.1) Numerical Operations (89.7) Essay Composition (92.5) Alphabet Writing Fluency (92.6*) | Oral Reading Fluency (93) Oral Reading Rate[a] (93.7) Early Reading Skills (93.8) | Early Reading Skills (89.2) Oral Expression (89.5) Oral Language Composite (90.4) Alphabet Writing Fluency (92.6) Listening Comprehension (93.9) |

Note: Mean composite or subtest scores are in parentheses. With the exception of the scores with asterisks (*) beside them, all scores from the groups with SLD are significantly lower ($p < 0.01$) that those of the nonclinical reference comparison groups.
Source: All WIAT-III data are from Tables 3.15–3.17 of the WIAT-III Technical Manual.
[a]Supplemental scores.

*KABC-II Study*

How does the pattern of scores on the KTEA-3 compare with those from the conormed KABC-II for children with Reading Disabilities? A sample of 141 students ages 6–18 (M = 13:2 years) with documented Reading Disabilities were administered the KABC-II, and the data were compared to a matched, nonclinical reference group (Kaufman & Kaufman, 2004b). Similar to the results on the KTEA-3, scores on all KABC-II subtests and composites were significantly lower for children with Reading Disabilities than for the nonclinical reference group (all differences were *p* < .001). The Reading Disability sample's mean scores on the Sequential/*Gsm*, Learning/*Glr*, and Knowledge/*Gc* scales bordered between the Below Average and Average classifications (see Rapid Reference 4.17). The largest difference between the nonclinical group and the reading disability group was found on the Learning/*Glr* scale (with a 1 SD difference between the mean scores). Kaufman, Lichtenberger, Fletcher-Janzen, and Kaufman (2005) provide an explanation for this low score in SLD samples:

> The Learning/*Glr* scale is a demanding scale because it requires that all of the cognitive processes work together. Children must use sequential abilities to listen and organize information in a serial manner and learn in a step-by-step fashion; they must use simultaneous processing to look, organize, and remember visual information; and they must use planning abilities to prioritize information processing. The whole process utilized for the Learning/*Glr* scale is very much like a functional symphony where the first and second functional units of the brain (measured by the Sequential/*Gsm* and Simultaneous/*Gv* scales) must interact and take direction and sustain interest from the third functional unit (measured by the Planning/*Gf* scale). A disability in any of these areas can affect scores on the respective scales, but may also affect the performance on the Learning/*Glr* scale where it all has to come together (pp. 213–214).

## ≡ *Rapid Reference 4.17*

### Notable Findings on the KABC-II Scales for Children With Reading Disabilities

| *Learning/*Glr* (84.3) Knowledge/*Gc* (84.8) | < | Sequential/*Gsm* (85.4) Planning/*Gf* (86.8) | < | Simultaneous/*Gv* (88.1) |
|---|---|---|---|---|

*Source:* Data from Kaufman and Kaufman (2004a, Table 8.31).

*Largest difference between SLD-R group and control group, and the task demands for the *Glr* scale notably require that all cognitive processes work together. Means are in parentheses.

*WISC-V Studies*

The WISC-V was administered to 30 children aged 7–16 years who were identified as SLD-R according to *DSM-5* criteria. When compared to the control group, children with SLD-R obtained significantly lower mean scores for all primary index scores, with the largest large effect sizes for the VCI and WMI. The lowest primary index score was 87.8 for WMI, followed by the VCI (89.1). This finding is consistent with research that indicates a relationship between reading achievement and working memory (Swanson & Howell, 2001).

Further, the WISC-V study reports that the SLD-R sample had significantly lower scores (with large effect sizes) on three of the four VCI subtests: Vocabulary, Information, and Similarities. Plus, significantly lower scores (with large effect size) on all three WMI subtests: Digit Span, Picture Span, and Letter-Number Sequencing. Two of the FRI subtests, Matrix Reasoning and Arithmetic, were also significantly lower subtests for the SLD-R sample, as well as the Visual Puzzles Subtest. The lower scores on VCI subtests may reflect, in part, a deficiency in the general fund of information that is usually acquired through reading. The lower scores on WMI subtests suggests the role working memory may play in reading disorders. Some of the scores from the Complementary Index Scales also showed large effect sizes for the SLD-R sample, including Naming Speed and Immediate Symbol Translation. Rapid Reference 4.18 summarizes some notable findings in an SLD-R sample on the WISC-V.

The WISC-V Integrated and the WISC-V were administered to 29 children aged 6–13 years who were diagnosed with SLD-R (Wechsler & Kaplan, 2015). The results of this study were consistent with those reported on the WISC-V alone. Specifically, verbal comprehension and working memory functioning is impaired compared to students who are in the matched control group. On the WISC-V Integrated, the Multiple Choice Verbal Comprehension Index and the Visual Working Memory Index showed large effect sizes with significantly lower scores in the SLD-R group. These results are consistent with research that suggests children with Reading Disorder have difficulty on verbally mediated tasks and measures of working memory (Stanovich & Siegel, 1994; Wolf & Bowers, 1999).

## ≡ Rapid Reference 4.18

### Notable Findings in SLD-R Sample on WISC-V

↓ Low Working Memory compared to controls
- WISC-V WMI (87.8)
- WISC-V Integrated VWMI (92.2)

↓ Low General Fund of Information compared to controls
- WISC-V VCI (89.1)
- WISC-V Integrated MCVCI (90.4)

↓ Low Rapid Automatic Naming compared to controls
- WISC-V Naming Speed Literacy (88.9)
- WISC-V Naming Speed Quantity (89.7)

Note: Mean scores are in parentheses.

## Writing Disability

Reading disorders are often comorbid with disorders in the area of written expression. Coexisting difficulties in reading and writing may be related to common cognitive processes and shared neurological mechanisms that are required to develop these skills (Berninger & Richards, 2010). Because these disorders commonly co-occur, the tests' manuals report samples of students with specific learning disabilities in the area of written expression that have at least a portion of the sample with comorbid disorders in reading.

### KABC-II Study

A sample of 122 students ages 6 to 18 ($M = 13{:}3$ years) with disorders in the area of written expression were administered the KABC-II. The results of this study were very similar to the results of the sample with reading disabilities, which is not surprising given that about one third of the students with written expression disabilities also had reading disabilities. On all KABC-II scales, the group with writing disabilities scored significantly worse than the nonclinical reference group (which was a sample matched on gender, race, and parent education). The range of mean scores across the KABC-II scales was small (only about 4 points). The lowest index for the writing disability sample was on the Learning/*Glr* scale (see Rapid Reference 4.19). Kaufman, Lichtenberger, Fletcher-Janzen, and Kaufman (2005) provide some insight on why this score may be depressed in children with writing disabilities:

> Written expression does place a large [cognitive] demand on examinees, not only in terms of integrating all levels of information, but also in terms of rapidly changing thoughts and ideas as the material develops. This type of activity stretches every cognitive functional system, and perhaps the Learning/*Glr* scale suffers the most when a child has problems with overall sequential, simultaneous, and planning activities. Indeed, it follows that the evidence-based intervention techniques that work best for children with written expression deficits are those that are based on cognitive and metacognitive strategies (p. 219).

## ≡ Rapid Reference 4.19

### Notable Small Range of Scores in Writing Disability Sample on KABC-II Scales

| | |
|---|---|
| Simultaneous/*Gv* (87.7) | *Highest* |
| Planning/*Gf* (86.8) | |
| Knowledge/*Gc* (85.2) | ↓ |
| Sequential/*Gsm* (84.6) | |
| Learning/*Glr* (83.9) | *Lowest* |

Notes: Adapted from Table 8.33 in Kaufman and Kaufman (2004a). Means are in parentheses.

## WIAT-III Study

A sample of 86 students in grades 2–12, ages 7–19 ($M = 12$:2 years), diagnosed with a learning disability in the area of written expression were administered the WIAT-III. Performance was compared to a matched control group (based on sex, age and grade/semester, ethnicity/race, parent education level, and geographic region). Approximately 18 percent of the LD students were also identified with a comorbid diagnosis of Reading Disorder, contributing to weaknesses on reading-related subtests. Performance of the LD group was significantly different ($<.01$) from the matched control group on the Sentence Composition, Essay Composition, and Spelling subtests as well as on the Written Expression composite. Specifically, the mean scores of the LD group on Sentence Composition, Essay Composition, and Spelling were 84.2, 88.9, and 78.3, respectively, compared to a mean of 98.7, 98.4, and 99.6, respectively, in the control group. The Written Expression composite score for the LD group ($M = 80.7$) was significantly lower than for the non-LD group ($M = 98.5$). Rapid Reference 4.16 lists the Writing Disability sample's average WIAT-III scores.

## KTEA-3 Study

A sample of 67 students in grades 1–12 with specific learning disabilities in reading and/or written expression were administered the KTEA-3 Comprehensive Form (mean age 12:4) (Kaufman & Kaufman, 2014b). About 40% of the students were identified has having a specific learning disability in the area of reading only, 5% (3 students) had a disorder in written expression only, and just over half had a disorder in both reading and writing. The scores of these students were compared to those of a nonclinical reference group that was matched on gender, ethnicity, and parent education. Compared to a matched control group, scores on all KTEA-3 subtests and composites were significantly lower ($p < .001$) for the sample with Reading or Written Expression Disabilities. The KTEA-3 core composite scores ranged from highs of 87.1 on Math to a low of 79.0 on Reading. The mean scores for Reading-Related composites were at a level comparable (i.e., about 1–2 points different) to the low score on the Reading core composite. Of the Cross-Domain composites, the Orthographic Processing showed the most impairment in the Reading Disability sample (mean 79.2). In contrast, scores in the Average range of academic ability on the Oral Language and Oral Fluency composite (albeit in the lower end of Average) indicate that oral language skills were an area of relative integrity for the Reading/Writing Disability sample. Compared to the matched sample, the Reading/Writing Disorder sample, showed the largest effect size for the Decoding, Academic Skills Battery, Reading, and Orthographic Processing composites. Rapid Reference 4.20 highlights notable results from this sample.

## WISC-V Study

A sample of 22 students ages 6–14 who were diagnosed with a specific learning disorder–reading and written expression (SLD-RW) based on the DSM-5 criteria were administered the WISC-V (Wechsler, 2014b). Compared to the matched control group, the SLD-RW group showed significant differences on the VCI, FRI, and WMI primary index scores. The largest effect size was noted for the

## ≡ *Rapid Reference 4.20*

### Notable KTEA-3 Results for Students With Specific Learning Disabilities in Reading or Writing

**KTEA-3 Subtests and Composites With Largest Effect Sizes for Reading/Writing Disability Sample**

Decoding composite (78.0)

Letter & Word Recognition (78.1)

Reading composite (79.0)

Spelling (79.3)

Word Recognition Fluency (79.6)

Academic Skills Battery composite (80.5)

Nonsense Word Decoding (80.6)

Reading Comprehension (82.1)

*Note:* All KTEA-3 data on Specific Learning Disabilities (SLD) are from the *KTEA-3 Technical & Interpretive Manual* (Kaufman & Kaufman, 2014b).

WMI index. Complementary index scores with the largest effect sizes included Auditory WMI, Naming Speed Index, and Storage and Retrieval Index. Not surprising was the fact that the subtests with the largest effect sizes were in the domain of working memory, including Digit Span and Letter-Number Sequencing, in addition to Naming Speed Literacy, a rapid naming task. Rapid Reference 4.21 highlights notable findings on the WISC-V for the SLD-RW sample.

## ≡ *Rapid Reference 4.21*

### Notable Findings in SLD-RW Sample on WISC-V

↓ **Lower scores and large effects on Working Memory compared to controls**
- WISC-V WMI (85.8)
- Digit Span Subtest (7.2)
- Letter-Number Sequencing (7.4)

↓ **Lower scores on Verbal Comprehension tasks compared to controls**
- WISC-V VCI (86.5)

↓ **Lower scores on Fluid Reasoning tasks compared to controls**
- WISC-V FRI (88.4)

↓ **Lower scores on Rapid Naming tasks compared to controls**
- WISC-V Naming Speed Literacy (85.6)

## Math Disability

### KTEA-3 Study

A sample of 51 students in grades 1–12 with specific learning disabilities in mathematics were administered the KTEA-3 Comprehensive Form (mean age 12:7) (Kaufman & Kaufman, 2014b). Similar to the KTEA-3 studies on other SLD, the scores of these students were compared to those of a matched control group. Compared to the control group, scores on all KTEA-3 subtests and composites were significantly lower ($p < .001$) for the sample with Math Disabilities. An important characteristic to note about this Math Disability sample was that 15 percent had comorbid Reading Disabilities, which may have contributed to deficits in achievement domains such as reading and writing. The overall pattern of KTEA-3 scores for the Math Disability sample included weaknesses across domains with notably lower scores in areas related to mathematics (see Rapid Reference 4.22). The lowest average KTEA-3 scores and the largest effect sizes for the Math Disability sample were on the Math composite ($M = 76.8$), Math Concepts & Applications ($M = 77.1$), and Math Computation ($M = 78.9$). In addition, one non-mathematics task had a lower mean score than Math Fluency ($M = 82.7$) and a strong effect size for this group, which was Written Expression ($M = 81.5$).

---

## ≡ Rapid Reference 4.22

......................................................................................................

### Notable KTEA-3 Results for Students With Specific Learning Disabilities in Math

**KTEA-3 Subtests and Composites With Largest Effect Sizes for Math Disability Sample**

Math composite (76.8)

Math Concepts & Applications (77.1)

Math Computation (78.9)

Math Fluency (82.7)

Written Expression (81.5)

Note: All KTEA-3 data on Specific Learning Disabilities (SLD) are from the *KTEA-3 Technical & Interpretive Manual* (Kaufman & Kaufman, 2014b).

---

### KABC-II Study

How do scores on the KTEA-3 of children with mathematics disabilities compare with measures of cognitive ability? A sample of 96 students ages 6 to 18 ($M = 13:7$ years) with learning disabilities in mathematics were administered the KABC-II. Like in the Reading Disability sample, all scales were significantly lower for the group with mathematics disabilities than in the matched control group. The nonclinical reference group's average standard score for all scales was about 1 SD higher than that of the Mathematics Disability group. The greatest standard score difference between the mathematics disability group and the clinical reference group (about 16 points) was on the Planning/*Gf* scale (see Rapid Reference 4.23). Other studies have found that children with mathematics disabilities can be helped by implementing remediation strategies related to planning and fluid reasoning. Examples of such interventions include using meta-cognitive approaches, teaching problem solving rules, and planning solutions to mathematical problems with step-by-step problem solving (Rourke, 1989; Teeter & Semrud-Clikeman, 1998).

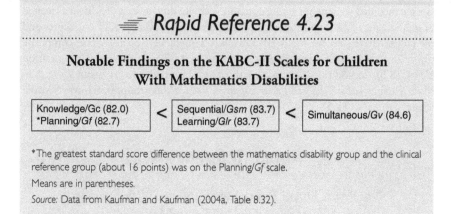

## ≡ *Rapid Reference 4.23*

### Notable Findings on the KABC-II Scales for Children With Mathematics Disabilities

| Knowledge/Gc (82.0) *Planning/Gf (82.7) | < | Sequential/Gsm (83.7) Learning/Glr (83.7) | < | Simultaneous/Gv (84.6) |

*The greatest standard score difference between the mathematics disability group and the clinical reference group (about 16 points) was on the Planning/*Gf* scale.

Means are in parentheses.

Source: Data from Kaufman and Kaufman (2004a, Table 8.32).

### *WIAT-III Study*

WIAT-III was administered to a sample of 90 students in grades 2–12, aged 7–19 (*M* = 12:8 years), diagnosed with a learning disability in mathematics (see Rapid Reference 4.24 for a summary of notable findings). Approximately 9 percent of these students had a comorbid diagnosis of reading disability, which contributed to significant weaknesses in reading and writing subtests as well. Performance was compared to a matched control group (based on sex, age, and grade/semester, ethnicity/race, parent education level, and geographic region). The lowest mean scores for the LD group were on the mathematics subtests: *M* = 80.5 on Math Problem Solving; *M* = 82.4 on Numerical Operations; *M* = 84.1 on Math Fluency—Addition; *M* = 81.6 on Math Fluency—Subtraction; and *M* = 85.0 on Math Fluency—Multiplication. At the composite level, the lowest scores for the LD group were Mathematics (*M* = 80.6) and Math Fluency (*M* = 82.4) compared to the non-LD sample (*M* = 99.5 and 100.1, respectively). These results suggest that the WIAT-III may be useful in identifying achievement weaknesses among individuals with learning disabilities in the area of mathematics. Rapid Reference 4.16 highlights the lowest and highest WIAT-III scores (composites and subtest together) from the sample of subjects with Mathematics Disorders.

*WISC-V Studies*

The WISC-V was administered to 28 children aged 9–13 years, who were diagnosed with a specific learning disorder-Mathematics (SLD-M) according to *DSM-5* criteria, and the WISC-V Integrated was administered to 37 children ages 7–16 who met the criteria for SLD-M. Means, standard deviations, and correlation coefficients are reported in Table 5.32 of the *WISC-V Technical and Interpretive Manual* (Wechsler, 2014) and Table 5.10 of the *WISC-V Integrated Technical and Interpretive Manual* (Wechsler, 2015). All and all the results from both the WISC-V and WISC-V integrated show a consistent pattern for students with SLD-M. The means scores on WISC-V primary and ancillary index scores were significantly lower for the SLD-M group than matched controls, except for the WMI. However, on the WISC-V Integrated the WMI was significantly lower for the SLD-M group. The largest effects on the WISC-V were noted on the Quantitative Reasoning Index ($M = 79.9$), the Nonverbal Index ($M = 81.5$), and the Visual Spatial Index ($M = 85.4$). These findings were supplemented by the WISC-V Integrated, which found the largest effects in this SLD-M sample for the Multiple Choice VCI, and moderate effects for the VIC, WMI and Auditory WMI. On both tests, the largest

## ≡ *Rapid Reference 4.24*

### Notable Findings in SLD-M Sample on WISC-V

↓ **Lower scores and large effects on Quantitative Reasoning compared to controls**
- WISC-V Quantitative Reasoning Index (79.9)
- WISC-V Arithmetic (6.4)
- WISC-V Integrated Arithmetic Process Approach (5.5 and 5.3)
- WISC-V Integrated Written Arithmetic (6.0)

↓ **Lower scores and large effects on Working Memory compared to controls**
- WISC-V Integrated WMI (90.2)
  *But on WISC-V, WMI was not significantly different from controls*
- WISC-V Integrated Auditory WMI (87.9)

↓ **Lower scores and large effects on Nonverbal tasks compared to controls**
- WISC-V Nonverbal Index (81.5)
- WISC-V Visual Spatial Index (85.1)
- WISC-V Integrated Figure Weights Process Approach (6.9)

↓ **Lower scores and moderate effects on Processing Speed compared to controls**
- WISC-V Integrated Coding (8.0)
- WISC-V Integrated Coding Copy (7.4)

Note: Mean scores are in parentheses.

effect sizes were for scores that required arithmetic calculation (Arithmetic, Arithmetic Process Approach A & B, and Written Arithmetic). Additional subtests with large effect sizes included WISC-V Visual Puzzles and WISC-V Integrated Figure Weights Process Approach, which indicated that additional time did not help the subjects with SLD-M. Generally, these combined findings suggest that students with SLD-M have the most significant difficulties with quantitative reasoning, visual-spatial ability, fluid reasoning, working memory, and processing speed.

### Conclusions From KTEA-3 and WIAT-III SLD Clinical Studies

The profiles of KTEA-3 and WIAT-III scores for the three types of learning disabilities reviewed here are similar to what would be expected based upon the skill deficits commonly present in students with SLD. In all of these SLD samples, relative weaknesses were seen across the board in specific areas of reading and written expression. In contrast, oral language was an area of relative integrity for all samples with LD. Readers must be cautious in generalizing from the data that we have summarized from the test manuals for several reasons. Most of these SLD samples were not homogenous groups; they included students that had disabilities in more than one area (e.g., the WIAT-III and KTEA-3 samples with Mathematics Disabilities included students with comorbid Reading Disorders). The students were not randomly selected for the studies, and for the KTEA-3 and KABC-II studies, independent clinicians were typically responsible for determining whether students fit LD criteria. Finally, these are group data that may not be representative of all individuals in a diagnostic class. Therefore, these data summarized from the manuals of the tests should be considered a preliminary estimate of how SLD samples perform on the measures. More research would be a welcome addition to the literature on the latest editions of these achievement instruments, using well-defined samples of SLD who are assessed using multiple measures.

> **DON'T FORGET**
>
> Examiners who are assessing children with referral concerns in particular academic areas (e.g., reading, writing, math) will find the "Decision Tree for KTEA-3 and WIAT-III Subtests" to be a useful reference. Found in the Digital Resources for this book, the Decision Tree provides recommendations for selecting subtest based on specific reasons for referral based on difficulty in a specific academic area.
>
> A comprehensive evaluation is preferable to fully understand an examinee's learning strengths and weaknesses, and to create an individualized approach to recommendations and remediation. However, these Decision Trees can help create a targeted assessment plan if it is warranted.

### Models for the Identification of a Specific Learning Disability

The WIAT-III and KTEA-3 are frequently used in the process of diagnosing learning disabilities to examine individual achievement and to compare achievement with cognitive ability. The requirements for diagnosing specific learning disabilities (SLD) have been debated in recent years (Flanagan, Ortiz, & Alfonso, 2013; Fletcher, Lyon, Fuchs, & Barnes, 2007; Kaufman & Kaufman, 2001). Many researchers and clinicians have put forth strong arguments against the use of achievement-ability discrepancies as criteria for determining SLD (Beninger, Dunn, & Alper, 2005; Flanagan et al., 2002; Siegel, 1999; Stanovich, 1999; Vellutino, Scanlon, & Lyon, 2000). Furthermore, changes to the Individuals with Disabilities Education Act (e.g., PL 108-446) formerly eliminated an achievement-ability discrepancy as a necessary part of determining SLD (Rapid Reference 4.25 lists where more information can be found on PL 108-446). Thus, assessment professionals (depending on how state and local educational authorities decide to implement PL 108-446) no longer need to utilize a rigid discrepancy formula including scores from tests such as the WIAT-III and KTEA-3 in conjunction with IQ scores. Rather, WIAT-III and KTEA-3 scores may be used as a mechanism to determine interindividual academic abilities, and to evaluate how academic deficits are related to or caused by deficits in basic cognitive processes. Procedures for diagnosing SLD without using an achievement-ability

## ≡ Rapid Reference 4.25

### Resources for the Individuals With Disabilities Education Improvement Act of 2004 (PL 108-446)

**National Association of School Psychologists**
http://www.nasponline.org/research-and-policy/current-law-and-policy-priorities/current-law/individuals-with-disabilities-education-improvement-act-(idea)

**National Center for Learning Disabilities**
http://www.ncld.org/archives/action-center/learn-the-law/individuals-with-disabilities-education-act-idea

**Council for Exceptional Children (CEC): Public Policy and Legislative Information**
http://www.cec.sped.org/Policy-and-Advocacy/Current-Sped-Gifted-Issues/Individuals-with-Disabilities-Education-Act

**Learning Disabilities Association of America**
http://www.ldanatl.org/

**Council for Exceptional Children (CEC): A Primer on the IDEA 2004 Regulations**
http://www.cec.sped.org/Policy-and-Advocacy/Current-Sped-Gifted-Issues/Individuals-with-Disabilities-Education-Act/A-Primer-on-the-IDEA-2004-RegulationsIDEA

**Wrights Law: IDEA 2004 Changes in Key Statutes**
http://www.wrightslaw.com/law/idea/index.htm

**U.S. Department of Education, Office of Special Education Programs' (OSEP's) IDEA Website**
http://idea.ed.gov/explore/view

discrepancy have been articulated by Berninger and colleagues (Berninger, Dunn, & Alper, 2005; Berninger & O'Donnell, 2005) and Flanagan and colleagues (Flanagan, Ortiz, Alfonso, & Mascolo, 2002; Flanagan, Ortiz, & Alfonso, 2007).

Results from a KTEA-3 and/or WIAT-II assessment may be integrated with cognitive ability assessment results as part of a comprehensive evaluation for the identification of specific learning disabilities, either within the context of the traditional ability-achievement discrepancy (AAD) model or within the context of several alternative models for identifying specific learning disabilities. Two alternative models will be described in the sections that follow:

- The Modern Operational Definition of SLD developed by Flanagan and colleagues (Flanagan, Ortiz, Alfonso, & Mascolo, 2006; Flanagan, Ortiz, & Alfonso, 2007).
- The Concordance-Discordance model of SLD identification developed by Hale and Fiorello (2004), which is described in the WIAT-III Technical Manual and the KTEA-3 *Technical & Interpretive Manual* as the pattern of strengths and weaknesses (PSW) discrepancy model.

Each of these models may be used within established cognitive and neuropsychological approaches to assessment (e.g., cognitive hypothesis-testing model, the Cross-Battery assessment approach, Cattell-Horn-Carroll theory, Lurian model).

### Modern Operational Definition of SLD

As shown in Figure 4.2, the Modern Operational Definition of SLD specifies several essential elements for identifying a specific learning disability that are organized into three levels: Level I involves specific academic skills measurement and evaluation of exclusionary factors; Level II involves measurement of broad abilities, processes, and learning aptitudes; and Level III involves evaluation of underachievement. Meeting each of these levels of criteria is necessary before a diagnosis of SLD is recommended. The details of levels of this definition of SLD are summarized below.

### Level I: Specific Academic Skills Measurement and Evaluation of Exclusionary Factors

For children identified as at-risk by RTI Tier 1 universal screening, learning dysfunction or the presence of academic deficits that fall below normal limits on norm-referenced tests (e.g., standard scores <85) must be documented at Level I. During this first level, practitioners must also determine whether the academic skill deficits are primarily the result of factors other than cognitive deficit (e.g., cultural or language differences, insufficient instruction, poor motivation, performance anxiety, psychiatric disorders, sensory impairments, medical conditions).

### Level II: Measurement of Broad Abilities, Processes, and Learning Aptitudes

The focus of a comprehensive assessment at Level II is on measurement of cognitive abilities, processes, and learning aptitudes. A comprehensive assessment should determine whether an examinee's cognitive abilities or process measures are below

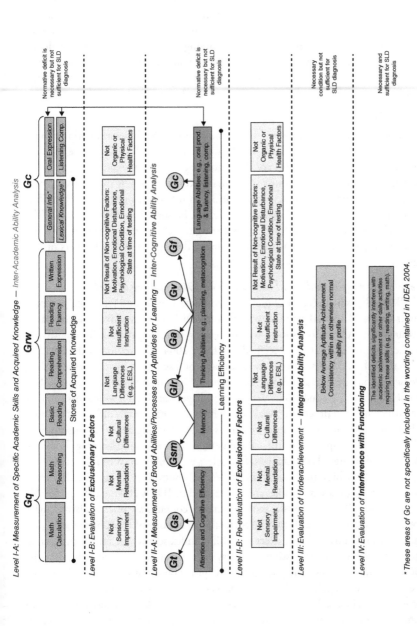

**Figure 4.2 Modern Operational Definition of SLD**

Source: Flanagan, Ortiz, and Alfonso (2007).

normal limits relative to the general population. If these deficits in cognitive abilities or processes exist, then the practitioner should determine whether they are related to the academic skill deficit. (For example, determine whether CHC specific or Narrow Abilities and processes have established relations to academic outcomes). A fundamental part of SLD identification is identifying related cognitive and academic deficits, or *below-average aptitude-achievement consistency*. At Level II, practitioners also must examine comorbid conditions and rule out exclusionary factors as the primary cause for cognitive deficits not evaluated at Level I (e.g., mental retardation).

### Level III: Evaluation of Underachievement

When moving to Level III, four necessary conditions for SLD determination should be documented: (1) academic deficit(s), (2) cognitive deficit(s), (3) cognitive and academic deficits are related, and (4) consideration of exclusionary factors.

At the third level, all data must be evaluated to determine if the below-average aptitude-achievement consistency exists within an otherwise normal ability profile. That is, in addition to areas of deficit, there must be spared cognitive abilities. The presence of spared cognitive abilities helps distinguish children with SLD from those who have more pervasive cognitive and academic deficits (e.g., slow learners or low achievers).

### Pattern of Strengths and Weaknesses (PSW) Discrepancy Model

The PSW model is included in Q-global's web-based scoring and reporting platform for users of the WIAT-III or KTEA-3. This model is an alternative research-based procedure to the AAD and response to intervention (RTI) approaches for identifying a specific learning disability as specified by IDEA 2004. The results of the AAD or PSW analysis should be used to generate, support, or disconfirm hypotheses regarding a specific referral question and should be supported by other relevant sources of information before making educational decisions or diagnoses. The PSW analysis requires the identification of a processing weakness, which differentiates a student with a specific learning disability from a student who is underachieving for other reasons, and is a fundamental component of the federal definition of a specific learning disability.

When conducting a PSW analysis, first select a KTEA-3 or WIAT-III subtest or composite as the achievement weakness. Selecting a subtest or composite that measures one of the eight areas of achievement specified by IDEA 2004 may be preferable in many settings. If the composite score of interest contains significant discrepancies between subtest-level scores, it may be preferable to use one of the subtest scores that comprise that composite. Next, select two ability index scores, one for the processing strength and one for the processing weakness, from a test of cognitive ability like the KABC-II or the WISC-V. The processing strength should not be empirically related to the achievement weakness, but the processing weakness should be related to the achievement weakness. Measures of processing speed, working memory, short-term memory, or long-term storage and retrieval are not empirically recommended as processing strengths within this model because these scores have lower psychometric *g* loadings (Prifitera, Saklofske, & Weiss, 2005) and are thought to be less representative of the true nature of SLD. For this reason, the Processing Speed and Working Memory Indexes from the WISC-V and the Sequential and Learning Indexes from the KABC-II are not typically recommended cognitive strengths within the PSW model.

As shown in Figure 4.3, in order to meet the criteria of the PSW model for a specific learning disability, two score comparisons must be significantly different (discrepant): the processing strength versus the achievement weakness, and the processing strength versus the processing weakness. If one or both score comparisons are not statistically different, the results do not support the identification of a specific learning disability. If the student is underachieving in more than one area, you may calculate the model more than once. Clinical judgment may be needed for cases that approach significance because some of these students may have a specific learning disability, but the results were not significant due to the student's use of compensatory strategies or due to other psychological processes lowering the cognitive strength. Remember that some differences are clinically significant even if not statistically significant.

## Pattern of Strengths and Weaknesses Analysis

Area of Processing Strength: WISC-V Fluid Reasoning Index: 109
Area of Processing Weakness: WISC-V Auditory Working Memory Index: 89
Area of Achievement Weakness: KTEA-3 Decoding: 80

| Comparison | Relative Strength Score | Relative Weakness Score | Difference | Critical Value (.05) | Significant Difference Y/N | Supports SLD hypothesis? Yes/No |
|---|---|---|---|---|---|---|
| Processing Strength/ Achievement Weakness | 109 | 80 | 29 | 9 | Y | Yes |
| Processing Strength/ Processing Weakness | 109 | 89 | 20 | 11 | Y | Yes |

*Note:* The PSW model is intended to help practitioners generate hypotheses regarding clinical diagnoses. The analysis should only be used as part of a comprehensive evaluation that incorporates multiple sources of information.

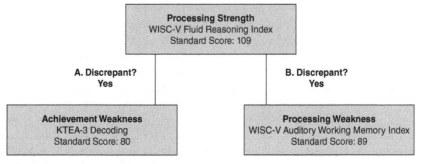

**Figure 4.3  Criteria of the PSW Model**

As recommended by Hale and Fiorello (2004), Q-global uses the standard error of the difference (SED) to evaluate the statistical significance of each score comparison in the PSW model. A standard formula is used to calculate SED, which is available through published references (e.g., Hale & Fiorello, 2004; Rust & Golombok, 1999). SED is preferred over the standard error of the residual (regression method) for comparing a processing strength and weakness because there is no implicit causal relationship between these scores (as in the AAD model). For this reason, and for consistency and simplicity, SED is used to calculate both score comparisons in the PSW model.

A third score comparison requiring consistency between the achievement weakness and the processing weakness is not a statistical requirement of the PSW model, but it is important to consider. The cognitive processing weakness should be theoretically related to the achievement weakness to provide an explanation for the learning disability (Hale, Fiorello et al., 2008). To select a processing weakness that is theoretically related to the achievement weakness, consult relevant research (e.g., Hale, Fiorello, Kavanagh, Hoeppner, & Gaither, 2001; Hale, Fiorello, Bertin, & Sherman, 2003; Fiorello, Hale, & Snyder, 2006) for information regarding theoretical relationships between cognitive processes and achievement domains.

### Learning Disability Subtypes

Identification of SLD typically involves meeting a set of criteria for recognized categories of learning disabilities. Categories of SLD will vary depending on whether the examiner relies on national or international published classification manuals (e.g., DSM-5; ICD-10), federal regulations (e.g., IDEA 2004), or a research-based framework (e.g., Berninger, 2015). Table 4.2 summarizes the categories of SLD described by the DSM-5, IDEA 2004, and Virginia Berninger to exemplify the different approaches. The DSM-5 and IDEA 2004 categorize SLD by achievement area. However, a research-based approach like Berninger's categorizes SLD by broader profiles of symptoms that consider developmental, learning, and cognitive characteristics.

### Intervention Guide for LD Subtypes

Subtypes of learning disabilities have also been proposed for the purpose of providing differentiated instruction based upon individual learning characteristics. A lack of consensus exists in the research literature about the validity and reliability of learning disability subtype classifications. Researchers (e.g., Gresham, 2009) have questioned whether better instructional outcomes are achieved when instruction is tailored to individual characteristics. However, researchers at the Florida Center for Reading Research (see Connor et al., 2013; Connor et al., 2011) have provided strong evidence in support of individualizing student instruction based on rigorous standardized assessment data of each student's academic strengths and weaknesses.

Table 4.3 presents an overview of the subtypes proposed in the research literature for reading-related learning disabilities along with key references. These seven subtypes are supported by the Intervention Guide for LD Subtypes, a web-based application in Q-global (invented by Kristina Breaux, patent pending). The Intervention Guide helps users analyze a student's learning profile to determine skill strengths and

**Table 4.2 Three Approaches to Subtyping Learning Disabilities for Differential Diagnosis or Identification**

| DSM-5 | IDEA 2004 | Research-Based (Berninger, 2015) |
|---|---|---|
| Specific learning disorder with impairment in one or more areas: | Underachievement despite appropriate instruction in one or more of the following areas: | Differential diagnosis of SLDs: |
| • Reading | • Oral expression | • Dyslexia |
| Word reading accuracy; Reading rate or fluency; Reading comprehension | • Listening comprehension | • Dysgraphia |
| • Written expression | • Written expression | • Oral and Written Language Learning Disability (OWL–LD) |
| Spelling accuracy; Grammar and punctuation accuracy; Clarity or organization of written expression | • Basic reading skills | • Dyscalculia |
| • Mathematics | • Reading fluency skills | • Nonverbal learning disabilities |
| Number sense; Memorization of arithmetic facts; Accurate or fluent calculation; Accurate math reasoning | • Reading comprehension | |
| | • Mathematics calculation | |
| | • Mathematics problem solving | |
| | *Dyslexia, dyscalculia,* and *dysgraphia* are allowable terms.[*] | |

*Dyslexia* and *dyscalculia* are allowable terms.

*Note:* In October of 2015, the U.S. Department of Education's Office of Special Education & Rehabilitative Services issued guidance to states and schools, clarifying that "there is nothing in the IDEA that would prohibit the use of the terms dyslexia, dyscalculia, and dysgraphia in IDEA evaluation, eligibility determinations, or IEP documents" (Yudin, 2015).

[*] In October of 2015, the U.S. Department of Education's Office of Special Education & Rehabilitative Services issued guidance to states and schools, clarifying that "there is nothing in the IDEA that would prohibit the use of the terms dyslexia, dyscalculia, and dysgraphia in IDEA evaluation, eligibility determinations, or IEP documents" (Yudin, 2015).

## Table 4.3 Subtypes of Reading-Related Learning Disabilities for Intervention Planning

| Subtypes | Key Features |
|---|---|
| Phonological Dyslexia | • Exhibit a phonological core deficit, or difficulty using the phonological route to reading and spelling.<br>• Rely on visual and orthographic cues, may memorize whole words as a strategy for word recognition.<br>• Rarely use letter-to-sound conversion.<br>• Read irregular or exception words better than pseudowords.<br>• Listening comprehension is stronger than reading comprehension. |
| Orthographic Dyslexia | • Difficulty using the visual-lexical route to reading and writing words.<br>• Rely on the phonological route, sounding words out letter by letter, overrelying on sound-symbol relationships.<br>• Pseudoword reading is better than irregular or exception word reading.<br>• Listening comprehension is stronger than reading comprehension. |
| Mixed Phonological-Orthographic Dyslexia | • Severely impaired with difficulty using the phonological route as well as the visual-lexical route to reading and writing words.<br>• Error patterns may not show consistent pattern of errors.<br>• Difficulty with regular, irregular, and pseudoword reading.<br>• Listening comprehension is stronger than reading comprehension. |
| Language | • Sometimes referred to as Oral and Written Language Learning Disability (OWL-LD), (Grammatical) Specific Language Impairment (SLI or G-SLI), or Language Learning Disability (LLD).<br>• Problems in both oral and written language with particular difficulty processing grammar and syntax.<br>• Nonverbal cognitive ability is intact (at least average).<br>• Poor listening and reading comprehension. |
| Fluency | • Poor reading fluency due to a naming speed deficit.<br>• Able to read and decode words accurately with adequate phonological processing skills.<br>• According to the Double-Deficit Hypothesis, reading disorders can be classified into two single-deficit subtypes that are relatively independent of each other (phonological or rate deficit) or as one combined double-deficit subtype. |

**Table 4.3** (Continued)

| Subtypes | Key Features |
|---|---|
| Comprehension | • Specific comprehension deficit, sometimes referred to as hyperlexia, is relatively rare and sometimes a symptom of a pervasive developmental disorder.<br>• Poor listening and reading comprehension.<br>• Fluency and accuracy of word recognition and decoding skills are intact, sometimes even far above average.<br>• Relative strengths are also observed in phonological processing and naming speed. |
| Global | • Individuals with global reading impairment are sometimes referred to as garden-variety poor readers.<br>• Skills are similar to younger children reading at the same level.<br>• Difficulty with all reading-related skills (word recognition, decoding, fluency, reading comprehension, and listening comprehension).<br>• May also show phonological deficits.<br>• No deficits in adaptive functioning (do not qualify for mild intellectual disability).<br>• Low verbal and nonverbal cognitive abilities (IQ standard scores between 70 and 90) with achievement scores similarly low.<br>• Given that these students have learning problems that are consistent with estimates of their cognitive ability (in other words, their learning difficulties are not unexpected), these students may not meet contemporary operational definitions of a specific learning disability. |

*Note:* References for the Phonological Dyslexia, Orthographic Dyslexia, and Mixed Phonological-Orthographic Dyslexia subtypes include the following: Feifer (2011); Feifer and De Fina (2000); Stanovich, Siegel, and Gottardo (1997). References for the Language subtype include: Berninger (2009); Bishop and Snowling (2004); Schwartz (2011). References for the Fluency subtype include: Lovett (1984; 1987); Meisinger, Bloom, and Hynd (2010); Wolf and Bowers (1999); Wolf, Bowers, and Biddle (2000). References for the Comprehension subtype include: Catts, Hogan, & Fey, 2010; Cain and Oakhill (2007); Gough and Tunmer (1986); Nation (1999); Henderson, Snowling and Clarke (2013); Tong, Deacon, & Cain, 2014. References for the Global subtype include: Gough and Tunmer (1986); Stanovich (1988, 1991); Stoodley, Ray, Jack, and Stein (2008); Vellutino, Scanlon, and Lyon (2000).

weaknesses, and then the application compares the student's skill levels with specific learning disability (LD) subtypes. If the student's profile matches the expected profile for a subtype, a report is provided with tailored, research-supported intervention suggestions. Essential information about how to use the Intervention Guide is provided in Rapid Reference 4.26.

## ≡ Rapid Reference 4.26

### FAQs About the Intervention Guide for LD Subtypes in Q-global

**What is the Intervention Guide for LD Subtypes?**

The Intervention Guide for LD Subtypes organizes a student's assessment data and guides the user in creating a skill level profile. This Intervention Guide compares the student's skill levels with specific learning disability (LD) subtypes and provides a report with tailored, research-supported intervention suggestions. *This Intervention Guide is not intended to identify or diagnose specific learning disabilities. Students may benefit from the interventions provided in the report regardless of whether or not they have been previously identified as having a learning disability.*

**How does it work?**

The student's Q-global assessment data is displayed according to skill area. The user may enter additional scores or observations beyond those in Q-global. After evaluating all available assessment data, the user determines whether a skill area is a weakness. These ratings are used to determine whether the student's pattern of relative strengths and weaknesses is consistent with the typical pattern observed for one of the learning disability subtypes currently supported by this Intervention Guide.

**What assessment data do I need?**

Information about the student's cognitive processing, language, and achievement skills are required. Results from clinical assessments in these areas are recommended; however, both quantitative and qualitative data are considered.

Use more than one source of data for each skill whenever possible. Performance across multiple measures provides cross-validation of the student's skill level. For example, a Spelling test score might be cross-validated with performance in the classroom and a curriculum-based measure before the user decides whether Spelling is an area of weakness.

**Which assessments are compatible with this Intervention Guide?**

To assist the user in creating a skill level profile, the user may choose to include a student's Q-global assessment data, which will be displayed and automatically organized by skill area. The user may select one or more of the following seven assessments:

1. KTEA-3
2. WIAT-III
3. WISC-V
4. WPPSI-IV
5. KABC-II
6. CELF-5
7. WRMT-III

(continued)

*(Continued)*

## How does this Intervention Guide report differ from the one generated for the KTEA-3 or WIAT-III error analysis results?

Error analysis results provide fine-grained information about which skills to teach in a particular area and provide recommendations for teaching those skills.

This Intervention Guide considers the student's patterns of performance across cognitive, language, and achievement areas when making recommendations about *how* to approach instruction and *why*. Recommendations are designed to utilize areas of relative strength for remediating weaknesses.

## Which subtypes are supported?

Currently, seven LD subtypes and a co-occurring condition are supported by this Intervention Guide:

- Phonological
- Orthographic
- Mixed Phonological-Orthographic
- Language (a.k.a., OWL-LD, SLI, or LLD)
- Specific comprehension deficit
- Reading fluency subtype/naming speed deficit
- Global
- Dysgraphia (included as a co-occurring condition with one of the other listed subtypes)

## What kinds of difficulties are not addressed?

Subtypes with primary weaknesses in mathematics, written expression, and nonverbal learning disabilities are not currently supported by this Intervention Guide.

The recommendations provided by the Intervention Guide are not comprehensive enough to address the following:

- Uncorrected visual or auditory impairment
- Moderate to severe intellectual disability
- Impoverished educational background/inadequate instruction
- Language or cultural differences
- Emotional, behavioral, or psychological conditions

## Who has access to the Intervention Guide for LD Subtypes?

At the time this book was published, Q-global users with a subscription for either the KTEA-3 or the WIAT-III have access to the Intervention Guide for LD Subtypes at no additional cost.

## How much does a report cost?

At the time this book was published, the Intervention Guide report is free of charge.

*(continued)*

(Continued)

## What criteria should I use to determine if a skill/ability is an area of weakness?

Weakness means the skill/ability is generally weak or difficult for the student. If not a weakness, then the skill is considered a relative strength. The rating is not based on statistics or formulas. Rely primarily on your own evaluation of all available evidence—both quantitative and qualitative. Consider the following data when evaluating each skill/ability:

- The Q-global assessment data that are provided
- Assessment data that are not in Q-global
- Criterion-referenced or curriculum-based measures
- Qualitative observations (e.g., test-taking or classroom observations).

## What if the student's skill profile doesn't fit one of the subtypes?

There are several reasons why the student's profile may not fit one of the supported subtypes. For example, the student's profile may be consistent with a subtype not yet supported by the Intervention Guide, or the student may be underachieving for reasons other than those accounted for by the LD subtypes. If the student's performance is not consistent with one of the subtypes supported by the Intervention Guide, a report may still be generated based on smaller clusters of weaknesses that are identified. Very rarely, a skill profile is not consistent with any subtypes or clusters and no report can be generated.

Source: Intervention Guide for LD Subtypes FAQ in Q-global. Copyright © 2015 NCS Pearson, Inc. Reproduced with permission. All rights reserved.

### Achievement Testing in Children with Attention-Deficit Hyperactivity Disorder

About 5% of children are affected with ADHD (American Psychiatric Association, 2013). Specific learning disabilities are often comorbid with ADHD. Estimates of the rates of learning disabilities coexisting with ADHD reveal that 8 to 39 percent of children with ADHD have a reading disability, 12 to 30 percent have a math disability, and 12 to 27 percent have a spelling disorder (Barkley, 1990; Faraone, Biederman, Lehman, & Spencer, 1993; Frick et al., 1991). Standardized achievement tests administered along with a comprehensive battery (including tests of cognitive ability, behavioral and emotional functioning) can help differentially diagnose ADHD from other learning and psychiatric disorders, and help determine the existence of comorbid disorders.

Children with attention-deficit/hyperactivity disorder (ADHD) have tremendous difficulty in their academic performance and achievement. These difficulties include both their work productivity in the classroom and the level of difficulty children have in mastering the expected academic material (Barkley, 1998). Given these difficulties, it is not surprising that ADHD is one of the most common referrals to school psychologists and mental health providers (Demaray, Schaefer, & Delong, 2003). Typically, children who are referred to a clinic for ADHD are doing poorly at school and are underperforming relative to their known levels of ability as determined by intelligence and academic tests. Their poor performance is likely related to their inattentive, impulsive, and restless behavior in the classroom. On standardized tests of academic achievement, children with ADHD typically score 10–30 standard score points lower than their peers in reading, spelling, math, and reading comprehension (Barkley, Dupaul, & McMurray, 1990; Brock & Knapp, 1996; Casey, Rourke, & Del Dotto, 1996). "Consequently, it is not surprising to find that as many as 56% of ADHD children may require academic tutoring, approximately 30% may repeat a grade in school, and 30–40% may be placed in one or more special education programs ... [and] 10–35% may drop out [of school] entirely" (Barkley, 1998, p. 99).

While achievement tests such as the WIAT-III and KTEA-3 and intelligence tests such as the WISC-V and KABC-II do not, and never were intended to, diagnose ADHD, they are of significant importance in the assessment of children with ADHD. Having knowledge of the specific areas of academic skill deficits coupled with awareness of the cognitive processing abilities of a child with ADHD is a great benefit in planning behavioral and educational programming.

## WIAT-III

Given what previous research on children with ADHD has shown, we would predict that children with ADHD tested on the WIAT-III would have significant areas of academic deficit compared to those without ADHD. A study of the performance of students with ADHD on the WIAT-III was not included in the test manual; however, previous studies using the WIAT-II are relevant to testing the assumption that students with ADHD would also demonstrate significant weaknesses on the WIAT-III because of the similarities between the two measures.

The WIAT-II was administered to a group of 178 individuals, ages 5–18 ($M = 13$ years), diagnosed with ADHD, as defined in the *DSM-IV*, and a control group matched on age and grade, gender, ethnicity/race, and parent education level. The lowest scores for the ADHD group were on the Written Expression (92.1) and Spelling (94.0) subtests and the Written Language (92.1) composite. The highest scores for this group were on the Listening Comprehension (100.1) and Oral Expression (98.2) subtests and the Oral Language composite (98.4). Significant differences ($p < .01$) occurred between the two groups across all subtests and composites except the Oral Expression subtest, with actual differences in mean scores ranging from 2.05 (Oral Expression) to 8.17 (Numerical Operations).

In a second study that included 51 children, aged 7–18 ($M = 12$ years), diagnosed with both ADHD and learning disabilities, a very different profile emerged. The differences between mean scores for the ADHD-LD and the control groups are significantly large (ranging from 8.78 for Oral Expression to 25.67 on Spelling). The lowest mean composite score for the ADHD-LD group was on Written Language (80.7), where sustained attention and effort, planning, organizing, and self-monitoring are required. The highest scores for this group were on Listening Comprehension (96.2) and Oral Expression (91.9).

A subsequent study conducted by McConaughy, Ivanova, Antshel, and Eiraldi (2009) investigated test session behavior and performance on the WIAT-II and other measures among 177 children, ranging in age from 6 to 11 years, who were classified as either ADHD–Combined type (ADHD-C), ADHD–Inattentive type (ADHD-I), nonreferred controls, or non-ADHD referred controls (students who were clinically referred for other diagnoses; NON-ADHD-Ref). This study found that, compared to the nonreferred control group, children with ADHD-C and ADHD-I scored significantly ($p < .05$) lower on all three WIAT-II composites that were evaluated: Reading ($M = 96.3$ and 97.9 for each subtype, respectively), Mathematics ($M = 97.4$ and 95.5 for each subtype, respectively), and Written Language ($M = 98.5$ and 97.6 for each subtype, respectively). In addition, there was no significant difference between the ADHD-C and ADHD-I groups in their performance on the WIAT-II composites. These researchers conclude that the WIAT-II was effective in differentiating the performance of children with ADHD and the control group; however, the WIAT-II scores did not differentiate subtypes of ADHD. Only test session observations differentiated ADHD subtypes.

Based upon the WIAT-II research results described here, it is reasonable to expect that students with ADHD are likely to demonstrate significantly lower performance on the WIAT-III reading, written expression, and mathematics subtests and composites; however, research with the newest edition of the WIAT is needed to confirm this finding.

### KTEA-3 Study

A sample of 91 students in Kindergarten through grade 12 (mean age 11:2) with ADHD (but no language disorder or learning disability) were administered the KTEA-3 along with a matched sample of students with no noted disability. Most KTEA-3 composite scores for the ADHD sample were not significantly lower than the nonclinical reference group. The Written Language, Academic Skills Battery, Oral Language, and Oral Fluency composites were significantly lower ($p < .01$) than the control group, and showed a moderate effect size. However, unlike the SLD samples whose composite scores were frequently more than 1 SD below the normative mean, the ADHD sample's KTEA-3 composite scores were in the average range, and they ranged from 3 to 4 points below the normative mean of 100. The mean composite scores for Reading (98.4), Mathematics (97.4), and Written Language (95.6) were not highly variable as they differed only by about 3 points. Although the mean Oral Language composite and Oral Fluency composite were higher at 98.0 and 98.2, respectively, it was significantly lower than the control group's mean score. Overall findings from the ADHD sample tested on the KTEA-3 do not support previous research that found depressed academic functioning for such children. However, this sample was not as impaired as samples of children with SLD, with all of the ADHD sample's mean scores classified within the average range of ability. Future research administering the KTEA-3 together with tests of cognitive ability to samples of children with ADHD and samples of children with comorbid ADHD and SLD will provide useful information to clinicians who work with such children.

## PART TWO: NEW COMPOSITE SCORES, SPECIAL CONSIDERATIONS, AND ONGOING RESEARCH

### Interpretation and Use of Three New Composite Scores

Included with this book are normative tables for generating three new composite scores. The new composite scores include four Dyslexia Index scores, two for the KTEA-3 and two for the WIAT-III, and a new KTEA-3 Oral Reading Fluency composite. The specific tables provided as Digital Resources are listed in the Don't Forget box.

## DON'T FORGET
..................................................................................................

### New Scores Tables Included as Digital Resources With This Book

For the Dyslexia Index Scores, the following tables are provided for the KTEA-3 and the WIAT-III:
- Grade-Based and Age-Based Composite Standard Scores
- Bands of Errors (95%, 90%, 85% Confidence Intervals) for Grade-Based Standard Scores and Age-Based Standard Scores
- Split-Half Reliability Coefficients for Subtests and Composites by Grade and by Age
- Reading/Writing Disorder Sample Mean Scores

For the KTEA-3 Oral Reading Fluency composite score:
- Grade-Based and Age-Based Composite Standard Scores
- Bands of Errors (95%, 90%, 85% Confidence Intervals) for Grade-Based Standard Scores and Age-Based Standard Scores
- Composite Score Comparisons for KTEA-3 Oral Reading Fluency Composite versus KTEA-3 Decoding Composite Score: Significance and Frequency of Standard Score Differences by Grade and by Age
- Split-Half Reliability Coefficients for Subtests and Composites by Grade (3–12) and by Age (8–25)

### Dyslexia Index Scores

The Dyslexia Index scores were designed to provide theoretically sound and research-based composite scores that maximize clinical sensitivity for identifying young children at-risk for dyslexia as well as students and adults who may have dyslexia. However, no single score is sufficient to identify or diagnose dyslexia.

Best practice for identifying dyslexia typically involves consideration of developmental, medical, and family history as well as a comprehensive evaluation of oral language, cognitive processing abilities, and academic skills. Dyslexia is best identified by a qualified professional based on a thoughtful synthesis of all available quantitative and qualitative evidence.

As specified in the international definition of dyslexia adopted by the IDA and NICHD (see Don't Forget box), the core symptoms of dyslexia typically include poor spelling, basic reading (accuracy and/or fluency), decoding, and phonological processing. In addition to poor phonological awareness, research indicates that poor letter knowledge and rapid automatic naming (naming facility) are core symptoms or predictors of dyslexia before children have begun reading (grades K and 1).

## DON'T FORGET

### International Definition of Dyslexia

"Dyslexia is a specific learning disability that is neurobiological in origin. It is characterized by difficulties with accurate and/or fluent word recognition and by poor spelling and decoding abilities. These difficulties typically result from a deficit in the phonological component of language that is often unexpected in relation to other cognitive abilities and the provision of effective classroom instruction. Secondary consequences may include problems in reading comprehension and reduced reading experience that can impede growth of vocabulary and background knowledge."

This Definition is also used by the National Institute of Child Health and Human Development (NICHD).

Source: www.eida.org. Adopted by the IDA Board of Directors, November 12, 2002.

The most powerful predictors of reading difficulty in the earliest grades are letter knowledge, rapid automatic naming, and phonological awareness (Kirby, Parrila, & Pfeiffer, 2003; Schatschneider & Torgesen, 2004). Measures of letter-name knowledge (early kindergarten) or letter-sound knowledge (later kindergarten) are excellent predictors of early word reading difficulties (Schatschneider & Torgesen, 2004). In addition, slow naming speed, especially in combination with phonological difficulties, predicts later reading difficulties (Kirby, Parrila, & Pfeiffer, 2003). Naming speed is important as a prerequisite for developing orthographic skill (Wolf & Bowers, 1999). As Bowers (1996, p. 1) explained, "naming speed influences the ability to learn the orthographic pattern of words." Since later reading development relies upon orthographic skill, naming speed is predictive of later reading skill. Hence, both phonological awareness and naming speed measures are useful for the early identification of children at-risk for dyslexia. However, once children begin reading, the best diagnostic indicators of dyslexia are measures of decoding fluency and text reading fluency, not measures of phonological awareness and rapid automatic naming (Schatschneider & Torgesen, 2004).

Based on this research, the KTEA-3 Dyslexia Index for grades K-1 includes measures of naming facility, phonological awareness, letter knowledge, letter-sound correspondence, and word recognition. The WIAT-III Dyslexia Index for grades K-1 includes measures of phonological awareness, letter knowledge, letter-sound correspondence, word recognition, and the orthographic loop. Both composites scores may be considered highly reliable and theoretically sound. The primary difference between these composites is that only the KTEA-3 includes a measure of rapid automatic naming/naming facility and only the WIAT-III includes a measure of the orthographic loop (early spelling of phonemes and words). The KTEA-3 includes a more comprehensive measure of phonological processing skills than the WIAT-III, which also contributes to a longer administration time (6–8 minutes longer) for the KTEA-3 Dyslexia Index as compared to the WIAT-III Dyslexia Index for grades K–1.

Based on the core symptoms agreed-upon by the international definition of dyslexia (see Don't Forget box) and the associated research support, the KTEA-3 Dyslexia Index for grades 2–12 includes measures of oral *word* reading fluency, decoding, and spelling. The WIAT-III Dyslexia Index for grades 2–12 includes measures of oral *contextual* reading fluency, decoding, and spelling. The primary difference between these composites is with the oral reading fluency measures: the KTEA-3 includes single word reading fluency whereas the WIAT-III includes passage reading fluency. The administration times are comparable for both composites (12–15 minutes).

The composite structures and estimated administration times for the four new Dyslexia Index scores are summarized in Rapid Reference 4.27. Any of the four Dyslexia Indexes may be administered in 20 minutes or less on average.

As shown in Table 4.4, the split-half reliability coefficients for the new Dyslexia Index scores are excellent, and the index scores showed large effect sizes in differentiating students with reading/writing disabilities from their normally achieving peers. Generally, reliabilities of .90 or higher support the use of a score for making educational decisions.

### KTEA-3 Oral Reading Fluency Composite

The new KTEA-3 Oral Reading Fluency (ORF) composite is designed to measure oral reading fluency of single words and pseudowords. This new composite score is especially useful for two purposes: (1) identifying students who exhibit weaknesses in oral reading fluency but not in silent reading fluency; and (2) facilitating a direct comparison of a student's basic reading accuracy and basic reading fluency by comparing the KTEA-3 ORF composite score with the KTEA-3 Decoding composite score.

## ≣ Rapid Reference 4.27

### Composite Structure of the Dyslexia Index Scores

| Score | Grades K–1 or Ages 5–7 | Grades 2–12+ or Ages 7–25 |
|---|---|---|
| KTEA-3 Dyslexia Index | Phonological Processing + Letter Naming Facility + Letter & Word Recognition | Word Recognition Fluency + Nonsense Word Decoding + Spelling |
| WIAT-III Dyslexia Index | Early Reading Skills + Spelling | Oral Reading Fluency + Pseudoword Decoding + Spelling |

### Estimated Administration Time for the Dyslexia Index Scores

| Score | Grades K–1 or Ages 5–7 | Grades 2–12+ or Ages 7–25 |
|---|---|---|
| KTEA-3 Dyslexia Index | 18–20 minutes | 12–15 minutes |
| WIAT-III Dyslexia Index | 12 minutes | 12–15 minutes |

**Table 4.4 Split-Half Reliability Coefficients and Clinical Validity Data for the New Dyslexia Index scores**

| Score | Mean Grade-Based Reliability | Mean Age-Based Reliability | Reading/Writing Disability Group Age-Based Mean (SD) | Matched Control Age-Based Mean (SD) | Effect Size |
|---|---|---|---|---|---|
| KTEA-3 Dyslexia Index: Grades K–1 | .93 | .92 | 79.4 (7.4) | 98.2 (12.8) | 1.79 |
| KTEA-3 Dyslexia Index: Grades 2–12+ | .97 | .97 | 80.0 (6.8) | 100.8 (13.0) | 2.01 |
| WIAT-III Dyslexia Index: Grades K–1 | .95 Fall .94 Spring | .94 | 82.6 (10.6) | 102.2 (12.9) | 1.66 |
| WIAT-III Dyslexia Index: Grades 2–12+ | .98 | .98 | 74.4 (9.2) | 96.8 (12.7) | 2.01 |

*Note:* All scores from the Reading/Writing Disorder groups were significantly lower ($p < .01$) than those of the nonclinical matched control groups. *N*-count for the Reading/Writing Disorder group at Grades K–1 was insufficient for clinical group comparison; for this reason, group means and effect sizes were based on a sample of students in grades 1–4, ages 6–10 (KTEA-3 $n = 20$; WIAT-III $n = 36$).

The Decoding composite provided in the KTEA-3 measures oral reading accuracy of single words and pseudowords. The main difference between LWR and WRF, and between NWD and DF, is that LWR and NWD are untimed measures and WRF and DF are speeded tasks. Clinically useful information may be obtained by comparing analogous measures of basic reading accuracy and basic reading fluency. Many struggling readers exhibit poor performance in both accuracy and fluency. Other struggling readers exhibit poor performance that is specific to fluency or only detected on a speeded measure. For this reason, score comparison tables are provided as Digital Resources for comparing the ORF and Decoding composite scores.

The new ORF composite differs from the Reading Fluency composite provided in the KTEA-3 (see Rapid Reference 4.28). The Reading Fluency composite provides a measure of reading fluency that includes silent contextual reading fluency as well as oral reading fluency of single words and pseudowords. This composite is useful for measuring broad reading fluency deficits that include silent and oral reading as well as contextual and single word reading.

## ≡ Rapid Reference 4.28

### KTEA-3 Oral Reading Fluency (ORF) Composite Structure

| New KTEA-3 Score | Grade/Age | Subtests | Utility |
|---|---|---|---|
| Oral Reading Fluency Composite | Grades 2–12 or Ages 7–25 | Word Recognition Fluency + Decoding Fluency | Measures oral reading fluency of single words and pseudowords |

### Related KTEA-3 Composites

| Related KTEA-3 Composites | Grade/Age | Subtests | Utility |
|---|---|---|---|
| Reading Fluency Composite | Grades 3–12 or Ages 8–25 | Silent Reading Fluency + Word Recognition Fluency + Decoding Fluency | Measures silent contextual reading fluency and oral reading fluency of single words and pseudowords |
| Decoding Composite | Grades 1–12 or Ages 6–25 | Letter & Word Recognition + Nonsense Word Decoding | Measures oral reading accuracy of single words and pseudowords |

**Table 4.5 Split-Half Reliability Coefficients for the New KTEA-3 ORF Composite Score**

| KTEA-3 Composite | Mean Grade-Based Reliability | Mean Age-Based Reliability |
|---|---|---|
| Oral Reading Fluency composite (new) | .91 | .92 |
| Reading Fluency composite | .93 | .93 |
| Decoding composite | .98 | .98 |

*Source:* Reading Fluency and Decoding composite reliabilities are from the *KTEA-3 Technical & Interpretive Manual* (Kaufman & Kaufman, 2014b); Grade-based reliability data are from Table 2.1 and age-based reliability data are from Table 2.2. Oral Reading Fluency composite reliabilities are in the Digital Resources for this book.

As shown in Table 4.5, the split-half reliability coefficients for the new ORF composite are excellent. For comparison purposes, reliability coefficients are also provided for the Reading Fluency and Decoding composite scores. As these data show, the new ORF composite score is highly reliable and comparable to other KTEA-3 composite scores. Generally, reliabilities of .90 or higher support the use of a score for making educational decisions.

## Accommodations for Visual, Hearing, and Motor Impairments

### Visual Impairments

The digital (Q-interactive) and paper content of the KTEA-3 and WIAT-III were designed with accessibility guidelines in mind to facilitate use by individuals who are visually impaired or color blind. To the extent possible, font contrast and color was carefully chosen to enhance text readability, reliance on color coding was avoided except on color critical items, and colors used on color critical items were selected carefully to ensure that contrast was maintained when viewed with common variations in color-vision (color-blindness).

Large-print editions and braille editions are not published by Pearson. However, the American Printing House for the Blind (APH) has adapted previous editions of the KTEA and WIAT to provide customers with large-print and braille editions. Examiners who create or use large print editions of the KTEA-3 or WIAT-III Stimulus Books for visually impaired examinees must report the assessment results as a non-standard administration and explain how the materials were changed.

### Hearing Impairments

As a group, examinees that are hard of hearing have a range of hearing differences, which should be considered in the administration and interpretation of the KTEA-3 and WIAT-III. Note, however, the KTEA-3 and WIAT-III are not intended for use with examinees who are deaf. If an examinee uses assistive technology (e.g., hearing aids, cochlear implants, or assisted listing device such as an FM system), examiners should ensure that the device is working properly prior to beginning assessment (Wechsler, 2015). Those that are hard of hearing will benefit from a testing environment that has limited background noise. For examinees with hearing impairments, the volume of the audio files used to present listening comprehension items to examinees may be adjusted as needed to the suit the preference of the examinee. Similarly, examiners may adjust the volume of the audio files presented on the iPad using Q-interactive. Finally, consider that some examinees who are hard of hearing may also depend heavily on visual cues from speech reading.

### *Motor Impairments*

The KTEA-3 and WIAT-III items require examinees to provide pointing, oral, or written responses. Subtests on the KTEA-3 and WIAT-III that depend on graphomotor speed or production are not appropriate to use with examinees with severe motor impairments, such as measures of written expression, written spelling, math fluency, and writing fluency. However, examinees with severe motor impairments may respond orally on the following KTEA-3 and WIAT-III subtests that typically require a written response but are not designed to measure written expression or graphomotor skills:

- KTEA-3 Math Computation
- WIAT-III Numerical Operations

### Ongoing Research on Gender Differences in Writing and the Utility of Error Analysis

Developmental gender differences in academic achievement have been reported by many researchers, but the size and consistency of those findings appear to vary depending on the academic area (e.g., math, reading, writing), the general ability level, and the age of the subjects (Scheiber, Reynolds, Hajovsky, & Kaufman, 2015). In reading, small and occasionally moderate advantages are seen in school-age females (Mullis, Martin, Kennedy, & Foy, 2007; Reynolds, Scheiber, Hajovsky, Schwartz, & Kaufman, 2015). In data reported from NAEP reading assessment, females in both fourth and eighth grades outperformed males (National Center for Education Statistics, 2012). However, other researchers have not consistently found these gender differences across all age groups. For example, Kaufman, Kaufman, Liu, and Johnson (2009) did not find significant gender differences in reading in their adult sample, nor did Camarata and Woodcock (2006).

Similar inconsistency has been reported in gender differences in math. In kindergarten, elementary school, or middle school samples, Camarata & Woodcock (2006) found no gender differences in math. However, in high school, males outperform females in mathematics problem solving (Hyde, Fennama, & Lamon, 1990). Generally, gender differences in the domains of math and reading are small (to moderate), and are deemed inconclusive during school-age years (Scheiber et al., 2015). In contrast, across the domain of writing, females have an advantage over males that appears to increase with age (Camarata & Woodcock, 2006; Malecki & Jewell, 2003). These gender differences in various academic domains have been specifically researched using the KTEA-II Comprehensive and KTEA-II Brief, and key findings are detailed in the sections that follow.

## Female Advantage in Writing on KTEA-II Brief and Comprehensive Forms

Reynolds and his colleagues (2015) used the KTEA-II Comprehensive form as the primary instrument to measure gender differences in reading, math, and writing, and Scheiber and her colleagues (2015) utilized the KTEA-II Brief form to study these differences. On both the KTEA-II Comprehensive and Brief forms, a small advantage for females was found in reading. However, in these samples no gender differences in math achievement were found overall on the KTEA-II Comprehensive or Brief Forms. Reynolds et al. (2015) did find that females did show an advantage in a specific area of math on the KTEA-II Comprehensive form: Math Computation.

Relative to the other areas of achievement, on both the KTEA-II Comprehensive and Brief Forms, females show larger advantages over males in written language (Reynolds et al., 2015; Scheiber et al., 2015). In research with the KTEA-II Brief Form, females showed a small advantage in writing through age 10, that became an even more pronounced effect by ages 15–18. Research using the Comprehensive Form, also found a female advantage in writing, but an increase in the female advantage in writing was not found with age. One difference between the Comprehensive and Brief forms that may have affected results of these studies is that the KTEA-II Brief Form includes spelling in the scoring criteria for writing, but on the Comprehensive Form, spelling is not part of the Written Expression subtest. However, even though the developmental trend was not equally shown on research with these instruments, girls had an advantage in writing even at the youngest age levels in studies with the KTEA-II Brief and Comprehensive Form. These findings are also supported with findings from other individually administered writing tests (e.g., Camarata & Woodcock, 2006).

Hypotheses about why females may have an advantage in writing have been put forth by researchers. Reynolds and his colleagues (2015) noted that $Gf$ and $Gc$ are two cognitive abilities required for successful writing, but processing speed ($Gs$) may also have a role in writing. Gender differences favoring females have been found on some $Gs$ measures, and have been noted in studies that examine both writing and $Gs$ in the same sample (Camarata & Woodcock, 2006). Reynolds et al. (2015) hypothesized that "$Gs$ may differentially affect writing and because gender differences in $Gs$ emerge early on, those differences may also contribute to the early sustained gender difference in writing" (p. 230). Although this finding of a female cognitive advantage in processing speed is a robust finding across many instruments, including the WPPSI-IV and WISC-V, research has yet to establish a causal link between processing speed and writing (Kaufman, Raiford, & Coalson, 2015; Palejwala & Fine, 2015).

# ✒ TEST YOURSELF ✒

1. **The samples with specific learning disabilities (SLD) reported from the KTEA-3 and WIAT-III normative data were unique because they were pure samples of SLD-Reading, SLD-Writing, and SLD-Math (e.g., no comorbid SLDs).**

   (a) True
   (b) False

2. **Both the Modern Operational Definition of Specific Learning Disabilities and the Pattern of Strengths and Weaknesses Model that were described in this chapter can be used with the WIAT-III and KTEA-3.**

   (a) True
   (b) False

3. **The CHC Broad ability of *Ga* and Lurian sequential processing are measured by the**

   (a) KTEA-3 Phonological Processing subtest
   (b) WIAT-III Early Reading Skills subtest
   (c) Both
   (d) Neither

4. **Which of the following is not one of the seven reading-related learning disability subtypes included in the Intervention Guide for LD Subtypes in Q-global?**

   (a) Phonological subtype
   (b) Deep (acquired) dyslexia
   (c) Language subtype/Oral and Written Language Learning Disability (OWL-LD)
   (d) Comprehension subtype

5. **The KABC-II Knowledge/*Gc* Index correlated most highly with the KTEA-3 Academic Skills Battery and Reading Composites. Which KABC-II Index showed the lowest correlations across all KTEA-3 composites (Rapid Reference 4.6)?**

   (a) Sequential/*Gsm*
   (b) Simultaneous/*Gv*
   (c) Learning/*Glr*
   (d) Planning/*Gf*

6. **Administration of which of the following process subtests from the WISC-V Integrated can be especially important when evaluating a student with a possible language-based learning disorder?**

   (a) Written Arithmetic, Vocabulary, Visual Digit Span
   (b) Block Design No Time Bonus, Digit Span Forward, Digit Span Backward
   (c) Longest Digit Span Forward, Longest Digit Span Backward, Cancellation
   (d) Vocabulary Multiple Choice, Similarities Multiple Choice, and Comprehension Multiple Choice

7. **In addition to five CHC Broad Abilities measured by the KABC-II, the KTEA-3 Comprehensive Form measures which three additional Broad Abilities?**
   (a) Auditory Processing (*Ga*)
   (b) Processing Speed (*Gs*)
   (c) Reading and Writing (*Grw*)
   (d) Quantitative Knowledge (*Gq*)
   (e) Decision Speed/Reaction Time (*Gt*)

8. **The KTEA-3 and WIAT-III Dyslexia Index Scores (provided in the Digital Resources for this book) are intended for which the following purposes?**
   (a) To provide a reliable and valid measure of the key symptoms of dyslexia
   (b) To be used on their own to diagnose dyslexia
   (c) To identify subtypes of dyslexia
   (d) None of the above

9. **The new KTEA-3 Oral Reading Fluency (ORF) composite (provided as a Digital Resource for this book) is useful for which of the following purposes?**
   (a) Measuring oral reading fluency of single words and pseudowords
   (b) Identifying students who exhibit weaknesses in oral reading fluency but not in silent reading fluency
   (c) Facilitating a direct comparison of a basic reading accuracy and basic reading fluency by comparing the KTEA-3 ORF composite score with the KTEA-3 Decoding composite score
   (d) All of the above

10. **Research has shown that females tend to score higher than males in the area of writing. Females also tend to show an advantage in which cognitive processing area that is related to writing ability?**
    (a) Fluid Reasoning (*Gf*)
    (b) Processing Speed (*Gs*)
    (c) Working Memory (*Gwm*)
    (d) Auditory Processing (*Ga*)
    (e) Females do not show an advantage in any particular area of cognitive processing.

*Answers:* 1. b; 2. a; 3. c; 4. b; 5. a; 6. d; 7. a, c, d; 8. a; 9. d; 10. b.

Five

# STRENGTHS AND WEAKNESSES
# OF THE KTEA™-3 AND WIAT®-III

## John O. Willis

*Senior Lecturer in Assessment, Department of Education,*
*Rivier University, Nashua, NH*

## Ron Dumont

*Director, School of Psychology, Fairleigh Dickinson University,*
*Teaneck, NJ*

The authors of this chapter consider the KTEA-3 (Kaufman & Kaufman, 2014) and the WIAT-III (Pearson, 2009) to be very good instruments. Both of us have had extensive experience with the KTEA (Kaufman & Kaufman, 1985, 1997), KTEA-II (Kaufman & Kaufman, 2004a), WIAT (Psychological Corporation, 1992), WIAT-II (Psychological Corporation, 2001), and WIAT-III, and other achievement assessment instruments, using them in our own evaluations and teaching them in graduate classes and workshops, and we are rapidly gaining similar experience with the newer KTEA-3. One of us (JW) consulted from time to time with the publisher during the development of the KTEA-II and KTEA-3, and has used the KTEA, KTEA-II, and KTEA-3 more often than other achievement tests. However, we do, of course, have some complaints and quibbles. That is our nature and our task. Some general issues discussed below apply to both the KTEA-3 and the WIAT-III, and some issues (or rants) apply to academic achievement testing in general. For example, we do not encourage the use of grade-equivalent scores with any test. We have tried not to duplicate material unnecessarily, so such commentary may appear in either the WIAT-III or KTEA-3 section of this chapter. Some characteristics of a test may be both assets and limitations, so the reader will find some complaints within discussions of assets and some commendations within comments on limitations.

## STRENGTHS AND WEAKNESSES OF THE KTEA-3

We previously reviewed (Dumont & Willis, 2010) the KTEA-II (Kaufman & Kaufman, 2004a) and concluded, "Although we have identified some concerns with the KTEA-II, we consider it to be one of the best currently available comprehensive achievement batteries" (p. 265). We find that the KTEA-3 has maintained the strengths of the KTEA-II and offers significant improvements. The KTEA-3 offers an efficient, thorough, practical, and statistically reliable and valid assessment of academic abilities. It is designed with features that enhance useful interpretation. The strengths and weaknesses we perceive in the KTEA-3 are listed in Rapid Reference 5.1.

≡ *Rapid Reference 5.1*

### Strengths and Weaknesses of the KTEA-3

| Strengths | Weaknesses |
|---|---|
| **Test Development** | |
| • Item selection using curriculum consultants and content of widely used textbooks. | • Limited ceiling for some subtests for the oldest students in the Above Average range. See Table 5.2 for specific data on highest possible subtest and composite scores for ages 21–25 and grade 12. |
| • Almost all Reading Comprehension questions are appropriately passage-dependent (see Keenan & Betjemann, 2006). | |
| • Subtests in all eight specific learning disability areas identified in the Individuals with Disabilities Education Improvement Act (IDEA, 2004). | • Although most subtests have a ceiling that is at least 2 SD above the mean, at Grade 12, the ceilings for Nonsense Word Decoding, Reading Comprehension, Listening Comprehension, and Letter Naming Facility range from 124 to 129. At the highest age range, 12 of the 19 subtests have ceilings ≤150. |
| • Subtests in each of the three DSM-5 areas of impairment (Reading, Written Expression, and Math). | |
| • Extensive tryout data using samples with approximate proportional representation by gender and ethnicity. | • Limited floor for some subtests for the youngest students with the lowest ability levels. For students younger than age 6, raw scores of 0 correspond to standard scores ranging from 78 to 40. For Pre-K through grade 1, raw scores of 0 correspond to standard scores ranging from 73 to 40. See Table 5.3 for specific data. |
| • Easel format for presenting subtest items. | |
| • Reading-related subtests contribute to eight composites and yield five reading-related composites. | |

*(continued)*

(Continued)

| Strengths | Weaknesses |
|---|---|
| **Test Development** | |
| • Innovative item types, especially in Reading Comprehension, Written Expression, and Phonological Processing. | • It is not until age 11:8 that all subtests (with the exception of Nonsense Word Decoding) have a complete floor (standard score 40) and ceiling (standard score of 160). Nonsense Word Decoding does not have both a complete floor and ceiling at any age. |
| • Use of extensive item analysis procedures to eliminate biased items (gender or race) and items with poor psychometric properties. | |
| • Expanded error analysis procedures with item-level analyses for Reading Comprehension, Listening Comprehension, Written Expression, Oral Expression, Phonological Processing, Math Concepts and Applications, Math Computation, Letter and Word Recognition, Nonsense Word Decoding, and Spelling. | • Although Form A and Form B generally produce similar standard scores by age or grade, some large differences do occur. For Spelling, at 5:0–5:2, a raw score of 0 corresponds to standard scores of 55 for Form A and 80 for Form B. |
| • Novel and stimulating artwork is used throughout the test. | • Error analysis procedures may be difficult for examiners lacking any background in curriculum. In rare instances, examiner knowledge and judgment are required to override potentially misleading error-analysis scores. |
| **Standardization** | |
| • The standardization sample is well stratified to match the U.S. population and included 48 states (no examiners reported for Alaska or Maine). | • The grade-norm sample has smaller upper-grade norm samples than for the younger-grade samples. For grades Pre-K–8 the sample size is 100 (for each form), while for grades 9–12 the sample size is 75 (for each form). The 18-year-old sample is $N = 100$, age 19 sample is $N = 80$, and $N = 125$ for the sample ages 20–22 and 125 for the ages 23–25 sample. |
| • Stratification included age or grade, gender, ethnicity geographic region, special education group, and parent's education level. | |
| • Standardizations were conducted, one in the fall and one in the spring, yielding a large normative group ($N = 2,050$ for the age-norm sample and $N = 2,600$ for the grade-norm sample). | • The age-norm sample has smaller adult norm samples than for the younger age samples. For ages 4–18 the samples range in size from 100 to 160, while for 19–20 and 21–25 the sample sizes are 75 each. |

(continued)

(Continued)

| Strengths | Weaknesses |
|---|---|
| **Standardization** | |
| • The standardization sample included students receiving special education services.<br><br>• Very detailed information on standardization procedures and sample are included in the *Technical & Interpretive Manual*.<br><br>• Expanded age range down to 4 years 0 months and up to 25 years 11 months for both Forms A and B. | • There are no separate norms for postsecondary students. Percentages of 19–20-, and 21–25-year-olds in high school or dropped out, graduated from high school with no further education, began 2-year postsecondary program, and began 4-year postsecondary program roughly approximated U.S. Census data in most cases, but the examiner still lacks norms specifically for students enrolled in postsecondary programs. |
| **Reliability and Validity** | |
| • Good to excellent mean split-half reliabilities of subtests and composites (range from .81 to .98, with the exception of Written and Oral Fluency which range from .62 to .76).<br><br>• Two alternate forms are available for the KTEA-3, resulting in reduced practice effects for children who are assessed more than once.<br><br>• Alternate form reliability coefficients (adjusted for the variability of the norm group) are generally strong, ranging from .69 to .96 for the composites. Oral Fluency is the weakest, ranging from .69 to .74.<br><br>• The *Technical & Interpretive Manual* offers correlational data with two other tests of academic achievement and the KTEA-II as well as with a test of language (CELF-IV). | • The Oral Language subtests have variable correlations with similar measures on the other achievement instruments. However this may be due to the very different approaches taken by different test batteries in measuring and defining oral expression and listening comprehension.<br><br>• Standard Errors of Measurement (SEm) are high for the age- and grade-norm sample for the Oral Fluency composite (ranging from 7.58–8.28) and several other subtests: Writing Fluency mean = 7.31, Associational Fluency mean = 9.28, Object Naming Facility mean = 8.31, and Letter Naming Facility mean = 8.81. |

(continued)

*(Continued)*

| Strengths | Weaknesses |
|---|---|
| **Reliability and Validity** | |

- Moderate to high correlations between most KTEA-3 and other measures of achievement for concurrent validity (.86–.90).
- Strong face validity based on use of textbook content and skill development in reading and mathematics.
- Construct validity indicated by increasing scores across grades and ages.

| **Administration and Scoring** | |
|---|---|

| Strengths | Weaknesses |
|---|---|
| • The test protocol has a user-friendly layout. | • Test protocol does not include a summary page for recording scores. If hand-scoring the test, these pages are available for printing from the flash drive. |
| • Easel format simplifies administration. | |
| • Starting points, basal and discontinue rules are clearly labeled on the record form and easels for all subtests. | • Need to write responses phonetically to use error analysis for Letter & Word Recognition and Nonsense Word Decoding, which can be especially challenging when testing students who respond very quickly. |
| • Although no longer provided or required, young children often find the use of a puppet (Pepper) very engaging in Phonological Awareness. | |
| • Students find the storybook format of Written Expression much less tedious than a more traditionally formatted test of written expression. | • Hand scoring is particularly time consuming. Computation forms must be downloaded and printed. Norms tables for converting raw scores to standard scores may be difficult to read and navigate. |
| • Most test items are scored in a dichotomous manner. | |
| • Both age and grade norms are available. | • Specific error analysis norms tables are difficult to locate quickly in the PDF Manual. Some examiners are tempted to interpret raw error-category scores instead of using norms, which can yield misleading results. |
| • An entire 200+ page manual provides many scoring examples for Reading and Listening Comprehension, Associational and Writing Fluency, and Written and Oral Expression. | |

*(continued)*

(Continued)

| Strengths | Weaknesses |
|---|---|
| **Administration and Scoring** | |

| Strengths | Weaknesses |
|---|---|
| • Table for error analysis categories is provided on the record form for five subtests. | • Need to remember to use conversion table to convert points earned in a set to the raw score for Reading Comprehension, Written Expression, Listening Comprehension, Word Recognition Fluency, and Oral Expression. Conversion tables are in the PDF Manual. |
| • Separate error analysis pages are provided for subtests that have large numbers of skill categories, thereby making the main record form less cumbersome. | |
| • New choices for descriptive categories allows examiners to base ability levels on either a 10- or 15-point scale. | • Although scoring of most of the Oral Expression and Written Expression items seems clear to us (especially with the aid of the explanations, examples, and Glossary), questions from graduate students, colleagues, and workshop attendees suggest that the scoring can be confusing for some examiners. |
| • The record form for Letter & Word Recognition and Nonsense Word Decoding includes phonetic pronunciation keys and, when needed, indicates correct stress of syllables. There is ample space to record the examinee's pronunciations. | |
| | • When Associational Fluency and Object Naming Facility are administered, they must be given out of easel order, which is easy to forget for some examiners. |
| • The flash drive provides audio files for instructing the examiner about the correct pronunciations for administration and scoring purposes. | • Subtests required for computing Core Composites and the Academic Skills Battery are not contained in a single easel. Only Reading and Math composites can be obtained using the materials in Stimulus Book 1. |
| • Even though they lack sufficient top, norms for Phonological Processing, Letter & Word Recognition, Nonsense Word Decoding, and Reading Comprehension above age 12 and grade 6 may be helpful with weak readers. | • The undifferentiated "Average" range for the 15-point score classification system extends from 85 to 115. This range may make sense statistically and psychologically, but we find it much too broad (more than two thirds of the population) for interpreting educational performance. |

(continued)

(Continued)

| Strengths | Weaknesses |
|---|---|
| Interpretation | |

### Strengths

- Both composites and subtests can be interpreted due to high reliability coefficients.
- Error analysis procedures pinpoint specific skill deficits.
- Qualitative observations for 15 KTEA-3 subtests, identified by both IDEA domain as well as by potential cognitive processing weaknesses, are especially helpful.
- The composites and error analysis yield much diagnostic information directly relevant to instructional remediation.
- Subtest and composite intercorrelations are presented by grade (Pre-K–12) and age (17–18, 19–20, 21–25) in the KTEA-3 Technical & Interpretive Manual.
- Interpretive procedures were simplified by comparing composites and subtests to ASB rather than to the mean of all composites.
- Integrated normative and ipsative comparisons are included in the interpretive process.
- Pairs of KTEA-3 Comprehensive subtests (i.e., Reading Comprehension and Listening Comprehension, and Written Expression and Oral Expression) have similar formats and allow for useful comparisons that can help the examiner distinguish specific problems in reading or writing from more general language problems.

### Weaknesses

- Caution needs to be taken when interpreting the scores with a nonoptimal ceiling or a nonoptimal floor for children under age 6.
- If all of the ASB subtests are not administered, then the Composite and Subtest Analysis cannot be completed because the ASB is used in all of these comparisons. However, pairwise composite comparisons or pairwise subtest comparisons are still possible.
- Many evaluators want to know if the component subtests in each composite are significantly and uncommonly different from each other, which should require cautious interpretation of the composite score. This information is available in Appendix G of the Manual, but is buried among all the other subtest comparisons.
- The comparison between Reading Comprehension and Listening Comprehension is very useful because of the almost identical formats of the two subtests. Differences between the formats of Written Expression and Oral Expression make that comparison less persuasive.
- Insufficient information is provided in the Technical & Interpretive Manual on how to utilize the Growth Scale Values (GSV).
- The Growth Scale Values (GSV) allow for comparisons between an individual's change across time but do not provide statistical comparisons to expected growth ("closing the gap").

(continued)

(Continued)

| Strengths | Weaknesses |
|---|---|
| **Interpretation** | |
| • Significance and base-rate levels are provided for those and other comparisons. | • Confidence bands can be calculated for age- or grade-equivalent scores (if those scores must be used at all), but this procedure is laborious and is not suggested in the Manual. |
| • Growth Scale Values (GSV) are provided to provide a mechanism by which a student's absolute (rather than relative) level of performance can be measured. | |
| • The Manual encourages examiners to verify hypotheses with other data. | |
| • The KTEA-3 Analysis & Comparisons Form provides a place to record the basic analysis of the scale composites, including normative and personal strengths and weaknesses, composite comparisons, subtest comparisons, and ability-achievement discrepancies. The specific comparisons are helpfully labeled with the identifying numbers of the relevant tables in the Manual. | |
| • Tables are provided in the *Technical & Interpretive Manual* for predicting KTEA-3 standard scores from ability standard scores based upon the correlation between the tests. | |

## ASSETS OF THE KTEA-3

### Test Development

Although, as with any test, there are a few weak or debatable items, the publisher's extensive efforts to enlist guidance from curriculum experts, to base items on popular textbooks and to complete a very thorough tryout produced an instrument with very useful, relevant content for educational assessment in all eight achievement areas specified by IDEA 2004 regulations for assessment of specific learning disabilities. Reading and reading-related skills are covered extensively, including normed tests of word and nonsense word reading, oral and silent reading fluency, phonetic decoding, phonological processing, and rapid naming and a criterion referenced letter naming measure. This is much broader coverage than is found on most broad spectrum achievement tests and many reading tests. Reading comprehension is now measured with two subtests: Reading Comprehension and Reading Vocabulary (which we consider an extremely valuable addition to the KTEA-II selection of subtests). Reading comprehension questions are read by the examinee and themselves pose appropriate reading challenges. In a few cases, the questions appear to be more difficult than the passages (which would be a problem for a test of content knowledge but adds to the depth of measurement of a reading comprehension test). Unlike some other tests (see, for example, Keenan & Betjemann, 2006), very few KTEA-3 reading comprehension questions can be answered correctly on the basis of prior knowledge and deduction without reading the passage. Reading Comprehension also includes some direction-following items, similar to "Turn around in your chair and then stand up."

Three subtests now measure aspects of written expression. The Written Expression subtest format of having the examinee fill in missing letters, words, punctuation, and sentences in a story book as the examiner tells the story and gives instructions, and then write a summary of the entire story is engaging, and it produces useful data, including the error analysis. There are four different Written Expression levels, three of which require separate storybooks. The need to keep three different storybooks in stock is a mild but worthwhile inconvenience. The artwork in the test easels and the storybook is attractive and appears to appeal to the students whom we have tested. The Spelling subtest begins with letter- or word-writing items with pictures and continues with words presented in the traditional and effective format of the examiner saying the word, using it in a prescribed sentence (printed on the record form), and repeating the word. The Writing Fluency subtest (new to the KTEA-3) asks the examinee to write "good, short" sentences about what is happening in each picture in the response booklet. After the sample and teaching items, the examinee is told to "Keep your sentences short and work as fast as you can." We strongly approve of fluency tests that explicitly tell the examinee to work fast (which is not the case with many tests).

The extensive error analysis procedures do require some time and attention if done by hand, but they provide genuinely useful information if the norms are used. The error categories are detailed and educationally meaningful. Error analysis worksheets are included in the KTEA-3 flash drive. The norms tables for the error analyses (*Technical & Interpretive Manual, Appendix H*) are clear and helpful. Breaux (2015) provides clear instructions on how to perform error analyses on subtests that use item sets when examinees reverse to a lower level item set. Examiners can use the analyses when necessary and omit them when there are no unanswered questions about remediation, as in the case of a high score or when an examinee's weakness in a domain is obvious, extreme, and pervasive. Unlike error analyses on many tests, the KTEA-3 weakness-average-strength categories are based on test norms rather than arbitrary cutoffs. It is essential that examiners use the norms, which requires some initial bullying of graduate students and supervisees. Raw scores in error categories (like any raw scores) can be very misleading.

During the KTEA-3 standardization, the KTEA-3 and KABC-II (Kaufman & Kaufman, 2004b) were administered to 99 examinees and the KTEA-3 and Differential Ability Scales (DAS-II; Elliott, 2007) to 122 examinees. Data from those studies were used to create tables of correlations between the several composite ability scores of the KABC-II and DAS-II and all of the KTEA composites and subtests. Those correlations can be used to look up predicted achievement scores and significant difference and base rate data for predicted and actual achievement. These easily used tables are very valuable. Our only complaints are that there are also tables for simple differences, which might inspire someone to actually use the simple-difference method (see McLeod, 1968, 1974), and that similar tables are not provided for the Wechsler Preschool and Primary Scale of Intelligence (4th ed.) (WPPSI-IV; Wechsler, 2012a), Wechsler Intelligence Scale for Children (4th ed.) (WISC-IV; Wechsler, 2003), Wechsler Adult Intelligence Scale (4th ed.) (WAIS-IV; Wechsler, 2008), and other popular tests such as the Woodcock-Johnson IV Tests of Cognitive Abilities (WJ IV COG; Schrank, McGrew, & Mather, 2014a). Those data would be very helpful to examiners who administer the KTEA-3 while another examiner selects and administers a test of cognitive ability. The WISC-V *Technical and Interpretive Manual* (Wechsler, 2014b, pp. 96–101) provides WISC-V correlations with the KTEA-3.

## Two Forms

The availability of two forms (A and B) of the KTEA-3 is extremely helpful in many situations. As discussed below, with very few exceptions, the two forms are statistically equivalent, so examiners bent on retesting students can alternate forms. An alternate form is also extremely useful when there is reason to doubt the validity of scores in a recent assessment.

We do need to offer one caveat. Even with alternate forms, individually administered achievement tests, such as the KTEA-3, WIAT-III, or WJ-IV ACH (Schrank, Mather, & McGrew, 2014) are not well suited for measuring short-term academic progress, especially in the higher grades. Table 5.1 shows the raw scores equivalent to a standard score of 100 by Winter norms for grades 1 through 12 on five of the KTEA-3 subtests without time limits or weighted or transformed scores. In grades 1 through 4, expected annual growth on these five subtests was 4.5 to 11 raw score points. In grades 5 through 8, however, the average student gained only 1.5 to 5.5 raw score points per year. In high school, expected annual growth was only 0 to 3.5 raw score points. With such small anticipated annual gains to maintain a standard score of 100, it could be difficult to distinguish growth or stagnation from random variation in test scores, especially in the higher grades. This is *not* a flaw of the KTEA-3, which

**Table 5.1 Raw Scores Corresponding to Standard Scores of 100 by Winter Grade Norms on the KTEA-3 Form A: Five Untimed Subtests Without Weighted or Transformed Scores**

| Grade | Letter-Word Identification | | Nonsense Word Decoding | | Math Computation | | Math Concepts & Applications | | Spelling | |
|---|---|---|---|---|---|---|---|---|---|---|
| | Raw Score | Growth | Raw Score | Growth | Raw Score | Growth | Raw Score | Growth | Raw Score | Growth |
| 1 | 38.5 | | 11 | | 22.7 | | 31.5 | | 22 | |
| 2 | 49.5 | 11.0 | 16 | 5.0 | 29 | 6.3 | 40 | 8.5 | 32 | 10.0 |
| 3 | 57 | 7.5 | 21 | 5.0 | 34.5 | 5.5 | 48 | 8.0 | 39.5 | 7.5 |
| 4 | 62 | 5.0 | 25.5 | 4.5 | 41 | 6.5 | 54 | 6.0 | 45.5 | 6.0 |
| 5 | 66 | 4.0 | 29.5 | 4.0 | 46.5 | 5.5 | 59 | 5.0 | 49 | 3.5 |
| 6 | 69.5 | 3.5 | 32 | 2.5 | 52 | 5.5 | 63 | 4.0 | 52 | 3.0 |
| 7 | 71.5 | 2.0 | 34 | 2.0 | 56.5 | 4.5 | 66 | 3.0 | 54 | 2.0 |
| 8 | 74 | 2.5 | 36 | 2.0 | 61 | 4.5 | 68 | 2.0 | 55.5 | 1.5 |
| 9 | 77.5 | 3.5 | 38 | 2.0 | 63 | 2.0 | 69.5 | 1.5 | 57 | 1.5 |
| 10 | 79.5 | 2.0 | 39.5 | 1.5 | 64 | 1.0 | 71 | 1.5 | 58 | 1.0 |
| 11 | 81 | 1.5 | 40.5 | 1.0 | 64 | 0.0 | 71.5 | 0.5 | 59 | 1.0 |
| 12 | 83 | 2.0 | 41.3 | 0.8 | 65 | 1.0 | 72 | 0.5 | 59.7 | 0.7 |

*Note: From Tables D.2 of the KTEA-3 Technical & Interpretive Manual (Kaufman & Kaufman, 2014b). Raw scores with tenths shown as decimals were interpolated.*

is better than many individually administered achievement tests in this regard, but a warning to be very cautious in using any individually administered test for measuring annual academic progress. Curriculum-based measurement (CBM) can be used as frequently as desired and may be a better way of measuring short-term progress. Group, multiple-choice achievement tests that take hours or days to administer have more items and, therefore, expected growth of more items per year than do individually administered achievement tests. The KTEA-3 does provide examiners with an additional way to track growth across time: Growth Scale Values (GSV). The KTEA-3 GSVs are similar to the GSV scales on the WIAT-III and the Woodcock Reading Mastery Tests-Third Edition (WRMT-III; Woodcock, 2011). The KTEA-3 GSVs are equal-interval scale and they can be used to monitor progress over time.

## Standardization

Please see Chapter 2 for detailed information on the standardization of the KTEA-3, which is also described at length in Chapter 1 of the *Technical & Interpretive Manual* (Kaufman & Kaufman with Breaux, 2014b). The large, national sample of students tested in the fall and in the spring was stratified to match then-current U. S.

Census data, including interactions of variables, such as ethnicity *and* average educational attainment of the child's parents or guardians. Special efforts were made to ensure randomization within the variables. Students receiving special education and gifted/talented services were included. Students with attention-deficit/hyperactivity disorder and students who were academically gifted or talented were underrepresented; students with specific learning disabilities, speech/language impairments, and developmental delays were slightly underrepresented; and students with intellectual disabilities were very slightly overrepresented. According to the *Technical & Interpretive Manual,* "a review of the data indicated that some individuals in the grade norm samples performed similarly to students with special education classifications" (p. 34).

## Reliability and Validity

The reliability and validity of the KTEA-3 are discussed in detail in the *Technical & Interpretive Manual.* Except for Oral Language, the mean split-half and alternate-form reliabilities are strong. Correlations with three other achievement tests and one language test are moderate to strong, showing good concurrent validity. Correlations with global scores on two cognitive ability tests are lower, indicating divergent validity: an achievement test should correlate reasonably highly with cognitive ability tests, but it should not be one.

The KTEA-3 subtests appear to be legitimate and reasonable measures of the intended constructions (face validity), which is reassuring to examiners, parents, and teachers, and helpful in maintaining the examinee's motivation and cooperation.

## Administration and Scoring

The easels, separate stimulus sheets, and record forms are easy to use (with one exception noted below). The easels are printed so test items face the examinee on one side of the easel and instructions and scoring information face the examiner on the other side, rather than, for example, having test items for different subtests printed on the two sides of each page so the examiner turns the easel around half-way through the examination and continues testing with the remaining subtests. The KTEA-3 arrangement uses twice as many pages, so the subtests fill two easels rather than just one. The bulk of two easels is a small price to pay for the convenience of having information for the examiner printed on the back of every test page.

For the most part, scoring (usually dichotomous) is straightforward with clear explanations. An entire 208-page *Scoring Manual* (Kaufman & Kaufman with Breaux, 2014d) provides scoring examples for many items on the Reading Comprehension, Listening Comprehension, Associational Fluency, Writing Fluency, Written Expression, and Oral Expression subtests. The age-based and grade-based norms are readily available and clearly labeled in the *Technical & Interpretive Manual* on the KTEA-3 flash drive, facilitating scoring and reducing the likelihood of errors. The record form encourages and simplifies the use of confidence bands, which happily do not extend lower than 85% confidence.

The KTEA-3 Graphical Profiles, printable from the flash drive, allow users to use either one of two standard score divisions to help describe results. One divides the standard score range by a seven category, "traditional" 10-point scale, which defines Average as standard scores from 90 to 109, while the other uses a seven category, 15-point scale in which Average is defined as scores of 85 to 115. The KTEA-II defined and the WIAT-III (Pearson, 2009a) defines Average as 85 to 115. We consider the 31-point average range a reasonable definition of "within normal limits," but an excessively broad educational definition of "average" achievement. Since classifications are arbitrary and opinions differ (e.g., Roid, 2003, p. 150; Wechsler, 2014b, p. 152), the choice of two interpretive scales strikes us as helpful, although it may lead to some confusion in team meetings. We urge examiners always to carefully explain either the various verbal classifications labels they are using on different tests or the single classification system they have elected to apply to all of the tests in an assessment.

## Interpretation

Interpretation of the KTEA-3 is enhanced by having subtests and/or composites that measure all eight areas of achievement specified by IDEA (2004) legislation as important for identifying and classifying learning disabilities: (1) oral expression (one subtest), (2) listening comprehension (one subtest), (3) written expression (composite based on two subtests), (4) basic reading skill (composite based on two subtests), (5) reading fluency skills (composite based on three subtests), (6) reading comprehension (composite based on two subtests), (7) mathematics calculation (one subtest), and (8) mathematics problem solving (one subtest). The KTEA-3 also includes subtests of rapid automatized naming (RAN) and phonological processing, two skills considered by many experts to be essential foundations for reading skills (e.g., Wolf & Bowers, 1999), a subtest measuring associational fluency, and writing fluency and math fluency subtests. In addition to the written expression (Written Language), basic reading skill (Reading Decoding), Reading Fluency, and Reading Comprehension composites mentioned above, the KTEA-3 provides composite scores for Reading, Math, Sound Symbol, (reading and listening) Comprehension, (written and oral) Expression, Orthographic Processing, Academic Fluency, Oral Language, and Oral Fluency. The recategorization of the 19 subtests into these 13 composite provides the examiner with a sound foundation for further interpretation. There is also an Academic Skills Battery (ASB) composite based on three prekindergarten, four kindergarten, or six subtests for grades 1 and above. This composite is not a total score (which would be practically meaningless), but a summary of reading, writing, and math skills (two each for grade 1 and above) to which scores on other composite and subtests can be statistically compared to determine relative strengths and weaknesses.

The generally high reliabilities of the composites and subtests permit separate interpretation, and the *Technical & Interpretive Manual* provides the necessary data on significant differences and base rates (as well as intercorrelations), which makes it easy to guard against overinterpretation of composite scores in which subtests are significantly or uncommonly different from each other.

We find that the subtests, composites, and error analyses are practical and that the information they provide is educationally meaningful, leading to useful recommendations. The 30-page chapter on interpretation and the 14 interpretive Tables in the *Technical & Interpretive Manual* provide the necessary information in a clear, concise format, and encourage the use of additional data to verify hypotheses.

Composite and subtest scores can be compared to each other with readily available data for significant differences and base rates. The contrast between Reading Comprehension and Listening Comprehension subtests (which can also be joined together in the Comprehension composite) is extremely valuable, as the two subtests have essentially identical formats with the only difference being who does the reading. That comparison is often far more useful than a comparison between levels of cognitive ability and achievement. The comparison between Written Expression and Oral Expression is less exact, as the formats differ, but it is still useful. The Analysis & Comparisons Form (which must be printed from the KTEA-3 flash drive for each examinee) includes spaces for recording these comparisons (and for writing in other comparisons of interest).

Growth Scale Values (GSV) are provided as an Item-Response-Theory-based statistic that would be much better for assessing growth over time than would be raw scores or grade-equivalent scores.

The Analysis & Comparisons Form makes it easy to record both normative strengths and weaknesses and personal (ipsative) ones. There are a simple chart for recording behavioral observations (disruptive and enhancing), a two-page Qualitative Observations list, and a six-page Qualitative Observations Hand Scoring Form with a very helpful discussion in the *Technical & Interpretive Manual* (Kaufman & Kaufman with Breaux, 2014b, pp. 116–120) written in collaboration with Elaine Fletcher-Janzen. There is also a table for recording ability-achievement discrepancies. Tables G.9 through G.14 permit comparison of KTEA-3 scores with those of the KABC-II and the DAS-II (but not, as mentioned above, with scores from the Wechsler intelligence scales). Each chart on the Analysis & Comparisons Form helpfully lists the identifying number of the table in the *Manual* that is to be used for the scores or comparisons in that chart.

### Phonological Processing

The norms for Phonological Processing now extend from age 4:0 (where the standard score for a raw score of 0 is 73) to age 25 (where the highest possible score is 130) and from Fall of Pre-Kindergarten (raw score 0 = standard score 69) to Spring of grade 12 (highest possible standard score is 132). This expansion of the KTEA-II age range for assessment of phonology is a welcome change. Weaknesses in phonological abilities are just as likely to contribute to weaknesses in reading and spelling in older students as in young ones.

## KTEA-3 Flash Drive

Hand-scoring the KTEA-3 requires use of files provided on a flash drive included in the kit. The contents of the flash drive can and should be copied to a computer hard drive before you lose the flash drive in spite of the convenient lanyard. Examiners familiar with the WIAT-III or other tests with electronic manuals will be accustomed to finding the *Technical & Interpretive Manual*, including test norms, in an Adobe pdf file. Those who have not used electronic manuals will need to adjust and learn to appreciate the advantages (if someone who used to administer the original WISC [Wechsler, 1949] can do it, you can, too). It would obviously be impractical (although if cost were not a factor, extremely useful) to print the 688-page manual in addition to the 66-page *Administration Manual* and 208-page *Scoring Manual*. As noted in Chapter 1, you can separately purchase a printed *Technical & Interpretive Manual* from the publisher (see Rapid Reference 1.4). With a little practice, it becomes easy to navigate the digital manual. Page 1 provides blue "quick links" to each chapter, each appendix, and the references.

The first page of each of the nine appendices is a table of contents. Although the contents are printed in black, each entry is also a quick link, so only two clicks are needed to take you, for example, to "Age Based Subtest Standard Scores for Subtest Raw Scores: Ages 9:8–9:11." (You would need three clicks to reach norms for ages 11:8 or above or norms for composite scores because those appear on the second page of the table of contents for that appendix.) At the bottom of each page, there are triangles pointing left and right and, between them, an icon that, if sufficiently enlarged, appears to be a house. Clicking on those icons takes you a page back, a page forward, or home to the Quick Links page. You can also use the arrow keys on your keyboard. All of the tables appear on the screen in a readable orientation. Tables presented in landscape layout are not rotated sideways, which avoids any need to tip one's laptop on its side to read a table. However, in order to be able to read the tables on a laptop screen, many examiners will need to zoom so much that the full table more than fills the screen. Then you must zoom out again or scroll down to use the navigation icons. We have found it helpful to print out and store within the *Scoring Manual* frequently used pages, especially the eight pages of grade- and age-based composite scores and four pages of confidence bands.

The chapters (Development and Standardization, Technical Characteristics, Interpretation, and Content Development) do not have tables of contents, but the CONTROL + F (or Command + F for Mac) "find" utility in Adobe makes it easy to locate, for example, "retest" in Technical Characteristics. In addition to the test norms, the appendices include Contributors, Intercorrelation Tables, Conversion Tables, Other Scoring Tables, Interpretive Tables, Error Analysis Norms, and Charting Growth Scale Values.

The flash drive also includes Audio Files, Hand Scoring Files, the Qualitative Observations Form, and the Letter Checklist, with instructions, a page of lowercase letters and a page of uppercase letters for the examinee to read, and a record form for each page. We have learned that the answer to about half the questions asked by new users of the KTEA-3 is, "It's on the flash drive." We consider the flash drive material to be a significant asset of the KTEA-3.

## LIMITATIONS OF THE KTEA-3

Although we find the KTEA-3 to be a valuable, flexible, and generally sound test, no test is without limitations.

### Test Development

Table 5.2 provides data on the highest possible subtest scores for the oldest examinees and for examinees in grade 12. Although most subtests have a ceiling that is at least 2 SD above the mean at Grade 12, the ceilings for Nonsense Word Decoding, Reading Comprehension, Listening Comprehension, and Letter Naming Facility range from 124 to 129. At the highest age range, 12 of the 19 subtests have ceilings ≤150.

Similarly, there is insufficient floor on some subtests for students younger than age 6 as shown in Table 5.3. For students younger than age 6, raw scores of 0 correspond to standard scores ranging from 78 to 40. For Pre-Kindergarten through grade 1, raw scores of 0 correspond to standard scores ranging from 73 to 40. See Table 5.3 for specific data. It is not until age 11:8 that all subtests (with the exception of Nonsense Word Decoding) have a complete floor (standard score 40) and ceiling (standard score of 160). Nonsense Word Decoding does not have both a complete floor and ceiling at any age. Before selecting any achievement test for a student, the examiner should always see what scores would be earned by a recently deceased child of the same age as the examinee (Dumont & Willis, 2009; Goldman, 1989).

Although Form A and Form B generally produce similar standard scores by age or grade, some large differences do occur. For Spelling, at 5:0–5:2, a raw score of 0 corresponds to standard scores of 55 for Form A and 80 for Form A (Table 5.4).

Although we find them very useful, and better than those on most other tests, including the KTEA-II, and we commend the normative data, the KTEA-3 error analysis procedures may be challenging for examiners who do not have any background in curriculum and instruction. There are occasional instances in which a student may miss an item for the wrong reason (for example, an addition error in the subproducts of an otherwise flawless long multiplication example), which require the examiner to override the official categorization of the item.

The KTEA-3 provides very good tests of silent reading fluency and oral reading fluency with word lists and lists of phonetically regular nonsense words. It does not

**Table 5.2  Ceiling for Students Age 21:0–25:11 and Grade 12: Highest Possible Subtest Score[a]**

| KTEA-3 Subtest | Ages 21:0–25:11 | | Grade 12[a] | |
|---|---|---|---|---|
| | Form A | Form B | Form A | Form B |
| Letter & Word Recognition | 131 | 131 | 134 | 134 |
| Nonsense Word Decoding | 124 | 124 | 124 | 124 |
| Reading Comprehension | 128 | 128 | 129 | 129 |
| Reading Vocabulary | 137 | 137 | 142 | 142 |
| Word Recognition Fluency | 160 | 160 | 160 | 160 |
| Decoding Fluency | 160 | 152 | 160 | 152 |
| Silent Reading Fluency | 153 | 148 | 156 | 152 |
| Math Concepts & Applications | 136 | 136 | 135 | 135 |
| Math Computation | 136 | 136 | 136 | 136 |
| Math Fluency | 160 | 160 | 160 | 160 |
| Written Expression | 160 | 160 | 156 | 156 |
| Spelling | 142 | 137 | 146 | 137 |
| Writing Fluency | 160 | 151 | 159 | 149 |
| Listening Comprehension | 136 | 136 | 129 | 129 |
| Oral Expression | 130 | 130 | 131 | 131 |
| Associational Fluency | 160 | 160 | 160 | 160 |
| Phonological Processing | 130 | 130 | 132 | 132 |
| Object Naming Facility | 141 | 141 | 145 | 145 |
| Letter Naming Facility | 137 | 137 | 128 | 128 |

[a]Spring grade norms are reported here. The values for Fall grade norms (available in Table D.1 of the KTEA-3 *Technical & Interpretive Manual*) for 12th-grade students are very similar to those reported here.

*Note:* From Tables D.3 and E.1 of the KTEA-3 *Technical & Interpretive Manual* (Kaufman & Kaufman with Breaux, 2014b). The maximum standard score on all subtests is 160. Scores >130 (+2 SD) are in the High range and scores 116 to 130 (+1 to +2 SD) are in the Above Average range.

include a test of oral reading fluency with passages. The KTEA-3 includes tests of phonological processes, reading of phonetically regular nonsense words, and reading fluency with nonsense words. A test of spelling dictated nonsense words would have completed the phonetic assessment, but there had to be a limit to the number of subtests.

## Standardization

The normative samples of adults are smaller than those for the younger students. The number of examinees per year of age is 100 for age 4, 160 for each year from 5 through

**Table 5.3 Floor for Students Age 4:0–5:11 and Pre-Kindergarten, Kindergarten, and Grade 1: Lowest Possible Subtest Score**

| KTEA-3 Subtest | Ages | | | | | | | | Grade[a] | | |
|---|---|---|---|---|---|---|---|---|---|---|---|
| | 4:0–4:2 | 4:3–4:5 | 4:6–4:8 | 4:9–4:11 | 5:0–5:2 | 5:3–5:5 | 5:6–5:8 | 5:9–5:11 | Pre-K | K | 1 |
| Letter & Word Recognition | 78 | 72 | 66 | 61 | 55 | 50 | 45 | 42 | 60 | 43 | 40 |
| Nonsense Word Decoding | — | — | — | — | — | — | — | — | — | — | 73 |
| Reading Comprehension | 58 | 52 | 47 | 42 | 40 | 40 | 40 | 40 | 43 | 40 | 40 |
| Reading Vocabulary | — | — | — | — | — | — | — | — | — | — | 62 |
| Word Recognition Fluency | — | — | — | — | — | — | — | — | — | — | 57 |
| Decoding Fluency | — | — | — | — | — | — | — | — | — | — | — |
| Silent Reading Fluency | — | — | — | — | — | — | — | — | — | — | 72 |
| Math Concepts & Applications | 65 | 62 | 58 | 55 | 52 | 49 | 47 | 45 | 48 | 41 | 40 |
| Math Computation | — | — | — | — | 65 | 59 | 53 | 49 | — | 49 | 40 |
| Math Fluency | — | — | — | — | — | — | — | — | — | — | 57 |
| Written Expression | 66 | 62 | 50 | 40 | 40 | 40 | 40 | 40 | 52 | 40 | 40 |
| Spelling | — | — | — | — | 55 | 50 | 46 | 43 | — | 40 | 40 |
| Writing Fluency | — | — | — | — | — | — | — | — | — | — | — |
| Listening Comprehension | 69 | 66 | 63 | 60 | 57 | 54 | 52 | 50 | 57 | 49 | 40 |
| Oral Expression | 54 | 48 | 44 | 40 | 40 | 40 | 40 | 40 | 40 | 40 | 40 |
| Associational Fluency | 49 | 45 | 40 | 40 | 40 | 40 | 40 | 40 | 40 | 40 | 40 |
| Phonological Processing | 73 | 68 | 64 | 61 | 58 | 56 | 52 | 49 | 59 | 47 | 40 |
| Object Naming Facility | 61 | 58 | 55 | 52 | 50 | 48 | 46 | 44 | 50 | 40 | 40 |
| Letter Naming Facility | — | — | — | — | 64 | 57 | 54 | 51 | — | 55 | 44 |

[a]Spring grade norms are reported here. The values for Fall grade norms (available in Table D.1 of the KTEA-3 *Technical & Interpretive Manual*) for Pre-Kindergarten, Kindergarten, and first-grade students are very similar to those reported here.

From Tables D.3 and E.1 of the KTEA-3 *Technical & Interpretive Manual* (Kaufman & Kaufman with Breaux, 2014b). The minimum standard score on all subtests is 40. Scores <69 (−2 SD) are in the Low range and scores 70 to 84 (−1 to −2 SD) are in the Below Average range. Data are reported for Form A only. However, in most cases the data for Form B are equivalent to Form A. Values shown here are standard scores corresponding to raw scores of zero.

**Table 5.4  Raw Scores Corresponding to Standard Scores of 100 by Winter Grade Norms on the WIAT-III: Five Untimed Subtests Without Weighted or Transformed Scores**

| Grade | Word Reading Raw Score | Growth | Pseudoword Decoding Raw Score | Growth | Math Computation Raw Score | Growth | Math Concepts & Applications Raw Score | Growth | Spelling Raw Score | Growth |
|---|---|---|---|---|---|---|---|---|---|---|
| 1 | 14 | | 7 | | 14.5 | | 31.7 | | 11 | |
| 2 | 29 | 15.0 | 19 | 12.0 | 19.2 | 4.7 | 37 | 5.3 | 17.3 | 6.3 |
| 3 | 36 | 7.0 | 24.5 | 5.5 | 23.3 | 4.1 | 42 | 5.0 | 20 | 2.7 |
| 4 | 42 | 6.0 | 28 | 3.5 | 27.8 | 4.5 | 45.5 | 3.5 | 24 | 4.0 |
| 5 | 47 | 5.0 | 29 | 1.0 | 30.7 | 2.9 | 48.3 | 2.8 | 28 | 4.0 |
| 6 | 51 | 4.0 | 32 | 3.0 | 33.3 | 2.6 | 50 | 1.7 | 31 | 3.0 |
| 7 | 54.5 | 3.5 | 35 | 3.0 | 36 | 2.7 | 52.5 | 2.5 | 34.5 | 3.5 |
| 8 | 57 | 2.5 | 36 | 1.0 | 38.5 | 2.5 | 54.5 | 2.0 | 38 | 3.5 |
| 9 | 59 | 2.0 | 38 | 2.0 | 39.5 | 1.0 | 55 | 0.5 | 40.5 | 1.5 |
| 10 | 61 | 2.0 | 39.5 | 1.5 | 40.5 | 1.0 | 56 | 1.0 | 43 | 2.5 |
| 11 | 62 | 1.0 | 40 | 0.5 | 41 | 0.5 | 57.3 | 1.3 | 45 | 2.0 |
| 12 | 62.5 | 0.5 | 40.5 | 0.5 | 42 | 1.0 | 58 | 0.7 | 47 | 2.0 |

From Tables D.2 of the WIAT-III *Technical Manual with Adult Norms* (Pearson, 2010a). Raw scores with tenths shown as decimals were interpolated.

10, 120 for each year from 11 through 16, 120 for ages 17 and 18 (an average of 60 per year of age), 75 for ages 19 and 20 (an average of 37.5 per year), and 75 for ages 21–25 (an average of about 15 for each year of age).

Had the sample of older students been larger, it would have been helpful to have separate norms for postsecondary students in 2- and 4-year programs. The age based norms for older students were based on the roughly same proportions as the U.S. Census of high-school students and dropouts, students who had graduated from high school and not continued their educations, students who had begun 2-year programs, and students who had begun 4-year programs.

### Reliability and Validity

As noted below, under Interpretation, assessment of oral language, especially on achievement tests, is problematic. On the KTEA-II (Kaufman & Kaufman, 2004a), the Oral Language Composite had variable correlations with the various oral language measures on other achievement tests. Interpretation of oral language achievement measures on tests of academic achievement should always be undertaken carefully and thoughtfully. The KTEA-3 *Technical & Interpretive Manual* (Kaufman & Kaufman with Breaux, 2014b) provides correlations of KTEA-3 oral language subtests with only one oral language instrument subtest, the Clinical Evaluation of

Language Fundamentals–Fourth Edition (Wiig, Semel, & Secord, 2003) Formulated Sentences subtest, which had correlations of .64, .53, and .47 with the KTEA-3 Oral Expression, Written Expression, and Listening Comprehension subtests, respectively. The correlation between the KTEA-3 Oral Language composite and the WIAT-III Oral Language composite was .73 with correlations of .48 between the Listening Comprehension subtests and .56 between the Oral Expression subtests of the KTEA-3 and WIAT-III.

Similarly, the reliabilities are low and the Standard Errors of Measurement high for the age-norm sample for Oral Language (SEm 4.85 to 6.34) and Oral Fluency (SEm 6.99 to 8.81). Therefore, differences needed for statistical significance between these tests and between these and other tests are large.

## Administration and Scoring

Error analysis for Letter & Word Recognition and Nonsense Word Decoding requires phonetic transcription of the examinee's pronunciations. Unless the examinee reads very rapidly, this is not difficult for examiners with some background in reading instruction or speech pathology, but might be challenging for those lacking this background. One reviewer (RD), for whom this description is valid, has had great difficulty accurately recording the phonemic responses of several students. Thankfully, the *Administration Manual* (Kaufman & Kaufman with Breaux, 2014c, p. 28) notes, "Recording oral responses verbatim may be recommended or required on some subtests, depending on the purpose of the evaluation and the depth of information required. Use of an audio recorder during these subtests is highly recommended to ensure accuracy of recording and scoring." We hope that examiners will record the oral responses even though the need to audio record responses increases the amount of equipment needed for test administration. A pocket-size audio recorder is not much to add to the kit along with a machine to play the audio files.

Weighted raw scores for Reading Comprehension, Written Expression, Listening Comprehension, Word Recognition Fluency, and Oral Expression are taken from conversion tables in Appendix C of the *Technical & Interpretive Manual* based on the item set(s) administered and the number of items passed within the set(s) and there are also Raw Score Lookup tables in Appendix C for Writing Fluency, Object Naming Fluency, and Letter Naming Fluency. The Subtest Composite Score Computation Form on the KTEA-3 flash drive should make it easy to enter the correct raw scores and weighted raw scores, but examiners new to the concept of item sets sometimes encounter difficulties.

We do not find significant difficulties with scoring most of the Written Expression and Oral Expression items, but some of our graduate students, workshop attendees, and colleagues report uncertainty in scoring some items, even with the explanations, examples, and Language Glossary in the *Scoring Manual* (Kaufman & Kaufman with Breaux, 2014d).

## Test Items

Some potentially ambiguous or confusing items on the KTEA-II were improved in the KTEA-3. However, several of the KTEA-3 Reading Comprehension and Listening Comprehension items list as "incorrect" responses that appear to us to be merely incomplete. Some of these are marked (say, **Tell me more**), but several are not and querying is permitted only for the responses so marked on the easel. Laconic examinees with adequate reading comprehension might be penalized on those items.

## Interpretation

As noted above, under Test Development and in Tables 5.2 and 5.3, examiners must be very cautious when interpreting scores on subtests that limit possible high scores for older examinees and possible low scores for younger ones. Near-perfect raw scores producing only modestly high standard scores and near-zero raw scores with moderately high standard scores must be interpreted with extreme care and may require assessment with another instrument. When an examinee's skills are extremely weak, criterion referenced assessment may be more useful than norm-based assessment.

If the six Academic Skills Battery (ASB) subtests for older students or the five for kindergarten or three for prekindergarten are not administered, then subtests and other Composites cannot be compared to the ASB. However, subtests and composites can still be statistically compared to each other.

Appendix G in the *Technical & Interpretive Manual* lists differences needed for statistical significance and base rates for differences between Composites (Tables G.3 and G.7 for grade and age, respectively) and between subtests (Tables G.4 and G.8), which is essential information. However, in Tables G.4 and G.8, it would have been helpful to highlight the two subtests that make up each composite. Most examiners want to know whether the components of a total score are sufficiently consistent with one another to permit confident interpretation of that total score. This is another instance in which examiners may want to print out and store copies of tables, which they could highlight manually. We find it helpful to use the blank space in the "Composite" columns on the Subtest & Composite Score Computation Form (which must be printed from the KTEA-3 flash drive for each examinee) to note whether the difference or differences between the two or three subtests in each composite are significant and unusual (base rate). We write either "$p < .05$" or "n.s." and either "$f \le 10\%$" or "$f \ge 10\%$" in the blank space for each composite.

As noted above, the comparison between the Reading Comprehension and Listening Comprehension subtests is extremely valuable diagnostically because the formats of the two subtests are so similar and the correlation between them is fairly high (e.g., .61 in grade 5), so a difference of 22 points has a base rate $\le 10\%$ in grades 1 through 6. The comparison between Written Expression and Oral Expression is somewhat less helpful because of substantial differences in test format and a lower correlation (e.g., .46 in grade 5) between the subtests, so a difference of 25 points is needed for a base rate $\leq$10% in grades 1 through 6.

The Growth Scale Values (GSV) seem to be potentially very useful, and the *Technical & Interpretive Manual* does provide more information on their use (pp. 36–37, 98–100, and 678–679) than did the KTEA-II *Manual*. However, there does not appear to be any provision on the record form or the materials provided on the flash drive, for recording or interpreting Growth Scale Values when one is hand-scoring the KTEA-3 (the online scoring provides these data).

If, for some unusual reason, an examiner wished to report grade-equivalent or age-equivalent scores, it would be helpful to report them as confidence bands rather than as single points. To do this, the examiner must translate the standard scores at the end points of the standard score confidence bands back to raw scores and then convert those raw scores to age- or grade-equivalent scores, a laborious process often requiring interpolation. In fairness, we know of no test that simplifies, encourages, or even mentions computation of confidence bands for age- and grade-equivalent scores.

Assessment of oral language is always a vexatious issue. Oral language is tested, of course, in oral language tests, such as the Clinical Evaluation of Language Fundamentals (CELF-5; Wiig, Semel, & Secord, 2013), Oral and Written Language Scales (OWLS-II; Carrow-Woolfolk, 2012), or Comprehensive Assessment of Spoken Language (CASL; Carrow-Woolfolk, 1999), where it is treated as a separate domain. Oral language is also assessed by most cognitive ability measures, such as the Differential Ability Scales (DAS-II; Elliott, 2007) or Wechsler Intelligence Scale for Children (WISC-V; Wechsler, 2014a), where it is treated as one broad ability within overall cognitive functioning. Oral language is also included in tests of academic achievement, such as the WIAT-III and KTEA-3, where it is a domain of school achievement, comparable to reading or math. This situation is, at best, confusing to evaluators when they attempt to decide whether oral expression or listening comprehension on an achievement test is weaker than would be expected from the student's scores on cognitive ability tests that require very similar speaking and listening skills.

In our opinion, efforts to create good tests of oral language as aspects of academic achievement, as opposed to tests of oral language as its own domain or oral language as part of cognitive abilities, have met with only moderate success. The KTEA-3 oral language and oral fluency subtests strike us as being as good as any currently available oral language *academic achievement* tests and better than most, but the reliability and validity coefficients are much weaker than those for most other KTEA-3 subtests (see Chapter 2 and Rapid Reference 5.1).

## FINAL COMMENT

Although we have identified some concerns with the KTEA-3, we consider it to be one of the best currently available comprehensive achievement batteries. It preserves the best aspects of the KTEA and KTEA-II, and the changes are, in our opinion, significant improvements.

## STRENGTHS AND WEAKNESSES OF THE WIAT-III

We previously reviewed the WIAT-III (Lichtenberger & Breaux, 2010, pp. 239–269) and concluded, "that, all in all, the WIAT-III is a very good instrument … a vast improvement over the prior edition.... The WIAT-III provides an efficient, thorough, reasonable and statistically reliable and valid assessment of academic abilities. It is designed with features that enhance useful interpretation" (pp. 239–240). The authors of this chapter still believe that the WIAT-III (Pearson, 2009a) is a very good instrument. Although we find the test to be overall a vast improvement over the prior edition and have welcomed many of the changes in the new edition, we still find several aspects of the test annoying or problematic. Admittedly, we are easily annoyed. The WIAT-III provides an efficient, thorough, reasonable, and statistically reliable and valid assessment of academic abilities. It is designed with features that enhance useful interpretation. Rapid Reference 5.2 provides a summary of the WIAT-III Strengths and Weaknesses. Because of limitations to the length of this chapter, several but not all points will be elaborated on below.

## ≡ Rapid Reference 5.2

### Strengths and Weaknesses of the WIAT-III

| Strengths | Weaknesses |
|---|---|
| **Test Development** | |
| • Improved the floor and ceiling of several subtests.<br>• Expanded the number and type of subtests to measure all eight areas of achievement specified by IDEA 2004 legislation.<br>• New or newly separate subtests include Early Reading Skills, Alphabet Writing Fluency, Sentence Composition, Essay Composition, Oral Reading Fluency, and three Math Fluency subtests. | • Limited ceiling for some subtests for the oldest students in the Above Average range. Although most subtests have a ceiling that is at least 2 SD above the mean, the ceilings for Sentence Building, Word Reasoning, Expressive Vocabulary, Oral Reading Accuracy, and Math Fluency (Addition, Subtraction, Multiplication) range from 117 to 128. At the highest age range, 15 of the 26 possible subtests have ceilings ≤144. |

*(continued)*

(Continued)

| Strengths | Weaknesses |
|---|---|
| **Test Development** | |
| • The Spelling subtest no longer includes an excessive number of potential homonym confusions. | • Limited floor for some subtests for the youngest students with the lowest ability levels. For students age 6, raw scores of 0 correspond to standard scores in the "average range" (i.e., SS $\geq$ 85) for Sentence Combining, Sentence Building, and Math Fluency (subtraction). |
| • Oral Discourse Comprehension is presented from a CD recording rather than being read aloud by the examiner. | |
| • Extensive tryout data using samples with approximately proportional representation by sex and ethnicity. | |
| • Easel format for presenting many subtest items. | |
| • Error analysis procedures were expanded. | |
| • Established links with the most recent Wechsler scales (i.e., WPPSI-III, WPPSI-IV, WISC-IV, WISC-V, WAIS-IV, WNV), and the DAS-II to enable clinicians to compare ability and achievement scores. | |
| **Standardization** | |
| • The standardization sample is well stratified to match the U.S. population. | • We hope that examiners will take the time to read, study, and annotate their PDF copies of the *Technical Manual*. |
| • Data were obtained from a stratified sample of 2,775 students in grades pre-K–12 (1,375 in the spring of 2008 and 1,400 students in the fall of 2008). From the overall grade sample, an overlapping stratified sample of 1,826 students ranging in age from 4 through 19 was also obtained. | • There are no college-age norms provided. |
| • The standardization sample included students receiving special education services. | |

(continued)

(Continued)

| Strengths | Weaknesses |
|---|---|
| **Standardization** | |

- Very detailed information on standardization procedures and sample are included in the manual.
- Extensive (over 500 pages) *Technical Manual* is provided as a "green" PDF file rather than a printed manual.

| **Reliability and Validity** | |
|---|---|

| | |
|---|---|
| • The average reliability coefficients for the WIAT–III composite scores are all excellent (.91–.98). | • No alternative forms are available. |
| • Average subtest reliability coefficients range from good (.83–.89) to excellent (.90–.97), with the exception of Alphabet Writing Fluency, which has an average reliability of .69. | • Standard Errors of Measurement (SEm) are high for the Alphabet Writing Fluency (8.35 for Fall, Spring, and Age samples). |
| • Correlations between the WIAT-III Total Achievement score and overall cognitive ability scores range from .60 to .82 and are consistent with research-based expectations regarding typical correlations between ability and achievement measures. Such correlations provide evidence of divergent validity, suggesting that different constructs are being measured by the WIAT-III from those measured by each ability test. | • The only academic achievement comparison was to the WIAT-II when the WIAT-III initially published (the KTEA-3 later provided correlations with the WIAT-III). |
| • Strong face validity based on item content and skill development in reading, writing, and mathematics. | |
| • Construct validity indicated by increasing scores across grades and ages. | |

(continued)

*(Continued)*

| Strengths | Weaknesses |
|---|---|
| **Administration and Scoring** | |

| Strengths | Weaknesses |
|---|---|
| • Easel format with tabbed separators simplifies administration. | • The test record form's layout is very busy and crowded in places – particularly on the first two Score Summary pages. |
| • Starting points and discontinue rules are clearly labeled on the record form for all subtests. | |
| • Many test items are scored in a dichotomous manner. | • The record form itself is 50 pages long. For those using the WIAT-III with younger children (pre-K and K), much of the record form is wasted (a separate Pre-K/K record form is available for purchase). |
| • Both age and grade norms are provided. | |
| • In an effort to improve ease of administration and shorten administration times, the same reverse rule and discontinue rule is used across all applicable WIAT-III subtests, and the discontinue rule has been shortened to 4 consecutive scores of 0. | • When hand scoring and filling in the summary pages, great care must be taken to avoid error. Normative tables are provided as a PDF file, which makes looking up score conversions awkward and at times difficult to read, especially on a small laptop screen (some tables are printed in landscape mode, not portrait layout). |
| • New descriptive categories reflect a simpler system of categorizing achievement level based on the test's SD of 15. | |
| • Scoring rules were improved in response to scoring studies, theoretical reviews by expert researchers, and usability reviews by teachers and clinicians. | • Not all correct or acceptable answers are provided on the record form. Examiners must be diligent to check the *Examiner's Manual* (Appendix B) and the *Scoring Workbook* for guidance. |
| • There are sufficient scoring examples and a 118-page *Scoring Workbook* to assist examiners in learning and using the scoring rules. | • Several questions appear to have more correct answers than are listed in the record form. |
| • Q-global and the Scoring Assistant computer program are valuable tools for score calculation, graphs, and subtest comparisons, saving time and eliminating possible human-made clerical errors. | • The new descriptive categories are different than those from the earlier versions of the WIAT as well as many other achievement and ability measures, which may be confusing to those familiar with the old categories. The undifferentiated "Average" range, extending from 85 to 115 may make sense statistically and psychologically, but we find it much too broad (more than 2/3 of the population) for interpreting educational performance. |
| • Error analysis for the subtests that have large numbers of skill categories is provided, both in the computer Scoring Assistant CD and as reproducible worksheets in the examiner's manual. | |

*(continued)*

(*Continued*)

| Strengths | Weaknesses |
|---|---|
| **Interpretation** | |
| • Composites and most subtests can be interpreted due to high reliability data. | • Caution needs to be taken when interpreting the scores with a nonoptimal ceiling or floor. |
| • Error analysis procedures pinpoint specific skill deficits. | • Subtest Score Summary column labeled "Standard Score" contains not only standard scores but weighted raw scores and sum of standard score, leading to possible misinterpretation of the actual numbers. |
| • The composites and error analysis yield much diagnostic information directly relevant to instructional remediation. | |
| • Pairs of WIAT-III subtests (i.e., Reading Comprehension and Listening Comprehension, and Written Expression and Oral Expression) were developed to have more similar formats than on the WIAT-II, which permits useful comparisons that can help the examiner distinguish specific problems in reading or writing from more general language problems. | • Insufficient information is provided in the *WIAT-III Technical Manual* on how to utilize the Growth Scale Values (GSV). |
| • The 4-point Oral Reading Fluency Prosody Scale is a useful observation. | |
| • The WIAT-III Scoring Assistant provides Growth Scale Values (GSV) to provide a mechanism of plotting two or more testing sessions by grade or age against a curve representing mean growth. | |

## ASSETS OF THE WIAT-III

### Test Development

The revisions made from the WIAT-II to the WIAT-III are, in general, excellent. The graphics and the content of the items appear to be excellent and much improved. The inclusion of the three new fluency measures in math, the broader coverage of academic achievement areas, improved scoring rules, a scoring workbook providing real-life examples, and the inclusion of the Scoring Assistant CD all add to the increased utility and user friendliness of the WIAT-III.

Expert advisory and user panels were consulted during the development of the WIAT-III. Surveys of the experts and of try-out and standardization examiners were conducted at several points during the development process.

The availability of the computer scoring program packaged with the test serves to alleviate numerical errors often associated with complex tests. The scoring program also offers several extremely useful features, including an enhanced skill analysis for core subtests as well as Intervention goal statements to assist with IEP development. Exclusive to the scoring program is the research-supported "pattern of strengths and weaknesses discrepancy analysis."

The 52-page Enhanced Record Form for the WIAT-III provides ample space for recording responses, calculating scores by hand, profiling scores, calculating and assessing differences between scores, and analyzing discrepancies between measures of cognitive abilities and WIAT-III scores by either the predicted achievement or, unfortunately, the simple difference method. The front page of the Enhanced Record Form, where subtest scores are recorded and composite scores calculated and profiled, helpfully lists the page number on which each subtest begins.

The Pearson web page for the WIAT-III offers valuable "Reference Materials," including *Assessing Writing Skills Using Correct-Incorrect Word Sequences* (Breaux & Frey, 2009), a *Quick Score Guide for WIAT-III Essay Composition*, two Technical Reports (one of which needs to be updated), *Patterns of Strengths & Weaknesses Models for Identifying SLD* (Daniel, Breaux, & Frey, 2010), and an explanation of WIAT-III Enhanced Content Modifications. We urge students and colleagues to make a habit of revisiting publishers' web sites for all of the tests they use to check for updates. In the case of the WIAT-III, this effort will be rewarded.

## Normative Sample

Normative samples are important for tests, just as for opinion polls. If the normative sample does not resemble the population to whom examinees will be compared, scores will be misleading. The normative sample of the WIAT-III is described in Chapter 2 of the WIAT-III *Technical Manual* (Pearson, 2010a) and we consider it to meet or exceed good current practice and to provide a trustworthy basis for an individual's scores.

Many examiners will be thrilled to have norms for adults. The WIAT-III provides norms for ages 20 through 25, 26 through 35, and 36 through 50 (Pearson, 2010a, Appendix L). Adult norms are rare in tests of academic achievement, and we welcome this addition.

Examinee candidates for the normative sample were extensively screened for potentially confounding issues that presumably might impair the validity of test performance. A complete list of the exclusionary criteria for the normative sample is presented in Table 2.1 (p. 15) of the *Technical Manual.* A representative proportion of students from various special clinical groups was also included in the normative samples to accurately represent the student population as a whole.

Special group studies were conducted to examine clinical utility of the WIAT-III with intellectually gifted students and students with mild intellectual disability and disorders of reading, written expression, mathematics, and expressive language (Pearson, 2010a, pp. 49–59).

## Reliability and Validity

The WIAT-III Composites, Indexes, and subtests generally have strong reliability. This topic is discussed at length in Chapter 3 of the *Technical Manual*. Test scores cannot be trusted unless the tests are internally consistent and likely to yield very similar scores for the same person under similar circumstances, so reliability is an essential foundation for any responsible use of test scores. It is a necessary, but not sufficient, basis for application of test scores. A test can be reliable, but still not valid for a particular purpose, but without reliability, it cannot be valid for any purpose.

The average reliability coefficients for the WIAT–III composite scores are all excellent (.91–.98). Short-term (2 to 32 days) stability coefficients for the WIAT–III subtest and composite scores at all grades (Pearson, 2010a, pp. 37–38), range from .73 (adequate) to .97 (reliable).

Validity data for the WIAT-III are discussed in Chapter 3 of this book, and in the WIAT-III *Technical Manual* (Pearson, 2010a, pp. 39–59). The subtest intercorrelations confirm expected relations between the subtests within composites and provide evidence of discriminant validity.

Validity evidence from comparisons with tests of tests of academic achievement and cognitive abilities supports the use of the WIAT-III for cognitive assessment and prediction of achievement. The relationships between the WIAT-III and the following cognitive measures were examined: WPPSI-III, WISC-IV, WAIS-IV, WNV, and DAS-II. It is very helpful for examiners to be able to predict WIAT-III achievement from both the DAS-II and Wechsler scales. The WISC-V *Technical and Interpretive Manual* (Wechsler, 2014b, pp. 101–105) provides WISC-V correlations with the WIAT-III. The WPPSI-IV *Technical and Interpretive Manual* (Wechsler, 2012b, pp. 104–108) provides WISC-V correlations with the WIAT-III. Unfortunately, the only academic achievement comparison was to the WIAT-II. However, the KTEA-3 *Technical & Interpretive Manual* (Kaufman & Kaufman with Breaux, 2014b) provides correlations, based on 73 examinees, between WIAT-III and KTEA-3 subtests and composites in Table 2.11 (pp. 64–65).

## Administration and Scoring

The administration of the WIAT-III seems to flow a bit more efficiently than did that of the WIAT-II, and one reason for this may be the revised discontinue rules (for most subtests there is a consistent discontinuation rule of four consecutive failures), which have for the most part been shortened. Entry points and other essential information have generally been made clear and user-friendly on the record form and sufficient space is provided for recording responses. Scoring for many tests is made easier than on the WIAT-II because it is dichotomous (0 or 1 point).

The tabbed, two-sided stimulus book contains five subtests and has an easel back that allows it to stand freely on the table. Most materials needed to properly administer the WIAT-III are provided and are generally light and do not appear at all cumbersome. It is much more reasonable for the examiner to provide several other materials (e.g., blank paper, CD or MP3 player, and stopwatch) than to have to keep purchasing such materials from the publisher of each test the examiner uses. One recommendation made in the *Examiner's Manual* that we wholeheartedly endorse is to add to the materials for administration an audio recorder to record the examinee's verbatim responses. Although certainly not needed for the entire test, the proper scoring of four subtests (Word Reading, Pseudoword Decoding, Oral Expression, and Oral Reading Fluency) can be greatly aided by the audio recording.

The inclusion of a CD containing the Oral Discourse Comprehension subtest is a welcomed addition. There has always been the problem of different examiners reading a comprehension passage differently from each other or even differently for different examinees. The inclusion of the oral discourse passages on the CD makes the administration of this subtest much more universally standardized so all examinees get the same pronunciation and word emphasis in the recitation of the stories. Many may remember the CHEWIES story on the original WIAT. (That story, as are several other original WIAT stories, is once again used for the Oral Discourse Comprehension passages.) Although the story passage that was to be read aloud to the examinee was printed clearly on the easel, there was no instruction as to whether or not an examiner was to read the passage with a normal tone, and without any special emphasis on any passage part or word (despite the fact that the word **CHEWIES** was always bolded in the story). This problem has been successfully eliminated on the WIAT-III by the use of the CD.

## INTERPRETATION

Interpretation of the WIAT-III is enhanced by having subtests and/or composites that measure all eight areas of achievement specified by IDEA (2004) legislation as important for identifying and classifying learning disabilities: (1) oral expression (one subtest), (2) listening comprehension (one subtest), (3) written expression (composite based on two or three subtests), (4) basic reading skill (composite based on two subtests), (5) reading fluency skills (one subtest), (6) reading comprehension (one subtest), (7) mathematics calculation (one subtest), and (8) mathematics problem solving (one subtest).

The 28 WIAT-III component subtests are organized into 16 subtests and seven composites plus a Total Achievement composite. The first page of the Enhanced Record Form makes it easy to enter the subtest scores and calculate the composite scores.

Footnotes are provided to facilitate correct summation of scores (e.g., Total Reading includes Reading Comprehension, Word Reading, and Pseudoword Decoding at all grade levels, but Oral Reading Fluency only for grades 2 through 12+). The distinctions between the composites for Total Reading, Basic Reading, and Reading Comprehension and Fluency are helpful, as are the separate composites for Mathematics and Math Fluency. Appendix H of the *Technical Manual* provides all of the necessary information for checking critical values and base rates for comparisons between composites and between subtest scores by age norms and grade norms.

### Better Listening Comprehension Measure

Historically, one wonderful aspect of the original WIAT was the lovely contrast between Reading Comprehension and Listening Comprehension. You had two tests, normed on the same sample, that were (except for the memory demand of Listening Comprehension) nearly identical in format, with one requiring reading and the other only listening. This contrasting pair was tremendously helpful in distinguishing reading comprehension problems from more pervasive language comprehension problems and in documenting the severity of a reading problem compared to an expectation based on oral comprehension. That contrast was lost in the WIAT-II where the Listening Comprehension test was primarily two very brief vocabulary subtests (Receptive Vocabulary and Expressive Vocabulary) with an extremely brief sentence comprehension test thrown in. The WIAT-III now has a much better Listening Comprehension measure made up of the Oral Discourse Comprehension and Receptive Vocabulary subtests. It may still be a bit difficult to interpretively contrast examinee's performance on the Reading Comprehension test to that of the Oral Discourse Comprehension subtest because the tables in the *Technical Manual* that provide the relevant critical values and base rate necessary for pairwise comparisons do so only for the Listening Comprehension versus Reading Comprehension measures, but not for the Oral Discourse Comprehension versus Reading Comprehension.

### Technical Manual

The WIAT-III *Technical Manual* (Pearson, 2010) is provided as a 627-page pdf file is obviously extensive and is easy to navigate. All headings and subheadings in the Main Table of Contents (TOC) can be clicked to go to the desired page. Readers can also move through the *Manual* with keyboard arrow keys. At the bottom of each page there is a button to return to the "Main TOC." Some of the tables are in landscape format and appear sideways, at least on a small laptop screen. We find it helpful to print and keep copies of frequently used pages, in which case, the orientation is not an issue. As mentioned in Chapter 1 of this book, a hard copy of the *Technical Manual* can be purchased from the publisher (see Rapid Reference 1.3).

## LIMITATIONS OF THE WIAT-III

### Floor and Ceiling

Table 5.5 shows the highest possible subtest scores for the oldest school-age and adult examinees and for examinees in Spring of grade 12. Although most subtests have a ceiling that is at least 2 SD above the mean, at grade 12, the ceilings for Word Reading, Oral Reading Accuracy (one component of the Oral Reading Fluency subtest, which has a ceiling of 160), the three Math Fluency subtests, Sentence Combining and Sentence Building (the two components of Sentence Composition, which has a ceiling of 160), and Expressive Vocabulary (a component of Oral Expression, which has a

**Table 5.5 Ceiling for Students Ages 21:0–25:11 and 36:0–50:11 and Grade 12: Highest Possible Subtest Score**

| WIAT-III Subtest | Ages 17:0 to 19:11 | Spring Grade 12 | Ages 36:0 to 50:11 |
|---|---|---|---|
| Word Reading | 123 | 122 | 120 |
| Pseudoword Decoding | 132 | 132 | 128 |
| Reading Comprehension | 160 | 160 | 156 |
| Oral Reading Fluency | 160 | 160 | 160 |
| Oral Reading Accuracy | 120 | 119 | 117 |
| Oral Reading Rate | 160 | 160 | 160 |
| Math Problem Solving | 138 | 134 | 139 |
| Numerical Operations | 142 | 137 | 152 |
| Math Fluency–Addition | 117 | 116 | 112 |
| Math Fluency–Subtraction | 122 | 120 | 113 |
| Math Fluency–Multiplication | 123 | 122 | 118 |
| Sentence Combining | 133 | 128 | 133 |
| Sentence Building | 121 | 128 | 116 |
| Sentence Composition | 160 | 160 | 160 |
| Word Count | 160 | 160 | 160 |
| Theme Development & Text Org. | 141 | 137 | 144 |
| Grammar and Mechanics | 160 | 1160 | 160 |
| Essay Composition | 160 | 160 | 160 |
| Spelling | 136 | 132 | 125 |
| Receptive Vocabulary | 139 | 138 | 127 |
| Expressive Vocabulary | 128 | 125 | 122 |
| Oral Discourse Comprehension | 136 | 135 | 133 |
| Oral Word Fluency | 148 | 148 | 147 |
| Sentence Repetition | 149 | 146 | 142 |
| Listening Comprehension | 160 | 160 | 160 |
| Oral Expression | 160 | 160 | 160 |

From Tables B.1 and C.1 of the WIAT-III *Technical Manual* (Pearson, 2010). The minimum standard score on all subtests is 40.

ceiling of 160) range from 116 to 128. Examiners should check for similar ceiling effects with any instrument we use. For example, if a 12th-grader scores 160 for Reading Comprehension and only 122 for Word Reading on the WIAT-III, we do not know if the student's word reading is really weaker than the student's comprehension since the student passed every item on both subtests.

Similarly, there is insufficient floor on some subtests for students of ages 6:0 and younger as shown in Table 5.6. For students of ages 6:0 to 6:3, raw scores of 0 correspond to standard scores ranging from 88 to 40 (88 for Sentence Building and 90 for Sentence Combining, which are components of Sentence Construction, which has a floor of 40). For First Grade Winter Norms raw scores of 0 correspond to standard

**Table 5.6  WIAT-III Floor for Students age 4:0–6:0 and Pre-Kindergarten, Kindergarten, and Grade 1: Lowest Possible Subtest Score**

| WIAT-III Subtest | Ages | | | Grades: Winter[a] of | | |
|---|---|---|---|---|---|---|
| | 4:0–4:3 | 5:0–5:3 | 6:0–6:3 | Pre-K | K | 1 |
| Early Reading Skills | 72 | 54 | 40 | 65 | 43 | 40 |
| Word Reading | | | 84 | | | 71 |
| Pseudoword Decoding | | | 84 | | | 76 |
| Reading Comprehension | | | 79 | | | 67 |
| Oral Reading Fluency | | | 40 | | | 40 |
| Oral Reading Accuracy | | | 40 | | | 40 |
| Oral Reading Rate | | | 48 | | | 40 |
| Math Problem Solving | 65 | 51 | 40 | 56 | 43 | 40 |
| Numerical Operations | | 71 | 59 | | 63 | 45 |
| Math Fluency–Addition | | | 75 | | | 68 |
| Math Fluency–Subtraction | | | 88 | | | 80 |
| Alphabet Writing Fluency | 80 | 70 | 60 | 77 | 65 | 52 |
| Sentence Combining | | | 90 | | | 83 |
| Sentence Building | | | 88 | | | 78 |
| Sentence Composition | | | 40 | | | 40 |
| Spelling | | 70 | 60 | | 65 | 59 |
| Receptive Vocabulary | 69 | 64 | 57 | 67 | 60 | 54 |
| Expressive Vocabulary | 71 | 65 | 59 | 69 | 62 | 55 |
| Oral Discourse Comp. | 74 | 66 | 57 | 72 | 61 | 54 |
| Oral Word Fluency | 57 | 50 | 42 | 55 | 46 | 40 |
| Sentence Repetition | 69 | 63 | 57 | 66 | 60 | 55 |
| Listening Comprehension | 40 | 40 | 40 | 40 | 40 | 40 |
| Oral Expression | 40 | 40 | 40 | 40 | 40 | 40 |

[a]Winter grade norms are reported here.
From Tables B.1 and C.1 of the WIAT-III *Technical Manual* (Pearson, 2010). The minimum standard score on all subtests is 40.

scores ranging from 83 to 40. See Table 5.6 for specific data. Zero raw scores are always risky to interpret on any test, partly because you do not know if it was a "high zero" (almost one point) or a "low zero" (it may be years before the examinee is able to pass a single item). Zero raw scores that yield relatively high standard scores are potentially misleading on any test. We advise examiners to check all tests they use for ceiling and floor effects, especially at the age or grade level of their current examinee.

## Test Coverage

The WIAT-III provides a very good test of oral reading fluency of passages with scores for rate, accuracy, and total fluency. It does not test silent reading fluency or oral reading fluency with word lists and lists of phonetically regular nonsense words. The WIAT-III assesses phonics skills with reading of phonetically regular nonsense words and reading fluency with nonsense words. A test of spelling dictated nonsense words would have completed the phonetic assessment, but there were already 28 scored subtests and composites.

## Poor Instructions for Scoring Certain Tasks

Although the instructions provided in the *Examiner's Manual* (Pearson, 2009b) are typically clear and unambiguous, there remain, in our opinion, several aspects of administration and scoring that need clarification. Some specific instructions may be confusing to examiners. Two examples are for the "Reverse Rules" and for the "Discontinuation Rules."

Four subtests (Oral Discourse Comprehension, Math Problem Solving, Numerical Operations, and Spelling) utilize the reverse rule. This rule states that if a student scores 0 points on any of the first three items given, administer the items in reverse order from the start point until three consecutive items are passed or item 1 is reached. At that point the examiner should "proceed forward" until the discontinuation rule has been reached. For the Oral Discourse Comprehension subtest, if a student starts at item 6, and passes 6 and 7 but fails 8, the reverse rule should be employed and the examiner must administer items in reverse order, starting with item 5, and continue until three consecutive items

> ## DON'T FORGET
>
> ### Tips for Administering Oral Discourse Comprehension
>
> As explained in Chapter 3 of this book, the reverse rule should not be applied too rigidly on Oral Discourse Comprehension. If the examinee has answered three consecutive items incorrectly and there is one additional item remaining that pertains to a given passage, do not reverse immediately to the preceding passage. Rather, administer the remaining question that pertains to the passage before reversing, and then reverse to the preceding passage.

are passed. However, because items 8 and 9 are for the same passage, is the examiner really supposed to employ the reverse rule after item 8? If so, do you replay the story again (the record form says "Do not repeat CD tracks"), ask the question associated with item 9 without the child hearing the story again, or administer item 9 even if item 8 is scored as a 0? If this is the answer, this may in fact cause more confusion with scoring. What if item 9 is passed, but during the reverse rule administration the child receives four consecutive scores of 0 below item 9? Would the score on item 9 count or not count?

For eight subtests, the discontinuation rule on the record form notes that the examiner is to "Discontinue after 4 consecutive scores of 0." Although technically correct, this applies only to discontinuing when the examiner is moving forward toward establish a ceiling. However, if an examiner has had to employ the Reverse Rule and administer items in reverse in order to establish a basal, it is quite possible that an examinee could have four consecutive failures while being administered the items in reverse order. In such a case, the examiner *should not discontinue* after four consecutive errors since these errors occurred while moving in a reverse order in an attempt to establish a basal.

## Item Scoring

Several subtest items appear to have more correct answers than are listed in the record form or *Examiner's Manual*. Clarification of certain responses from the test authors will be helpful.

### *Reading Comprehension*

The Reading Comprehension scoring rules should, we think, provide more guidance on querying. Acceptable answers still, as on the WIAT-II, place a premium on the examinee guessing what the question really is asking or what the passage in meant to imply, so there are many possible answers that suggest good understanding but receive no credit and apparently warrant no query. Several questions appear to have more correct answers than are listed in the record form. Examples are listed below:

Item #38 asks that the examinee give the word that "best describes Gobbledee-glue." Several 2-point responses are allowed (no 1-point responses are provided) and answers such as "homemade" or "rolled" are not scored or queried.

Item #54 requires the examinee to give three dangers encountered by the family on their journey. Unfortunately, "getting lost" is not listed as an acceptable answer despite the fact that the story features an Indian guide who helps them survive and guides them to the destination. Item #73 requires the examinee to explain what caused whales to begin to make a recovery, and two specific answers are necessary to obtain maximum points. Listed as a possible 1-point response is "Placed on endangered species list." This specific response requires a query by the examiner of "Tell me more." There doesn't appear to be any clear reason why this acceptable 1-point response, followed by either one of the two other acceptable 1-point response would not cumulatively be scored as 2 points but apparently only two of the three 1-point responses are acceptable in the 2-point scoring.

# CAUTION

## Scoring Reading Comprehension Items

Chapter 3 of this book discussed the following items that tend to raise questions for examiners about how the scoring rules were determined. Additional explanation is provided here.

Item 73 requires the examinee to explain what caused whales to begin to make a recovery, and two specific answers are necessary to obtain full credit. Only two of the three 1-point responses are acceptable in the 2-point response. A 1-point response is "Placed on endangered species list," which requires a query by the examiner of "Tell me more." However, "Placed on endangered species list" does not qualify as one of the necessary 2-point responses. This response is queried to encourage the examinee to elaborate and possibly provide a 2-point response.

Item 76: Identify the three consequences that would result if zoo prices are not raised. The answers that receive credit (i.e., zoo closes, animals sold off, children lose learning experiences, families lose entertainment) are the most salient consequences listed in the passage, because the passage clearly states that the zoo would close if zoo prices are not raised, and these are the consequences of the zoo closing. There are alternative responses that could be derived from the passage, such as the employees not receiving raises or the facilities not being kept up; however, these are not the most salient consequences because none of these would be relevant if the zoo were no longer open.

# DON'T FORGET

## Reminder to Use Paper and Pencil

As stated in Chapter 3 of this book, if an examinee appears to struggle on one of the later items without attempting to work the problem on paper, you may remind the examinee that using paper and pencil is permitted. Administer the prompt by saying, "You may use this paper and pencil at any time to help work a problem."

## Math Problem Solving

On item 13 (chip counting), what if the child counts incorrectly but gives a correct total? Could two wrongs may make a right: the child might point wrong (missing a chip) and count wrong (skipping a number) and come up with the right answer.

Two items (47 and 54) seem to be attempting to measure how well a student knows 90 and 180 degrees respectively, but it also takes a good amount of visualization skills (*Gv*) to do the problem successfully. Reminding the examinee that he or she can use the paper and pencil provided may help alleviate the problem, but there do not appear to be any such cues. Before you start the subtest, you do include the instruction, "You may use this paper and pencil at any time to help work a problem" but there is no indication that this reminder can be given to a student who might be struggling with the problems.

## Pseudoword Decoding

One word, diminecial, has two correct pronunciations listed on the record form. Is there actually a third: die-min-ə-shel?

## Numerical Operations

There appears to be a potential scoring problem with Item 2: Item 1 asks a child to count a number of balls and then tell how many there are. Item 2 asks the child to "write the number of the balls you counted" into a box on the record form. How does one score it if the child miscounts the number of balls (e.g., says 4 instead of 5), thus getting

> **DON'T FORGET**
> ..........................................................
> ### Acceptable Pseudoword Pronunciations
>
> As mentioned in Chapter 3 of this book, only the pronunciations listed in the record form may be scored as correct. Correct responses were determined by reviewing the tryout and standardization data and consulting with speech and language experts.

Item 1 wrong, but then, for item 2, correctly writes in the box "4"? Although the child has done exactly what the directions ask—"write the number of the balls you counted"—the answer key gives 5 as the only correct answer.

> **DON'T FORGET**
> ..........................................................................................................
> ### Scoring Numerical Operations Items
>
> As explained in Chapter 3 of this book, the following items tend to raise questions for examiners about how the scoring rules were determined. Additional explanation is provided here.
>
> **Item 1:** Asks the examinee to count the number of balls and tell how many there are, then Item 2 asks the examinee to write the number of balls counted. If the examinee miscounted the number of balls for Item 1 (e.g., says 4 instead of 5), which would be scored 0, and then writes that number for Item 2 (writes "4"), Item 2 is also scored 0. Why is the response for Item 2 incorrect even though the examinee followed the directions correctly? Numerical Operations is primarily a test of *written* math computation, so writing the correct answer is required on Item 2; however, these early items were designed to provide additional information about how the examinee arrived at their answer by asking the examinee to provide an oral response first.
>
> (continued)

*(Continued)*

**Item 52:** The answer is 5.375. If the examinee wrote 5.3, is it scored as correct? No, the answer must be 5.375 because the purpose of this item is division of a number with a decimal point.

**Item 53:** The answer is 17. If the examinee wrote the square root of 289, is it scored as correct? Yes, this is an equivalent answer that reflects an understanding of how to work the problem.

---

# DON'T FORGET

## Timing Oral Reading Fluency

As explained in Chapter 3 of this book, after reading the instructions and "**Start here. Begin,**" start timing as soon as the examinee begins reading the first word.

---

# CAUTION

## Scoring Oral Reading Fluency Passage "The Moon"

As Chapter 3 of this book mentions, the comprehension questions asks, "What does the author like to do by moonlight?" The first sentence of the passage reads, "I like to watch the moon as it shines at night." "Watch the moon" is not listed as a correct response (and was not given as a response during tryout or standardization); however, this response is well supported by the first sentence of the passage and should be considered as an alternate correct response. Since the comprehension questions are for qualitative purposes only, accepting this alternate response will not alter standardized procedures or affect the validity of the scores.

---

## Oral Reading Fluency

Although the directions for timing the reading passages are clear in the box at the top of the record form ("start timing when the student reads the first word of the passage"), the instructions simply say, "**Start here. Begin**. Start timing." Shouldn't they say "Start timing when the student reads the first word"?

One story, "Amelia the pigeon" seems awfully implausible. A WW1 "tiny camera" being sent to a great-granddaughter is supposed to still work AND have film available to use!

The passage "The Moon" asks "What does the author like to do by moonlight?" The very first sentence says "I like to watch the moon as it shines at night." Is "watch the moon" an acceptable answer?

### Audio Recorder

An audio recorder is specified for recording the student's oral responses to several subtests (Word Reading, Pseudoword Decoding, Oral Expression, and Oral Reading Fluency). Will examiners actually do this, since it is a recommendation rather than a requirement? The need to audio record an examinee's responses increases the amount of equipment needed to correctly administer the test, although pocket-size audio recorders are now readily available. Given that the Oral Discourse Comprehension subtest requires the use of a separate CD player, examiners should transport to testing sessions both a CD player and an audio recorder or a machine with both functions.

## FINAL COMMENT

Although we have identified some concerns with the new WIAT-III, we definitely consider it a significant improvement over the WIAT-II and, on balance, find it to be a very valuable instrument with significant strengths.

## CONTENT COVERAGE OF THE KTEA-3 AND WIAT-III

Perhaps the most striking difference between the WIAT-III and KTEA-3 is the approach to assessing written expression. In addition to the Spelling subtest, which is included in the written language composite on both instruments, the KTEA-3 offers a single Written Expression subtest, which for all but the youngest examinees requires the examinee to write missing letters, words, punctuation, and sentences according to the examiner's instructions given while the examiner reads a multi-page story book with the examinee. At the end, the examinee writes a summary of the entire story. Many, but not all, examiners find this format to be very effective and consider it a strength of the KTEA-3. However, although there is a detailed error analysis, the Written Expression subtest yields only a single normative score. The WIAT-III provides Alphabet Writing Fluency for grades K through 2 and, for grades 3 through 12+, includes a Sentence Composition subtest with separate scores for Sentence Combining and Sentence Building. The WIAT-III Essay Composition subtest for grades 3 through 12+ involves a single, 10-minute essay with very specific instructions. The essay yields a total subtest score based on standard scores for Word Count and for Theme Development and Text Organization. There is also an optional standard score for Grammar and Mechanics based on the highly effective measure of Correct Word Sequences minus Incorrect Word Sequences (Breaux & Frey, 2009). Some examiners find the WIAT-III Written Expression subtests to be extremely useful. Others dislike or have difficulty mastering the Essay Composition scoring even with the aid of the WIAT-III *Examiner's Manual* (Pearson, 2009b), *WIAT–III Essay Composition: "Quick Score" for Theme Development and Text Organization* (Pearson, 2010b), the clear and efficient *WIAT-III Scoring Tutorial* (Lichtenberger & Breaux, 2010), and helpful archived Webinars (Pearson, n.d.). Examiners, in our experience, tend to have very strong opinions about and preferences between the KTEA-3 and WIAT-III measures of written expression.

The WIAT-III and KTEA-3 provide very broad coverage of academic achievement and cover many of the same achievement domains, but there are important differences between the two instruments. Rapid Reference 5.3 attempts to show those differences by listing the measures that provide normative scores on each instrument. Examiners may want to compare the skill coverage of the KTEA-3 and WIAT-III before selecting one test or the other for a particular examinee. For example, both instruments provide a normative score for math fluency, but only the WIAT-III provides separate scores for addition, subtraction, and multiplication. Both instruments include assessment of foundation reading skills, but only the KTEA-3 offers separate scores for phonological processing, associational fluency, object naming facility, and letter naming fluency. Both instruments assess reading fluency, but the WIAT-III gives scores for both rate and accuracy as well as total fluency for reading passages and a composite reading comprehension and fluency score, while the KTEA-3 gives scores for speed of accurately reading lists of words and lists of nonsense words, for speed of silently reading sentences, and a reading fluency composite. A thoughtful examiner will often have a good reason for selecting one instrument or the other on the basis of the examinee's history and the referral questions and concerns.

## ≡ Rapid Reference 5.3

### Scored Measures on the KTEA-3 and WIAT-III

|  | KTEA-3 | WIAT-III |
|---|:---:|:---:|
| **Reading Foundation Skills** | | |
| Early, precursor reading skills | | ✓ |
| Separate phonology subtest | ✓ | |
| Separate rapid naming subtest | ✓ | |
| Associational fluency | ✓ | |
| Sound-symbol (phonology & phonics) composite | ✓ | |
| **Oral Reading Accuracy** | | |
| Reading words aloud from a list | ✓ | ✓ |
| Reading pseudowords aloud from a list | ✓ | ✓ |
| Composite of reading real and nonsense words | ✓ | ✓ |
| Oral reading accuracy for passages | | ✓ |
| **Reading Fluency** | | |
| Oral reading accuracy for passages | | ✓ |
| Oral reading speed for passages | | ✓ |
| Total oral reading fluency | | ✓ |
| Silent reading fluency | ✓ | |
| Fluency reading words aloud from a list | ✓ | |
| Fluency reading pseudowords aloud from a list | ✓ | |
| Reading fluency composite | ✓ | ✓ |

*(continued)*

(*Continued*)

| | KTEA-3 | WIAT-III |
|---|:---:|:---:|
| **Reading Comprehension** | | |
| Reading vocabulary | ✓ | |
| Comprehension of passages | ✓ | ✓ |
| *Reading comprehension composite* | ✓ | |
| *Comprehension and fluency composite* | | ✓ |
| *Reading composite* | ✓ | ✓ |
| **Written Expression** | | |
| Alphabet writing fluency | | ✓ |
| Writing fluency | ✓ | |
| Sentence combining | | ✓ |
| Sentence building | | ✓ |
| *Sentence composition subtest* | | ✓ |
| Word count in an essay | | ✓ |
| Theme development & text organization | | ✓ |
| Grammar and mechanics | | ✓ |
| *Essay composition subtest* | | ✓ |
| Written expression subtest with items and essay | ✓ | |
| Writing fluency | ✓ | |
| Spelling dictated words | ✓ | ✓ |
| *Written language/expression composite* | ✓ | ✓ |
| **Mathematics** | | |
| Math computation | ✓ | ✓ |
| Math problem-solving and concepts | ✓ | ✓ |
| *Math composite* | ✓ | ✓ |
| Math fluency–addition | | ✓ |
| Math fluency–subtraction | | ✓ |
| Math fluency–multiplication | | ✓ |
| *Math fluency composite* | ✓ | ✓ |
| **Oral Language** | | |
| Receptive vocabulary | | ✓ |
| Oral discourse comprehension | | ✓ |
| *Listening comprehension composite* | ✓ | ✓ |
| Expressive vocabulary | | ✓ |
| Oral word fluency | | ✓ |
| Sentence repetition | | ✓ |
| *Oral expression composite* | ✓ | ✓ |
| *Oral language composite* | ✓ | ✓ |

(continued)

*(Continued)*

|  | KTEA-3 | WIAT-III |
|---|:---:|:---:|
| **Other Composites** | | |
| Reading and listening comprehension composite | ✓ | |
| Written and oral language composite | ✓ | |
| Orthographic processing composite | ✓ | |
| Academic (reading, writing, math) fluency composite | ✓ | |
| Academic Skills Battery Composite | ✓ | |
| Total Achievement Composite | | ✓ |

# 🖋 TEST YOURSELF 🖋

1. **The revised discontinue rules for the WIAT-III are**
   (a) A strength because they provide a consistent discontinuation rule of four consecutive failures for most subtests.
   (b) A strength because they provide a flexible discontinuation rule based on the examinee's overall level of performance.
   (c) A weakness because they provide a consistent discontinuation rule of four consecutive failures for most subtests.
   (d) A weakness because they provide a flexible discontinuation rule based on the examinee's overall level of performance.

2. **A strength of the WIAT-III scoring program is that it offers which of the following among its useful features?**
   (a) An enhanced skill analysis for core subtests.
   (b) Intervention goal statements to assist with IEP development.
   (c) A research-supported pattern of strengths and weaknesses discrepancy analysis.
   (d) All of the above.

3. **The specification of an audio recorder for recording the student's oral responses to several WIAT-III subtests is**
   (a) A strength because the audio recorder is included in the WIAT-III kit.
   (b) A strength because an accurate record of responses is essential for correct scoring.
   (c) A weakness because it adds to the equipment the examiner must schlep around.
   (d) a and b.
   (e) a and c.
   (f) b and c.

4. **A strength of the KTEA-3 is that, unlike error analyses on many tests, the categories of weakness-average-strength are based on the test norms.**
   (a) True
   (b) False

5. **Having subtests and/or composites that measure all eight areas of achievement specified by IDEA legislation as important for identifying and classifying specific learning disabilities is a strength of**
   (a) The WIAT-III.
   (b) The KTEA-3.
   (c) Both the WIAT-III and KTEA-3.
   (d) Neither the WIAT-III nor the KTEA-3.

6. **Norms for examinees of ages 26 through 50 is a strength of**
   (a) The WIAT-III.
   (b) The KTEA-3.
   (c) Both the WIAT-III and KTEA-3.
   (d) Neither the WIAT-III nor the KTEA-3.

7. **Correlations of KTEA-3 subtest scores with the WISC-V (for calculating predicted achievement) are found in the technical manual for**
   (a) The KTEA-3.
   (b) The WISC-V.
   (c) Both tests.
   (d) Neither test; more research is needed.

8. **Correlations of WIAT-III subtest and composite scores with KTEA-3 subtest and composite scores are found in the technical manual for**
   (a) The KTEA-3.
   (b) The WIAT-III.
   (c) Both tests.
   (d) Neither test; this is a weakness of both tests.

9. **Availability of alternate forms for retesting is a strength of**
   (a) The KTEA-3.
   (b) The WIAT-III.
   (c) Both tests.
   (d) Neither test.

10. **Separate subtest scores for sentence composition and essay composition is a strength of**
    (a) The KTEA-3.
    (b) The WIAT-III.
    (c) Both tests.
    (d) Neither test.

11. **Composite scores for Expression (oral and written) and for Comprehension (oral and written) are a strength of**
    (a) The KTEA-3.
    (b) The WIAT-III.
    (c) Both tests.
    (d) Neither test.

12. **Confidence bands for age-equivalent and grade-equivalent scores can be calculated, but are also directly available in tables in the technical manual of**
    (a) The KTEA-3.
    (b) The WIAT-III.
    (c) Both tests.
    (d) Neither test.

13. **A state-of-the-art norming sample is a strength of**
    (a) The KTEA-3.
    (b) The WIAT-III.
    (c) Both tests.
    (d) Neither test.

14. **A weakness is that oral language subtests have lower reliability than most other subtests on**
    (a) The KTEA-3.
    (b) The WIAT-III.
    (c) Both tests.
    (d) Neither test.

*Answers:* 1. a; 2. d; 3. f; 4. a; 5. c; 6. a; 7. b; 8. a; 9. a; 10. b; 11. a; 12. d; 13. c; 14. c.

# Six

# ILLUSTRATIVE CASE REPORTS

his chapter presents case studies of three students who were referred for psychoeducational evaluation. The first student, Jenna, age 9, was referred for a re-evaluation for attention, math, and reading comprehension and fluency difficulties. She was administered the WIAT–III and WISC-V, as well as measures of her neuropsychological and behavioral functioning. The second student, Oscar, age 11, was administered the KTEA-3 and WISC-V, as well as additional measures of language and processing abilities and behavioral functioning, to evaluate concerns regarding his attentional and emotional difficulties along with his oral language, reading, spelling, and written expression problems. The third student, Rob, age 15, demonstrated difficulties in the areas of academic fluency and visual motor integration. He was administered the KTEA-3 and KABC-II along with supplemental measures to assess his difficulties. A summary of the key attributes of these three case studies is provided in Table 6.1.

The goals of this chapter are to bring all other facets of this book together to demonstrate how the KTEA-3 and WIAT–III may be used as part of a comprehensive battery, and to demonstrate the cross-validation of hypotheses with behavioral observations, background information, and supplemental test scores. The basic outline for each report includes the following: reason for referral, background information, appearance of client and behavioral observations, tests administered, test results and interpretation, summary and diagnostic impression, and recommendations. All of the test data are presented in a psychometric summary at the end of each report.

As in all illustrative cases presented throughout this book, the personally identifying information of the clients have been changed to protect their confidentiality.

## CASE REPORT 1: JENNA

**Age at Evaluation:** 9 years, 1 month
**Grade:** 3
**Norms Reported:** Age-Based

**Table 6.1 Overview of Case Studies**

| | Referral Concern | Primary Achievement and Cognitive Ability Tests | Diagnoses |
|---|---|---|---|
| Case 1: Jenna, age 9 | Re-evaluation for Attention, Math, Reading | WIAT–III, WISC-V | ADHD Predominately Inattentive Type Specific Learning Disorder: Reading, Written Expression, and Mathematics Language Disorder |
| Case 2: Oscar, age 11 | Attention, Reading, Spelling, Writing | KTEA-3, WISC-V | Oral and Written Language Learning Disability Dysgraphia |
| Case 3: Rob, age 15 | Academic Fluency, Visual Motor Integration | KTEA-3, KABC-II | Specific Learning Disorder: Reading and Mathematics Dysgraphia |

## Reason for Evaluation

Jenna Bronson is a 9-year-old girl who lives with her parents and her 12-year-old brother. Jenna is entering the third grade at a special education school in a major metropolitan city. Jenna was tested by this examiner at age 6. The results of this prior evaluation indicated developmental reading disorder, mathematics disorder, and mixed receptive-expressive language disorder, along with possible attention-deficit/hyperactivity disorder (ADHD). Mr. and Mrs. Bronson requested this current evaluation in order to obtain an updated assessment of Jenna's neurocognitive and psychological functioning.

## Background Information

Jenna is the product of a high-risk pregnancy complicated by preeclampsia. Jenna was delivered at 34 weeks and she weighed 7 lbs. She remained in the NICU for 2 1/2 weeks due to breathing difficulties. All motor milestones were reached within appropriate limits. Surgeries and hospitalizations include ear tubes at age 2. Jenna's vision and hearing are described as intact.

She struggles with ongoing sensory integration issues, including sensitivity to sounds and food textures. Jenna is a picky eater who eats mainly carbohydrates. She was treated with occupational therapy and physical therapy from ages 3 to 6 to address these struggles. She also participated in speech therapy due to a lisp. Jenna evidenced a tic in the form of a head jerk last school year.

Jenna is a very athletic girl with a tall and skinny build who loves sports and is a gifted baseball player. She also excels in soccer and basketball. She falls asleep easily at night and sleeps well.

Regarding her academic history, Jenna evidenced difficulties with attention and response control at age 3 and difficulties with phonics at age 4. She struggled with increasing academic difficulties in kindergarten and was diagnosed with significant learning, language, and anxiety struggles, as well as possible attentional deficits. There is a maternal family history of ADHD, anxiety, and depression. Jenna began stimulant medication under the care of a psychiatrist in first grade, which was reported to be very beneficial.

At present, Jenna is described as having strong reading skills, particularly in terms of her recognition of sight words. Her reading comprehension is reportedly intact, although she does not read for pleasure. Jenna experiences great difficulty in math. She struggles with the concepts of time and money, and some visual-spatial difficulties are apparent in terms of lining up numbers and regrouping. Homework is a struggle for Jenna, especially her math worksheets. Mrs. Bronson noted that Jenna does not appear to recall the math lesson she has learned that same day. Jenna finds the timed computerized math exercises particularly frustrating and anxiety-provoking.

> ## DON'T FORGET
>
> Jenna's recent background indicates "strong" reading skills, which will be examined carefully in contrast to her previously diagnosed reading disorder.
>
> From a psychosocial perspective, Jenna is a sweet and happy girl who wants to please others and is highly cooperative. However, Mrs. Bronson is concerned about Jenna's high anxiety, as well as her self-esteem and attitude towards school. Jenna has no social struggles. She is well-liked by her peers and has good relationships with family members, although Mrs. Bronson reported that Jenna does not play well alone and spends too much time on electronics. In addition to sports, Jenna participates in Girl Scouts and regular playdates.

## Behavioral Observations

Jenna presented as a happy and friendly young girl. Her cute smile was contagious and rapport was very easily established. Jenna separated easily from her mother. She never complained about tasks, and for the most part, even when it was clear that Jenna was fatigued or challenged, she persevered. Jenna was a little reluctant to attempt more challenging math computation problems involving two-digit addition. However, with the promise that she would be able to choose one sports trading card for each problem she attempted, Jenna was a little more willing to persist with the task. Her mood and affect were normal although some tasks were somewhat frustrating for her. At no time was Jenna observed to be anxious or overtly upset by the testing.

Jenna was talkative, and no expressive or receptive language deficits were noted. Jenna's attentional stamina and endurance were somewhat poor for her age. Although she was alert both mornings as testing began, she became fatigued after working for a short period of time. Nonetheless, with support from the examiner, Jenna was able to work for at least an hour before needing a short break. Jenna was not observed to be restless or distractible. However, at times Jenna appeared to rush through tasks, and she was reminded to slow down and respond carefully. Her rushing was most evident on reading comprehension tasks.

Jenna took one or two breaks on each day of testing. During her breaks she played with Legos but refused snacks. She transitioned back to structured testing with no difficulty. Testing results, along with these behavioral observations, indicate that the test results appear to be valid measures of Jenna's current functioning.

> **DON'T FORGET**
> ........................................................
> Jenna's quick fatigue might be related to the symptoms of ADHD and difficulty with sustaining attention.

For this evaluation, Jenna was assessed without stimulant medication on the first day of testing but with stimulant medication (Focalin XR) on the second day to assess the effects of her medication on neurocognitive symptoms related to attention and learning.

### Assessment Procedures and Tests Administered

Clinical interviews with Mr. and Mrs. Bronson and Jenna Bronson
Exchange of information with Jenna's tutor and psychiatrist

*Intellectual Functioning and Executive Functions*
California Verbal Learning Test–Children Version (CVLT-C)
Comprehensive Test of Phonological Processing–Second Edition (CTOPP-2)
Integrated Visual & Auditory Continuous Performance Test (IVA+Plus CPT)
Medical Symptom Validity Test (MSVT)
NEPSY: A Developmental Neuropsychological Assessment–Second Edition (NEPSY-II), Selected Subtests
Test of Everyday Attention for Children (TEA-Ch), Selected Subtests
Wechsler Intelligence Scale for Children–Fifth Edition (WISC-V)
Wisconsin Card Sorting Test-64: Computer Version 2 (WCST-64)

> **DON'T FORGET**
> ........................................................
> With a wide variety of tests administered, it can be beneficial to the reader to organize them thematically (e.g., intellectual functioning, behavioral and socioemotional functioning, and so forth).

*Behavioral and Socioemotional Functioning*
Beck Youth Inventories–Second Edition (BYI-II)

Conners Comprehensive Behavior Rating Scales (Conners CBRS) Parent and
Teacher Forms
Kinetic Family Drawing
Millon Pre-Adolescent Clinical Inventory (M-PACI)
Achenbach Child Behavior Checklist (CBCL) and Teacher Report Form (TRF)
Behavior Rating Inventory of Executive Function (BRIEF): Parent Form

*Academic Achievement*
Kaufman Test of Educational Achievement–Third Edition (KTEA-3)

## Test Results

### Intellectual Functioning

In order to assess Jenna's intellectual and cognitive abilities, she was administered the
WISC-V. This test has six composite scores: Verbal Comprehension Index, Visual
Spatial Index, Fluid Reasoning Index, Working Memory Index, Processing Speed
Index, and Full Scale IQ. A score derived from a combination of subtest scores from
these composites is considered the most representative estimate of Jenna's global intellectual ability, which is in the Average to Low Average range when compared to
other children her age (Full Scale IQ/FSIQ = 88, 21st percentile). Jenna's general
intelligence can also be summarized by a score that is less impacted by working memory and processing speed, and in that case, her overall intellectual ability is in the
Average range and at the 30th percentile (General Ability Index/GAI = 92). The difference between these two scores representing her global ability indicates that Jenna's
cognitive proficiency, as measured by
working memory and processing speed,
led to a lower overall FSIQ. While the
FSIQ and GAI provide a broad representation of her cognitive functioning, a
description of Jenna's specific cognitive
abilities is provided below for a more
thorough understanding of her current
level of functioning.

## DON'T FORGET

A complete score report is given at the
end of the report in Tables 6.2–6.9, but
for the ease of reading, only key scores
are reported in the body of the report.

### Verbal Reasoning and Word Knowledge Abilities

Jenna's ability to access and apply acquired word knowledge was in the Average range.
Specifically, her ability to verbalize meaningful concepts, think about verbal information, and express herself using words was reflected in Jenna's performance on subtests
within the Verbal Comprehension Index (VCI), which was typical for her age and
emerged as a relative strength for Jenna (VCI = 100, 50th percentile). She performed
comparably across verbal reasoning and word knowledge tasks, indicating that these
abilities are similarly developed.

## Visual-Spatial Abilities

Similar to her average verbal reasoning and word knowledge, Jenna's ability to evaluate visual details and understand visual spatial relationships in order to construct geometric designs from a model were typical of a child her age. These tasks require visual spatial reasoning, integration and synthesis of part-whole relationships, attentiveness to visual detail, and visual-motor integration. During this evaluation, visual-spatial processing was one of Jenna's strengths, with performance in the Average range (Visual Spatial Index/VSI = 102, 55th percentile). Jenna showed Average to High Average performance when putting together geometric designs using a model. Her mental rotation skills and ability to understand part-whole relationships may be particularly strong when compared to her other abilities. However, Jenna had difficulty on a measure (on the NEPSY) of her visuoconstructional ability and visuomotor integration assessing her ability to reproduce simple abstract designs with paper and pencil.

## Reasoning Abilities

In contrast, Jenna's ability to detect the underlying conceptual relationship among visual objects and to use reasoning to identify and apply rules was in the Low Average range. Overall, Jenna's performance on tasks that required identification and application of conceptual relationships, inductive and quantitative reasoning, broad visual intelligence, simultaneous processing, and abstract thinking was slightly low for her age (Fluid Reasoning Index/FRI = 85, 16th percentile). Thus, she may experience some difficulty solving complex problems that require her to identify and apply rules. Her pattern of strengths and weaknesses suggests that she may currently experience relative difficulty applying logical reasoning skills to visual information, but she may have relatively strong ability to verbalize meaningful concepts.

## Memory Abilities

### Working Memory

Jenna evidenced impaired ability to register, maintain, and manipulate visual and auditory information in conscious awareness on the Working Memory Index (WMI). Working memory was one of Jenna's weakest areas of cognitive performance, with scores that were below most other children her age (WMI = 79, 8th percentile, Very Low range). Jenna showed significant difficulty recalling and sequencing series of pictures and lists of numbers. Her visual and auditory working memory appear to be similarly impaired.

To further understand how well she takes in, stores, and remembers information presented both visually and verbally, Jenna was administered tasks from the NEPSY. Some memory deficits were noted on both symptom validity tasks as well as structured memory tasks.

### Visual Memory

Jenna had no difficulty on a task assessing her encoding of facial features, as well as face discrimination and recognition, and she scored in the High Average to Superior range on this task (with stimulant medication). In contrast, on the same day of testing, Jenna's performances were very impaired on a test of spatial memory for novel visual material assessing both spatial recall and visual content recognition. Both her immediate recall and her delayed recall were weak on this task.

### Verbal Memory

Jenna struggled on a measure of narrative memory assessing her contextual verbal memory for organized verbal information (with stimulant medication). Her free recall, cued recall, and her recognition memory were all weak on this task. Without stimulant medication, Jenna was administered a measure of the strategies and processes involved in learning and recalling verbal material within the context of an everyday shopping task. On this task, Jenna's ability to repeat a list of words the first time she heard it indicates a Low Average initial attention span for auditory-verbal information. Similarly, on her fifth learning attempt, her performance was also Low Average. In addition, her total recall of the word list across the five learning trials was Low Average compared to others her age. After both a short delay and a longer delay, Jenna's recall of the list was Low Average. Category cueing helped Jenna about the same as others her age. Jenna's ability to discriminate between words that were on the list and those that were not was Low Average for her age. Jenna's ability to recognize information was about the same as her ability to recall it.

Taken together, these findings suggest that Jenna experienced difficulty in encoding verbal information and more complex visual information into memory.

### Processing Speed Abilities

Jenna's overall processing speed was low for her age on tasks that measured Jenna's speed and accuracy of visual identification, decision making, and decision implementation. Her ability to rapidly identify, register, and implement decisions about visual stimuli was in the Low Average Range (Processing Speed Index/PSI = 80, 9th percentile). It is important to note that Jenna's relatively slow processing speed may have inhibited her performance on tasks involving complex mental operations, such as verbal reasoning and visual spatial reasoning tasks. The PSI consists of two timed subtests, and performance across these tasks was similar, suggesting that Jenna's associative memory, graphomotor speed, and visual scanning ability are similarly developed.

### Sensory-Motor Functioning

Jenna is right-handed. On written tasks, her letters were clearly formed and she evidenced a mature pencil grip. Her simple and complex finger dexterity and motor speed was intact bilaterally. In contrast, Jenna had difficulty on a measure of rapid motor programming assessing her ability to learn and automatize a series of rhythmic movements. She clearly struggled with motor regulation on this task. In addition, her performance was mildly impaired on a measure of Jenna's graphomotor skills. She tended to work quickly but a little carelessly on this task when required to draw a line through a curved track.

### Attention and Executive Functions

Various subtests and rating scales were used to assess how well Jenna is able to plan, organize, change, and control her behavior. Although Jenna's sustained attention tended to be intact with stimulant medication, her executive functioning was variable.

With medication, Jenna struggled on a task assessing her ability to formulate basic concepts, to sort these objects into categories, and to shift set from one concept to another. This subtest is a measure of executive functioning assessing initiation, cognitive flexibility, and self-monitoring. Similarly, her nonverbal behavioral productivity was impaired on a measure of her ability to generate unique designs by connecting up to five dots, presented in two arrays: structured and random. In contrast, her verbal behavioral productivity was strong on a task assessing verbal fluency. Some difficulties were noted on a computerized assessment of her concept formation skills assessing her ability to form abstract concepts and to maintain set. Jenna did appear to benefit from computerized feedback indicating when her responses were incorrect; however, she struggled to generate alternate problem solving strategies, reflecting some deficits in concept formation.

> **DON'T FORGET**
> ...........................................................
> The results of this section highlight the effect of her stimulant medication on attention and inhibition since she was assessed both on and off medication.

On a measure of inhibition, Jenna's performance was variable on a task designed to assess the ability to inhibit automatic responses in favor of novel responses and the ability to switch between response types. Although Jenna struggled with response control difficulties on this task, intact cognitive flexibility was noted as well as overall good self-monitoring. She performed in the Low Average range on another task of inhibition that required Jenna to learn tones that allow progression (go) or required inhibition (no-go).

Jenna's auditory sustained attention was intact with stimulant medication. She had no difficulties on an auditory continuous performance task measuring selective and sustained attention, response inhibition, and executive functioning, and in fact Jenna evidenced High Average performance on the first part of this subtest that is designed to assess selective auditory attention and the ability to sustain it (i.e., vigilance). Her performance was intact on the second part of this subtest designed to assess the ability to shift and maintain a new and complex set involving both inhibition of previously learned responses and correctly responding to matching or contrasting stimuli. She also evidenced Average performance on a task requiring Jenna to listen to a recording of single-digit numbers and to respond with the number that precedes the occurrence of all specific double-digit stimulus presentations.

Without stimulant medication, Jenna's sustained attention and response control was further assessed by means of a computerized task that is intended to be mildly boring and demanding of sustained attention over a 13-minute period of time. Jenna did not validly respond to visual test stimuli. She may have been impaired in her ability to shift sets from the auditory to the visual modality and therefore her performance in the auditory domain only can be interpreted. In terms of her response control, Jenna's ability to inhibit responses to auditory stimuli was strong. This ability indicates that she is not likely to make careless errors to auditory stimuli and that she has the ability to stop and think rather than overreact when stressed in her daily life. If there are functional problems with inhibition or self-control with respect to auditory stimuli, causal emotional factors other than ADHD could be considered. Jenna had no deficits in her ability to be consistent in her responses to auditory stimuli. She is able to process new information in a reliable manner and "keep up the pace." She can usually ignore ordinary auditory distractions in the environment. Jenna's response time to auditory stimuli became faster over the course of the test. In a school setting, she is likely to be capable of meeting the demand to perform and to achieve goals in a timely manner unless other psychological or emotional factors are present that impair her functioning. Jenna is unlikely to exhibit problems with inappropriate off-task behavior in her home or school environment. She does not engage in fidgety or impulsive behaviors to any significant degree. She may be reasonably tolerant of "boring" tasks.

In contrast, Jenna showed some problems with her general auditory attentional functioning on the computerized task. At times she was inattentive to key auditory stimuli. Consequently, she is likely to demonstrate occasional problems in the school environment in maintaining her auditory attention and her efforts to listen. Environmental stressors and social distractors may exacerbate her auditory attentional problems at times. She may also have "good and bad days" with respect to her attentional abilities. Her ability to pay attention under low demand conditions to the auditory targets was moderately to severely impaired. In other words, she had significant problems remaining alert when the nontargets were prevalent. This dysfunction in auditory attention indicates that she is likely to "tune out" periodically when there is little demand to perform, unless she is actively engaged in the task at hand. Behavioral interventions need to be considered to keep her on task and better manage her problems sustaining attention. She was able to maintain her attention and remain alert under high demand conditions. Jenna did not show any problems with her overall auditory processing speed. Her recognition reaction time falls within the normal range.

Further measures of Jenna's attentional functioning were obtained by having Jenna's parents and teacher complete various rating scales. Jenna was rated by both her parents and her teacher as evidencing moderate to severe deficits in her attention, but somewhat less severe concerns were noted regarding her hyperactivity/impulsivity. Some significant executive functioning deficits were identified by her mother in terms of extreme problems with emotional control, moderate deficits with task initiation, working memory, and organization of materials, and only mild concerns regarding response inhibition and problems planning and organizing tasks.

## Oral Language Processing

### Phonological Processing

In order to assess her phonological processing, Jenna was administered measures of phonological awareness, phonological memory, and rapid naming. Phonological awareness refers to the ability to understand the sound structure of oral language.

For example, it includes a child's ability to understand that letters represent sounds, how sounds are blended, and how those sounds can build words. Phonological memory is the ability to hold a sound in one's short-term or working memory. Rapid naming measures one's ability to retrieve language information from long-term or permanent memory. Research indicates that these three kinds of phonological processing appear to be especially relevant for developing reading and writing skills.

In the area of phonological awareness, Jenna's overall score falls within the Poor range. Within this skill area, consistent difficulty was evident. Jenna evidenced Below Average performance when required to remove sounds from spoken words to form other words, such as removing the "b" from "bold" to say "old." Her performance was also Below Average on a subtest requiring her to combine sounds to form words, as in blending the sounds "c-oh-n" together to form the word "cone." More difficulty was noted on a task assessing Jenna's ability to identify target sounds in words (such as the second sound in the word "dog"), and she performed in the Poor range on this task.

In contrast to these difficulties, Jenna evidenced intact performance overall on tasks that assessed her ability to code information phonologically for temporary storage. However, some inter-subtest variability was observed. Jenna evidenced Low Average performance when asked to recall a series of numbers of varying length; however, she performed in the Average range when asked to repeat nonwords, such as "mistruf."

Jenna displayed Above Average ability in her efficient retrieval of phonological information from long-term memory. Efficiency and fluency allow the reading process to become automatic, which allows mental energy to be directed to the higher-level skill of comprehension. Her speed of naming letters and numbers was within the Average range.

### Oral Language

Jenna's oral language skills were assessed by means of the WIAT-III and one subtest from the NEPSY-II.

Jenna exhibited relatively strong oral vocabulary skills. On a measure of receptive vocabulary that required Jenna to point to the picture that best represented a given word/concept, Jenna scored in the Average range. Similarly, on a measure of expressive vocabulary that required Jenna to say the names of pictured concepts, Jenna also scored in the Average range.

Two measures of sentence and passage-level listening comprehension were administered. The first measure (NEPSY-II Comprehension of Instructions) required Jenna to respond to oral instructions of increasing complexity, and Jenna scored in the Average range. The second measure (WIAT-III Oral Discourse Comprehension) required Jenna to listen to an oral passage and then orally respond to literal and inferential comprehension questions that she read on her own. Her performance was Below Average on this task. To some degree, Jenna's difficulties on this listening task may be related to her difficulties with maintaining auditory attention and poor working memory. However, Jenna exhibits language comprehension weaknesses during listening as well as reading tasks, which suggest a broader language comprehension concern.

Jenna's oral expression abilities were assessed further with measures of verbal fluency and sentence repetition. A measure of oral word (verbal) fluency required Jenna to say things belonging to a given category by retrieving words from memory quickly and efficiently, and Jenna scored in the Very Superior range. A measure of sentence repetition required Jenna to listen to sentences of increasing length and complexity and repeat each one verbatim. Jenna scored in the Below Average range. Her errors on this task suggested weaknesses in grammar and auditory verbal working memory.

### Academic Skills
Jenna's academic skills were assessed by means of the WIAT–III, in the areas of reading, math, and writing.

### Reading
Jenna's overall reading skills measured in the Average range; however, variability was noted in her skills. Jenna's basic reading skills are relatively strong, but her reading comprehension and fluency skills are relatively weak. Her ability to read real words and to decode "fake" words were both in the Average range. However, Jenna evidenced difficulty in reading comprehension, scoring in the Below Average range. Jenna appeared to misunderstand details from the text, and she was somewhat careless in her response style. Her reading style was somewhat passive in that she did not appear to comprehend details as she was reading and she reread passages numerous times in order to answer questions. When asked to read grade-level passages aloud, Jenna evidenced Below Average performance in her reading fluency, rate, and accuracy. Her reading errors included omissions, additions, and substitutions.

> **DON'T FORGET**
>
> Information in the Background section highlighted her stronger reading skills, but the more sensitive tasks parsed out her areas of deficit.

### Mathematics
Jenna's math skills were estimated in the Low range overall. Her math problem solving performance was Below Average, and her math calculation skills were Low. In contrast, she performed in the Average range on timed tests of addition and subtraction math fluency, which required her to complete as many simple math problems as possible under a time limit.

### Spelling and Written Expression
Jenna evidenced Average performance on a measure of her spelling skills. However, Jenna exhibited significant weaknesses in specific areas of written expression. On a test of sentence composition that required her to combine sentences and then build sentences using a target word, Jenna scored in the Below Average range. She had particular difficulty writing grammatically correct sentences with target words. When asked to write a short essay, Jenna's word count and productivity was in the Average range, but her performance in the areas of theme development, text organization, and grammar and mechanics were in the Low to Below Average range.

## Psychosocial Functioning

Jenna evidenced a strong self-concept. Despite her history of anxiety, she did not report any serious struggles in this regard. She did indicate that she becomes worried when her teacher makes her finish a task at recess or after school, but no significant anxiety was noted. Likewise, her testing did not indicate a high level of depression or anger. Jenna values her relationships with others. She seeks out interesting peers and wants to be seen as socially appealing. She tends to deny troublesome emotions and she seeks harmony with others. Jenna attempts to restrain negative emotions and to avoid losing control. However, at times her need to maintain proper appearances may result in a rigid behavior pattern and conformity to the rules of others.

Jenna is strongly connected to her family and she spoke positively about her mother, father, and brother. On rating scales, Jenna was rated by her mother as evidencing mild internalizing concerns in terms of anxiety. Her teacher indicated no concerns. No other psychological struggles were noted.

### Neuropsychological Implications and Diagnostic Impressions

Jenna Bronson is a pleasant third-grade girl who is struggling with variable neurocognitive functions. Testing suggests that Jenna struggles to efficiently process information when involved in learning and problem solving. Her higher-order cognitive abilities like verbal reasoning and visual spatial skills appear to be a strength compared to abilities that facilitate cognitive processing efficiency, like speed of processing and certain parts of her memory. As a result, relative weaknesses in her mental control and her speed of visual scanning may sometimes create challenges as Jenna engages in more complex cognitive processes, such as learning new material or applying logical thinking skills. This is clearly evident on memory tasks and tasks of executive functioning.

Jenna continues to meet diagnostic criteria for ADHD. Although she does appear to benefit somewhat from stimulant medication in terms of improved sustained attention, Jenna's deficits in executive functioning, learning, inhibition, and nonverbal fluency are not impacted by medication. Clearly, Jenna is a hard-working child who wants to please, and it is a daily struggle for her to cope with these enduring deficits. Her parents, doctors, teachers, and tutors share in this struggle as they work to ease Jenna's difficulties with inconsistent results.

Jenna's academic functioning is highly variable and she continues to show some areas of serious impairment. Significant deficits are evident in Jenna's math computation and problem solving skills, reading and listening comprehension skills, reading fluency, and written expression. Jenna's phonological awareness was also observed as an area of weakness, although her basic reading and spelling skills are commensurate with her grade level peers. Jenna continues to meet diagnostic criteria for Language

Disorder with impairments in language comprehension, vocabulary, and grammatical knowledge.

Jenna has made great strides in her personal development over the past 2 1/2 years. She is no longer the highly anxious and unhappy child who was assessed by this examiner just over 2 years ago, and she presents as a more confident and content girl who is proud of her athletic endeavors. She does not evidence serious school avoidance, and she has managed to make some significant gains in her reading skills. Jenna's hard work in these areas is commendable.

Based upon these neuropsychological findings, the following diagnoses are made:

314.00 ADHD; Predominately Inattentive Type
**Specific Learning Disorder with impairments in**
315.1 Mathematics (Accurate calculation; Accurate math reasoning)
315.2 Written Expression (Grammar and punctuation; Clarity and organization)
315.0 Reading (Comprehension; Fluency)
315.39 Language Disorder

## Recommendations

### *Academic Interventions*

1. Ongoing placement at her elementary school is critical. At this stage it would be anticipated that this will continue to be an excellent placement for Jenna through middle school.
2. It is critical that Jenna has her full recess period and is not required to complete academic tasks during this time.
3. Thirty minutes of academic support after school would be beneficial should Jenna have difficulty completing her work during classtime.
4. In addition, sessions with her tutor should be scheduled at least twice a week, preferably during the school day to address Jenna's severe math difficulties.
5. Fifty percent extended time on standardized and class tests is critical.
6. Jenna will learn new information at a rate that is somewhat slower than other children her age, and may have particular difficulty with abstract thinking. Preteaching and reteaching lessons learned in school will give her additional exposure to new concepts and may facilitate her comprehension and recall of information. Due to deficits in auditory attention and listening comprehension, it may be helpful to present new content material in multiple modalities, using relatively simple vocabulary and sentence structure.
7. Encourage Jenna to subvocalize when working on visual tasks. Her verbal fluency skills are strong and might help her on these tasks.
8. Jenna may need more repetition of material to learn it. Care should be taken not to frustrate her by presenting too much information too quickly. She may

benefit from shorter periods of learning and longer breaks between periods of learning. Jenna would also likely benefit from memory training exercises designed to enhance her encoding skills.

9. Teach Jenna to chunk information and connect new information to concepts that she already knows (e.g., use preparatory sets).

10. Jenna likely has a relative strength in explaining concepts aloud, but may have more difficulty applying logical thinking to visual information. It may be beneficial for Jenna to talk herself through problems rather than attempting to solve them in her head. It may also be useful for her to leverage her verbal skills when attempting to memorize information.

11. Due to deficits in fluid reasoning, Jenna may benefit from structure and practice when approaching tasks that are challenging to her. Asking questions about stories or movies (What is the main idea? What might happen next?) can further build fluid reasoning skills. Reinforcing her ideas with positive feedback may encourage her to grow in this area.

12. Ongoing involvement in enjoyable extracurricular activities is critical in order to build Jenna's competency in a variety of arenas.

*Psychopharmacological Interventions*

13. Mr. and Mrs. Bronson are encouraged to discuss these test results with Jenna's psychiatrist in order to determine her ongoing course of treatment.

*Ongoing Monitoring of Jenna's Progress*

14. A re-evaluation of Jenna's neuropsychological functioning in fifth grade would likely be prudent.

Thank you for this opportunity to assess Jenna. It has been my pleasure to spend time with this engaging and interesting girl once again. Please let me know if I may be of any further assistance.

*Michelle Lurie, Psy.D.; ABPdN*
*Clinical Neuropsychologist*
*Diplomate of the American Board of Pediatric Neuropsychology*

## Psychometric Summary for Jenna

### Table 6.2 Medical Symptom Validity Test

| Paired Associates | Free Recall |
| --- | --- |
| Good effort; Normal range memory | Good effort; Poor memory |

**Table 6.3 Wechsler Intelligence Scale for Children–Fifth Edition (WISC-V)**

| Composite | Composite Score | Percentile Rank | 90% Confidence Interval | Qualitative Description |
|---|---|---|---|---|
| Verbal Comprehension (VCI) | 100 | 50 | 92–108 | Average |
| Visual Spatial (VSI) | 102 | 55 | 94–109 | Average |
| Fluid Reasoning (FRI) | 85 | 16 | 79–93 | Low Average |
| Working Memory (WMI) | 79 | 8 | 73–88 | Very Low |
| Processing Speed (PSI) | 80 | 9 | 73–91 | Low Average |
| Full Scale (FSIQ) | 88 | 21 | 83–94 | Low Average |

| Ancillary Composite | Index Score | Percentile Rank | 90% Confidence Interval | Qualitative Description |
|---|---|---|---|---|
| Quantitative Reasoning (QRI) | 82 | 12 | 77–89 | Low Average |
| Nonverbal (NVI) | 87 | 19 | 81–94 | Low Average |
| General Ability (GAI) | 92 | 30 | 87–98 | Average |
| Cognitive Proficiency (CPI) | 76 | 5 | 70–85 | Very Low |

| Verbal Comprehension Subtests | Scaled Score | Percentile Rank |
|---|---|---|
| Similarities | 11 | 63 |
| Vocabulary | 9 | 37 |

| Visual Spatial Subtests | Scaled Score | Percentile Rank |
|---|---|---|
| Block Design | 9 | 37 |
| Visual Puzzles | 12 | 75 |

| Fluid Reasoning Subtests | Scaled Score | Percentile Rank |
|---|---|---|
| Matrix Reasoning | 8 | 25 |
| Figure Weights | 7 | 16 |
| (Arithmetic) | 7 | 16 |

| Working Memory Subtests | Scaled Score | Percentile Rank |
|---|---|---|
| Digit Span | 7 | 16 |
| Picture Span | 6 | 9 |

| Processing Speed Subtests | Scaled Score | Percentile Rank |
|---|---|---|
| Coding | 8 | 25 |
| Symbol Search | 5 | 5 |

**Table 6.4 California Verbal Learning Test–Children's Version (CVLT-C)**

| Level of Recall | Standard Score |
|---|---|
| Trial 1 | −1 |
| Trial 5 | −1 |
| Trial 1–5 Total | T = 36 |
| Short Delay Free Recall | −1 |
| Short Delay Cued Recall | −1 |
| Long Delay Free Recall | −1 |
| Long Delay Cued Recall | −1.5 |

**Table 6.5 Test of Everyday Attention for Children (TEA-Ch)**

| Subtest | Scaled Score | Percentile Rank |
|---|---|---|
| Walk, Don't Walk | 7 | 16 |
| Code Transmission | 11 | 63 |

**Table 6.6 NEPSY: A Developmental Neuropsychological Assessment–Second Edition (NEPSY-II)**

| | Scaled Score | Percentile Rank |
|---|---|---|
| **Attention and Executive Functioning** | | |
| Animal Sorting | 7 | 16 |
| Auditory Attention | 13 | 84 |
| Response Set | 9 | 37 |
| Design Fluency | 3 | 1 |
| Inhibition–Inhibition | 7 | 16 |
| Inhbition–Switching | 13 | 84 |
| **Language** | | |
| Comprehension of Instructions | 11 | 63 |
| **Memory** | | |
| Memory for Designs | 4 | 2 |
| Memory for Designs Delayed | 5 | 5 |
| Memory for Faces | 13 | 84 |
| Memory for Faces Delayed | 15 | 95 |
| Narrative Memory Free and Cued | 5 | 5 |
| Narrative Memory Recognition | — | 6–10 |
| **Sensorimotor** | | |
| Fingertip Tapping–Repetitions | 9 | 37 |
| Fingertip Tapping–Sequences | 11 | 63 |
| Manual Motor Sequences | — | 3–10 |
| Visuomotor Precision | 8 | 25 |
| **Visuospatial Processing** | | |
| Design Copying | — | 6–10 |

**Table 6.7 Wisconsin Card Sort Test–64: Computer Version 2 (WCST-64)**

| WCST Scores | Standard Scores | Percentile |
|---|---|---|
| Perseverative Errors | 109 | 73 |
| Nonperseverative Errors | 80 | 9 |

**Table 6.8 Comprehensive Test of Phonological Processing–Second Edition (CTOPP-2)**

| Composite Scores | Standard Score | Percentile Rank |
|---|---|---|
| Phonological Awareness | 75 | 5 |
| Phonological Memory | 95 | 37 |
| Rapid Symbolic Naming | 110 | 86 |

| Subtests | Scaled Score | Percentile Rank |
|---|---|---|
| Elision | 7 | 16 |
| Blending Words | 7 | 16 |
| Phoneme Isolation | 4 | 2 |
| Memory for Digits | 8 | 25 |
| Nonword Repetition | 10 | 50 |
| Rapid Digit Naming | 12 | 75 |
| Rapid Letter Naming | 12 | 75 |

**Table 6.9 Wechsler Individual Achievement Test–Third Edition (WIAT-III)**

| | Standard Score (mean = 100) | Percentile Rank | Descriptive Category |
|---|---|---|---|
| Total Reading | 92 | 30 | Average |
| Basic Reading | 107 | 68 | Average |
| Word Reading | 108 | 70 | Average |
| Pseudoword Decoding | 107 | 68 | Average |
| Reading Comprehension & Fluency | 79 | 8 | Low |
| Reading Comprehension | 88 | 21 | Below Average |
| Oral Reading Fluency | 80 | 9 | Below Average |
| Oral Reading Accuracy | 80 | 13 | Below Average |
| Oral Reading Rate | 84 | 9 | Below Average |
| Mathematics | 79 | 8 | Low |
| Numerical Operations | 78 | 7 | Low |
| Math Problem Solving | 83 | 13 | Below Average |
| Math Fluency–Addition | 93 | 32 | Average |
| Math Fluency–Subtraction | 90 | 25 | Average |

(continued)

**Table 6.9** (Continued)

| | Standard Score (mean = 100) | Percentile Rank | Descriptive Category |
|---|---|---|---|
| Written Expression | 86 | 18 | Below Average |
| Spelling | 96 | 39 | Average |
| Sentence Composition | 82 | 12 | Below Average |
| Sentence Combining | 87 | 19 | Below Average |
| Sentence Building | 79 | 8 | Low |
| Essay Composition | 89 | 23 | Average |
| Word Count | 97 | 42 | Average |
| Theme Development and Text Organization | 80 | 9 | Below Average |
| Grammar and Mechanics | 79 | 8 | Low |
| Oral Language | 91 | 27 | Average |
| Listening Comprehension | 84 | 14 | Below Average |
| Receptive Vocabulary | 92 | 30 | Average |
| Oral Discourse Comprehension | 82 | 12 | Below Average |
| Oral Expression | 101 | 53 | Average |
| Expressive Vocabulary | 100 | 50 | Average |
| Oral Word Fluency | 134 | 99 | Very Superior |
| Sentence Repetition | 70 | 2 | Below Average |
| **Total Achievement** | 85 | 16 | Average |

## CASE REPORT 2: OSCAR

**Age:** 11 years, 5 months
**Grade:** 5
**Norms Reported:** Grade-Based for Achievement Scores, Age-Based for Cognitive Ability and Language Scores

### Reason for Evaluation

Oscar attends fifth grade at a public, suburban elementary school. He has received special education services under the eligibility criteria of Emotional Disability since second grade. Mrs. Drogan, Oscar's aunt and legal guardian, requested the evaluation to determine if Oscar has a learning disability and/or attention disorder, and to obtain recommendations for instructional approaches that will improve his reading and spelling.

### Background Information

Background information was obtained from interviews with Mrs. Drogan and his fourth-grade special education teacher, Mrs. Hawthorne.

## Family History

Oscar has been living with his aunt, uncle, and two cousins (ages 13 and 16) for the past 9 months and their family life is reported to be very happy and stable. Oscar and his family speak English only.

Oscar's biological mother passed away 3 years ago after a battling cancer for several years. Oscar's two younger brothers live nearby with their father, who is not Oscar's biological father. The identity of Oscar's biological father is unknown. Oscar has good relationships with his siblings, although they sometimes teased him because he is naïve and easily upset. After Oscar's mother passed away while he was in third grade, Oscar showed signs of anxiety and refused to go to school.

Oscar's mother had been diagnosed with a reading disability and also had difficulty with math. She earned an associate's degree and worked in the home. Oscar's half siblings have not experienced learning difficulties.

Mrs. Drogan describes Oscar as a sweet kid with a great laugh. He enjoys interacting with children and animals, being outdoors, and playing video games. Oscar seems to have good retention of information when he is paying attention, and he can explain things well. Science is a relative strength for him (when reading is not involved) and he enjoys doing science experiments at home. He has good social skills and makes friends with all types of people. Although he has good social skills, Mrs. Drogan reported that Oscar's thinking is very concrete and literal, so he often does not understand a joke or figure of speech. When this happens, he will ask for explanation. Oscar is compliant and wants to please others, sometimes to a fault. He tends to be naïve and will follow others or go along with the crowd.

## Medical/Developmental History

Oscar is small for his age in both height and weight, and Mrs. Drogan reported that he is a very picky eater. Oscar was the result of a full-term, healthy pregnancy and did not experience complications at birth, according to his aunt's report. Oscar met most developmental milestones as expected, although he was delayed in speech and language. Oscar was born with a congenital hearing defect in his left ear, which was diagnosed when he was a preschooler. Due to his hearing impairment, Oscar was a late talker and had speech delays. Mrs. Drogan reported that Oscar occasionally does not produce certain speech sounds clearly. He has very little hearing in his left ear, but he's learned to compensate in academic and social settings and his overall hearing is within normal limits. His vision is also reported to be within normal limits.

Oscar is physically healthy with no history of surgeries or significant injuries. Mrs. Drogan indicated that Oscar is accident prone and somewhat clumsy. Oscar's teachers report that he's fidgety and tends to be moving constantly. To diminish these behaviors during class, he has a "chewie" that he can hold or manipulate, which has been helpful. He is currently taking a low dose of Imipramine for anxiety and mood stability. Imipramine is a tricyclic antidepressant that is sometimes used off-label to treat attention disorders. Although Imipramine can have a sedative effect, Mrs. Drogan reported that Oscar does not seem drowsy. Oscar is typically exhausted by the end of the school day, but Mrs. Drogan does not attribute his exhaustion to the medication.

### Emotional and Social History

Oscar has a history of anxiety. In addition to refusing to attend school for a semester of fourth grade, he has refused to go on airplanes, ride in elevators, etc. Since he began living with the Drogan family, however, he has had excellent school attendance and no longer demonstrates anxious or avoidant behaviors. Mrs. Drogan described Oscar as fairly "even keel," although he does not like change. Oscar saw a therapist after his mother passed away, but he is not seeing a therapist at this time and he is reported to be emotionally stable. Mrs. Drogan cautioned that Oscar quickly learns how to get away with things and softly manipulate people, especially when work demands are placed on him. For example, he might suddenly report feeling sad or missing his mom to avoid schoolwork.

### Educational History

Mrs. Drogan does not have detailed information about Oscar's early academic performance, but she reported that reading difficulties were evident early on. Oscar repeated second grade because his reading skills were below grade level. He has qualified for special education services since second grade, which have provided behavioral and academic support as needed. In fourth grade, he incurred excessive absences after refusing to attend school for one semester, which caused him to fall further behind. He was tutored over the summer by his fourth-grade teacher.

Oscar is currently reading about one grade level behind, according to school records. Mrs. Drogan reported that Oscar has poor fluency and comprehension, and he often loses track of where he is on the page. He tends to guess at words or sometimes he will laboriously "sound it out." In other academic areas, Mrs. Drogan reported that Oscar needs improvement in handwriting, spelling/mechanics, and written expression. Writing by hand is not easy for him, so he writes as little as possible to get by. However, he types well and uses this accommodation at school for writing assignments. In math, he has difficulty with column alignment and word problems, but his conceptual and procedural knowledge are reportedly good. Keeping his schoolwork organized and remembering to bring things home are also challenging for him.

At school, Oscar receives in-class support and accommodations such as math visual aids, math word problems and reading comprehension questions read aloud, no penalty for spelling errors on most writing assignments, and a computer for typing essays. During testing, he receives extra time with items read aloud as requested by him. His grade averages include Bs and Cs. Oscar has an effective behavior plan in place, which provides supports such as redirection, prompts, and quiet time as needed. Oscar also receives prompts and frequent reminders to stay on task because he tends to be extremely distractible.

### Previous Test Results

On a behavior rating scale from 3 years ago, Oscar's behavior indicated clinically significant or at-risk levels of both internalizing and externalizing problems. His teacher last year witnessed very few "emotional breakdowns," but said Oscar distracted easily, needed excessive reassurance, and had difficulty organizing and finishing his work. Oscar did not meet fourth-grade standards or benchmarks on the statewide assessment for reading, writing, and math.

## Behavioral Observations

Oscar was dressed casually when he arrived for the test session. He had a friendly smile and made eye contact when introduced. Initially, Oscar was hesitant to speak at all. He responded as briefly as possible, with a voice as quiet as a whisper. His speech was difficult to understand at times because he spoke so quietly. He said his favorite part of school is recess, and his least favorite part is learning. Towards the second half of the test session, he began speaking comfortably and asking questions. Occasional grammatical errors were observed. Oscar was seated directly across from the examiner, which Mrs. Drogan indicated was an acceptable seating arrangement for his hearing impairment. He seemed to understand the examiner's instructions, though he occasionally asked for items to be repeated.

Oscar appreciated knowing how many things he would be asked to do and when his breaks would be. He counted the tasks and reminded the examiner of his progress. He did not seem particularly motivated by praise or success, and did not seem interested in whether his answers were right or wrong. However, he sustained motivation throughout the test session, knowing that his hard work would be rewarded with a new game when he got home. His attention waned frequently, but he reoriented to the task when prompted. Oscar was in motion throughout most of the testing, shifting in his seat, tapping a pencil on his head, biting his nails, or occasionally standing. The testing lasted about 4 hours, not including several short breaks and a 30-minute lunch break. During one cognitive ability subtest (Figure Weights, which has multiple choice responses), Oscar appeared to be guessing as he responded to the first few items quickly without much thought. As a result, the subtest ended quickly and he scored extremely low. His performance on this subtest was not consistent with his reasoning ability on other measures, so his low performance was attributed to insufficient effort. With the exception of this subtest, Oscar's levels of effort and motivation seemed adequate throughout the test session. Thus, these results are believed to provide a valid and reliable estimate of his current functioning.

> **DON'T FORGET**
>
> Most tests were administered on an iPad. Using the iPad for testing seemed to engage Oscar.

## ASSESSMENT PROCEDURES AND TESTS ADMINISTERED

Review of school records and sample of schoolwork

Interviews with Mrs. Drogan, Oscar Drogan, and Mrs. Hawthorne (SPED teacher)

Behavior Assessment Scale for Children–Third Edition (BASC-3) – Parent and Teacher Forms

Clinical Evaluation of Language Fundamentals–Fifth Edition (CELF–5)*

Kaufman Test of Educational Achievement–Third Edition (KTEA-3) Brief Form and Comprehensive Form*

Process Assessment of the Learner–Second Edition (PAL-II)

Wechsler Individual Achievement Test–Third Edition (WIAT–III): Selected Subtests

Wechsler Intelligence Scale for Children–Fifth Edition (WISC-V)*

*The CELF-5, KTEA-3, WIAT-III, and WISC-V were administered on Q-interactive with a touch tablet (iPad).*

> ### DON'T FORGET
> ............................................................
> Oscar was first administered subtests of the KTEA-3 Brief. Additional subtests from the KTEA-3 Comprehensive Form were subsequently added. A complete summary of scores is in Tables 6.10–6.24.

## Test Results

### Intellectual Functioning

Intellectual ability refers to an individual's overall capacity to reason, solve problems, and learn information in an efficient and timely manner. Oscar's intellectual functioning is made up of a profile of relative strengths and weaknesses, which provides far greater information than a single overall score. His profile of scores on the WISC-V suggests a level of aptitude in the normal range of cognitive ability.

Oscar's ability to apply and verbalize his word knowledge was in the Average range (Verbal Comprehension Index, 23rd percentile), a significant strength for Oscar. These tests included measures of verbal concept formation, categorical reasoning, and expressive vocabulary.

Oscar's visual-perceptual and visual-spatial skills are in the low average to average range (18th percentile). Oscar performed significantly lower on a task requiring visual-motor manipulation to copy designs with blocks (Block Design, 5th percentile) than a task requiring no visual-motor skill (Visual Puzzles, 50th percentile). His performance suggests that he may need support in developing his visual-motor skills to solve problems, but he does well in solving visual puzzles (without motor manipulation) and analyzing part-whole visual relationships.

Oscar's ability to reason about abstract and visual-conceptual relationships ranged from below average to the upper end of the average range (5th to 75th percentiles), depending on the task. Oscar's highest score on the WISC-V was a test of inductive and deductive reasoning and problem solving (Matrix Reasoning, 75th percentile). His lowest score on subtests assessing this domain was likely due to insufficient effort, and is not seen as a reflection of his true ability, as noted earlier (Figure Weights, 0.1 percentile). Although Oscar has strong nonverbal reasoning skills, he may need additional support and explicit strategy instruction—especially when a task involves novel concepts or when he perceives a task to be effortful or overwhelming.

> **DON'T FORGET**
> ·······················································
> The behaviors observed during Figure Weights administration were tied back into the interpretation of Fluid Reasoning subtests.

Oscar displayed impairment in his ability to hold and manipulate visual and auditory information in memory, scoring in the very low to low average range (4th percentile) on the Working Memory Index. This score is significantly weaker than his score on the Verbal Comprehension Index. Specifically, weaknesses were observed with auditory working memory for decontextualized information (digits) and visual nonverbal information (remembering pictures in order). He did not appear to use verbal mediation or any other strategy to help him on the working memory tasks.

Oscar also evidenced impairment in his ability to rapidly identify and respond to visual stimuli, scoring in the very low to low average range (4th percentile) on the Processing Speed Index. In the area of processing speed, Oscar scored very low on a task that required copying symbols quickly (Coding, 2nd percentile), suggesting a possible graphomotor weakness. He scored in the low average range on a visual matching task (Symbol Search, 16th percentile). On both measures, his performance was slow but accurate.

Oscar's performance on the Working Memory Index and the Processing Speed Index was significantly weaker than his score on the Verbal Comprehension Index. This pattern of performance indicates that his abilities to verbalize his word knowledge are more well developed than his abilities to process visual information quickly and to hold and manipulate visual and auditory information in memory.

### Academic Achievement
#### Reading
Reading skills include letter-sound correspondence (phonics), word recognition, decoding, fluency, and comprehension. Oscar's overall reading skills were estimated in the low average range, with skills ranging from below average to average.

Oscar showed relative strengths in phonological processing and decoding (21st and 25th percentiles, respectively). Phonological processing is the ability to isolate and manipulate the sounds within words, hold speech sounds in working memory to analyze or blend them together, and retrieve the sound of words from memory. Oscar performed well on blending, rhyming, sound matching, deleting sounds, and segmenting words into syllables, but had some difficulty segmenting longer words into phonemes—which places the highest demand on auditory working memory. Decoding is the ability to apply knowledge of letter-sound correspondences to read phonetically regular words and pseudowords.

His weakest skill was reading words in isolation (from a list), which was below average (6th to 8th percentile). In particular, Oscar struggled to read irregular words that do not follow consistent letter-sound correspondence. Oscar read words more accurately in context than in isolation, so he seems to benefit from contextual cues. On fourth-grade passages, Oscar's reading accuracy was in the average range (32nd percentile), but his reading rate and fluency were much lower (12th percentile). When asked to read fourth- and fifth-grade passages aloud, Oscar read slowly and haltingly with a monotonous quality. He gave very little attention to phrase boundaries or punctuation, and he did not attempt to resolve words or phrases that were nonsensical or ungrammatical.

His reading comprehension was estimated in the low average range (19th percentile) using texts appropriate for his reading level. His reading comprehension skills are certainly lower for grade-level passages due to the added difficulties of word recognition. Oscar had particular difficulty comprehending expository texts. However, Oscar's comprehension difficulties were not specific to reading. His reading comprehension and listening comprehension skills were highly similar, suggesting weak comprehension skills for both oral and written language.

## Mathematics

Oscar's math computation and arithmetic skills were estimated in the average range (32nd percentile), and his math problem-solving skills were in the low average range (14th percentile). In contrast to math computation, math problem solving places demands on language comprehension and also requires inhibition (the ability to suppress irrelevant information) and shifting (the ability to flexibly shift attention between tasks). His math problem-solving errors involved word problems, multistep problems, and time and money.

## Written Language

Oscar used an adaptive pencil grasp. He used incorrect letter formation for lowercase g, a, d, b, p, and q. His handwriting was mostly legible but generally poor. Writing fluency, the ability to write quickly and legibly, was difficult for Oscar. He was slow to write simple sentences (14th percentile) and copy a sentence (16th percentile). Oscar was slow in repeating a sequence of finger movements with either hand, suggesting low average ability to plan and execute serial finger maneuvers. Oscar avoids writing as much as possible and experiences writing fatigue after a short time. However, he enjoys drawing and his drawing and tracing skills seem age appropriate according to Mrs. Drogan.

Oscar showed considerably difficulty in the areas of spelling and written expression, scoring in the below average range (6th and 4th percentiles, respectively). His spelling errors reflected his relatively strong phonological awareness and weaker skills in orthography (memory for letter patterns) and morphology (knowledge of word structure). He usually represented all the sounds in the words but seemed to over-rely on phonology, rather than his memory for the correct spelling (e.g., "ledder" for letter). He correctly spelled common inflected endings (-s, -ed, -ing, -ly) but had difficulty with suffixes such as -al and -tion. Irregular words with unpredictable patterns were particularly difficult for him. Although Oscar has difficulty recalling the correct spelling of a word, he is quite good at recognizing the correct spelling of a word among misspelled alternatives. Hence, Oscar has word spellings stored in long-term memory, but these representations are "fuzzy" and not well developed.

On written expression tasks, Oscar wrote as little as possible. Spacing between words is inconsistent and his letters are not well positioned on the line. Oscar's writing errors indicate significant weaknesses in meeting task requirements, grammar and syntax, and capitalization.

## Cognitive Processes

### Auditory Processing

Auditory processes range from basic hearing and auditory perception to more integrated skills such as being able to understand directions. Oscar has limited hearing in his left ear, but his hearing in his right ear is within normal limits. He does not require a corrective hearing device. Oscar may have difficulty distinguishing and/or pronouncing certain speech sounds. Mrs. Drogan reported that Oscar sometimes pronounces certain words incorrectly, which were also observed during testing. For example, when Oscar was asked to repeat the word picnic, he responded "pignic." When prompted again, he was able to say picnic and hear the difference between picnic and pignic. Articulation and speech sound perception were not formally assessed as part of this evaluation.

### Oral Language

Oscar's performance across several oral language measures indicate that he is at-risk for a language disorder. His performance across these measures was fairly consistent, ranging from the 9th to 16th percentiles. When listening to passages, Oscar showed significant weakness in literal and inferential comprehension on both narrative and expository passages. When speaking, Oscar made grammatical errors that included incorrect pronouns, unclear referents, incorrect/nonspecific verbs, and subject-verb disagreement. When Oscar gave oral definitions of words or described how words were similar, sometimes his initial responses were vague or included details that were not pertinent, and it took him a few tries to give the correct response. He used nonspecific words like stuff. Oscar had particular difficulty using and understanding subordinating conjunctions, subordinate and relative clauses (complex sentence structures), and comparative terms. Oscar also has difficulty understanding jokes and figurative language, according to Mrs. Drogan. According to reports from Mrs. Drogan and Ms. Hawthorne, Oscar's functional communication skills are in the at-risk range.

### Visual Processing

Visual processes include visual acuity, basic visual perception, and visual-spatial recognition. Oscar has passed all his vision screenings at school, and no indications of vision difficulties were observed during testing. Oscar's performance on visual-spatial and visual-perceptual tasks were mixed with stronger performance on tasks that do not involve visual-motor manipulation.

*Fine and Gross Motor Functioning*

Motor functioning includes fine motor skills such as handwriting and tracing as well as gross motor skills such as balance, coordination, and gait. Mrs. Drogan reported that Oscar tends to be accident prone and clumsy. However, his clumsiness does not hinder his daily functioning and has not been observed by his teacher Ms. Hawthorne. Gross motor skills were not assessed as part of this evaluation.

*Behavioral and Social-Emotional Functioning*

Information about Oscar's behavior was gathered from Mr. and Mrs. Drogan, Oscar's guardians, and Ms. Hawthorne, Oscar's special education teacher from last year who provided in-class support for him. Oscar qualifies for special education services under the category of Emotional Disability. According to his guardians and teacher, Oscar can be anxious and very reserved in new situations and sometimes lies or deceives to avoid undesirable tasks. He has poor self-control and often acts without thinking. He can be pessimistic and irritable at times. He's not easily angered, but sometimes becomes upset or overly emotional. At home, he's often fearful. Over the last year, however, Oscar's teachers and guardians report that his emotional stability and anxious-avoidant behaviors have shown marked improvement. Both at home and school, Oscar exhibits strong social skills and gets along well with peers and adults. He also displays good coping skills and manages transitions well.

## Diagnostic Summary

Based on an evaluation of Oscar's history and background, guardian and teacher reports, school records, and test results, Oscar exhibits a pattern of strengths and weaknesses consistent with an oral and written language learning disability (OWL-LD) and dysgraphia. Oscar's behavior at school and at home indicates a high probability of attention-deficit/hyperactivity disorder (ADHD).

Oscar showed relative strengths in certain types of verbal and nonverbal reasoning, math computation, phonological awareness, and decoding. Oscar exhibited normative weaknesses in oral expression, listening comprehension, basic reading skill, reading fluency skills, reading comprehension, written expression, writing fluency, and handwriting. Processing weaknesses were identified in visual-motor skills, auditory and visual working memory, and processing speed. His most significant impairments involve language comprehension, grammar, reading fluency, spelling, and written expression (productivity, grammar, mechanics). Oscar's impairments are not better explained by a visual, hearing, or motor disability, intellectual disability, emotional disturbance, cultural factors, environmental or economic disadvantage, limited English proficiency, or a lack of appropriate instruction. Oscar's congenital hearing defect in one ear, his excessive absences from school last year, and his symptoms of emotional disturbance are not sufficient to explain the profile of academic strengths and weaknesses observed.

Oscar's cognitive and learning profile is consistent with OWL-LD, which is also known as a language processing disorder or language learning disability. Oscar's profile is not characteristic of dyslexia, which is typically characterized by core deficits in phonological awareness and decoding with adequate listening comprehension and grammar skills. Characteristics of OWL-LD include the following:

- Low oral reading and spelling with similarly low FSIQ (no discrepancy)
- Impaired morphological and syntactic awareness and often word retrieval
- Impaired working memory
- Relative strength in nonword reading/decoding but persisting impairments in comprehension and real word reading
- Difficulty understanding jokes and figurative language

Using the Diagnostic and Statistical Manual of Mental Disorders (DSM-V), the following diagnoses are well supported:

*Specific Learning Disorder with impairments in*
315.0 Reading (reading accuracy, fluency, and comprehension)
315.2 Written Expression (spelling accuracy, grammar, and punctuation, and clarity/organization of written expression)
315.39 Language Disorder

Oscar also exhibits a profile that is consistent with dysgraphia. Characteristics of dysgraphia include the following:

- Handwriting and spelling problems despite normal motor function
- Poor positioning of letters on the line and spacing of letters and words
- Poor and inconsistent letter formation
- Poor fluency in writing legible letters and copying
- Impaired orthographic coding and the orthographic loop of working memory
- Errors in math-related writing such as alignment and placement of numerals during computation
- Difficulty with finger sequencing/succession

> **DON'T FORGET**
>
> Because many parents (as well as other readers) may not be familiar with the term "dysgraphia," a description of the disorder was provided here.

Follow up testing with a speech and language pathologist and audiologist is recommended to provide more in-depth information about Oscar's articulation and speech sound perception abilities. In addition, further evaluation by a psychiatrist or pediatrician is recommended to provide additional treatment recommendations for ADHD.

## DON'T FORGET

Organizing the Recommendations section thematically by each of the domains that need remediation can be helpful for teams that are utilizing the information in the report for program planning or IEPs.

## Recommendations

On the basis of these findings, the following recommendations are made:

*Language and Literacy*

When teaching Oscar to read and spell new words, incorporate all five language blocks of word study: phonological awareness, orthographic knowledge, semantic and vocabulary knowledge, morphological knowledge, and mental orthographic images.

Plan complementary oral and written expression instruction to improve subject-verb agreement, pronoun and verb usage, and sentence structure.

Plan complementary reading and spelling instruction. Avoid using graded spelling lists that may include words above Oscar's reading level.

*Morphological Analysis (for reading and spelling)*

Improve Oscar's ability to recognize meaningful units of words, including (-an, -og), roots (aqua, gen), and affixes (-ed, pre-).

Study groups of derived words together (e.g., magic, magical, magically, magician) and words that share a common feature (e.g., librarian, politician, musician).

Study the ways in which adding derivational suffixes changes the pronunciation and/or syllable stress of the word.

*Reading Fluency*

Always emphasize accuracy and careful reading over speed. Discourage Oscar's tendency to "guess and go" while reading.

Improve reading fluency at the level of the word, phrase, sentence, and passage.

Practice reading new or challenging words in isolation prior to reading them in text.

Orally read "phrase cards" and track the time needed to read them accurately.

Neurological impress method: Paired reading where the student and an adult read the same text almost simultaneously.

*Listening and Reading Comprehension*

Simplify the language of instruction and allow Oscar extra time to process language.

Use visual supports and graphic organizers to support comprehension when listening and reading.

Prepare Oscar to listen or read. Give text previews. Prime background knowledge.
Teach self-monitoring strategies (summarize, paraphrase, question) and fix-up
strategies (reread, read aloud, question, ask for repetition).

*Writing*
Teach handwriting and letter formation skills to improve Oscar's writing fluency.
Keyboarding is an important skill, but should not replace handwriting alto-
gether. Encourage proper letter formation and work on speed only when letter
formation is well established and legible.
Provide an authentic context for communication. Write for a purpose and an
audience.
Use story starters and graphic organizers.
Provide instruction to strengthen both oral expression and written expression.
Strengthen grammatical knowledge (in speaking and writing). Ask Oscar to
recognize structurally correct sentences, build sentences with word cards,
and formulate sentences that follow a particular structure.

*Spelling*
Traditional spelling lists/tests are not likely to improve Oscar's spelling skills.
Provide spelling instruction that proceeds from recognition to partial recall
to full recall. For recognition, Oscar would circle/point to the correct spelling
among distractors. For partial recall, he spells words by filling in the missing
letters (e.g., b _ nd). Begin with only one or two missing letters, working up
to filling in all the blanks.
Teach explicit spelling strategies. Oscar can recognize the correct spelling of a
word, but he does not seem to use this knowledge as a strategy for spelling.
Teach Oscar to generate alternative spellings for words that are difficult for him
to spell (or whenever he spells a word that "doesn't look right"). This strategy
allows him to utilize his strength in recognition spelling.
Look-say-cover-write-check. Look carefully at the word you're trying to spell
and notice the parts of the word that are tricky. Say the word as you're
looking at it. Cover it up, and write the word as you say it. Finally,
uncover the word and check your spelling as you say the word again.
Repeat as needed.
Encourage morphological analysis and spelling by analogy as strategies for
spelling.

*Attention and Working Memory*
Discuss the option of an FM system with Oscar and his IEP team. Oscar is
extremely exhausted every day after school and he may be experiencing
auditory fatigue as a result of his hearing loss in one ear. An FM system
may reduce auditory fatigue and improve his attention during class.

Provide cues to signal off-task behavior and improve Oscar's self-awareness. Consider nonverbal cues (such as tapping a finger on the reminder card on his desk).

Use memory aids (e.g., pictorial graphic organizers) as a reminder of the instructions or to guide the completion of an activity.

Use preparatory sets to build background knowledge about a particular topic, focus attention on particular themes or words, and provide an expectation of what to look for or listen to in any new material.

## Resources

Examples of programs and resources to consider:

Process Assessment of the Learner (PAL) Research-Based Reading and Writing Lessons (www.pearsonclinical.com)

RAVE-O (www.voyagersopris.com)

Seeing Stars® Program for Reading Fluency and Spelling (www.lindamoodbell.com)

SPELL-Links to Reading and Writing (www.learningbydesign.com)

Berninger, V. W., & Wolf, B. J. (2016). *Teaching students with dyslexia, dysgraphia, OWL LD, and dyscalculia* (2nd ed). Baltimore, MD: Brookes.

Words: Integrated Decoding and Spelling Instruction Based on Word Origin and Word Structure–Second Edition (www.proedinc.com)

*Disclaimer: The examiner receives no royalties or compensation and has no significant financial interest in any of the products or programs recommended.*

*Reference for characteristics of dyslexia, dysgraphia, and OWL-LD:*

Berninger, V. W. (2009). Highlights of programmatic, interdisciplinary research on writing. *Learning Disabilities Research & Practice: A Publication of the Division for Learning Disabilities, Council for Exceptional Children, 24*(2), 69–80.

*Resource for further information about OWL-LD/Language Processing Disorder:*

Learning Disabilities Association of America: http://ldaamerica.org/

> ## DON'T FORGET
> ...........................................
> Not all reports will have a "Resources" section, but in Oscar's case the examiner determined that both his educational team and his parents would benefit from having some specific resources clearly laid out.
>
> *Kristina C. Breaux, PhD*

## Psychometric Summary for Oscar

### Table 6.10 WISC-V**

| Scale/Index<br>Subtest | Standard<br>Score | (90% Confidence<br>Interval) | Percentile<br>Rank | Qualitative Descriptor |
|---|---|---|---|---|
| Verbal Comprehension | 89 | (83–96) | 23 | Low Average to Average |
| Similarities | 8 | | 25 | |
| Vocabulary | 8 | | 25 | |
| Visual Spatial | 86* | (81–94) | 18 | Low Average to Average |
| Block Design | 5 | | 5 | |
| Visual Puzzles | 10 | | 50 | |
| Fluid Reasoning | 79** | (74–87) | 8 | Very Low to Low Average |
| Matrix Reasoning | 12 | | 75 | |
| Figure Weights | 1 | Insufficient effort | 0.1 | |
| (Picture Concepts) | 5 | Substitute for FW<br>in FSIQ | 5 | |
| Working Memory | 74 | (70–83) | 4 | Very Low to Low Average |
| Digit Span | 6 | | 9 | |
| Picture Span | 5 | | 5 | |
| Processing Speed | 75 | (70–86) | 5 | Very Low to Low Average |
| Coding | 4 | | 2 | |
| Symbol Search | 7 | | 16 | |
| Full Scale IQ | 77 | (73–83) | 6 | Very Low to Low Average |

*Note:* WISC-V Index standard scores have a mean of 100 and a standard deviation of 15, and the subtest standard scores have a mean of 10 and standard deviation of 10.
*Nonunitary composite score.
**The WISC-V was administered on Q-interactive with a touch tablet (iPad).

### Table 6.11 Index Level Strengths and Weaknesses

| Index | Score | Strength or Weakness (p < .05) | Base Rate |
|---|---|---|---|
| VCI | 89 | S | < = 15% |

Comparison score is the FSIQ. Base rates are reported by ability level.

### Table 6.12 Index Level Pairwise Difference Comparisons

| Index Comparison | Score 1 | Score 2 | Difference | Critical<br>Value | Significant<br>Difference<br>(p < .05) | Base Rate |
|---|---|---|---|---|---|---|
| VCI–WMI | 89 | 74 | 15 | 12.46 | Y | 9.7% |
| VCI–PSI | 89 | 75 | 14 | 13.79 | Y | 10.8% |

Base rates are reported by ability level.

**Table 6.13 Subtest Level Strengths and Weaknesses**

| Subtest | Score | Strength or Weakness | Base Rate |
|---------|-------|---------------------|-----------|
| MR | 12 | S | < = 2% |

**Table 6.14 Subtest Level Pairwise Difference Comparisons**

| Subtest Comparison | Score 1 | Score 2 | Difference | Critical Value | Significant Difference (p < .05) | Base Rate |
|--------------------|---------|---------|------------|----------------|----------------------------------|-----------|
| BD–VP | 5 | 10 | −5 | 3.04 | Y | 4.6% |

| Process Score | | Scaled Score |
|---------------|------|--------------|
| Block Design No Time Bonus | BDn | 6 |
| Digit Span Forward | DSf | 7 |
| Digit Span Backward | DSb | 9 |
| Digit Span Sequencing | DSs | 5 |

**Table 6.15 Process Level Pairwise Difference Comparisons**

| Process Score Comparison | Score 1 | Score 2 | Difference | Critical Value | Significant Difference (p < .05) | Base Rate |
|--------------------------|---------|---------|------------|----------------|----------------------------------|-----------|
| DSb–DSs | 9 | 5 | 4 | 3.66 | Y | 11.5% |

**Table 6.16 KTEA-3 Brief: Grade Norms**

| Subtest/Composite | Standard Score (90% CI) | Percentile Rank | Qualitative Descriptor |
|-------------------|-------------------------|-----------------|------------------------|
| Letter & Word Identification | 79 (74–84) | 8 | Below Average |
| Reading Comprehension | 87 (77–97) | 19 | Low Average |
| **Reading** | **81 (74–88)** | **10** | **Low Average** |
| Math Concepts and Application | 84 (79–89) | 14 | Low Average |
| Math Computation | 93 (88–98) | 32 | Average |
| **Mathematics** | **86 (82–90)** | **18** | **Low Average** |
| Written Expression | 74 (66–82) | 4 | Below Average |
| Spelling | 77 (71–83) | 6 | Below Average |
| **Written Language** | **75 (69–81)** | **5** | **Below Average** |
| **Academic Skills Battery** | **78 (74–82)** | **7** | **Below Average** |

**Table 6.17  KTEA-3 Comprehensive: Grade Norms**

| Subtest/Composite | Standard Score (90% CI) | Percentile Rank | Qualitative Descriptor |
|---|---|---|---|
| Phonological Processing | 88 (81–95) | 21 | Low Average |
| Nonsense Word Decoding | 90 (84–96) | 25 | Average |
| Word Recognition Fluency | 77 (66–88) | 6 | Below Average |
| Writing Fluency | 84 (73–95) | 14 | Low Average |
| Listening Comprehension | 83 (73–93) | 13 | Low Average |
| **Sound-Symbol** | **86 (81–91)** | **18** | **Low Average** |
| **Decoding** | **83 (79–87)** | **13** | **Low Average** |
| **Comprehension** | **83 (75–91)** | **13** | **Low Average** |

*Note:* The KTEA-3 was administered on Q-interactive with a touch tablet (iPad).

**Table 6.18  KTEA-3 Error Analysis: Phonological Processing**

| Error Category | Items Attempted | Average # of Errors | Student's # of Errors | Skill Status |
|---|---|---|---|---|
| Blending | 10 | 0–2 | 2 | Average |
| Rhyming | 8 | 0–1 | 0 | Average |
| Sound Matching | 6 | 0–1 | 1 | Average |
| Deleting | 6 | 0–1 | 1 | Average |
| Segmenting | 10 | 0–2 | 3 | Weak |

**Table 6.19  KTEA-3 Error Analysis: Listening Comprehension**

| Error Category | Items Attempted | Average # of Errors | Student's # of Errors | Skill Status |
|---|---|---|---|---|
| Literal Comprehension | 12 | 2–4 | 8 | Weak |
| Inferential Comprehension | 9 | 2–4 | 6 | Weak |
| Narrative Comprehension | 10 | 1–3 | 7 | Weak |
| Expository Comprehension | 11 | 2–5 | 7 | Weak |

**Table 6.20  KTEA-3 Error Analysis: Reading Comprehension**

| Error Category | Items Attempted | Average # of Errors | Student's # of Errors | Skill Status (N/A for out of level item set) |
|---|---|---|---|---|
| Literal Comprehension | 22 | N/A | 4 | N/A |
| Inferential Comprehension | 9 | N/A | 1 | N/A |
| Narrative Comprehension | 16 | N/A | 0 | N/A |
| Expository Comprehension | 15 | N/A | 5 | N/A |

**Table 6.21  KTEA-3 Error Analysis: Written Expression**

| Error Category | Items Attempted | Average # of Errors | Student's # of Errors | Skill Status |
|---|---|---|---|---|
| Task | 6 | 0–2 | 3 | Weak |
| Structure | 8 | 2–4 | 5 | Weak |
| Word Form | 8 | 0–2 | 4 | Weak |
| Capitalization | 14 | 3–7 | 10 | Weak |
| Punctuation | 24 | 9–14 | 13 | Average |

**Table 6.22  WIAT–III: Grade Norms**

| Subtest | Standard Score (90% CI) | Qualitative Descriptor |
|---|---|---|
| Oral Reading Fluency (Grade 4 item set) | 82 (75–89) | Low Average |
| Oral Reading Fluency Accuracy | 93 (83–103) | Average |
| Oral Reading Fluency Rate | 82 (75–89) | Low Average |

**Table 6.23  PAL-II: Grade Norms**

| Subtest | Scaled Score (90% CI) | Qualitative Descriptor |
|---|---|---|
| Finger Succession—Dominant Hand | 6 | Low Average |
| Finger Succession—Nondominant Hand | 6 | Low Average |
| Word Choice—Accuracy | 8 | Average |
| Word Choice—Fluency | 7 | Low Average |
| Alphabet Writing—Legible at 15 seconds | 11 | Average |
| Alphabet Writing—Legible Letter Writing | 6 | Low Average |
| Alphabet Writing—Total Time | 10 | Average |
| Sentence Copying—Legible at 15 seconds | 8 | Average |
| Sentence Copying—Legible Letter Writing | 13 | High Average |
| Sentence Copying—Total Time | 7 | Low Average |

**Table 6.24  CELF–5**

| Subtest/Composite | Scaled Score (90% CI) | Qualitative Descriptor |
|---|---|---|
| Word Classes | 6 (4–8) | Low |
| Formulated Sentences | 7 (5–9) | At Risk |
| Recalling Sentences | 7 (6–8) | At Risk |
| Semantic Relationships | 7 (6–8) | At Risk |
| **Core Language** | **81 (76–86)** | At Risk |

*Note:* The CELF–5 was administered on Q-interactive with a touch tablet (iPad).

## CASE REPORT 3: ROB

**Age at Evaluation:** 15 years, 9 months
**Grade:** 10
**Norms Reported:** Grade-Based for Achievement Scores, Age-Based for Cognitive Ability and Behavior Scores

### Purpose of the Evaluation

Rob is struggling to complete exams in school and he was unable to complete the PSAT in the standard allotted time. Rob has always taken longer to process information than others his age, especially when presented verbally (such as lectures), and when completing exams and homework. He had a previous psychoeducational evaluation by his school district after which he received accommodations through a 504 Plan. He needs an updated evaluation to qualify for accommodations through the school and for college boards.

### History and Background

Rob's mother, Ms. Abby Long, provided the following background information. Rob lives with both parents, Abby and Martin Long, his two younger sisters (ages 10 and 12), and his paternal grandmother. The primary language spoken at home is English. His grandmother also speaks Spanish in the home. There is a family history of autism in twin cousins. No other learning, speech or developmental problems were noted in Rob's family.

Rob's medical history is fairly unremarkable. He was born full-term, weighing 8 pounds 3 ounces. Rob's mother reported that he met early motor and language developmental milestones within a normal timeframe. He has not had any serious illnesses, injuries or hospitalizations and is not currently taking any medication. He had his most recent physical a year ago. His mother noted that due to his homework, he does not sleep much. During the week, he typically goes to sleep at 10 p.m. and wakes up at 4 a.m. to finish schoolwork. He sleeps in a little more on weekends, and typically sleeps 7 to 8 hours a night during the summer.

Rob's academic history began when he entered preschool at age 3, where he attended three days a week. He entered kindergarten at 5 years old, and did fine in school throughout his elementary school years. He consistently performed well on standardized state testing as well. Beginning in second grade, however, he had increasing difficulty completing tasks in a timely manner. In seventh grade, Rob was referred for psychoeducational evaluation by his school because he was taking an abnormally long time to complete classwork, and he had difficulty showing the steps involved in math reasoning. Results of the evaluation indicated that poor visual motor integration was impacting his ability to work rapidly and copy information. His overall cognitive abilities and academic achievement were all within the average to above average range. He was not eligible for special education; however, a 504 Plan for accommodations was put into place that allowed Rob extra time to complete assignments and tests, provided a peer note taker when the teacher was lecturing, provided Rob with a paper copy of PowerPoint presentations to use during lectures, and provided a small group format for state testing. During middle school, with these accommodations in place, Rob earned all As.

Currently, Rob is in his sophomore year of high school. His mother noted that he has an excellent work ethic, spending extra time to study and understand the material well. His teachers are no longer willing to provide additional time without a written plan for accommodations. Moreover, Ms. Long said that Rob has been stressed about not being able to finish his tests on time. She said that when he rushes, he makes careless errors because he does not have time to check his work. His mother mentioned that Rob not only struggles with finishing timed tasks, but he also struggles with processing too much information at one time (e.g., multistep directions, lectures in which the teacher says a lot at once).

Rob recently took the PSAT and he was not allowed extra time to complete the exam. He reportedly did well on the math that he finished, but he did not finish either the reading or math sections in the time given.

Socially, Rob's parents reported that he gets along well with his peers at school. He is on the school's tennis team. When not in school, his mother said he likes to play video games, write stories, and watch movies.

## Behavioral Observations

Rob presented as a tall, slim, well-groomed adolescent boy with short brown hair and brown eyes. He was dressed casually and appropriately for each testing session. Throughout the evaluation, Rob was kind, made good eye contact, and showed good social skills, answering the examiner's questions, elaborating appropriately in conversation, and telling the examiner relevant stories or information. Thus, rapport was easily established. Rob was always cooperative and appeared to try his best on all tasks. He willingly participated in all activities, even refusing breaks. Furthermore, he was polite and helpful, helping to clean up some of the testing material in between items.

**DON'T FORGET**

..............................................

Rob's request for repetition is consistent with background information noting that Rob has difficulty when too much information is presented at once.

Rob appeared motivated to perform well. He asked for clarification with many verbal directions, wanting to make sure he understood what to do and that he was following directions. For longer questions that were presented verbally, he frequently asked for repetition, suggesting some difficulty with spoken instructions.

Rob's approach to most problems was slow and methodical. He rarely responded quickly or impulsively, taking his time before answering and often taking quite a long time to solve problems. Even when the examiner told him she would be keeping track of how long it took him, Rob did not work quickly. He appeared more interested in focusing on accuracy than on speed. The exception was on a task in which he was told to work quickly and if the examiner asked him what his answer was, he was to tell her. On this task, he answered quickly, appearing to not want to run out of time to respond.

Even though Rob worked very slowly on many tasks, he did not appear to struggle, except on tasks that required handwriting or paper and pencil copying tasks. On these tasks, he frequently erased, made letters and numbers that were difficult to read, and had poor spacing on the line or page.

> **DON'T FORGET**
>
> A key part of this section of the report links the behaviors observed to the referral concerns regarding Rob's inability to work quickly.

Rob did not show any obvious signs of inattention or difficulties with sustaining his focus. In fact, he demonstrated good attention and concentration. No fidgety behaviors or extraneous motor movements were observed.

Given that Rob appeared motivated to do well and showed good attention and concentration, this evaluation is deemed a valid estimate of his current cognitive and academic abilities.

## ASSESSMENT PROCEDURES AND TESTS ADMINISTERED

Clinical interview with mother
Review of records
Behavior Assessment System for Children–Second Edition Parent Rating Scales–Adolescent (BASC-2, PRS-A)
Behavior Rating Inventory of Executive Function, Parent Form (BRIEF)
Kaufman Assessment Battery for Children–Second Edition (KABC-II)
Kaufman Test of Educational Achievement–Third Edition (KTEA-III)
Nelson Denny Reading Test
Wechsler Intelligence Scale for Children–Fifth Edition (WISC-V)—selected subtests (a summary of all test scores is provided in Tables 6.25–6.29)

### Results

#### Cognitive Abilities
Rob was administered the KABC-II to obtain a comprehensive picture of his mental processing and cognitive abilities. The KABC-II offers five scales:

1. Sequential/*Gsm* (short-term memory)
2. Simultaneous/*Gv* (visual processing)
3. Learning/*Glr* (long-term storage and retrieval)

4. Planning/ $Gf$ (fluid reasoning)
5. Knowledge/ $Gc$ (crystallized ability)

These five scales can be interpreted from two different perspectives: (1) a neuropsychological theory that focuses on attention, coding and storing information, and planning behavior (while de-emphasizing acquired knowledge), or (2) from the perspective of a data-driven (CHC) theory that divides abilities into those specific cognitive abilities listed parenthetically above.

In Rob's case, his cognitive abilities were interpreted from the perspective of the data-driven theory because his primary language is English, and the fact that his referral reason was to diagnose any processing or learning disability. Using this interpretive perspective, Rob's global measure of general cognitive ability was assessed by a combination of all five of the scales.

Rob's overall mental processing ability was in the Average range, as he earned a KABC-II Fluid Crystallized Index (FCI) of 107, ranking him at the 68th percentile. The chances are 90% that his true FCI is between 103 and 111. However, looking closely at Rob's skills revealed that his overall ability was just an average of highly discrepant skills and not a meaningful measure of Rob's global abilities. Specifically, Rob demonstrated a 41-point difference between his lowest and highest index scores, which is variability of large magnitude. Therefore, it is more meaningful to examine his performance on the separate indexes to gain a better understanding of his cognitive strengths and weaknesses.

Rob's short-term memory and his long-term storage and retrieval abilities are in the Average range compared to others his age. His skills were evident on his performance on two scale indexes: He earned a standard score of 91 on the Sequential/ $Gsm$ Index (27th percentile), and a standard score of 94 on the Learning/ $Glr$ Index (30th percentile). Although Rob's abilities are in the Average range, indicating that his short-term memory abilities and his associative memory abilities are all comparable to others his age, these skills are areas of relative weakness for him. Rob's short-term memory skills were shown on two tasks: (1) a task in which Rob was to repeat numbers presented verbally; and (2) a task in which he touched a series of silhouettes of common objects in the same order as the examiner said the names of the objects. His long-term memory ability was tapped in a task (Atlantis) that required him to learn nonsense names assigned to pictures of fish, plants, and shells, and a subtest (Rebus) requiring him to learn a new language, namely to associate new visual symbols with familiar words and to read sentences composed of these symbols. Even though Rob performed in the average range, he had some difficulty initially learning the material. However, the tasks provided repeated exposure. One task gave corrective feedback and the other enabled him to use context to help him. However, if he did not respond within 5 seconds, the examiner either told him to skip it or told him the answer. Thus, he was penalized for slower respond- ing. Overall, Rob's memory abilities were a personal weakness for him, even though they are still average compared to same-aged peers.

> **DON'T FORGET**
>
> The interpretation makes a clear distinction between Rob's personal weaknesses (relative to his own performance) and normative weaknesses (relative to his peers).

Rob demonstrated a personal strength in his knowledge based on what he has obtained through his environment. This personal strength was evident on his Above Average performance on the Knowledge/*Gc* Index, on which Rob earned a standard score of 115 (84th percentile). This index comprises tasks such as (a) a task of verbal knowledge in which the examiner said a word or asked a question and the was to point to the picture that showed what the word meant or showed the best answer (Verbal Knowledge), and (b) a task in which the examiner verbally provided several characteristics of a concrete or abstract verbal concept and Rob had to name it (Riddles). Rob worked slowly, spending ample time thinking about his responses (neither task was timed); however, he asked for very few questions to be repeated.

Rob's nonverbal problem-solving skills were a significant normative strength for him, as evidenced by his standard score of 132 (98th percentile) on the Planning/*Gf* Index, which is in the Upper Extreme range. Tasks that comprise this index include a test in which he was shown a row of pictures that tell a story and he was to complete the story with pictures he was given (Story Completion), and a task in which he was shown a series of stimuli that form a logical, linear pattern with one stimulus missing; he was to complete the pattern by selecting from an array of 4 to 6 options (Pattern Reasoning). It should be noted that typically, these tasks are timed, with bonus points being awarded for quick performance. However, given Rob's significant difficulty with timed tasks, his performance was scored without time restrictions. Without time constraints, Rob's nonverbal reasoning skills are extremely high; however, when scored with the bonus points for quick responding, his performance would be in the average range (standard score of 99; 47th percentile). This clearly demonstrates one of the ways Rob's slower speed of processing and responding interferes with his success if he is expected to work quickly.

Rob's visual processing and problem-solving was in the Average range. Rob earned a standard score of 100 (50th percentile) on Simultaneous/*Gv* Index, indicating aver- age visual processing and visual-motor skills. Both tasks are also timed, but there is not an option to score the task without timing (as can be done for the Planning/*Gf* Index). On one task in which Rob was shown a stack of blocks with some partially hidden and he was to count how many blocks he saw (Block Counting), he responded more quickly. On this task, the examiner told him that when time was up she would ask him to say his answer. This task was the only task on which he appeared to work more quickly, although he worked slowly before these directions were given. Furthermore, he made numerous errors when rushing. On the second task in which he was to move a toy dog on a grid to get its bone using the shortest path (Rover), Rob worked slowly and lost points for running out of time. Thus, it is likely that if Rob were not rushed and not penalized for slower responding, his overall visual processing abilities would be significantly higher than his Simultaneous/$Gv$ Index reflects.

Because Rob has a history of difficulties with handwriting and visual-motor integration, he was administered several supplemental paper-and-pencil tests, both timed and untimed. He was administered the Beery Buktenica Developmental Test of Visual Motor Integration (VMI), a paper-and-pencil design copying test (untimed). Rob earned a VMI standard score of 63 (1st percentile), which is in the Low range. Rob was also administered two tasks that make up the Processing Speed Index (PSI) from the Wechsler Intelligence Scale for Children–Fifth Edition (WISC-V). On the PSI, a measure of clerical speed and accuracy, Rob earned a standard score of 56, which is in 2nd percentile and in the Low range, indicating impairment in his ability to fluently and automatically perform relatively easy cognitive tasks, when under time pressure. Rob's ability was assessed by two tasks—one required him to quickly copy symbols that were paired with numbers according to a key (Coding), and the other required him to identify the presence or absence of a target symbol in a row of symbols (Symbol Search). As mentioned previously, Rob appeared more concerned with accuracy than with working quickly. He did not make any errors, but he worked extremely slowly, referring to the key for each code rather than using his memory to aid him (Coding).

### Academic Achievement

To assess Rob's academic achievement in reading, math, oral language and written language, he was administered the KTEA-3, which is an individually administered test of academic achievement. Rob's academic skills range from above average in some select areas to very low in other areas. Therefore, it is important to examine Rob's performance within each area to fully understand his difficulties and his areas of strength.

Rob's reading skills were mostly consistent with the exception of one area, Silent Reading Fluency. He performed in the Average range when he was reading real words (61st percentile on Letter and Word Recognition; 39th on Word Recognition Fluency) and reading made-up words (68th percentile on Nonsense Word Decoding; 37th on Decoding Fluency), although his performance was markedly better on the untimed reading tests as compared to the timed tests. His reading comprehension skills were also estimated in the Average range (45th percentile on Reading Comprehension). He exhibited a skill strength in his literal reading comprehension.

However, when quickly reading simple questions and indicating whether each is true or false, Rob performed in the Below Average range (13th percentile on Silent Reading Fluency), which is a personal weakness for him.

Rob was also administered the Listening Comprehension subtest, in which he listened to passages spoken aloud and then he answered questions read by the examiner. Rob earned a standard score of 90 on the Listening Comprehension subtest (25th percentile), which is in the low Average range. In comparing Rob's understanding of what he reads to his understanding of what he hears via passages, there is no significant difference. However, an analysis of Rob's errors indicates a specific skill weakness in inferential listening comprehension (having to infer or predict the answer).

Rob was also administered a Written Expression subtest to assess his ability to complete sentences, use punctuation, and write his own sentences and a short essay. Rob earned a standard score of 110 (75th percentile). However, on the untimed portion, he spent a significant amount of time writing sentences. When asked to write a short essay in 10 minutes, he ran out of time and was unable to add a concluding sentence. Rob's handwriting was difficult to read at times. The spacing between letters or words was not always accurate, and the size of the letters made it difficult to determine if he was capitalizing incorrectly. Rob's written expression of ideas was Average to Above Average, but punctuation was identified as a specific skill weakness.

## DON'T FORGET

The specific description of observations of how Rob wrote (in addition to specific scores on writing tasks) is instrumental in evaluation of possible dysgraphia.

Rob's performance on the Mathematics Composite reveals consistently Above Average to Superior skills both in his computation skills (93rd percentile) and in his ability to apply mathematical principles to solve word problems (87th percentile on Math Concepts & Application). Even though Rob performed quite well on both of the math tasks and he did not have any skill weaknesses, it should be noted that the errors he did make were primarily simple computational or careless errors (e.g., $7 \times 0 = 7$; transferring the wrong number/answer from his scratch paper).

To further examine Rob's academic fluency skills, he was administered several timed tasks from the KTEA-3: Silent Reading Fluency, Decoding Fluency (both mentioned briefly earlier), Math Fluency, and Writing Fluency. These fluency tasks involve solving simple arithmetic problems (the four basic operations); reading a list of made-up words; creating simple sentences to describe a picture. On the Academic Fluency Composite, which combines decoding fluency, math fluency and writing fluency, Rob earned a standard score of 80 (9th percentile), which is in the Below Average range. His fluency difficulties were most evident in the areas of

## DON'T FORGET

Most tasks are untimed on KTEA-3 except the fluency tasks, which are directly related to Rob's referral concerns. Making this distinction is clearly important to directly respond to the reason for this assessment.

Math Fluency (standard score of 89; 23rd percentile), Writing Fluency (standard score of 72; 3rd percentile), and Silent Reading Fluency standard score of 83 (13th percentile). In contrast, his ability to read individual real words aloud was at a level commensurate with other students his age (Decoding Fluency standard score of 95; 37th percentile).

When comparing Rob's performance on the simple fluency tests with his performance on the more complex untimed tests, he scores significantly lower under timed conditions. These differences range from 38 points in writing (over 2 standard deviations), 33 points in math (over 2 standard deviations), and 15 points in reading (1 standard deviation). It should be noted that Rob's decoding fluency versus his regular decoding skills did not show significant variability. When Rob's Fluency Composite is compared with his overall cognitive abilities, there are also significant differences.

Rob was also administered the Comprehension subtest of the Nelson-Denny Reading Test under standard and extended timed conditions. Rob's performance was in the 22nd percentile (standard time) and in the 35th percentile (extended time). He did not complete the test under either condition. In the standard administration, he only finished four passages. With extended time, he completed six out of the seven passages. Thus, even with 50% extra time, he was unable to finish.

### Social, Emotional, and Executive Functioning

Emotionally and behaviorally, Rob presented during the evaluation as a sweet, compliant young man who was willing to do his best. He was able to sustain his attention for long periods of time in this one-on-one interaction; however, it took him a long time to complete most of the tasks. Based on parent report, including rating scales such as the BASC-2 and the BRIEF, Rob is not currently exhibiting any significant emotional or behavioral symptoms, or executive dysfunction.

### Summary and Diagnostic Impressions

Specific Learning Disorder (DSM-V 315) with impairments in Reading (Reading Fluency) and Mathematics (Fluent Calculation)

Dysgraphia (ICD-9-CM 781.3)

Overall average cognitive abilities with highly variable skills

Normative strength in nonverbal problem-solving (upper extreme)

Normative weaknesses in processing speed and visual-motor integration (low)

Personal strength in verbal knowledge (above average)

Personal weaknesses in memory and associative learning (average)

Overall academic functioning all within average to above average range
> Normative weaknesses in academic fluency (contextual reading, writing, math)

Based on the current evaluation, Rob's cognitive abilities are not uniformly developed. He exhibits lower average memory and learning skills (personal weakness for him), average visual processing skills (negatively impacted by timed conditions), above average verbal knowledge, and upper extreme nonverbal problem solving skills. Rob demonstrates significant weakness in his visual-motor integration skills and his processing speed skills (both deficits). In fact, he appears slower in his processing of information, both input and output, which translates into his taking longer to respond.

Rob's academic skills vary from above average/superior to low. Most of his reading skills are average compared to same-grade peers, as are his written expression and listening comprehension skills. His math skills are above average/superior. However, Rob has significant deficits in his fluency (the speed with which he is able to encode, process, and respond to simple reading, writing and even math questions). These deficits are most notable when coupled with the need for quick writing; however, they also significantly impact his basic reading understanding and math when expected to work quickly.

Rob's academic functioning is significantly lower than his cognitive abilities. He has a processing deficit clearly related to his academic concerns (processing speed and fluency). Thus, he meets criteria for a Specific Learning Disorder with impairment in all areas (reading, writing, math) that are affected by time constraints. He also

> **DON'T FORGET**
>
> Clearly comparing Rob's cognitive processing deficits to his academic deficits lays the groundwork to support a Specific Learning Disability.

meets criteria for the diagnosis of dysgraphia (ICD-9-CM). Dysgraphia is the condition of impaired letter writing by hand, that is, disabled handwriting. Impaired handwriting can interfere with learning to spell words in writing and speed of writing text.

## Recommendations

Based on Rob's specific deficits in processing speed and visual-motor integration, which affect his fluency in writing, reading, and math, the following recommendations have been made:

1. Rob has significant deficits with his visual-motor integration that affect his handwriting, making it slow and laborious. In addition, it is often difficult to read his handwriting. It is strongly recommended that he learn keyboarding/typing skills so that he can complete in-class writing

assignments and exams via computer. Summer is a good time for him to practice keyboarding skills.

2. Until Rob becomes proficient with typing, he and his family may want to investigate dictation apps for his computer to help with longer written assignments at home (such as papers). Summer time is a good time to explore various programs to determine which ones Rob likes better.

3. It is recommended that Rob begin receiving educational services in the form of accommodations via his school's Learning Center. Based on his current diagnosis of specific learning disorder and dysgraphia and the accompanying processing speed and fluency deficits, the following are recommended:

   (a) Rob will need to have extra time to complete all exams and in-class assignments (up to double extra time). He should be taking exams in a separate place from the rest of the class so that he is not disturbed when others complete their work before him.

   (b) Rob should be given a copy of the teacher's lessons and notes (or a peer note taker) for each class to lessen the requirements for him to quickly copy notes from the board or lectures. He may also want to record the lectures to review.

   (c) Rob's counselor may be able to assist him in applying for special accommodations for standardized testing (e.g., SAT), which he will definitely require. He may need up to double time. In addition, he should mark his answers directly on the test booklet and not be required to transfer answers onto the scantron.

   (d) When taking exams requiring longer handwritten responses such as essays or short paragraphs, Rob should be allowed to use a laptop or iPad.

   *Debra Y. Broadbooks, PhD*
   *Licensed Psychologist*

## Psychometric Summary for Rob

### Table 6.25 Kaufman Assessment Battery for Children–Second Edition (KABC-II, CHC Model)

| Scale | Standard Score/Scaled Score | 90% Confidence Interval | Percentile Rank |
|---|---|---|---|
| **Sequential/*Gsm*** | 91 | 83–99 | 27 |
| Number Recall | 8 | | 25 |
| Word Order | 9 | | 37 |
| **Simultaneous/*Gv*** | 100 | 92–108 | 50 |
| Rover | 11 | | 63 |
| Block Counting | 9 | | 37 |

**Table 6.25** (Continued)

| Scale | Standard Score/Scaled Score | 90% Confidence Interval | Percentile Rank |
|---|---|---|---|
| **Learning/Glr** | **94** | **88–100** | **34** |
| Atlantis | 10 | | 50 |
| Rebus | 8 | | 25 |
| **Planning/Gf** | **132** | **119–139** | **98** |
| Story Completion* | 13 | | 84 |
| Pattern Reasoning* | 17 | | 99 |
| **Knowledge/Gc** | **115** | **107–121** | **84** |
| Verbal Knowledge | 14 | | 91 |
| Riddles | 12 | | 75 |
| **Fluid-Crystallized Index (FCI)** | **107** | **103–111** | **68** |

* *Note:* Scored without time points.

**Table 6.26 Beery Buktenica Developmental Test of Visual Motor Integration**

| Index | Standard Score | 90% Confidence Interval | Percentile Rank |
|---|---|---|---|
| Beery VMI | 63 | — | 1 |

**Table 6.27 Wechsler Intelligence Scale for Children–Fifth Edition (WISC-V, Selected Subtests)**

| Index/Subtest | Standard Score/Scaled Score | 90% Confidence Interval | Percentile Rank |
|---|---|---|---|
| **Processing Speed Index (PSI)** | **56** | **51–66** | **0.2** |
| Coding | 1 | | 0.1 |
| Symbol Search | 4 | | 2 |

**Table 6.28 Kaufman Test of Educational Achievement–Third Edition (KTEA-3, Form B)**

| Composite/Subtest | Standard Score (age-based) | 90% Confidence Interval | Percentile Rank |
|---|---|---|---|
| **Reading Composite** | **101** | **96–106** | **53** |
| Letter & Word Recognition | 104 | 99–109 | 61 |
| Reading Comprehension | 98 | 90–106 | 45 |
| *Silent Reading Fluency* | *83* | *72–94* | *13* |

(continued)

**Table 6.28** (Continued)

| Composite/Subtest | Standard Score (age-based) | 90% Confidence Interval | Percentile Rank |
|---|---|---|---|
| **Mathematics Composite** | **121** | **117–125** | **92** |
| Math Concepts & Applications | 117 | 112–122 | 87 |
| Math Computation | 122 | 117–127 | 93 |
| *Math Fluency* | *89* | *82–96* | *23* |
| **Written Language Composite** | — | — | — |
| Written Expression | 110 | 99–121 | 75 |
| *Writing Fluency* | *72* | *59–85* | *3* |
| **Comprehension Composite** | **93** | **86–100** | **32** |
| Listening Comprehension | 90 | 80–100 | 25 |
| Reading Comprehension | 98 | 90–106 | 45 |
| **Reading Fluency Composite** | **89** | **83–95** | **23** |
| Word Recognition Fluency | 96 | 88–104 | 39 |
| Decoding Fluency | 95 | 85–105 | 37 |
| **Academic Fluency** | **80** | **73–87** | **9** |

**Table 6.29 Nelson Denny Reading Test**

| Subtest | Percentile Rank |
|---|---|
| Comprehension and Rate, standard time | 22 |
| Comprehension and Rate, extended time | 35 |

Seven

## Q-INTERACTIVE FOR KTEA™-3 AND WIAT®-III

# Thomas Witholt*, Kristina C. Breaux*, and Elizabeth O. Lichtenberger

*Pearson Clinical Assessment, San Antonio, TX

## With Contributions by James A. Henke

Q-interactive Product Specialist, Pearson Clinical Assessment, Bloomington, MN

P ractitioners have the option to administer and score the KTEA-3 and the WIAT-III using Q-interactive, Pearson's digital system for tablet-based assessment. Q-interactive is designed to streamline the assessment process for the examiner to reduce administration and scoring errors, minimize scoring time, and allow the examiner to focus more on the examinee and less on the mechanics of assessment.

The information provided in this chapter is intended to benefit a wide audience. The basics of how to use Q-interactive are clearly explained for new and novice users, while more advanced tips and explanations are provided for more experienced users. This chapter is organized into five sections:

1. Q-interactive versus Q-global
2. Equivalency research
3. Essential Features of Q-interactive
4. Basic Steps to Using Q-interactive
5. Administering KTEA-3 and WIAT-III Subtests on Q-interactive

### Q-INTERACTIVE VERSUS Q-GLOBAL

Q-interactive and Q-global are both Pearson systems that facilitate digital scoring and reporting. However, only Q-interactive delivers tablet-based assessments. Q-global is used primarily for web-based scoring and reporting and does not support tablet-based administration.

Q-interactive key features include the following:

- Web-based management of clients and assessments with the capability to administer and score offline
- Administration of assessments using two iPads: one iPad functions as a stimulus book for the examinee, the other functions as a digital record form and manual for the examiner
- Offers digital scoring and reporting
- Provides digital resources such as manuals on the Central website (www.qiactive .com, for users only)

Q-global key features include the following:

- Delivers some self-administered on-screen assessments, which require only one screen
- Offers web-based scoring and reporting
- Provides digital resources such as manuals, scoring keys, and audio files in the Resource Library (qglobal.pearsonclinical.com, for users only)

For the most up-to-date information about Q-interactive and Q-global, visit www.helloq.com.

---

## DON'T FORGET

### Get Started with Q-interactive

Gather information and set up an account at www.helloq.com.

Devices you will need (not sold by Pearson):

- Two Apple® Full Size iPads® (iPad 2 or newer with 16 GB of memory or higher)
- iPad cases that allow the iPads to prop up (some tests require the Client Device to lay flat on the table while other tests require the Client Device to be propped up)
- A stylus for the examiner

Testing materials you will need:

- Pencils (with and without erasers) for written responses
- Scratch paper for KTEA-3 Math Concepts & Applications and WIAT-III Math Problem Solving
- Response Booklets: KTEA-3 and WIAT-III Response Booklets (and KTEA-3 Written Expression Booklets) are required. Subtests with written responses are still administered using Assess, but the examinee writes their responses in a booklet.

(continued)

(*Continued*)

Testing materials you will *not* need:
- Record forms
- Stimulus books
- Stopwatch
- Audio files/CD
- Audio playback and recording device

# DON'T FORGET

## Key Benefits of Q-interactive

- Create custom batteries that combine subtests from one or more tests
- Administer subtests correctly and efficiently
  - Guidance for choosing the correct item set and start/stop point for an examinee
  - Prompts the examiner to reverse or discontinue
  - Audio capture of oral responses happens automatically
  - Audio stimuli are available at the touch of a button
  - Timing capabilities are built in (no stopwatches are required)
  - Add new subtests or change the battery during administration to test hypotheses
- Score easily and quickly
  - All scoring is consolidated in one place with no need for additional forms, such as those used for error/skills analysis
  - Grade and age-based scores are displayed immediately after subtest administration and item scoring is complete
- Generate complete score reports
  - Data for interpretive score reports are collected directly from the software without the need to enter additional information
  - Sync data to generate a report

## EQUIVALENCY STUDIES

Before a test is delivered on Q-interactive, each new type of subtest undergoes an equivalency study to evaluate whether scores from Q-interactive testing are interchangeable with those scored from paper-and-pencil testing. If a subtest is similar

---

*Note:* Much of the information included in this section was adapted from the resources provided at www.helloq.com/research.

(in item type, stimulus presentation, response format, etc.) to one already tested in an equivalency study, then an additional study is not required because the prior research findings are assumed to generalize to similar tests. The primary goal of the equivalency studies has been to maintain raw score equivalence between paper and digital administration and scoring formats. The standard criterion that has been used to ensure equivalence in all studies is an effect size of 0.2 or smaller, which is equal to three standard score points or fewer on the KTEA-3 and WIAT-III. Effect size is the average amount of difference between scores on Q-interactive and paper administrations, divided by the standard deviation of scores. Equivalency of raw scores indicates that the norms, reliability, and validity information obtained using the paper and pencil tests can be applied to Q-interactive results.

For the KTEA-3 and WIAT-III, equivalency study results suggest that the scores obtained from the digitally adapted administrations are comparable to those obtained from traditional paper based administrations. No equivalency studies were conducted specifically for the KTEA-3 because all subtests were similar (in item type, stimulus presentation, response format, etc.) to subtests already included in previous equivalency studies. However, a technical report specific to the WIAT-III (available at www.helloq.com/research) outlines a study conducted for Oral Reading Fluency and the Sentence Repetition component of Oral Expression. The results indicated nonsignificant score differences with effect sizes of −0.05 to 0.11 for Oral Reading Fluency (Rate, Accuracy, Fluency scores) and −0.08 for Sentence Repetition. In addition, a preliminary readability study was conducted to ensure that readability was not affected by tablet presentation of text. For Word Reading and Pseudoword Decoding, the text size of the words/pseudowords were slightly reduced in size in order for the stimuli to fit on the tablet screen. For Oral Reading Fluency, no text size adjustments were needed because each reading passage in the printed stimulus booklet fit on the tablet screen without the need for scrolling. The results of this readability study indicated nonsignificant score differences with effect sizes of 0.18 for Word Reading/Pseudoword Decoding and −0.11 for Oral Reading Fluency. In summary, none of the score differences were statistically significant at the .05 level, and all effect sizes were 0.11 or smaller, well within the tolerance limits for equivalency.

A variety of clinical assessments also yielded comparable scores in the Q-interactive and paper administration formats, including the WAIS-IV, WISC-IV, NEPSY-II, WMS, and CELF-5.

## ESSENTIAL FEATURES OF Q-INTERACTIVE

This section reviews the key terminology used in Q-interactive, and then describes the essential features of Q-interactive's two main components: the Central website and the Assess application.

## Key Terminology

Understanding the key terminology that is used throughout Q-interactive, as explained in Rapid Reference 7.1, is helpful for new users. Some of the terms will be unfamiliar to new users because they are specific to the technology (e.g., Assess, Central). Other terms may differ from what is typically used in the KTEA-3 and WIAT-III because they are intended to be generic enough to apply across a diverse array of clinical assessments (e.g., pertaining to mental health, personality, behavior, neuropsychology, etc.); for example, the term *client* is used instead of *student* or *examinee*.

### ≡ Rapid Reference 7.1

#### Key Terminology in Q-interactive

*Q-i:* Q-interactive is also referred to as "Q-i" for short.

Applications

*Assess:* The iPad application through which examiners can administer and score assessments

*Central:* The website (www.qiactive.com) through which examiners create clients, assign assessments, and create reports for a specific assessment

Devices (iPads)

*Client Device:* The iPad used to present stimuli to the examinee

*Examiner Device* (also referred to as Practitioner Device in the Assess settings): The iPad used by the examiner to administer and score

Features and Actions

*Home Screen:* The entry point on Assess, where all assessments currently on the iPad can be accessed

*Assessment:* A battery of subtests assigned to a particular examinee for a particular testing event

*Card:* All of the Assess content that appears within one frame on the iPad without having to swipe forward or backward in the app (e.g., most subtests have one card for each item, while all items of the Spelling subtests are presented on a single card)

*Contextual Events:* Common events that examiners often want to track, such as the number of times a student says, "I don't know," does not respond, or requires repetition of an item prompt

*Pop-over:* A window that opens to display new information within Assess

*Swipe:* To move from one card to the next, swipe your finger horizontally across the screen

## Central Website

*Central* is the website (www.qiactive.com) where examiners access their account information, prepare for an assessment, and finalize reporting after an assessment. *Central is not used for administering tests.* Rather, Central is used by examiners to enter client data, plan an initial battery of assessments, access score reports post-administration, and so forth. Central also provides access to digital resources such as manuals and scoring keys. Step-by-step instructions for using the Central website (as well as the Assess application) is provided in the *Basic Steps to Using Q-interactive* section of this chapter.

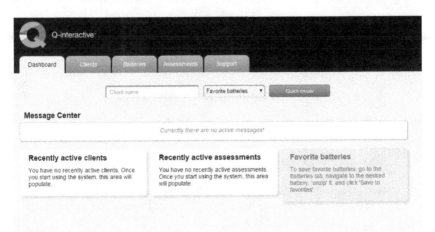

# DON'T FORGET

### Update the Assess App on Both iPads

The Assess application is updated fairly regularly with new features and functionality. Before test administration, always make sure that both of your iPads have the most up-to-date version. If one iPad is using an older version than the other iPad, complications may arise. Be sure to check the Updates section of the Apple App Store (found on the home screen of the device) for updates to Assess.

## Assess Application

*Assess* is a digital application downloaded from the Apple App Store onto two iPads connected by Bluetooth. After creating a client and planning an initial battery in Central, the examiner sends the assessment (via wireless internet connection) to Assess on the iPads for administration. In the application settings of the iPads, the examiner designates one iPad as the Client device and the other iPad as the Practitioner device. The Client device functions as a stimulus book for the examinee and the Practitioner's iPad functions as a digitally enhanced record form and manual for the examiner to use in administration and scoring.

Assess was designed to use similar design features and functionality across tests to make it easier for practitioners to learn and transition between tests. These basic features, found on the home screen and within the assessment screens, will be reviewed next.

### Home Screen: Interview, Battery, and Results Tabs

On the home screen, information is organized under three tabs: Interview, Battery, and Results. The *Interview* tab shows basic demographic information (birth date, gender) for the examinee as well as the date and time of the assessment. This tab also provides the option to write Notes relevant to the assessment (this feature can be used before or after the assessment and all notes will sync back to Central) or remove the assessment from the iPad.

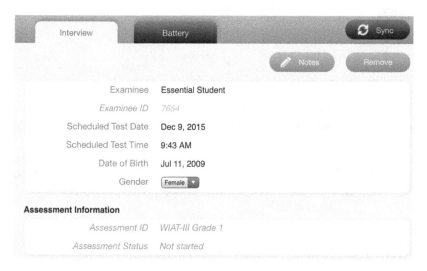

The *Battery* tab lists the subtests in the current assessment battery. Subtests already administered are grayed out, and the current subtest has a play button arrow. Tapping on the current subtest will take you to the last viewed screen in the assessment.

The "Edit Battery" button in the upper right corner of the Battery tab allows you to customize the battery from within the Assess app, by reordering or removing subtests that are part of the assessment (and have not yet been started), or by adding new subtests from a variety of tests.

The *Results* tab becomes available after a subtest is started. This tab presents the "end of subtest" results including raw scores and standard scores.

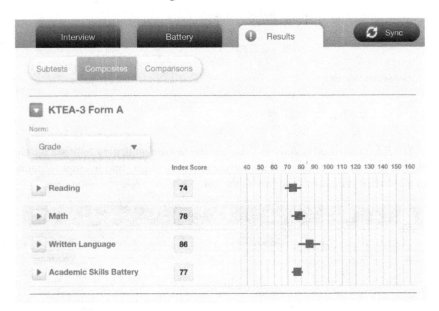

Each subtest in Assess will include the following standard features: The Global Bar, Beginning of Subtest Coverpage, Item Card, and End of Subtest Card.

## Global Bar

After beginning an assessment in Assess and leaving the home screen, a black bar with icons (referred to as the global bar) will remain at the top of each item or instruction screen. The global bar includes seven icons that provide features common to all subtests (see Rapid Reference 7.2 for a list of features). These features are meant for use while administering an item, so the global bar features are not available at other times (e.g., while reviewing an item already administered or previewing an item not yet administered).

Notes may be written by the examiner using a finger or stylus at any point before, during, or after an assessment session (see Notes button on Interview tab of Assess home screen to access Notes before or after an assessment session). During an assessment, in the upper right-hand corner of every screen is a pencil icon, which opens up an area for writing notes about the current item/subtest or the assessment as a whole. A drop-down menu in the top left allows you to switch between notes. This large recording area is the size of the iPad screen, so item responses that would require more than a few lines of writing or which would benefit from the large area, such as a drawn image, should be recorded here. As with verbatim responses, you can start another page of notes if you need more writing space, by tapping the pencil icon with a plus symbol. All notes are available for later review on Assess by touching the Notes icon and navigating to the appropriate note, by tapping the "All Notes" button under the Results tab of your assessment, or on the Central Website by clicking on Notes when viewing the assessment overview.

## ≡ Rapid Reference 7.2

### Global Bar Features

The global bar includes seven icons. These icons and their features are explained here in the order of their appearance in the figure (left to right).

**Home (Q)** Takes you back to the Assess home screen, where you can switch between assessments, edit your battery, or view general information and results for an assessment.

**Review pane (or "All to Do")** This drop-down lists all subtests and all items in the battery, allowing you to navigate between items and subtests for review. A red circle counter will display how many items in the battery need scoring or review ("All To Do"), and each of these items is flagged. These "to do" items must be resolved before an assessment can be considered complete and ready for reporting.

*(continued)*

(Continued)

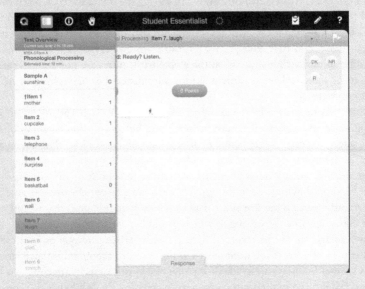

**Subtest information (i Button)** This pop-over contains subtest-specific information about materials needed, administration rules, scoring rules, and recommendations for recording responses and contextual events.

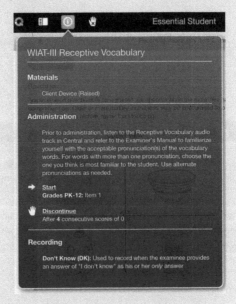

(continued)

(*Continued*)

**Manual discontinue (Hand icon)** Ends administration of the subtest or section. Once manually discontinued, a subtest cannot be resumed. Use with caution: If the discontinue point has not been reached, the subtest will be invalidated.

**Notes (Pencil)** Opens up a window in which to take handwritten notes about the battery as a whole, the subtest, or the current item. You may navigate between these three options using a drop-down menu. The note may be flagged for later review by clicking the exclamation point. Notes are stored on Assess and Central under the specific assessment for which they were taken.

**Picture-in-Picture (Double screen)** This pop-over displays a smaller version of what is being displayed on the client device. Only select subtests currently offer this feature.

**About (?)** This pop-over displays the current version of the App software, which is useful to note if you have any technical difficulties.

**Observational Checklist (KTEA-3 only)** The KTEA-3 includes an additional clipboard icon in the Global Bar (before the Notes pencil) for responding to a qualitative observations survey regarding general and subtest-specific behaviors. Based on the examiner's qualitative observations, a table will be included in the score report to suggest possible areas of cognitive processing weaknesses to investigate further.

### Beginning of Subtest Coverpage

A coverpage appears at the beginning of each subtest or subtest section. This coverpage informs the examiner that a transition will be made. If you decide *not* to proceed with the subtest or section, you may go back to the Assess home page to modify the battery but do *not* swipe past the coverpage. Once you swipe past the coverpage, the subtest becomes billable (the usage will be reflected in your account) and the subtest can no longer be edited out of the battery.

### Item Card

Subtests are administered using item cards, which may include one or more of the following features. Images showing examples of each feature are included as well.

- Administration prompts: text that is read aloud to the examinee is presented in a teal-colored font
- A button to present the item stimulus (audio or visual)
- Scoring options
- Response capture

- Contextual event buttons to record qualitative information. Specific contextual events vary by subtest and are explained in each subtest's i-button
- A pre-set timer
- Additional resources such as scoring rules

Many subtests show one item per card while other subtests show several or all items on a single card. For subtests with multiple item cards, the examiner is allowed to swipe backward by only one item, but this will clear any scores or responses collected for the current item. Use the Review button in the Global bar to return to an earlier item (see below).

## DON'T FORGET

### Using Timer Function

On subtests that require timing, you *must* use the timer function in Assess. Items with time limits count up by default, but tapping on the icon of the clock with a down arrow will set them to count down. With 5 or 10 seconds remaining (depending on the subtest's time limit), the number of seconds remaining turns red to alert the examiner that time is almost up.

If the examiner does not start or stop the timer fast enough and the elapsed time needs to be adjusted to reflect the accurate number of seconds, the examiner can touch the completion time to open the *Adjust Timer* window and then use the up and down arrows.

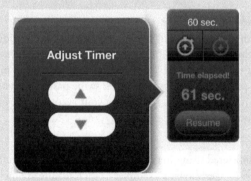

If the timer needs to be reset (e.g., the examiner starts the timer too soon or the examinee was not quite ready to begin), touch the timer while it is running and use the reset option.

The item bar, found just below the global bar, appears on each Item Card when administering items in Assess. The item bar indicates the item(s) currently being administered. Rapid Reference 7.3 lists the other primary features of the item bar.

# ≡ Rapid Reference 7.3

**Item Bar Features** The item bar includes three primary features/icons. These features are explained here in the order of their appearance in the figure (left to right).

**Special instructions (Speech Bubble)** This pop-over contains instructions and prompts for addressing common "If-Then" scenarios during administration of the subtest (e.g., If the examinee does X, then do/say Y).

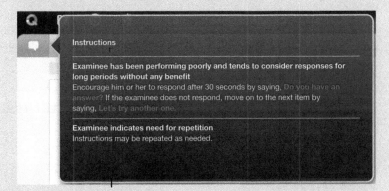

**Score** Displays the current raw score for any item(s) on the current card. Clicking on it will typically display a pop-over that includes more information, such as the total number of correct items and incorrect items on a card that has multiple items.

**Flag for Review (Flag)** Clicking the flag will change the flag's color from white to red, indicating that the item needs review (even if it is scored). Flagged items are easily accessed later in the Review sidebar and from the home screen's "Results" tab.

## *End of Subtest Card*

After an examinee discontinues or completes a subtest, the End of Subtest Card displays the following data:

- Standard scores
- Raw scores (total, item-level, and weighted, if any)
- Administration time
- Number of errors by error/skill category

# LEARN MORE

In order to keep this Essentials book within its page limits, only a preview of this Q-interactive chapter is provided in print. Chapter 7 may be viewed in its entirety by accessing the content online in the book's Digital Resources.

## 🖋 TEST YOURSELF 🖋

1. **Tablet-based assessments can be conducted on both Q-interactive and Q-global.**
   (a) True
   (b) False

2. **Equivalency study results suggest that the raw scores obtained from the digitally adapted administrations of the KTEA-3 and WIAT-III on Q-interactive are comparable to those obtained from traditional paper-based administrations.**
   (a) True
   (b) False

3. **After an examinee discontinues or completes a subtest, the End of Subtest Card displays the following data:**
   (a) Standard Scores
   (b) Raw Scores
   (c) Administration time
   (d) All of the above

4. **The digital administration process on Q-interactive makes examiner errors nearly impossible to make, so practicing the test administration is not necessary even for first-time users.**
   (a) True
   (b) False

5. **Which of the following statements about modifying an assessment battery (reordering, removing, or adding subtests) is false?**
   (a) Before administration of the assessment begins, a battery can be modified in Central or in Assess.
   (b) During administration in Assess, the examiner can modify subtests that have not yet started (i.e., progressed past the Beginning of Subtest Card).
   (c) During administration in Assess, all subtests can be modified.
   (d) After administering the complete battery, additional subtests can be added in Assess.

6. **Benefits of conducting assessments on Q-interactive's Assess application include which of the following?**

   (a) Automatic timing of timed subtests
   (b) Audio recording of subtests that have oral responses
   (c) Picklists for subtests that have common correct and incorrect responses
   (d) All of the above

7. **Even using Q-interactive, paper response booklets are required for administering subtests with written responses.**

   (a) True
   (b) False

8. **The Global bar in the Assess application provides access to all of the following features except:**

   (a) Review pane or "All to Do" items
   (b) Subtest information (i-button)
   (c) Notes
   (d) Manual discontinue
   (e) Audio recordings

9. **Which two of the following types of data are _not_ saved when the assessment is synced back to the Central website?**

   (a) Audio recordings
   (b) Verbatim capture entries
   (c) Notes
   (d) Examinee's touch responses
   (e) Picklist responses

10. **Which of the following statements about Q-interactive is false?**

    (a) Assess is an iPad app for administration and scoring
    (b) Score reports are generated using the Assess application.
    (c) An assessment is initially created on the Central website.
    (d) Assessment data collected in Assess is synced (saved) to the Central website.

*Answers:* 1. b; 2. a, 3. d; 4. b; 5. c; 6. d; 7. True; 8. e; 9. a, d; 10. b.

# References

Adams, M. (1990). *Beginning to read: Thinking and learning about print*. Cambridge, MA: MIT Press.

American Psychiatric Association. (2013). *Diagnostic and statistical manual of mental disorders* (5th ed.). Washington, DC: Author.

Archer, R. P., Maruish, M., Imhof, E. A., & Piotrowski, C. (1991). Psychological test usage with adolescent clients: 1990 findings. *Professional Psychology: Research & Practice, 22*, 247–252.

Barkley, R. A. (1990). *Attention-deficit hyperactivity disorder: A handbook for diagnosis and treatment*. New York, NY: Guilford Press.

Barkley, R. A. (1998). *Attention-deficit hyperactivity disorder: A handbook for diagnosis and treatment* (2nd ed.). New York, NY: Guilford Press.

Barkley, R. A. (2003). Attention-deficit/hyperactivity disorder. In E. J. Mash & R. A. Barkley (Eds.), *Child psychopathology* (2nd ed., pp. 75–143). New York, NY: Guilford Press.

Barkley, R. A., DuPaul, G. J., & McMurray, M. B. (1990). A comprehensive evaluation of attention deficit disorder with and without hyperactivity. *Journal of Consulting and Clinical Psychology, 58*, 775–789.

Berninger, V. W. (2009). Highlights of programmatic, interdisciplinary research on writing. *Learning Disabilities Research & Practice: A Publication of the Division for Learning Disabilities, Council for Exceptional Children, 24*(2), 69–80.

Berninger, V. W. (2015). Diagnosing specific learning disabilities and twice exceptionality. In *Interdisciplinary frameworks for schools: Best professional practices for serving the needs of all students* (pp. 221–247). Washington, DC: American Psychological Association. doi:10.1037/14437-002

Berninger, V., Dunn, A., & Alper, T. (2005). Integrated multilevel model of branching assessment, instructional assessment, and profile assessment. In A. Prifitera, D. Saklofske, L. Weiss, & E. Rolfhus (Eds.), *WISC–IV Clinical use and interpretation* (pp. 151–185). San Diego, CA: Academic Press.

Berninger, V., & O'Donnell, L. (2005). Research-supported differential diagnosis of specific learning disabilities. In A. Prifitera, D. Saklofske, L. Weiss, & E. Rolfhus (Eds.), *WISC–IV Clinical use and interpretation* (pp. 189–233). San Diego, CA: Academic Press.

Berninger, V., & Richards, T. (2010). Inter-relationships among behavioral markers, genes, brain, and treatment in dyslexia and dysgraphia. *Future Neurology, 5*(4), 597–617. doi:10.2217/fnl.10.22

Berninger, V., Vaughn, K., Abbott, R., Brooks, A., Abbott, S., Reed, E., Rogan, L., & Graham, S. (1998). Early intervention for spelling problems: Teaching spelling units of varying size within a multiple connections framework. *Journal of Educational Psychology, 90*, 587–605.

Berninger, V., Whitaker, D., Feng, Y., Swanson, H. L., & Abbott, R. D. (1996). Assessment of planning, translating, and revising in junior high writers. *Journal of School Psychology, 34*(1), 23–52

Berninger, V. W., & Wolf, B. J. (2016). *Teaching students with dyslexia, dysgraphia, OWL LD, and dyscalculia* (2nd ed). Baltimore, MD: Brookes.

Bishop, D. V., & Snowling, M. J. (2004). Developmental dyslexia and specific language impairment: Same or different? *Psychological Bulletin, 130*(6), 858.

Bowers, P. (1996). The effects of single and double deficits in phonemic awareness and naming speed on new tests of orthographic knowledge. Paper presented to the Annual Meeting of the Society for the Scientific Study of Reading. New York, NY.

Breaux, K. C. (2015). *Error analysis for out of level item sets* (KTEA-3 Technical Report #1). San Antonio, TX: Pearson. Retrieved from http://images.pearsonclinical.com/images/assets/ktea-iii/KTEA-3-Tech-Report-OutofLevelErrorAnalysis.pdf

Breaux, K. C., & Frey, F. E. (2009). *Assessing writing skills using correct–incorrect word sequences: A national study*. Poster Session, National Association of School Psychologists Conference. Retrieved from http://psychcorp.pearsonassessments.com/hai/images/products/wiat-iii/WIAT-III_NASP_Poster.pdf

Brock, S. W., & Knapp, P. K. (1996). Reading comprehension abilities of children with attention-deficit/hyperactivity disorder. *Journal of Attention Disorders, 1*, 173–186.

Camarata, S., & Woodcock, R. (2006). Sex differences in processing speed: Developmental effects in males and females. *Intelligence, 34*(3), 231–252.

Carroll, J. B. (1993). *Human cognitive abilities: A survey of factor-analytic studies*. Cambridge, UK: Cambridge University Press.

Carroll, J. B. (1997). The three-stratum theory of cognitive abilities. In D. P. Flanagan, J. L. Genshaft, & P. L. Harrison (Eds.), *Contemporary intellectual assessment: Theories, tests, and issues* (pp. 122–130). New York, NY: Guilford Press.

Carrow-Woolfolk, E. (1999). *Comprehensive Assessment of Spoken Language*. Circle Pines, MN: American Guidance Service.

Carrow-Woolfolk, E. (2012). *Oral and Written Language Scales*. Austin, TX: Pro-Ed.

Casey, J. E., Rourke, B. P., & DelDotto, J. E. (1996). Learning disabilities in children with attention deficit disorder with and without hyperactivity. *Child Neuropsychology, 2*, 83–98.

Castles, A., & Nation, K. (2006). How does orthographic learning happen? In S. Andrews (Ed.), *From inkmarks to ideas: Challenges and controversies about word recognition and reading* (pp. 151–179). London, UK: Psychology Press.

Cattell, R. (1943). The measurement of adult intelligence. *Psychological Bulletin, 40*, 153–193.

Cattell, R. (1963). Theory of fluid and crystallized intelligence: A critical experiment. *Journal of Educational Psychology, 54*, 1–22.

Cattell, R., & Horn, J. (1978). A check on the theory of fluid and crystallized intelligence with description of new subtest designs. *Journal of Educational Measurement, 15*, 139–164.

Catts, H. W., Hogan, T., & Fey, M. E. (2010). Subgrouping poor readers on the basis of individual differences in reading-related abilities. *Journal of Learning Disabilities, 36*(2), 151–164.

Connor, C. M., Morrison, F. J., Fishman, B., Crowe, E. C., Al Otaiba, S., & Schatschneider, C. (2013). A longitudinal cluster-randomized controlled study on the accumulating effects of individualized literacy instruction on students' reading from first through third grade. *Psychological Science, 24*(8), 1408–1419.

Connor, C. M., Morrison, F. J., Fishman, B., Giuliani, S., Luck, M., Underwood, P. S., … Schatschneider, C. (2011). Testing the impact of child characteristics × instruction interactions on third graders' reading comprehension by differentiating literacy instruction. *Reading Research Quarterly, 46*(3), 189–221.

Daniel, M. H. (2013). *User survey on Effect of Q-interactive examinee behavior*. Retrieved from http://www.helloq.com/content/dam/ped/ani/us/helloq/media/User_Survey_on_Effect_of_Q-interactive_Examinee_Behavior_final.pdf

Daniel, M. H., Breaux, K. C., & Frey, F. E. (2010). *Patterns of strengths & weaknesses models for identifying SLD*. Paper presented at the annual National Association of School Psychologists Convention, Chicago, IL. Retrieved from http://images.pearsonclinical.com/images/Products/WIAT-III/NASP_2010_%20PSW_Poster.pdf

Das, J. P., Naglieri, J. A., & Kirby, J. R. (1994). *Assessment of cognitive processes*. Needham Heights, MA: Allyn & Bacon.

Delis, D. (2014, October 31). *Cognitive assessment leaps into the digital age*. Retrieved from http://www.eschoolnews.com/2014/10/31/cognitive-assessment-digital-429/2/

Demaray, M. K., Schaefer, K., & Delong, K. (2003). Attention-deficit/hyperactivity disorder (ADHD): A national survey of training and current assessment practices in the schools. *Psychology in the Schools, 40*(6), 583–597.

Dumont, R., & Willis, J. O. (2009). *The evaluation of Sam McGee*. Retrieved from http://www.myschoolpsychology.com/testing-information/the-story-of-sam-mcgee/

Dumont, R., & Willis, J. O. (2010). Strengths and weaknesses of the WIAT-III and KTEA-II. In E. O. Lichtenberger & K. C. Breaux, *Essentials of WIAT-III and KTEA-II Assessment* (pp. 239–269). Hoboken, NJ: Wiley.

Elliott, C. D. (2007). *Differential Ability Scales* (2nd ed.). San Antonio, TX: The Psychological Corporation.

Faraone, S. V., Biederman, J., Lehman, B. K., & Spencer, T. (1993). Intellectual performance and school failure in children with attention deficit hyperactivity disorder and in their siblings. *Journal of Abnormal Psychology, 102*(4), 616–623.

Feifer, S. (2011). How SLD manifests in reading. In D. P. Flanagan & V. C. Alfonso (Eds.), *Essentials of specific learning disability* (pp. 21–42). Hoboken, NJ: Wiley.

Feifer, S. G., & De Fina, P. A. (2000). *The neuropsychology of reading disorders: Diagnosis and intervention workbook*. Middletown, MD: School Neuropsych Press.

Fiorello, C. A., Hale, J. B., & Snyder, L. E. (2006). Cognitive hypothesis testing and response to intervention for children with reading problems. *Psychology in the Schools, 43*(8), 835–853.

Flanagan, D. P., & Kaufman, A. S. (2004). *Essentials of WISC-IV assessment*. New York, NY: Wiley.

Flanagan, D. P., & Kaufman, A. S. (2009). *Essentials of WISC-IV assessment* (2nd ed.). Hoboken, NJ: John Wiley & Sons.

Flanagan, D. P., McGrew, K. S., & Ortiz, S. O. (2000). *The Wechsler intelligence scales and Gf-Gc theory*. Boston, MA: Allyn & Bacon.

Flanagan, D. P., & Ortiz, S. O. (2001). *Essentials of cross-battery assessment*. New York, NY: Wiley.

Flanagan, D. P., Ortiz, S. O., & Alfonso, V. C. (2007). *Essentials of cross-battery assessment* (2nd ed.). Hoboken, NJ: Wiley. See also the official site of the CHC Cross-Battery Approach by Dawn P. Flanagan and Samuel O. Ortiz at http://facpub.stjohns.edu/~ortizs/cross-battery, retrieved February 29, 2008.

Flanagan, D. P., Ortiz, S. O., & Alfonso, V. C. (2013). *Essentials of cross-battery assessment* (3rd ed.). Hoboken, NJ: Wiley.

Flanagan, D. P., Ortiz, S. O., & Alfonso, V. C. (2015). Cross-battery Assessment Software System (X-bass). Wiley.

Flanagan, D. P., Ortiz, S. O., Alfonso, V. C., & Mascolo, J. T. (2002). *The achievement test desk reference (ATDR): Comprehensive assessment and learning disabilities*. Boston, MA: Allyn & Bacon.

Flanagan, D. P., Ortiz, S. O., Alfonso, V. C. & Mascolo, J. T. (2006). *Achievement test desk reference (ATDR-II): A guide to learning disability identification* (2nd ed.). Hoboken, NJ: Wiley.

Fletcher, J. M., Lyon, G. R., Fuchs, L. S., & Barnes, M. A. (2007). *Learning disabilities: From identification to intervention*. New York, NY: Guilford Press.

Frick, P. J., Kamphaus, R. W., Lahey, B. B., Loeber, R., Christ, M. A. G., Hart, E. L., & Tannenbaum, L. E. (1991). Academic underachievement and the disruptive behavior disorders. *Journal of Consulting and Clinical Psychology*, *59*, 289–294.

Fry, A., & Hale, S. (1996). Processing speed, working memory, and fluid intelligence: Evidence for a developmental cascade. *Psychological Science*, *7*, 237–241.

Gathercole, S., Pickering, S., Ambridge, B., & Wearing, H. (2004). The structure of working memory from 4 to 15 years of age. *Developmental Psychology*, *40*, 177–190.

Goldberg, E., & Bougakov, D. (2000). Novel approaches to the diagnosis and treatment of frontal lobe dysfunction. In A. Christensen & B. P. Uzell (Eds.), *International handbook of neuropsychological rehabilitation* (pp. 93–112). New York, NY: Kluwer/Plenum.

Goldman, J. J. (1989). On the robustness of psychological test instrumentation: Psychological evaluation of the dead. In G. G. Ellenbogen (Ed.), *The primal whimper: More readings from the Journal of Polymorphous Perversity*. New York, NY: Ballantine/Stonesong Press.

Gough, P. B., & Tunmer, W. E. (1986). Decoding, reading, and reading disability. *Remedial and Special Education*, *7*(1), 6–10. doi:10.1177/074193258600700104

Gregg, N., Coleman, C., Davis, M., & Chalk, J. C. (2007). Timed essay writing: Implications for high-stakes tests. *Journal of Learning Disabilities*, *40*(4), 306–318.

Gresham, F. M. (2009). Using response to intervention for identification of specific learning disabilities. In A. Akin-Little, S. G. Little, M. A. Bray, & T. J. Kehle (Eds.), *Behavioral interventions in schools: Evidence-based positive strategies* (pp. 205–220). Washington, DC, US: American Psychological Association. doi:10.1037/11886-013

Hale, J. B., & Fiorello, C. A. (2004). *School neuropsychology: A practitioner's handbook*. New York, NY: Guilford Press.

Hale, J. B., Fiorello, C. A., Bertin, M., & Sherman, R. (2003). Predicting math achievement through neuropsychological interpretation of WISCIII variance components. *Journal of Psychoeducational Assessment*, *21*, 358–380.

Hale, J. B., Fiorello, C. A., Miller, J. A., Wenrich, K., Teodori, A., & Henzel, J. N. (2008). WISC-IV interpretation for specific learning disabilities identification and intervention: A cognitive hypothesis testing approach. In A. Prifitera, D. H. Saklofske, & L. G. Weiss (Eds.), *WISC-IV clinical assessment and intervention* (2nd ed., pp. 109–171). San Diego, CA: Academic Press.

Hammill, D. D., Fowler, L., Bryant, B., & Dunn, C. (1992). *A survey of test usage among speech/language pathologists*. Unpublished manuscript.

Henderson, L., Snowling, M., & Clarke, P. (2013). Accessing, integrating, and inhibiting word meaning in poor comprehenders. *Scientific Studies of Reading*, *17*(3), 177–198. doi:10.1080/10888438.2011.652721

Henry J. Kaiser Family Foundation. (2010). *Profiles of generation M2: Media in the lives of 8- to 18-year-olds*. Menlo Park, CA: Author.

Hooper, S. R., & Hynd, G. W. (1982, October). The differential diagnosis of developmental dyslexia with the Kaufman Assessment Battery for children. Paper presented at the meeting of the National Academy of Neuropsychologists, Atlanta, GA.

Hutton, J. B., Dubes, R., & Muir, S. (1992). Assessment practices of school psychologists: Ten years later. *School Psychologist Review*, *21*, 271–284.

Hyde, J. S., Fennema, E., & Lamon, S. J. (1990). Gender differences in mathematics performance: A meta-analysis. *Psychological Bulletin*, *107*(2), 139–155.

Individuals with Disabilities Education Improvement Act (IDEA or IDEIA) of 2004, Pubic Law No. 108–446.

James, E. M., & Selz, M. (1997). Neuropsychological bases of common learning and behavior problems in children. In C. R. Reynolds and E. Fletcher-Janzen (Eds.), *The handbook of clinical child neuropsychology* (2nd ed., pp. 157–203). New York, NY: Kluwer-Plenum.

Joint Committee on Testing Practices (2004). *Code of Fair Testing Practices in Education.* Washington, DC: American Psychological Association.

Kaufman, A. S., & Kaufman, N. L. (1985, 1997). *Kaufman Test of Educational Achievement.* Circle Pines, MN: AGS.

Kaufman, A. S., & Kaufman, N. L. (2001). *Specific learning disabilities and difficulties in children and adolescents.* New York, NY: Cambridge University Press.

Kaufman, A. S., & Kaufman, N. L. (2004a). *Kaufman Test of Educational Achievement (2nd ed.).* Circle Pines, MN: American Guidance Service. (KTEA-II)

Kaufman, A. S., & Kaufman, N. L. (2004b). *Manual Kaufman Assessment Battery for Children, Second Edition.* Circle Pines, MN: American Guidance Service.

Kaufman, A. S., & Kaufman, N. L. (2004c). *Kaufman Brief Intelligence Test, Second Edition Manual.* Circle Pines, MN: American Guidance Service.

Kaufman, A. S., & Kaufman, N. L. (2005). *Kaufman Test of Educational Achievement, Second Edition Brief Form.* Circle Pines, MN: American Guidance Service.

Kaufman, A. S., & Kaufman, N. L. (2014a). *Kaufman Test of Educational Achievement — Third Edition (KTEA-3).* Bloomington, MN: NCS Pearson.

Kaufman, A. S., & Kaufman, N. L. (with Breaux, K. C.) (2014b). Technical & interpretive manual. *Kaufman Test of Educational Achievement— Third Edition.* Bloomington, MN: NCS Pearson.

Kaufman, A. S., & Kaufman, N. L. (with Breaux, K. C.) (2014c). Administration manual. *Kaufman Test of Educational Achievement— Third Edition.* Bloomington, MN: NCS Pearson.

Kaufman, A. S., & Kaufman, N. L. (with Breaux, K. C.) (2014d). Scoring manual. *Kaufman Test of Educational Achievement–Third Edition.* Bloomington, MN: NCS Pearson.

Kaufman, A. S., & Kaufman, N. L. (2015a). *Kaufman Test of Educational Achievement Brief Form–Third Edition.* Bloomington, MN: NCS Pearson.

Kaufman, A. S., & Kaufman, N. L. (with Breaux, K. C.) (2015b). Administration manual. *Kaufman Test of Educational Achievement Brief Form–Third Edition.* Bloomington, MN: NCS Pearson.

Kaufman, A. S., Kaufman, J. C., Liu, X., & Johnson, C. K. (2009). How do educational attainment and gender relate to fluid intelligence, crystallized intelligence, and academic skills at ages 22–90 years? *Archives of Clinical Neuropsychology, 24*(2), 153–163.

Kaufman, A. S., Lichtenberger, E. O., Fletcher-Janzen, E., & Kaufman, N. L. (2005). *Essentials of KABC-II assessment.* Hoboken, NJ: Wiley.

Kaufman, A. S., Raiford, S. E., & Coalson, D. L. (2015). *Intelligent testing with the WISC-V.* Hoboken, NJ: Wiley.

Keenan, J. M., & Betjemann, R. S. (2006). Comprehending the Gray Oral Reading Test without reading it: Why comprehension tests should not include passage-independent items. *Scientific Studies of Reading, 10*(4), 363–380.

Kirby, J. R., & Williams, N. H. (1991). *Learning problems: A cognitive approach.* Toronto: Kagan and Woo.

Kirby, J. R., Parrila, R., & Pfeiffer, S. L. (2003). Naming speed and phonological awareness as predictors of reading development. *Journal of Educational Psychology, 80*, 437–447.

Laurent, J., & Swerdlik, M. (1992). *Psychological test usage: A survey of internship supervisors.* Paper presented at the annual meeting of the national Association of School Psychologists, Nashville, TN.

Lichtenberger, E. O. (2001). The Kaufman tests: K-ABC and KAIT. In A. S. Kaufman & N. L. Kaufman (Eds.), *Specific learning disabilities and difficulties in children and adolescents* (pp. 283–306). New York, NY: Cambridge University Press.

Lichtenberger, E. O., & Breaux, K. C. (2010). *Essentials of WIAT-III and KTEA-II Assessment.* Hoboken, NJ: Wiley.

Lichtenberger, E. O., Broadbooks, D. Y., & Kaufman, A. S. (2000). *Essentials of cognitive assessment with KAIT and other Kaufman measures.* New York, NY: Wiley.

Lichtenberger, E. O., & Smith, D. R. (2005). *Essentials of WIAT-II and KTEA-II assessment.* Hoboken, NJ: Wiley.

Lovett, B. J. (2011). Extended time testing accommodations: What does the research say? *Communique: The Newspaper of the National Association of School Psychologists, 39*(1), 14–15.

Lovett, M. W. (1984). A developmental perspective on reading dysfunction: Accuracy and rate in the subtyping of dyslexic children. *Brain and Language, 22*(1), 67–91. doi:10.1016/0093-934X(84)90080-4

Lovett, M. W. (1987). A developmental approach to reading disability: Accuracy and speed criteria of normal and deficient reading skill. *Child Development, 58*(1), 234–260. doi:10.2307/1130305

Luria, A. R. (1966). *Human brain: An introduction to neuropsychology.* New York, NY: Basic Books.

Luria, A. R. (1970). The functional organization of the brain. *Scientific American, 222,* 66–78.

Luria, A. R. (1973). *The working brain: An introduction to neuro-psychology.* London, UK: Penguin Books.

Lyon, G., Fletcher, J. & Barnes, T. (2003). Learning disabilities. In E. J. Mash & R. A. Barkley (Eds.), *Child psychopathology* (pp. 390–345). New York, NY: Guilford Press.

Lyon, G. R., Shaywitz, S. E., & Shaywitz, B. A. (2003). Defining dyslexia, comorbidity, teachers' knowledge of language and reading: A definition of dyslexia. *Annals of Dyslexia, 53,* 1–14.

Malecki, C. K., & Jewell, J. (2003). Developmental, gender, and practical considerations in scoring curriculum-based measurement writing probes. *Psychology in the Schools, 40*(4), 379–390.

Masterson, J., Apel, K., & Wasowicz, J. (2002). SPELL. Spelling Performance Evaluation for Language & Literacy: A prescriptive assessment of spelling on CD-ROM. Evanston, IL: Learning by Design.

Mather, N., & Wendling, B. J. (2015). *Essentials of WJ IV Tests of Achievement Assessment.* Hoboken, NJ: Wiley.

Mather, N., Wendling, B. J., & Woodcock, R. W. (2001). *Woodcock-Johnson III Tests of Achievement Examiner's Manual.* Itasca, IL: Riverside.

McConaughy, S. H., Ivanova, M. Y., Antshel, K., & Eiraldi, R. B. (2009). Standardized observational assessment of attention deficit hyperactivity disorder combined and predominantly inattentive subtypes. I. Test session observations. *School Psychology Review, 38*(1), 45–66.

McEvoy, C., & Woitaszewski, S. (2014). Q-interactive and the undiscovered country: A conversation on the new digital platform for assessment. *WSPA Sentinel, 13*(4), 21–23.

McGrew, K. S., & Flanagan, D. P. (1998). The intelligence test desk reference (ITDR): *Gf-Gc* cross-battery assessment. Boston, MA: Allyn & Bacon.

McLeod, J. (1968). Reading expectancy from disabled readers. *Journal of Learning Disabilities, 1,* 97–105.

McLeod, J. (1974). Educational underachievement: Toward a defensible psychometric definition. *Journal of Learning Disabilities, 12,* 322–330.

Meisinger, E. B., Bloom, J. S., & Hynd, G. W. (2010). Reading fluency: Implications for the assessment of children with reading disabilities. *Annals of Dyslexia, 60*(1), 1–17.

Mertler, C. A. (2002). *Using standardized test data to guide instruction and intervention.* College Park, MD: ERIC Clearinghouse on Assessment and Evaluation. (ERIC Document Reproduction Service No. ED470589).

Moats, L. C. (1993). Assessment of spelling in learning disabilities research. In G. R. Lyon (Ed.), *Frames of reference for the assessment of learning disabilities: New views on measurement issues* (pp. 333–349). Baltimore, MD: Brookes.

Mullis, I. V., Martin, M. O., Kennedy, A. M., & Foy, P. (2007). *PIRLS 2006 International Report.*

Naglieri, J. A. (2001). Using the Cognitive Assessment System (CAS) with learning disabled children. In A. S. Kaufman & N. L. Kaufman (Eds.), *Specific learning disabilities and difficulties in children and adolescents* (pp. 141–177). New York, NY: Cambridge University Press.

Nation, K. (1999). Reading skills in hyperlexia: A developmental perspective. *Psychological Bulletin, 125*(3), 338–355. doi:10.1037/0033-2909.125.3.338

National Center for Education Statistics (2012). *The Nation's Report Card: Writing 2011* (NCES 2012–470). Institute of Education Sciences, U.S. Department of Education, Washington, D.C.

National Governors Association Center for Best Practices, & Council of Chief State School Officers. (2010). *Common Core State Standards.* Washington, DC: Authors.

National Institute of Child Health and Human Development (NICHHD, 2000). *Report of the National Reading Panel. Teaching children to read: An evidence-based assessment of the scientific research literature on reading and its implications for reading instruction* (NIH Publication No. 00-4769). Washington, DC: U.S. Government Printing Office.

Nelson, J. R., Benner, G. J., Neill, S., & Stage, S. A. (2006). Interrelationships among language skills: Externalizing behavior. *Journal of Emotional and Behavioral Disorders, 14*(4), 209–216.

Neuhaus, G. F., & Swank, P. R. (2002). Understanding the relations between RAN letter subtest components and word reading in first grade students. *Journal of Learning Disabilities, 35*(2), 158–174.

Ofiesh, N., Mather, N., & Russell, A. (2005). Using speeded cognitive, reading, and academic measures to determine the need for extended test time among university students with learning disabilities. *Journal of Psychoeducational Assessment, 23*(1), 35–52.

Palejwala, M. H., & Fine, J. G. (2015). Gender differences in latent cognitive abilities in children aged 2 to 7. *Intelligence, 48*, 96–108.

Pearson. (2009a). *The Wechsler Individual Achievement Test—Third Edition.* San Antonio, TX: Author.

Pearson. (2009b). Examiner's manual. *Wechsler Individual Achievement Test—Third Edition.* San Antonio, TX: Author.

Pearson. (2010, April 22). *WIAT-III content and scoring modifications.* San Antonio, TX: Author. Retrieved from http://images.pearsonclinical.com/images/products/WIAT-III/WIAT-IIIEnhancedContentUpdates.pdf

Pearson (2010a). Technical manual with adult norms. *Wechsler Individual Achievement Test–Third Edition* San Antonio, TX: Author.

Pearson (2010b). *WIAT–III Essay Composition: "Quick Score" for theme development and text organization.* San Antonio, TX: Author. Retrieved from http://images.pearsonclinical.com/images/Products/WIAT-III/WIAT-III_Quick_Scoring_Guide.pdf

Pearson (n.d.). *Archived Webinars*. San Antonio, TX: Author. Retrieved from http://www
.pearsonclinical.com/psychology/products/100000463/wechsler-individual-achievement-
testthird-edition-wiatiii-wiat-iii.html#tab-training

Perlow, R., Jattuso, M., & Moore, D. (1997). Role of verbal working memory in complex skill
acquisition. *Human Performance, 10*, 283–302.

Pikulski, J. J., & Chard, D. J. (2005). Fluency: Bridge between decoding and reading comprehension. *The Reading Teacher, 58*(6), 510–519.

Prifitera, A., Saklofske, D. H., & Weiss, L. G. (2005). WISC-IV clinical use and interpretation. San Diego, CA: Elsevier Academic Press.

Psychological Corporation. (1992). *Wechsler Individual Achievement Test*. San Antonio, TX:
Author.

Psychological Corporation. (2001). *Wechsler Individual Achievement Test–Second Edition*. San
Antonio, TX: Author.

Rasinski, T. V. (2012). Why reading fluency should be hot! *The Reading Teacher, 65*(8),
516–522.

Reynolds, C. R., Kamphaus, R. W., Rosenthal, B. L., & Hiemenz, J. R. (1997). Applications of the Kaufman Assessment Battery for Children (K-ABC) in neuropsychological
assessment. In C. R. Reynolds & E. Fletcher-Janzen (Eds.), *The handbook of clinical child
neuropsychology* (2nd ed., pp. 253–269). New York, NY: Kluwer-Plenum.

Reynolds, M. R., Scheiber, C., Hajovsky, D. B., Schwartz, B., & Kaufman, A. S. (2015).
Gender differences in academic achievement: Is writing an exception to the gender similarities hypothesis? *The Journal of Genetic Psychology, 176*(4), 211–234.

Savage, R., Pillay, V., & Melidona, S. (2008). Rapid serial naming is a unique predictor of
spelling in children. *Journal of Learning Disabilities, 41*(3), 235–250.

Schatschneider, C., & Torgesen, J. K. (2004). Using our current understanding of dyslexia
to support early identification and intervention. *Journal of Child Neurology, 19*(10),
759–765.

Scheiber, C., Reynolds, M. R., Hajovsky, D. B., & Kaufman, A. S. (2015). Gender differences
in achievement in a large, nationally representative sample of children and adolescents.
*Psychology in the Schools, 52*(4), 335–348.

Schneider, W. J., & McGrew, K. (2012). The Cattell-Horn-Carroll model of intelligence.
In D. Flanagan & P. Harrison (Eds.), *Contemporary intellectual assessment: Theories, tests,
and issues* (3rd ed., pp. 99–144). New York, NY: Guilford Press.

Schrank, F. A., Mather, N. & McGrew, K. S. (2014). *Woodcock Johnson–IV Tests of Achievement*. Rolling Meadows, IL: Riverside.

Schrank, F. A., McGrew, K. S., & Mather, N. (2014a). *Woodcock-Johnson–IV Tests of Cognitive
Abilities*. Rolling Meadows, IL: Riverside.

Schrank, F. A., McGrew, K. S., & Mather, N. (2014b). *Woodcock-Johnson–IV*. Rolling Meadows, IL: Riverside.

Schwartz, R. (2011). *Handbook of child language disorders*. New York, NY: Psychology Press.

Semel, E., Wiig, E. H., & Secord, W. A. (2003). *Clinical evaluation of language fundamentals*
(4th ed.). San Antonio, TX: The Psychological Corporation.

Siegal, M. (1997). *Knowing children: Experiments in conversation and cognition* (2nd ed.).
Hove, UK: Psychology Press.

Siegel, L. S. (1999). Issues in the definition and diagnosis of learning disabilities: A perspective
on *Guckenberger v. Boston University. Journal of Learning Disabilities, 32*, 304–319.

Smith, D. K. (2001). *Essentials of individual achievement assessment*. New York, NY:
Wiley.

Spreen, O. (2001). Learning disabilities and their neurological foundations, theories, and subtypes. In A. S. Kaufman & N. L. Kaufman (Eds.), *Specific learning disabilities and difficulties in children and adolescents* (pp. 283–306). New York, NY: Cambridge University Press.

Stahl, S. A., & Murray, B. A. (1994). Defining phonological awareness and its relationship to early reading. *Journal of Educational Psychology, 86*(2), 221–234.

Stanovich, K. E. (1988). Explaining the differences between the dyslexic and the garden-variety poor reader: The phonological-core variable-difference model. *Journal of Learning Disabilities, 21*(10), 590–604. doi:10.1177/002221948802101003

Stanovich, K. E. (1991). Discrepancy definitions of reading disability: Has intelligence led us astray? *Reading Research Quarterly, 26*, 7–29.

Stanovich, K. E. (1992). Developmental reading disorder. In. S. R. Hooper, G. W. Hynd, & R. E. Mattison (Eds.), *Developmental disorders: Diagnostic criteria and clinical assessment* (pp. 173–208). Mahwah, NJ: Erlbaum.

Stanovich, K. E. (1999). The sociopsychometrics of learning disabilities. *Journal of Learning Disabilities, 32*, 350–361.

Stanovich, K. E., & Siegel, L. (1994). Phenotypic performance profile of children with reading disabilities: A regression-based test of the phonological-core variable-difference model. *Journal of Educational Psychology, 86*, 24–53.

Stanovich, K. E., Siegel, L. S., & Gottardo, A. (1997). Converging evidence for phonological and surface subtypes of reading disability. *Journal of Educational Psychology, 89*(1), 114–127. doi:10.1037/0022-0663.89.1.114

Stanovich, K. E., & West, R. (1989). Exposure to print and orthographic processing. *Reading Research Quarterly, 24*(4), 402–433.

Sternberg, R. (1995). *In search of the human mind*. Fort Worth, TX: Harcourt Brace College Publishers.

Stinnett, T. A., Havey, J. M., & Oehler-Stinnett, J. (1994). Current test usage by practicing school psychologists: A national survey. *Journal of Psychoeducational Assessment, 12*, 331–350.

Stoodley, C. J., Ray, N. J., Jack, A., & Stein, J. F. (2008). Implicit learning in control, dyslexic, and garden-variety poor readers. *Annals of the New York Academy of Sciences, 1145*(1), 173–183.

Swanson, H. (1996). Individual and age-related differences in children's working memory. *Memory & Cognition, 24*, 70–82.

Swanson, H., & Howell, M. (2001). Working memory, short-term memory, and speech rate as predictors of children's reading performance at different ages. *Journal of Educational Psychology, 9*, 720–734.

Teeter, P. A. (1997). Neurocognitive interventions for childhood and adolescent disorders: A transactional model. In C. R. Reynolds and E. Fletcher-Janzen (Eds.), *The handbook of clinical child neuropsychology* (2nd ed., pp. 387–417). New York, NY: Kluwer-Plenum.

Teeter, P. A., & Semrud-Clikeman, M. (1998). *Child clinical neuropsychology: Assessment and interventions for neuropsychiatric and neurodevelopmental disorders of childhood*. Boston, MA: Allyn & Bacon.

Tong, X., Deacon, S. H., & Cain, K. (2014). Morphological and syntactic awareness in poor comprehenders: Another piece of the puzzle. *Journal of Learning Disabilities, 47*(1), 22–33. doi:10.1177/0022219413509971

Vellutino, F. R., Scanlon, D. M., & Lyon, G. R. (2000). Differentiating between difficult-to-remediate and readily remediated poor readers: More evidence against the IQ-achievement discrepancy definition of reading disability. *Journal of Learning Disabilities, 33*, 223–238. doi:10.1177/002221940003300302

Wechsler, D. (1949). *Wechsler Intelligence Scale for Children*. New York, NY: The Psychological Corporation.

Wechsler, D, (2002). *Wechsler Preschool and Primary Scale of Intelligence—Third Edition*. San Antonio, TX: The Psychological Corporation.

Wechsler, D. (2003). *Wechsler Intelligence Scale for Children—Fourth Edition*. San Antonio, TX: Pearson.

Wechsler, D. (2008). *Wechsler Adult Intelligence Scale—Fourth Edition*. San Antonio, TX: Pearson.

Wechsler, D. (2012a). *Wechsler Preschool and Primary Scale of Intelligence—Fourth Edition*. San Antonio, TX: Pearson.

Wechsler, D. (2012b). Technical and Interpretive Manual. *Wechsler Preschool and Primary Scale of Intelligence—Fourth Edition*. San Antonio, TX: Pearson.

Wechsler, D. (2014a). *Wechsler Intelligence Scale for Children—Fifth Edition*. Bloomington, MN: Pearson.

Wechsler, D. (2014b). Technical and interpretive manual. *Wechsler Intelligence Scale for Children—Fifth Edition*. Bloomington, MN: Pearson.

Wechsler, D., & Kaplan, E. (2015). *Wechsler Intelligence Scale for Children-Fifth Edition Integrated*. Bloomington, MN: Pearson.

Wechsler, D., & Naglieri, J. A. (2006). *Wechsler Nonverbal Scale of Ability*. San Antonio, TX: The Psychological Corporation.

Wiig, E. H., Semel, E., & Secord, W. A. (2013). *Clinical evaluation of language fundamentals* (5th ed.). Bloomington, MN: Pearson.

Wilson, M. S., & Reschley, D. J. (1996). Assessment in school psychology training and practice. *School Psychology Review, 21*, 9–23.

Wolf, M. (1991). The word-retrieval deficit hypothesis and developmental dyslexia. *Learning Individual Differences, 3*(3), 205–223.

Wolf, M., & Bowers, P. G. (1999). The double-deficit hypothesis for the developmental dyslexias. *Journal of Educational Psychology, 91*(3), 415–438. doi:10.1037/0022-0663.91.3.415

Wolf, M., Bowers, P. G., & Biddle, K. (2000). Naming-speed processes, timing, and reading: A conceptual review. *Journal of Learning Disabilities, 33*(4), 387–407. doi:10.1177/002221940003300409

Woodcock, R. W. (2011). *Woodcock Reading Mastery Test–Third Edition*. Minneapolis, MN: NCS Pearson.

Woodcock, R. W., McGrew, K. S., & Mather, N. (2001). *Woodcock-Johnson III Tests of Achievement*. Itasca, IL: Riverside.

# Annotated Bibliography

Flanagan, D. P., Ortiz, S. O., & Alfonso, V. C. (2013). *Essentials of cross-battery assessment* (3rd ed.). Hoboken, NJ: Wiley.
*This third edition provides a comprehensive set of guidelines and procedures for organizing assessments based on contemporary CHC theory and research, integrating test results from different batteries in a psychometrically defensible way, and interpreting test results within the context of research on the relations between cognitive and academic abilities and processes. Also includes guidelines for assessing culturally and linguistically diverse populations and individuals suspected of having a specific learning disability. This book includes a CD-ROM containing three software programs for assisting in data management and interpretation, making decisions regarding specific learning disability, and discerning difference from disability in individuals whose cultural and linguistic backgrounds differ from the mainstream.*

Kaufman, A. S., & Kaufman, N. L. (2014). *Kaufman test of educational achievement* (3rd ed.). Bloomington, MN: NCS Pearson.
*Three manuals are included in the test kit:* Administration Manual, Scoring Manual, *and* Technical & Interpretive Manual. *The* Administration Manual *gives an overview of the KTEA-3 and provides detailed guidelines on administration and scoring. The* Scoring Manual *gives scoring instructions for the KTEA-3's subjectively scored subtests and instructions for conducting error analysis. The* Technical & Interpretive Manual *(provided digitally) gives detailed information about KTEA-3 test development, standardization, and the test's psychometric properties. It recommends an interpretive approach for analyzing test results, including error analysis. Norms tables are also included in the* Technical & Interpretive Manual *for examiners that prefer hand scoring (rather than using Q-global, the publisher's digital scoring and reporting platform).*

Kaufman, A. S., & Kaufman, N. L. (2015). *Kaufman test of educational achievement brief form* (3rd ed.). Bloomington, MN: NCS Pearson.
*The KTEA-3 Brief kit includes two manuals: a printed* Administration Manual *and the* Technical & Interpretive Manual *(in digital form). The* Administration Manual *gives an overview of the KTEA-3 Brief and provides detailed guidelines on administration and scoring. The* Technical & Interpretive Manual *reviews the test development, normative samples, and psychometric qualities. A suggested interpretive approach is provided in this manual for analyzing test results. Norms tables are also provided for hand scoring (as an alternative to using Q-global, the publisher's digital scoring and reporting platform).*

Kaufman, A. S., Lichtenberger, E. O., Fletcher-Janzen, E., & Kaufman, N. L. (2005). *Essentials of KABC-II assessment*. Hoboken, NJ: Wiley.
*Covers thoroughly the administration, scoring, and interpretation of the KABC-II, including treatment of how it can be integrated with the KTEA-II (which can also be applied to the KTEA-3). It includes sample case reports exemplifying use of the KABC-II with the KTEA-II.*

Kaufman, A. S., Raiford, S. E., & Coalson, D. L. (2015). *Intelligent testing with the WISC-V*. Hoboken, NJ: Wiley.
*Provides guidance on administration, scoring, and interpreting WISC-V profiles for informing diagnoses and making meaningful educational recommendations. It gives advice on clinically*

*applying the WISC-V by using a child's strengths and weaknesses to create a targeted, appropriate intervention plan. The best theory-based methods for interpreting each child's profile of test scores within the context of his or her background and behaviors are identified. Clinical case reports are presented with diverse referral reasons. Use of both the conventional WISC-V and WISC-V Digital is outlined in detail.*

Pearson (2009). *Wechsler Individual Achievement Test–Third Edition.* San Antonio, TX: Author.

*The Examiner's Manual of this test (included in the test kit) gives detailed information about WIAT-III subtests and composites, how to administer and score the subtests, and how to interpret the results. The Technical Manual CD (included in the test kit) describes the test's development, standardization, and the psychometric properties. It provides correlational data and information about how the WIAT-III is related to other tests. The Technical Manual reviews the test development, normative samples, and psychometric characteristics. Digital norms tables are provided for hand scoring (as an alternative to using Q-global, the publisher's digital scoring and reporting platform).*

Schneider, W. J., Lichtenberger, E. O., Mather, N., & Kaufman, N. L. (in press). *Essentials of assessment report writing* (2nd ed). Hoboken, NJ: Wiley.

*This book reviews the essential elements and structure of well-written psychological and psychoeducational reports. It covers all aspects of preparing a written report and provides numerous illustrative examples of clear, informative reports. The book's annotated case reports use a variety of cognitive, achievement, psychological, and neuropsychological assessment instruments to evaluate clients with a variety of referral concerns. The approach to assessment report writing advocated in this book suggests that writers present their conclusions using simple, lively prose, but omit unnecessary details about how they arrived at them, so that readers can focus on the key useful truths about the client.*

# About the Authors

**Kristina C. Breaux, PhD,** is a Senior Research Director with Pearson Clinical Assessment, a learning disabilities consultant, a researcher, and an author with expertise in the field of learning disabilities. Since receiving her clinical training at Northwestern University, Kristina has taught students of all ages as a licensed special educator and educational therapist and she has conducted numerous psycho-educational assessments for children, adolescents, and adults. In addition to coauthoring *Essentials of WIAT-III and KTEA-II*, Kristina is a published author of several book chapters and articles pertaining to assessment and learning disabilities. In her professional role at Pearson, Kristina led the development of the WIAT-III and worked in close collaboration with Alan and Nadeen Kaufman to develop the KTEA-3 Comprehensive and KTEA-3 Brief assessments. Kristina dedicates her professional work to improving the lives of individuals with learning disabilities by linking assessment and instruction, and bridging research and practice.

**Elizabeth O. Lichtenberger, PhD,** has worked as an Adjunct Faculty member at Alliant International University in San Diego and a researcher at the Laboratory for Cognitive Neuroscience at The Salk Institute for Biological Studies in La Jolla, California. Her work at The Salk Institute focused on the cognitive and neuropsychological patterns in children with genetic developmental disorders. Because of her expertise in psychological, psychoeducational, and neuropsychological assessment, Liz also serves as a psychoeducational test/measurement consultant and trainer for organizations and provides consultation to individual psychologists.

Liz is a published author of numerous books, book chapters, and articles on assessment and assessment instruments, including many books in the *Essentials* series, as well as *Assessing Adolescent and Adult Intelligence* (3rd ed.). In addition, Liz served as a consulting editor of the second edition of the *Encyclopedia of Special Education: A Reference for the Education of the Handicapped and Other Exceptional Children and Adults* and is currently on the editorial board of the journal *Psychology in the Schools*.

# ABOUT THE DIGITAL RESOURCES

Thank you for choosing the *Essentials of Psychological Assessment* series. *Essentials of KTEA-3 and WIAT-III Assessment* includes downloadable resources designed to enhance your education and practice.

To access your resources, please follow these steps:

Step 1 Go to http://www.wiley.com/go/psyessresources

Step 2 Enter your email address, the password provided below, and click "submit"
   Password: wiley123

Step 3 Select and download the listed resources

If you need any assistance, please contact Wiley Customer Care 800-762-2974 (U.S.), 317-572-3994 (International) or visit www.wiley.com.

## CONTENT INCLUDED IN THE DIGITAL RESOURCES

### Chapter 7: Q-INTERACTIVE FOR KTEA™-3 AND WIAT®-III
*This chapter is provided in its entirety as a digital file.*

### Decision Trees for KTEA-3 and WIAT-III Subtests
*This file includes the following decision tree tables to guide examiners in selecting subtests for specific referral concerns:*

- Decision Tree for KTEA-3 Subtest Selection Based on Referral Concerns in the Domain of Spelling and Writing
- Decision Tree for KTEA-3 Subtest Selection Based on Referral Concerns in the Domain of Reading
- Decision Tree for WIAT-III Subtest Selection Based on Referral Concerns in the Domain of Spelling and Writing
- Decision Tree for WIAT-III Subtest Selection Based on Referral Concerns in the Domain of Math
- Decision Tree for WIAT-III Subtest Selection Based on Referral Concerns in the Domain of Reading

### Min & Max KTEA-3 Subtest Scores

*This file includes tables that provide the lowest and highest possible standard scores for each KTEA-3 subtest at each age and grade level.*

### Min & Max WIAT-III Subtest Scores

*This file includes tables that provide the lowest and highest possible standard scores for each WIAT-III subtest at each age level.*

### New Score Data for the KTEA-3 and WIAT-III

*This file includes tables for five (5) new composite scores: two KTEA-3 Dyslexia Index Scores, two WIAT-III Dyslexia Index Scores, and a new KTEA-3 Oral Reading Fluency composite score.*

For each of the KTEA-3 and the WIAT-III Dyslexia Index Scores, the following tables are provided:

- Grade-Based and Age-Based Composite Standard Scores
- Bands of Errors (95%, 90%, 85% Confidence Intervals) for Grade-Based Standard Scores and Age-Based Standard Scores
- Split-Half Reliability Coefficients for Subtests and Composites by Grade and by Age
- Reading/Writing Disorder Sample Mean Scores

For the KTEA-3 Oral Reading Fluency composite score, the following tables are provided:

- Grade-Based and Age-Based Composite Standard Scores
- Bands of Errors (95%, 90%, 85% Confidence Intervals) for Grade-Based Standard Scores and Age-Based Standard Scores
- Composite Score Comparisons for KTEA-3 Oral Reading Fluency Composite versus KTEA-3 Decoding Composite Score: Significance and Frequency of Standard Score Differences by Grade and by Age
- Split-Half Reliability Coefficients for Subtests and Composites by Grade (3–12)

# INDEX

Page references followed by *fig* indicate an illustrated figure; followed by *t* indicate a table.